OLD FAMILIES OF
CARRICKFERGUS
& BALLYNURE

GRAVESTONE INSCRIPTIONS
COUNTY ANTRIM
VOLUME 3

OLD FAMILIES OF
CARRICKFERGUS
& BALLYNURE

from
Gravestone Inscriptions, Wills
and
Biographical Notes

•

compiled by
GEORGE RUTHERFORD
and edited by
RICHARD CLARKE

ULSTER HISTORICAL FOUNDATION
PUBLICATIONS

This book has received support from the Cultural Traditions Programme of the Community Relations Council which aims to encourage acceptance and understanding of cultural diversity (1995).

COVER IMAGE
'Carrickfergus Castle on Belfast Lough, Co. Antrim' by Henry Brocas
IMAGE COURTESY OF THE NATIONAL LIBRARY OF IRELAND

First published in 1995, reprinted 2016
by Ulster Historical Foundation,
The Corn Exchange,
31 Gordon Street, Belfast, BT1 2LG
www.ancestryireland.com
www.booksireland.org.uk

Except as otherwise permitted under the Copyright, Designs and Patents Act, 1988, this publication may only be reproduced, stored or transmitted in any form or by any means with the prior permission in writing of the publisher or, in the case of reprographic reproduction, in accordance with the terms of a licence issued by the Copyright Licensing Agency. Enquiries concerning reproduction outside those terms should be sent to the publisher.

© Ulster Historical Foundation, 1995
ISBN: 978-0-901905-52-9

Printed by SPRINT-print Ltd.
Cover design by FPM Publishing

CONTENTS

List of Illustrations	vi
Introduction	vii
Bibliography	xi
List of Abbreviations	xiii
Map of parishes of Carrickfergus and Ballynure	xiv
Ballygowan Townland, Knox Grave	1
Ballynure Old Graveyard	2
Ballynure Church of Ireland Church	49
Carrickfergus Old Graveyard (St. Nicholas')	52
Carrickfergus, St. Nicholas' Church of Ireland Church	148
Carrickfergus Congregational Church	157
Carrickfergus, First Presbyterian Church	160
Carrickfergus, North Road Cemetery	163
Carrickfergus, St. Nicholas' Roman Catholic Graveyard	189
Carrickfergus, Prospect Roman Catholic Cemetery	193
Carrickfergus, Victoria Cemetery	196
Loughmorne Presbyterian Graveyard	197
Straid Congregational Church	207
Appendix 1: Some Carrickfergus deaths, 1853-1872	209
Appendix 2: Summary Guides to documentary sources for Carrickfergus	211
Appendix 3: List of Subscribers to this volume	245

LIST OF ILLUSTRATIONS

Map of the Parishes of Carrickfergus and Ballynure	xiv
Ballynure Old Graveyard. Thomas Logan of Loganstown, Straidnahanna	27
Carrickfergus Old Graveyard. Marble bust of Alexander Johns, J.P.	89
Carrickfergus Old Graveyard. Kirk arms	94
Carrickfergus Old Graveyard. John Lattimore	97
Carrickfergus Old Graveyard. Pillar and Celtic cross to Laverty family	99
Carrickfergus Old Graveyard. Luke Livingston Macassey	104
Carrickfergus Old Graveyard. McGookin headstone	110
Carrickfergus Old Graveyard. Major-General Frederick Amelius Ogle	122
Carrickfergus Old Graveyard. Mrs Agnes Ogle (nee Reid)	123
Carrickfergus Old Graveyard. Baptistry and tablet to C. A. W. Stewart	135
Carrickfergus Old Graveyard. James Weatherup	140
Carrickfergus Old Graveyard. Elizabeth Weatherup nee Donel	141
Carrickfergus, St. Nicholas' C of I Church. Chichester monument	148
Carrickfergus, St. Nicholas' C of I Church. Arms of George Augustus, second Marquis of Donegall	154
Carrickfergus, St. Nicholas' C of I Church. George Hamilton, third Marquis of Donegall	155
Carrickfergus, First Presbyterian Church. The Rev. James White	162
Carrickfergus, North Road Cemetery. General view, under snow	163
Carrickfergus, North Road Cemetery. Cast iron plaque to James Edmonds	168
Carrickfergus, North Road Cemetery. Lappin headstone, now flaking	177
Loughmorne Presbyterian Graveyard. General view, under snow	197
Loughmorne Presbyterian Graveyard. Irwin headstone	200

INTRODUCTION

An old story tells of a king named Fergus. He sailed from his Scottish Kingdom in search of a cure for his leprosy. His destination was a healing well contained in a rock that jutted into the sea. A storm arose and wrecked the ship against this very rock. When the king's body washed ashore it was taken four miles west for burial at Monkstown. The rock was named after him - Carraig Fheargus or the Rock of Fergus.

The history of Carrickfergus really begins when the Norman knight, John de Courcy, rode north from Dublin to carve an earldom for himself from the territory of Ulster. He seems to have begun the building of the castle on the Rock of Fergus by 1178, and this became the chief military strong point, from which he and his successors held dominion over the colony. De Courcy is credited with founding St. Mary's Premonstratensian Abbey at Woodburn, one mile west of the Castle, and St. Nicholas' parish church, which was granted to the Abbey. Minting his own coinage at Carrickfergus and Downpatrick could be read as an act of a sovereign prince. So it is not surprising that King John replaced him in 1205 by appointing Hugh de Lacy as Earl of Ulster. But in 1210, after besieging the castle, the king deposed Hugh in turn and Carrickfergus became a royal castle. (John was the only king of England to sojourn in the castle, where he stayed for ten days in July 1210.)

After a period of crusading in France Hugh returned in another bid to gain lands. Despite his unsuccessful siege of Carrickfergus during 1224, he was again granted the Earldom in 1227. The first documentary evidence for a town is provided in 1223 with the mention of burgesses. In 1232 Hugh founded the Franciscan Friary at the opposite end of High Street and in 1443 was interred there. The earldom then reverted to the crown, but in 1264 was granted to Walter de Burgh.

During the Scottish War of Independence there was Irish contact with both sides and in 1315 (the year after victory at Bannockburn) Edward Bruce, heir presumptive to the Scottish throne, landed at Larne with an army to free Ireland from English rule. Carrickfergus Castle suffered a long and bitter siege, not surrendering to Edward's forces until September 1316. Meanwhile, the destructive war had been taken into the other provinces and Edward was crowned King of Ireland. After his death at the battle of Faughart, county Louth, the Scots left for home.

Economic recovery had still not been achieved by 1333 when William de Burgh, Earl of Ulster, was murdered, leaving his infant daughter as heir. As T.E. McNeill comments "little girls make poor marcher lords". The Earldom settled into a long decline. All subsequent earls were absentee and the Castle came under the crown. Irish expansion under the O'Neills pushed eastward from Lough Neagh until the County of Carrickfergus was reduced to a small enclave about five miles square. The town was burned by Niall O'Neill in 1384.

The highland Scots, now settling in north Antrim, were also troublesome. The town was burned by them in 1386, and again in 1402. From some time in the first half of the fifteenth century, the corporation paid "black rent" to the O'Neills of Clandeboy. It has been suggested that as a trading outpost Carrickfergus was useful to the Irish at this time as a source of foreign imports.

In 1513 a Scottish fleet under the Earl of Arran (and against his king's instructions) burned the town. A siege by Scots in 1555 was raised by the Lord Deputy, but in 1573 the Irish again burned the town. It suffered another attack by Scots in 1575. With such insecurity of property, it is hardly surprising that the streets featured two types of building: stone-built tower houses and huts of sod and thatch - one to withstand the raids, the other cheap and easily replaced. For most of the medieval period the town defences were a ditch or earthen wall and it was not until 1615 that a stone wall finally enclosed the town.

Renewed interest in Ulster by the Tudors is shown by repairs to the Castle from the mid-sixteenth century - notably its adaptation for cannon. Carrickfergus was the base for expeditions against Scots in 1545, 1551, 1556, 1558, 1568, and 1575. Sir James McDonnell and his Scots inflicted a spectacular defeat on the garrison in 1597, but after the accession of King James in 1603, both sides had a common loyalty.

To establish an English colony at the expense of the Irish, the Earl of Essex with the rank of Governor of the Province of Ulster had arrived with an army in 1573, but soon abandoned the enterprise. Essex Street and Governors Walk are memorials of his stay. The next development was to survey (in 1602 and 1606) much of the land within the boundary of the County of the Town and its division into regular plots which were then granted to the aldermen, burgesses and freemen. The surnames of recipients reveal three equal groups: Irish, Old English, and New English.

Meanwhile, the long war against Hugh O'Neill ended in 1603 leaving the way open for the confiscation of lands and the Plantation of Ulster. From 1599 Sir Arthur Chichester had been actively soldiering as governor of Carrickfergus. He received extensive land grants from the Crown and, in 1604, was appointed Lord Deputy, an office which allowed him to take a leading role in the scheme to plant Ulster with British emigrants. Carrickfergus now became a major port of entry for the settlers. Despite his position in the Dublin government, Chichester chose to build his stately home, Joymount, here, on the site of the friary. The town wall was completed in 1615.

The progress of plantation was uneven and often slow, but continued confidently until the abrupt shock of the Irish rebellion of 1641. To protect the British settlers an army was raised in Scotland with the approval of the English Parliament and landed at Carrickfergus in April 1642. The developing civil war in England and mistrust between the parliaments in London and in Edinburgh added to the confused political and military position in Ireland. Carrickfergus changed hands several times before the relative tranquillity of the Commonwealth in the 1650s. Later the town expanded beyond the walls: the west suburb became known as Irish Quarter and the east suburb, known as Scotch Quarter, was founded about 1665 by Scottish fishermen.

On the arrival of the Duke of Schomberg with a Williamite army a short vigorous siege caused the surrender of the garrison in August 1689. The following year William of Orange landed at the pier on his way to fight James II at the Boyne.

The Castle was captured for the last time in February 1760 when three French ships arrived under the command of Commodore Francois Thurot. Threats had the desired effect of procuring provisions from Belfast. When the squadron was loaded it sailed, leaving the local inhabitants with a long remembered impression of the polite manners of their French enemies.

In 1797 William Orr ("the bard of Ballycarry") of Farranshane in the parish of Antrim was tried for insurrection -administering the oath of the United Irishmen to two soldiers. He was hanged at Gallows Green on 14th October. Afterwards the body was waked in Ballynure Presbyterian Meeting House and buried at Templepatrick. "Remember Orr" became a rallying cry of the United Irishmen, but their rebellion of 1798 had little impact on Carrickfergus.

By this time Belfast had overtaken Carrickfergus as a commercial centre, but the latter remained the administrative seat for the County of Antrim and the County of the Town of Carrickfergus until the 1840s. The county was then absorbed into that of Antrim, the court and gaol relocated in Belfast, and Muncipal Commissioners were elected for the urban area. Like Belfast the town developed cotton industries and then turned to linen. Shipbuilding was established in 1845. The railway came in 1848 and gas lighting in 1855. About the same time a trial bore for coal revealed a thick bed of salt that provided a new mining industry.

Since the Second World War Carrickfergus has grown rapidly assisted by the new industries of artificial fibres. The closure of the three largest factories had a severe effect on employment through the 1980s, but also brought government sympathy and special help to refurbish the town centre and revitalise the old civic pride.

The village of Ballynure (Baile-an-Iubhair: town of the yew tree) was established between the ancient church and the castle built for John Dalway in Castletown. It did not prove an effective growth point - urban development took place in Ballyclare on the western edge of the parish. This is where the road from Carrickfergus to Antrim crossed the Six Mile Water. It was well placed as the market for the upper valley and its fairs became renowned while those at Fair Hill in Castletown died away. Linen manufacture was prominent in the area in the eighteenth century and into the nineteenth. An important paper mill was also located here.

The church of Ballynure was mentioned in the taxation roll of 1306 and described

Introduction

as decayed in the Visitation of 1622. In 1683 Richard Dobbs wrote of "a well called Toberdoney ... which in former times was very much frequented for sickness and distempers by the Irish, and still is on May-eve, Midsummer-eve, and Christmas...". The Dobbs family were landlords since 1626 when Hercules Dobbs had his title to the "Cynament of Ballynure" confirmed after a long and bitter legal battle with John Dalway. When a new family vault was constructed in the graveyard for the Dobbs in 1857 a protest meeting was held in the nearby Presbyterian Church and the Rev. Samuel Turner attacked the Establishment for interference with humbler graves. No memorial marks the grave of the radical weaver poet James Campbell who died in 1818.

The old church of Ballynure was repaired after the Restoration and appears to have been still in use in 1837 (Lewis: *Topographical Dictionary*) and 1847 (Reeves: *Ecclesiastical Antiquities*). It was, however, replaced in 1856 by the present building in the wave of enthusiasm of the mid-Victorian era. The baptismal register dates from 1812, marriage register from 1803 and burial register from 1852. The Presbyterian church, which has no graveyard, has baptismal registers from 1819 and marriage registers from 1827.

St. Nicholas' Church in Carrickfergus has the unusual feature of a nave shorter than its chancel. However, when Robert le Mercer completed work on the chancel in the early fourteenth century the church must have been a splendid building with nave much longer, aisle on either side, and side chapels issuing from the transepts. Later remodelling greatly reduced capacity and raised the floor level by about five feet. (A curious shift of meaning has resulted in the transepts being known as "Wills' Aisle" and "Donegall Aisle". The latter because the Lords Donegall occupied the north transept and the former from the Wills family, see under BURLEIGH inscription.) When the West Tower was added in 1778 it became the main entrance and allowed the porch of 1614 to be reused as a private sepulchre (see Wilson). But this was reopened in 1952 as a baptistry, furnished with a font retrieved from the site of Woodburn Abbey.

Two medieval coffin lids employed as building stone (presumably during the post-reformation rebuild) and rediscovered during alterations are displayed in the chancel. On the north wall is the "founder's tomb": the slab is decorated with a crozier and set under a low arch creating a niche within the thickness of the wall. Reassembled against the south wall are three pieces of a coffin lid decorated with a foliate cross.

The parish registers of baptisms, marriage and burial date from 1740, with a gap from 1800 to 1825.

The present Presbyterian Church in North Street was opened in 1829 on a site acquired in 1719. A second congregation was established at Joymount in 1852. A Non-Subscribing Presbyterian Church was opened on Joymount Bank in 1837 and continued to function into this century when the building was converted for use as a cinema. The baptismal register of the First Presbyterian Church dates from 1823 and the marriage registers from 1840.

None of the Presbyterians in the town have had a separate burial ground, but at Loughmorne, the covenanting congregation dating from 1804, began to bury in their meeting house yard as early as 1809. John Paul, the first minister became active in the theological disputes of the day and led his congregation out of the Reformed Presbyterian Synod (1843). In 1893 the congregation successfully applied for admission to the General Assembly of the Presbyterian Church in Ireland.

About 1662 Quakers settled at Crossgreen near Prospect and in 1680 established a burial ground there. The Society met considerable opposition and did not long survive. Their unmarked graves were forgotten. Among those who left were the ancestors of Richard Milhouse Nixon, thirty-seventh president of the United States of America.

Thomas Fagan, one of the compilers of Ordnance Survey memoirs, made the following note in 1839:-

> In the Middle Division, and Suburbs of Carrickfergus, there stands in the corner of a kitchen garden in the burial ground of a quaker and family, consisting of himself, his wife, and their children, all who are interred in this place of modern selection. As yet there are no headstones erected, though one has been lately cut for the purpose. The family name is Reilly. They at one period possessed considerable property within the Corporation. The last male of the

Introduction

family - Lazarus Reilly opened the above about 50 years back, but no other branch of the family have condescended to join him in his New Sepulture, though it is sheltered and carefully preserved from trespass.

Unfortunately an exact location is not given, but D. J. McCartney has drawn attention to John Wesley's Journal entry for Saturday 24th July 1756 when he was in Carrickfergus. Immediately after his sermon "a poor enthusiast began a dull, pointless harangue. James Reley began his bad work again as soon as I had done speaking. But I walked quietly away as did also the congregation." James Seton Reid explained that the parents of the interrupter were "of the Established Church, but he renounced that communion and had joined no other. He rigorously abstained from eating flesh, wore his beard, and by his express desire was buried in an erect position in his own garden".

During the eighteenth century there was no resident Catholic priest in Carrickfergus but mass was occasionally celebrated by a visiting priest at the Priest's Bush or a house belonging to some Catholic. In the early nineteenth century people assembled at the foot of Bryantang Brae, two miles from the town. In 1825 Father O'Neill obtained from E. Smith a lease, for 999 years, of ground at Barley Hill and erected the present church. The new building was dedicated in the following years by Dr William Crolly and Father O'Neill preached the opening sermon.

In 1840 Father O'Neill also established St. Columbkille's Chapel at Aldoo, about three miles to the north west. This was convenient for the labourers during the construction of Woodburn reservoirs, but is now derelict and deconsecrated. The ground was not used for burials.

Thanks are due to those members of the Carrickfergus Historical Society who assisted in transcribing inscriptions, especially Peggy Duncan and Edna M'Stea (St. Nicholas's Church of Ireland and North Road), Mary Mulvenna (Prospect) and also Neville McAllister (Loughmorne and Ballynure). The late Dr H.G. Calwell and Adrian Arbothnot translated the Latin epitaphs on the Gardner and Donegall monuments. Mrs. Bembridge and Mervyn kindly gave access to the Congregational and Presbyterian churches. Miss Ann Weatherup supplied biographical information and she, as well as Dr John Logan and Robin Cameron, made available photographic portraits. The watercolour by Andrew Nichol on the cover and the bust of Alexander Johns are reproduced with the kind permission of the Trustees of the Ulster Museum.

We are also grateful to the Carrickfergus Borough Council, the Carrickfergus Literary and Scientific Society (Union Hall) Trust Fund and the Carrickfergus and District Historical Society for help towards the cost of the publication. Mrs Sheela Speers of the Ulster Museum supplied much biographical information. She and Miss Pat Vizard also transcribed the Freeman's Rolls by kind permission of Carrickfergus Borough Council. Finally we wish to thank Mr Harold J. Twinem for information on the Burleigh family.

George Rutherford
Richard Clarke

BIBLIOGRAPHY

Anderson, E.B.: *Sailing Ships of Ireland*. Dublin, 1951 (reprinted, Coleraine, 1984).
Army List.
Bailie, W.D. (ed.): *A History of Congregations in the Presbyterian Church in Ireland 1610-1982*. Belfast, Presbyterian Historical Society, 1982.
Barkley, J.M.: *Fasti of the General Assembly of the Presbyterian Church in Ireland, 1840-1910 (Parts I-III)*. Belfast, Presbyterian Historical Society, 1986-7.
Basset, G.H.: *The Book of Antrim*. Dublin, 1888 (reprinted by Friars Bush Press, 1989).
Belfast and Ulster Directory. Published annually.
Belfast Newsletter. Published daily from 1737.
Brett, C.E.B.: *Buildings of Belfast, 1700-1914*. Second edition, Belfast, 1985.
Burke's Irish Family Records. London, 1976.
Burke, Sir Bernard: *Dictionary of the Landed Gentry of Great Britain and Ireland*. London, 1866.
Burke, Sir Bernard: *A Genealogical and Heraldic History of the Landed Gentry of Ireland*. London, 1912
Burke, Sir Bernard: *A Genealogical and Heraldic History of the Landed Gentry of Ireland*. London, 1958.
Burtchaell, G.D. and Sadleir, T.U.: *Alumni Dublinenses*. London, 1924.
Calwell, H.G.: *Andrew Malcolm of Belfast, 1818-1856, Physician and Historian*. Belfast, 1977.
Cameron, R: "Carrick's Pacific Colony" in *Carrickfergus and District Historical Journal*. 1985, 1:35.
Campbell, G. and Crowther, Susan: *Historic Buildings in the Town of Carrickfergus*. Belfast, Ulster Architectural Heritage Society, 1979.
Carmody, W.P.: *Lisburn Cathedral and its Past Rectors*. Belfast, 1926.
Carrickfergus Advertiser. Published weekly since 1883.
Carrickfergus and District Historical Journal. From 1985 to the present.
Carrickfergus Freeman. Published weekly in 1865-1866.
Chambers, G.: Faces of Change: *The Belfast and Northern Ireland Chambers of Commerce and Industry, 1783-1983*. Belfast, 1984.
Chichester, Sir A.P.B., Bart.: *History of the Family of Chichester from 1086 to 1870*. London, 1871.
Clarke, D.: *Arthur Dobbs Esquire 1689-1765*, Chapel Hill, North Carolina, 1957.
Clarke, R.S.J.: *Gravestone Inscriptions, Belfast, Volume 3*. U.H.F., Belfast, 1986.
C[ockayne], G.E. (ed.): *Complete Peergage, Volume 4*. London, 1916.
Corcoran, Doreen: *A Tour of East Antrim*. Belfast, Friar's Bush Press, 1990.
Corran, *Journal of the Larne and District Folklore Society*. Published quarterly from 1976.
Crickard, Eilis (ed.) *Return to Carrick, Please*. WEA Oral History Class 1992 (ISBN 0 9507812 6 6)
Crookshank, C.H.: *History of Methodism in Ireland*. Volumes I-III. Belfast and London, 1885-1888.
Dictionary of National Biography, London, 1909.
Dobbs, Richard, *The Town Records of Carrickfergus 1569-1747*. Typescript by John Logan, 1982, held by Northeastern Education and Library Board.
Fanning, David: *St Joseph's, Penarth*. 1990
Hewitt, John: *Art in Ulster, I* Belfast, 1977.
Hill, E.D.: *Guide to the Ancient Church of St. Nicholas*. Belfast, 1832.
Hill, G.: *The Macdonnells of Antrim*. Belfast, 1873 (reprinted Coleraine, 1976).
Irish Church Directory. Published annually.
Journal of the Association for the Preservation of the Memorials of the Dead in Ireland or Memorials of the Dead (M.D.) Vols 1-13, 1888-1934.
Kennedy, B. *British Art, 1900-1937*. Belfast, 1982.
Leslie, J.B.: *Armagh Clergy and Parishes*. Dundalk, 1911. Supplement to the above. Dundalk, 1948.
Leslie, J.B.: *Clogher Clergy and Parishes*. Enniskillen, 1929.

Leslie, J.B.: *Ossory Clergy and Parishes*. Enniskillen, 1933.
Leslie, J.B.: *Derry Clergy and Parishes*. Enniskillen, 1937.
Leslie, J.B.: *Clergy of Connor from Patrician times to the present day*. U.H.F., Belfast, 1993.
Leslie, J.B. and Swanzy, H.B.: *Biographical Succession Lists of the Clergy of Diocese of Down. Enniskillen, 1936*.
Loudan, Jack: *In Search of Water, being a History of the Belfast Water Supply*. Belfast, 1940.
Loughridge, A.: *Fasti of the Reformed Presbyterian Church of Ireland, Part 1*. Belfast, 1970.
Loughridge, A.: *The Convenanters in Ireland: A History of the Reformed Presbyterian Church of Ireland*, Belfast, 1984.
McCartney, D.J.: *Nor Principalities nor Powers: A history of First Presbyterian Church*. Carrickfergus, 1991.
McCaughan, M.: "Paul Rodgers, an Ulster Shipbuilder and his Welsh Connections". Maritime Wales. 1983
McConnell, C.: *Carrickfergus: A Stroll through Time*. 1994
McConnell, J.: *Fasti of the Irish Presbyterian Church, 1616-1840*. Belfast, 1951
McFetridge, L.: *Carrickfergus - a Booklist*. Carrickfergus, 1986.
McKinney, J.: *Where the Six Mile Water Flows: Historic photographs of the Ballyclare area*. Belfast, Friar's Bush Press, 1991.
MacNeice, J.F.: *Carrickfergus and its contacts*. Belfast, 1928.
McNeill, T.E.: *Anglo Norman Ulster: the history and archaelology of an Irish barony 1177-1400*. Edinburgh, 1980.
McNeill, T.E.: *Carrickfergus Castle*. Belfast, H.M.S.O., 1981.
McSkimin, S.: *The History and Antiquities of the County of the Town of Carrickfergus*. Belfast, 1811 etc. New edition with notes by E.J. McCrum. Belfast, 1909.
Maguire, W.A.: *Living like a Lord: The Second Marquis of Donegall, 1769-1844*. Belfast, 1984.
Millin, J.S.: *Additional Sidelights on Belfast History*. Belfast, 1938.
Mitchell, G.A.: *A Guide to Saint Nicholas' Church*. Carrickfergus, 1962.
MOPIA KPATEOMENH ...... *being a collection of all the addresses, squibs and songs, which appeared before, and at the Carrickfergus midsummer election, 1808*. Carrickfergus, 1808.
Morison, S.E.: *John Paul Jones: a sailor's biography*. Boston, 1959.
Northern Whig, The. Published daily from 1824.
O'Laverty, J.: *An Historical Account of the Diocese of Down and Connor*. Volume 3, Dublin, 1884 (reprinted, Ballynahinch, 1981).
Rankin, D. Helen and Nelson, E.C. (ed.), *Curious in Everything: the Career of Arthur Dobbs of Carrickfergus 1689-1765*. Belfast, 1990.
Reeves, W.: *Ecclesiastical Antiquities of Down and Connor and Dromore*. Dublin, 1847.
Robinson, P.S.: *Historic Towns Atlas: Fascicle No. 2, Carrickfergus*. Dublin, Royal Irish Academy, 1986.
Scott, A.B., and Martin, F.X., (ed), *Expugnatio Hibernia: The Conquest of Ireland by Giraldus Cambrensis*. Dublin, 1978.
Speers, Sheela: "A Note on Castle Lugg, West Division" in *Carrickfergus and District Historical Journal*, 1986, 2:56.
Speers, Sheela: *Under the Big Lamp*. Belfast, Friar's Bush Press, 1989.
Stevenson, D.: *Scottish Covenanters and Irish Confederates*. Belfast, 1981.
Stewart, Iris. *Loughmorne Presbyterian Church, Graveyard and Surrounding District*. 1994.
Vicars, A.: *Index to the Prerogative Wills of Ireland, 1536-1810*. Dublin, 1897.
White, W.M.: *Im Memoriam: the Late Rev. James White*. Belfast, 1890.
Who Was Who
Young, G.V.C., and Foster, Caroline: *Captain Francois Thurot*. Peel, 1986.
Young, R.M. and Pike, W.T.: *Belfast and the Province of Ulster in the 20th Century: with Contemporary Biographies*. Brighton, 1909.

LIST OF ABBREVIATIONS

A.D.	Anno Domini
ae	aetatis
A.R.H.A.	Associate of the Royal Hibernian Academy
B.A.	Bachelor of Arts
B.A.O.	Bachelor of the Arts of Obstetric
B.Ch.	Bachelor of Surgery
B. & N.C. Ry.	Belfast & Northern Counties Railway
C.B.	Commander of the Order of the Bath
D.D.	Doctor of Divinity
D.L.	Deputy Lieutenant
F.R.C.S.E.	Fellow of the Royal College of Surgeons of England
H.E.I.C.S.	Honourable East India Company's Service
H.M.	Her Majesty
H.M.S.	Her Majesty's Ship
I.H.S.	*Iesus Hominum Salvator* or *In Hac (cruce) Salus* or *In Hoc Signo (vinces)*
J.P.	Justice of the Peace
K.C.B.	Knight Commander of the Order of the Bath
K.C.S.I.	Knight Commander of the Star of India
LL.D.	Doctor of Laws
M.A.	Master of Arts
M.B.	Bachelor of Medicine
M.D.	Doctor of Medicine
M.D.	*Memorials of the Dead (Journal of the Association for the Preservation of the Memorials of the Dead in Ireland)*
M.R.I.A.	Member of the Royal Institute of Architects
N.S.W.	New South Wales
N.Y.	New York
P.M.	Past Master (Freemasons)
P.P.	Parish Priest
P.R.O.N.I.	Public Record Office of Northern Ireland
q.v.	quid vides
R.A.	Royal Artillery
R.C.	Roman Catholic
R.I.C.	Royal Irish Constabulary
R.I.P.	*Requiesca(n)t In Pace*
R.I.R.	Royal Irish Rifles
R.N.	Royal Navy
R.P.	Reformed Presbyterian
T.C.D.	Trinity College, Dublin
U.D.C.	Urban District Council
U.K.	United Kingdom
U.S.A.	United States of America
vid. inf.	vide infra (see below)

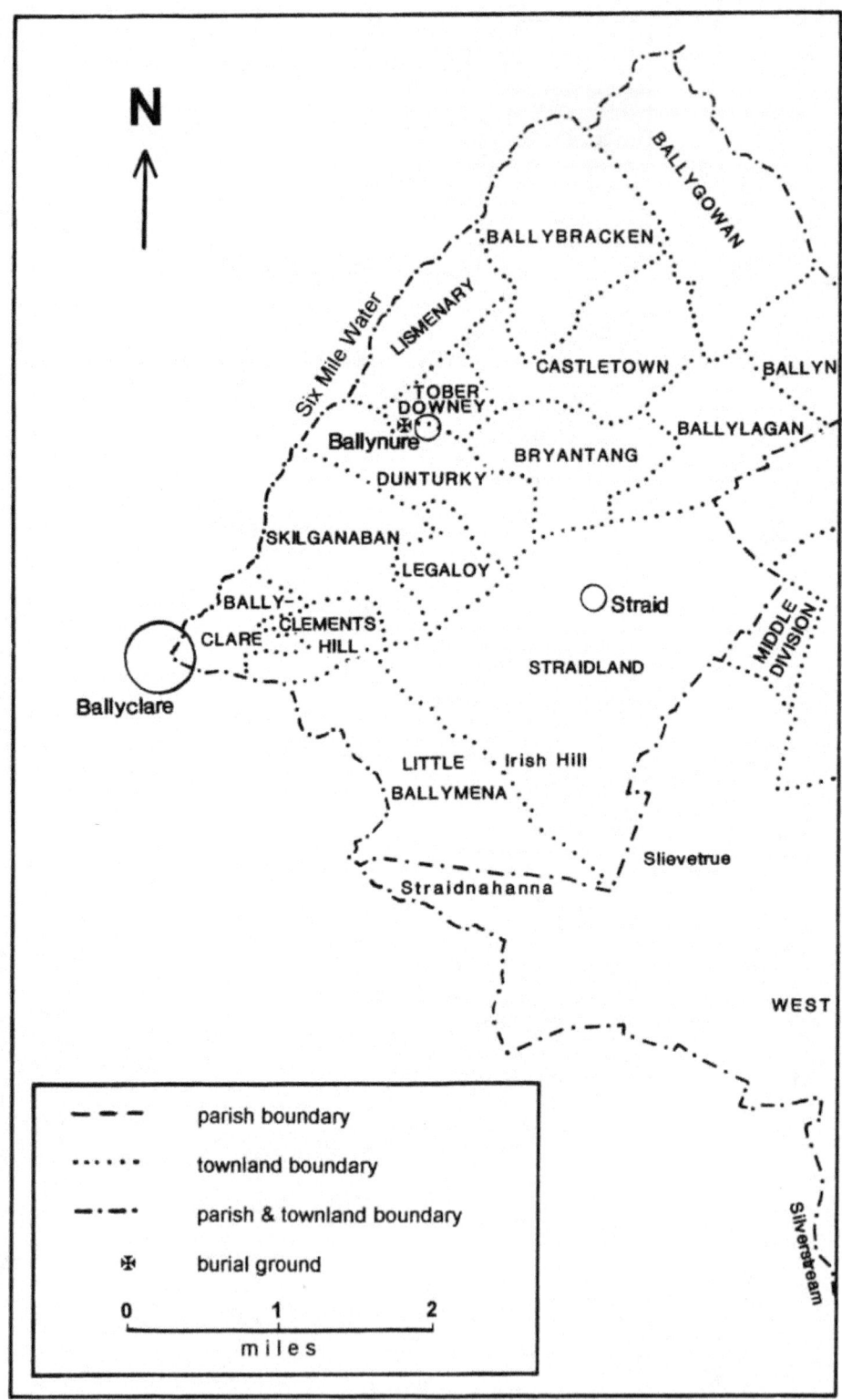

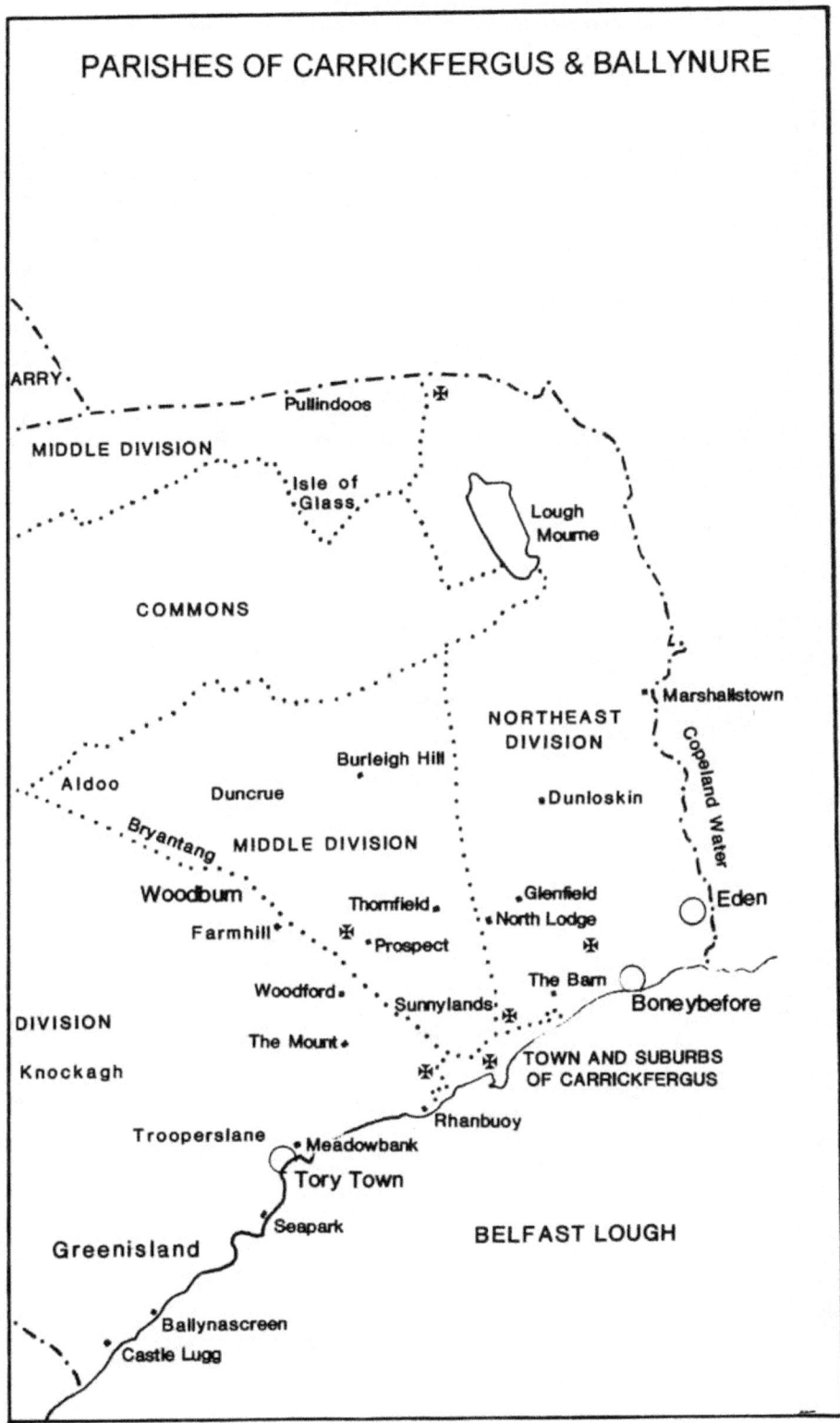

BALLYGOWAN TOWNLAND, KNOX GRAVE

O.S. 46 Grid Ref. J349950

This is an isolated grave on a farm in the townland of Ballygowan, two miles north east of Ballynure. According to his desire Mr Knox was buried on his own farm two field lengths from the house. The simple sandstone memorial is in a railed enclosure planted with laurels and of sufficient size to accommodate his large, but absent, family.

In the front garden of the farmhouse and at the base of a shed gable is the inscription "James Knox 1778", said to commemorate the arrival of the family at this farm. Higher on the wall a painted face, cast in plaster, survived until about 1978. This was identified as James Knox who was a brother of Joseph and who emigrated to America in 1840 eventually settling near Hebron, Nebraska. Eaves protected the plaster cast from the weather and the "shrine" was completed by a shelf which could carry vases of flowers.

KNOX

Sacred to the memory of Joseph Knox who departed this life on the 24th day of January in the year of our Lord 1900 in his 73rd year. Erected by his family.

BALLYNURE OLD GRAVEYARD

O.S. 45 Grid Ref. J315936

This is in the townland of Toberdowney, parish of Ballynure, and barony of Lower Belfast and is severed from the older part of the village by the main road. A tributary of the Six Mile Water flows past on one side of the graveyard. Newtownabbey Borough Council keeps the grass neatly trimmed. Of the old parish church of Saint Mary Magdalene which stood within the graveyard, only the west doorway and part of a later porch now remain standing. Near the ruins are three family vaults. One (Dobbs) is Victorian with steeply pitched roof, while the earlier two (Dobbs and Ellis) are barrel vaulted.

A relic from the days of resurrectionists, or body snatchers, is the corpse house by the entrance gate. It is sturdily built of locally quarried basalt, and buttresses flank a doorway defended by a heavy iron grill. When Thomas Fagan was taking notes for the Ordnance Survey memoir in 1839 he said it was erected by the parish for a safe depository for bodies lying there a number of days previous to interment - a plan lately adopted against resurrectionists taking up or carrying off the bodies in a fresh state.

Fagan noted sixty-one surnames from gravestones. The following names are included in his list but cannot now be found on pre-1840 stones: Anderson, Barklimore, McConaghy, McCrom, Morrow, Macky, Rogers, Stephenson, Stevenson, Watson and Wiley. The earliest date of death to be read is 1628 (Clements), although Fagan has 1717 as the oldest legible stone.

As this was the old parish burial ground all religious denominations buried here. A low area with few headstones in the south east was used for the unbaptised and suicides. The burial register dates from 1852. All stones with dates of death up to 1900 have been copied.

ADAMSON
[Flaking sandstone.] Erected by ...... (m) Adamson of Castletown in memory of his father (Ro)bert Adamson who died 23rd Dec. 1848 aged (5)9 years. Also his mother Jane Adamson who died 13th Dec. 18(5)8 aged 70 years.

ADAMSON
[Lead lettering in white marble, next to foregoing.] Erected by William Adamson of Castletown in memory of his mother Ann SIMMS who died 21st October 1904. Also his father William Adamson who died 6th April 1906. Also his sister Jenny who died 8th January 1921. Also his brother Samuel H. who died 6th February 1897. His sisters: Jean died 29th March 1923 aged 75 years; Margaret died 3rd June 1936 aged 78 years. Also his brother James died 1st November 1937 aged 68 years. Also his wife Annie SCOTT died 18th November 1952 aged 75 years. Also their infant son William Scott died 13th September 1905 aged 10 weeks. And the above William Adamson died 29th September 1947 aged 84 years. [Mason:-] T. Holden, Larne.

ADRAIN
[Cast iron plaque.] John Adrain, Ballynure, 2 graves. [Cast by:-] Samuel Millar, Ballyclare Foundry.

ADRAIN
[White marble with granite surround.] Erected to the memory of John Adrain who died 2nd Octr. 1892 aged 82 years. His wife Mary Adrain who died 19th Novr. 1865 aged 49 years. Their eldest daughter Margaret who died 2nd Octr. 1897 aged 50 years. And three of their children, Susanna, John, and Hugh, who died in infancy. Also of Robert Adrain who died 13th January 1902 aged 62 years, son of John and Mary Adrain. Also their sons William Adrain who died on board the troopship 'Nankin' 8th August 1878 aged 39 years, and was buried at sea. Hugh C. Adrain, master mariner, who died at Mackay, Queensland, 11th September 1903 aged 51 years. William Kearns Adrain, 2nd lieut. 5th Batt. Royal Irish Regiment,

killed in action in France, 24th August 1916 aged 20 years, third son of Robert Adrain. Jane, wife of Robert Adrain, died 10th April 1931 aged 74 years. John Adrain, eldest son of Robert and Jane Adrain, died 4th November 1942. Robert Adrain died 30th August 1976. Margaret Adrian, born 17th July 1897, died 25th June 1986. Charlotte STEWART, born 8th March 1899, died 30th August 1986.

[The will of John Adrain, late of Carntall, county Antrim, farmer, who died 2 October 1892 at same place, was proved at Belfast 13 July 1894 by Robert Adrain of Ballyclare, in said county, draper, and Stafford Clair of Carntall, farmer, the executors. Effects £175.]

AGNEW
[Lead lettering in white marble, now broken in two.] Erected by Ann Agnew of Belfast in memory of her beloved husband William Agnew who departed this life 9th January 1888 aged 54 years. Also Agnes Agnew, youngest child, who departed this life 22nd November 1883 aged 4 years. Also the above-named Ann Agnew who died 20th Nov. 1916 aged 80 years. Also Margaret Agnew died 12th July 1(921). Blessed are the dead which die in the Lord. 2 graves each side.

ALCORN
[A very low stone. The name of the deceased has been chiselled out.] 1869. Erected by Ann Jane Alcorn in memory of .... in 1846.

ALEXANDER
See McCAY

ALLEN
[Sandstone.] Sacred to the memory of a beloved father and mother Samuel and Mary Allen of Ardboley. Also two daughters Martha and Maryann.

ALLEN
[Sandstone, a wreath is carved between two quatrefoils.] Erected by William Allen, Ballyfore, in memory of his son Samuel Allen who died February the 12th 1871 aged 33 years in full assurance and blessed hope of a glorious resurrection. Also his two daughters Sarah and Jane who died in infancy. 4 graves north.

ANDERSON
Erected by Thomas Anderson to the memory of his beloved daughter Alice Jane who departed this life August 11th 1858 aged 19 years. Also his beloved daughter Susan who departed this life July 20th 1862 aged 27 years. The above-named Thomas Anderson died at Ballynure on 17th Septr. 1883 aged 75 years. Also his wife Jane Anderson who died 7th March 1888 aged 80 years.

AULD
[Lead lettering in white marble.] Erected by John Auld in memory of his wife Matilda Auld who died 28th Sept. 1913 aged 59 years. The above named John Auld who died 7th Jan. 1926 aged 83 years. Also their son Samuel who died 21st Jan. 1898 aged 19 years. [Mason:-] Holden, Larne.

BAIRD
[White marble panel set into sandstone with capstone missing.] Erected by J. & E. WILSON in affectionate remembrance of their niece Eliza Baird who died 23rd March 1862 aged 36 years. Also her three children: Margaret Wilson Baird died 1850 aged 2 years, Huston Wilson Baird died 1859 aged 14 months, Ann Baird died 1861 aged 13 months. Also R. T. W. Baird, M. J. Baird, and E. STRAIGHT (nee Baird).

BANKHEAD
See CHAMBERS and HILL

(B)ARCLY
See FORSYTH

BARKLIE

[Sandstone, now fallen face downward.] Erected by James Barklie of Lismenary in memory of his uncle Jas. Barklie who departed this life in the year 1818 aged 68 years. And his wife Nancy JAMFREY who died in the year 1843 aged 84 years. And also of my own beloved wife Elizabeth HAY who died 15th of July 1852 aged 59 years. Likewise the above named James Barklie who died 8th July 1873 aged 89 years. Also his daughters Elia who died 31st July 1905 aged 71 years. And Isabella who died 10th July 1912 aged 75 years.

BARKLIMORE

[Sandstone within railing.] Erected by Hugh B. SEMPLE of Thornfield in memory of his aunt Mary Barklimore who departed this life 23rd of Jan. 1855 aged 84 years. Also his aunt Elizabeth Barklimore who departed this life 29th of April 1859 aged 70 years and his mother Jane Semple who departed this life 7th Feby. 1864 aged 90 years. Also the said Hugh B. Semple who departed this life 20th April 1873 aged 78 years. He was respected by all who knew him. Jane Semple died in Carnlough 11th March 1892 aged 62 years. Archibald B. Semple died in Australia 11th February 1915.

[The will of Hugh Barklimore Semple, late of Jordanstown, county Antrim, gentleman, who died 20 April 1873 at same place, was proved at Belfast 30 July 1873 by the oath of William McQuillan of Cushendall, schoolmaster, and James Moreland of Ballyduff, farmer, both in (Carnmoney), said county, the executors. Effects under £3,000.]

BARTON

See WILSON

BATES

See GREENFIELD

BEATTIE

[Sandstone.] In memory of Edward Beattie who died 29th Dec. 1842 aged 80 years. Also Margaret Beattie his wife aged 84. And her daughters: Agnes HUME died 3rd September 1887 and Margaret HALL died 5th September 1895. At rest.

[The will of Margaret Hall, late of Ballyboley, Ballyeaston, county Antrim, widow, who died 5 September 1895 at same place, was proved at Belfast 25 September 1895 by Robert Hutchison of City Lane, Ballyloggan, and Robert James Wilson of Ballyalbana, both in said county, farmers, the executors. Effects £359. 13s. 4d.]

BEATTY

Erected to the memory of John Beatty of Ballynure who died October 29th 1825 aged 52 years. And his wife Ann HAY who died on the 16th December 1871 aged 86 years. Sarah Jane BOYD, wife of Robert Beatty, died 19th June 1897 aged 82 years. Robert Beatty died 24th April 1899 aged 85 years. Also in loving memory of Elizabeth Hay Beatty, youngest daughter of Robert Beatty, died 23rd July 1936 aged 81 years.

[The will of Ann Beatty, late of Rushvale, near Ballyclare, county Antrim, widow, who died 16 December 1871, at same place, was proved at Belfast 12 February 1872 by the oaths of William Andrew Wylie of Little Ballymena, Ballynure, farmer, and Robert Beatty of Ballynure, merchant, both in said county, two of the executors. Effects under £1,000.]

BEATTY

[White marble stone next to foregoing.] In loving memory of Maggie Boyd eldest child of Robert Beatty, Ballynure, whose spirit gently passed away on the 2nd January 1858 in the 18th year of her age. And of Bobbie the youngest who after a short life of most patient suffering found his rest on the 31st March 1861 aged 3 years and 10 months. Also of John, second son, who on the 24th January 1871 slept in Jesus aged 25 years. 'Blessed are the dead which die in the Lord.' Rev. XIV, 13.

BEATTY
See SMILEY and WYLIE

BEGGS
See HILL

BELL
[A very low stone. Arms: three bells. Crest: a ......statant (the head was worn off.)] Here lyeth the body of John Bell who died 5th Sept. 1738 aged 2(5) years. Also John Bell who died 29 May 1775 aged 48.

BELL
[Ledger stone next to foregoing. In giving the age a two occupies the same space as the four, therefore it could be intended as either '28' or '48'. Arms: three bells disposed. Crest: a bell. Motto: Love is the sign of peace. Two square and compass symbols are scratched on the stone.] In memory of William Bell surgeon and apothecary of Ballyclare who departed this life March the 13th 1794 aged (4)8 years. He lived beloved & died much lamented by all who knew him.

BELL
Erected to the memory of John Bell glazier at Ballynure who departed this life 22d. (Octr. 181)7 aged 4(.) years. Also two of his children who died in childhood.

BELL
[Ten fragments of this stone were collected and assembled.] Erected in memory of Andrew B......(a)rne who died .... aged 63. Also his son William Bell who died in Demerara 25th Se.. 1831 aged 23. And his son Jam.. (wh)o died in infancy.

BELL
[An unusual wheeled cross of sandstone. On the north arm is a coronet above an anchor. On the south arm 'I.H.S.' The inscription is on white marble set into the plinth.] In affectionate remembrance of Anne, the beloved wife of Richard Bell, who departed this life 3rd Jan. 1866 aged 30 years.

BELL
[Panel of white marble set into sandstone, within railings.] Erected by John Bell of Tildarg in memory of his parents: Elizabeth Bell who died April 1867 aged 7(3) years and William Bell who died September 1871 aged 78 years. Also their grandchild Wm. Jno. Bell who died Nov. 1876 aged 13 years. Also their friend Js. McLATCHIE died June 2nd 1882 aged 31 yrs. Also above named John Bell died May 17th 1893 aged 76 yrs. & their daughter Margt. GREENLES died Feb. 14th 1897 aged 70 yrs. [Mason:-] R. Love, York St., Belfast.

BELL
[Polished granite next to William Bell, died 1794.] In memory of David Bell, Saint Catherines, Carrickfergus, who departed this life 18th July 1886 aged 80 years. 'I know that my Redeemer liveth.' Job, XIX, 25.
[The will of David Bell, late of St. Catherine's, Carrickfergus, gentleman, who died 18 July 1886 at same place, was proved at Belfast 4 August 1886 by Sarah Kirk, widow, and Anna Molyneux, spinster, both of Marsden Villa, Antrim Road, the executrixes. Effects £2,549. 11s. 4d.]

BELL
[White marble.] Sacred to the memory of Mary, wife of Robert John Bell of Ballybracken, Doagh, who departed this life 19th April 1896 aged 64 years. [Mason:-] Holden, Larne. 3 graves.

BELL
See FALLOON

BIRNIE
[Sandstone.] Erected to the memory of Jane Birnie who departed this life 26th February 1805 aged 62 years. Also her husband Samuel Birnie who departed this life 5th June 1815 aged 65 years.

BILSHER
[Sandstone in the east of graveyard.] Erected by Eliza Jane REA in memory of her beloved husband John Rea Bilsher who died 9th December 1856 aged 29 years. Also the above named Eliza Jane Rea who died 13th May 1873 aged 33 years.

BLAIR
[Broken white marble in enclosure beside church ruins.] Erected by William Park Blair and Lizzie Crawford Blair, Ballynure, in memory of their infant daughter, born 19th January 1882, died 1st February 1882. "He shall gather the lambs with his arm." Isaiah, XL, II.

BLAIR
See MAWHINNEY

BOYD
[Unconventional arms: a fess chequy. Crest: a dexter hand giving a victory salute.] Here lieth the body of William Boyd, late burgess of Carrickfergus, who departed this life 23d. day of February 1783 aged 72 years.

BOYD
[Tall sandstone on the west edge of the graveyard.] Sacred to the memory of Samuel Boyd who departed this life November 24th 1838 aged 75 years. Also his son Samuel who died November 17th 1824 aged 11 months.

BOYD
[Sandstone on the western edge of graveyard.] Here lieth the body of John Boyd who departed this life the 15th August 182(5) aged 35 years.

BOYD
[Tilting stone within iron railings.] Erected by John Boyd in memory of his daughter Eally who departed this life 27th May 1826 aged 17 years. Also Samuel Boyd her brother who departed this life on the 29th October 1832 aged 26 years. And James Boyd his brother who departed this life on the 8th November 1833 aged 18 years. Likewise Elizabeth Boyd their mother who departed this life 9th April 1849 aged 66 years. And the said James Boyd their father who departed this life the 30th March 1850 aged 74 years.

BOYD
[Lead lettering on white marble set into sandstone.] Erected by Joice Boyd, Straid, in memory of her beloved husband James Boyd, who departed this life 16th Jany. 1868 aged 53 years. The above named Joice Boyd died 16th Feby. 1877 aged 53 years. Also their son Wm. Andrew who died 17th April 1874 aged 6 years. Also their son James who died 16th Decr. 1881 aged 33 years. Also their son Robert Dixon Boyd who died 17th April 1912 aged 65 years. And their son Thomas Boyd who died 18th April 1938 and Mary, wife of Thomas Boyd, died 8th June 1914. [Mason:-] R. McCormick, Belfast.

[The will of James Boyd, late of Straid, Ballynure, Co Antrim, innkeeper, who died 16 January 1868 at same place, was proved at Belfast 10 February 1868 by John Wilson of Dunturkey (Ballynure) and Alexander Kirk of Leggaloy, Ballynure, farmers, the executors. Effects £4,000.

The will of Joice Boyd, late of Straid, county Antrim, widow, who died 16 February 1877 at same place, was proved at Belfast 8 November 1878 by the oath of James Boyd of Straid, Ballyclare, same county, farmer, one of the executors. Effects under £2,000.

The will of James Boyd, late of Straid, county Antrim, farmer, who died 16 December 1881 at same place, was proved at Belfast 13 January 1882 by Robert

Hugh Gamble and Thomas Wilson, both of Straid, farmers, the executors. Effects £1,053. 10s. 3d.]

BOYD
[Polished granite beside McComb ledger.] Erected by David Boyd, Ballynure, in memory of his beloved wife Sarah Boyd died 12th April 1878 aged 60 years. Also the above David Boyd died 20th Dec. 1880 aged 69 years.

[The will of David Boyd, formerly of Ballynure, county Antrim, and late of Ballylaggan, Carrickfergus, publican, who died 20 December 1880 at latter place, was proved at Belfast 18 March 1881 by the oath of Hugh Whiteford of Ballylaggan, farmer, one of the executors. Effects under £500.]

BOYD
[White marble with lead lettering beside that of John Boyd who died 182(5).] Erected to the memory of John Boyd, Straid, who died 28th Novr. 1884 aged 83 years. Also his wife Mary who died 27th Decr. 1882 aged 74 years. Also their son Andrew Boyd died 4th May 1920 aged 75 years. Also his wife Jenny LOGAN died 1st Nov. 1909 aged 70 years. And their son John Boyd died 14th Nov. 1893 aged 19 years. Mary Agnes Boyd died 6th June 1946. Her sister Martha Ross Boyd died 20th January 1955.

BOYD
See BEATTY, McCAMON and McCAY

BRENAN
See DOBBS

BUCHANAN
[Lead lettering in white marble.] Erected by Robert Buchanan in memory of his sister Eliza Buchanan who died 28th Jan. 1876 aged 42 years. Also his father John Buchanan who died 24th May 1878 aged 91 years. Also his mother Eliza Buchanan who died 12th May 1886 aged 95 years. Also his brother John Buchanan who died 4th Feb. 1902 aged 83 years. Also his sister Margaret Buchanan who died 19th July 1904 aged 81 years. Also the above-named Robert Buchanan who died 21st March 1923 aged 92 years. [Mason:-] T. Holden, Larne.

CAIRNS
See SIMM

CALHOON
See LOVE

CAMPBELL
[A large stone broken into many pieces. It has a late 18th century style.] Here lyeth ye body of John Campbell merchant in Belf... son of George Campbell at Belynur(e) who departed this life ye 9 o(f) February ...(7).

CAMPBELL
Erected by Agnes Campbell in memory of her beloved mother Agnes Campbell who departed this life 15th June 1847 aged 46 years. And of her father William Campbell who departed this life 7th Novr. 1863 aged 65 years. The above-named Agnes Campbell died 25th Jany. 1898 aged 60 years.

CARMICHAEL
[Concrete tablet next to vault.] 1894. Family burying ground, erected by Jenny Carmichael. 4 graves W.C. J.S.

CARSON
[Blue slate.] William Carson.

CHAMBERS
[White marble in sandstone frame, loose, in same enclosure as Rev. Adam Hill, 1827.] In memoriam Janie BANKHEAD, the beloved wife of Robert Chambers, ob. Sunday 13th October 1861 AE 24 years and is now a saint in heaven.

CINNAMOND
[Lead lettering on white marble set into wall of vault beside Dobbs tablet. Crest: a dove statant, in its beak a fern leaf. Motto: Pro amore et pace.] Erected to the memory of Eliza Cinnamond, daughter of James and Elizabeth PARK, who departed this life 12th September 1875. Also her son Thomas Cinnamond, solicitor, who died 22nd March 1880 aged 49 years. And his daughter Mary who died 25th January 1888 aged 17 years.

CLARKE
See SCOTT

CLEMENTS
[Two tablets (Castle Espie limestone and sandstone) flank the sealed entrance of a basalt vault.] Here lyeth the body of Ellinor, the wife of Edward Clements of Mvlligan-Hill gent. and eldest daughter of Alexander DALLVAY of Bally Hill Esqr., who departed this life the 3th day of March 1628 aged 35 years.

This tablet to mark the burying place of the ELLIS family of Straid & Prospect was placed here by direction of their last representative Jane Anne Clements NICOLEY in July 1884. Tablet in opposite pillar has been placed there for safety.

[Captain Robert Ellis obtained a burgess share in the 1606 division of Carrickfergus lands. He had three sons John, Edmond and Henry. Edmond was provost-marshall under Sir Henry Dockwra and had five sons Foulk, Edmond, Francis, Anthony, and Henry, who were all active in the military struggles of the civil wars. Edmond was governor of Carrickfergus in 1649. Henry served as a major under the Commonwealth, acquired lands in Leinster, and had four sons Henry, Francis, Hercules, and Edward, of whom the eldest (Henry) married Sarah, daughter of Edward Clements, Straid, and was sovereign of Belfast 1717, 1720, and 1722. Francis settled at Prospect and married Anne, another daughter of Edward Clements. They had two sons Henry and Hercules. Hercules was the mayor of Carrickfergus in 1770 and 1774. He married Catherine Barry, a granddaughter of Sir Robert Adair, but left no children. The elder brother Henry was mayor 1754-57 and again in 1773. He married Eleanor, daughter of Waterhouse Crymble of Clements Hill. They had three daughters. Millicent married Charles Adair of Loughanmore in 1775; Nancy married Rev. Dr C. Benning; and Mary did not marry. Their only son Henry Clements Ellis inherited Straidland on the death of his uncle Edward Crymble and married firstly Jane, daughter of William Burleigh of Dublin, who died in 1795 without surviving children. His second wife was Jane, a daughter of James Craig of Carrickfergus (q.v.) and their daughter Jane married firstly Duncan Wilson, and secondly Christian William Nicolay. See McCrum ed. of McSkimin: *History and Antiquities of Carrickfergus* (1909).]

CLEMENTS
[Red sandstone next to Mary Clements who died in 1867.] Erected by Mary McCURDY in memory of her husband Henry Clements who died on the 2nd March 1831 aged 75 years. The above-named Henry Clements' first wife Martha SIMM died the 9th July 1800 aged 48 years.

CLEMENTS
[Small unshaped stone.] Here lyeth the body of Frances Clements aged 82 years. 1812.

CLEMENTS
In memory of Mary Clements, the beloved wife of Wm. Clements, who departed this life on 5th March 1867 aged 63 years. And an infant son. Also her son Andrew who was lost at sea in May 1852 aged 22 years. Also the above-named Wm. Clements who died 16th March 1882 aged 76 years.

CLEMENTS
See PHILIPS

COBAIN
[Sandstone on western edge of graveyard.] Erected by Robert Cobain in memory of his beloved wife Mary who departed this life on the 9th of December 1854 aged 50 years. Also the erector Robert Cobain of Coldhaim who departed this life the 27th January 1889 aged 91 years.

[The will of Robert Cobain, late of Caldhame, Ballynure, county Antrim, farmer, who died 27 January 1889 at same place, was proved at Belfast 18 March 1889 by Sarah Beattie, wife of David Beattie of Caldhame, Straid, and Samuel Kirk of Clement's Hill, Ballynure, farmer and carpenter, both in said county, the executors. Effects £560. 9s.]

COBAIN
[Red sandstone.] Erected by Robert Cobain in memory of his daughter Rose who died on the 8th August 1867 aged 3 months.

COYNE
See PARK

CRAIG
[Polished granite.] In memory of Hugh Craig, Ballyboley, who departed this life 7th April 1881 aged 59 years. Also of his brother John Craig, Ballyboley who died 25th July 1885 aged 65 years. Rachel Craig who died 6th June 1897. Anne Jane Craig died 28th May 1913. Hugh Craig died 19th May 1934. Also their daughter Jane Eleanor died 3rd Oct. 1900.

[Letters of administration of the personal estate of Hugh Craig, late of Ballyboley, county Antrim, farmer, who died 7 April 1881 at Belfast, were granted at Belfast 6 May 1881 to John Craig of Ballyboley, farmer, a brother. Effects under £1,000.

The will of John Craig, late of Ballyboley, county Antrim, farmer, who died 25 July 1885 at same place, was proved at Belfast 21 August 1885 by James Craig of Cogry and John Stewart and William Stewart, both of Ballycorr, all in said county, farmers, the executors. Effects £1,914. 15s. 9d.

Probate of the will of Rachel Craig, late of Ballyboley, county Antrim, spinster, who died 6 June 1897, granted at Belfast 18 January 1898 to John and William Stewart, both of Ballyboley, farmers, and the Reverend William John McCracken of Ballyeaston, county Antrim, Presbyterian minister. Effects £906. 8s. 8d.]

CROOKS
The burying ground of Andrew & John Crooks. 1883. [Cast by:] Ulster Foundry.

CROSS
[Unshaped local stone next to following plaque.] P. Cross. J.C.

CROSS
[Cast iron plaque mounted on low railing.] The family burying ground of James Cross. [Cast by:-] The Millfield Foundry 1925. 3 graves.

CROWE
[Sandstone originally of the Phillips family.] The family burying place of John Crowe, Straid. In memory of his mother Margery Crowe who died 2nd June 1884 aged 82 years. Also his father Samuel Crowe who died 28th Aug. 1889 aged 94 years. Also his daughter Elizabeth Jane who died 21st June 1905 aged 12 years. Also his wife Mary Agnes who died 17th March 1922 aged 63 years. The above-named John Crowe died 14th October 1936 aged 92 years. Samuel, son of John and Mary Crowe, died 29th April 1946, interred in Walnut Hills Cemetery, Boston, U.S.A. Also their son John died 31st March 1958.

CRYMBLE

[Sandstone.] Erected by Robert Crymble of Ballyboley in memory of his father Joseph Crymble who departed this life 3rd Feb. 1875 aged 77 years. Also his mother Jenny Crymble who died 14th Jan. 1896 aged 92 years. Also his sister Ellen who died 29th Feb. 1892 aged 60 years. Also his sister Maggie who died 23rd May 1911 aged 65 years. Also the above named Robert Crymble who died 26th Oct. 1912 aged 78 years. Also his sister Sarah who died 21st Jan. 1925 aged 85 years.

[The will of Joseph Crymble, late of Ballyboley, county Antrim, farmer, who died 3 February 1875 at same place, was proved at Belfast 7 January 1876 by the oaths of Jenny Crymble, widow, James Blair, farmer, and John Hill, farmer, all of Ballyboley, the executors. Effects under £300.

The will of Ellen Crymble, late of Ballyboley, Ballynure, county Antrim, spinster, who died 29 February 1892 at same place, was proved at Belfast 11 April 1892 by Hugh Bailie of Rorysglen, Kilwaughter, said county, farmer, the sole executor. Effects £187. 6s. 10d.]

CURRAN

[Beside vault.] Erected by David Curran, Ballynerry, in memory of his father William Curran who died 15th Novr. 1853 aged 64 years. Also his mother Agnes Curran who died 11th March 1888 aged 85 years. And his brother John who died 20th March 1886 aged 57 years. The above-named David Curran died 9th July 1908 aged 64 years. Nancy KNOX, beloved wife of David Curran, died 25th Aug. 1948 aged 92 years. "Blessed are the dead who die in the Lord."

[The will of John Curran, late of Ballynerry, Ballynure, county Antrim, farmer, who died 20 March 1886 at same place, was proved at Belfast 30 April 1886 by David Curran of Ballynerry, David Jamison of Ballynure and Henry Wilson of Ballygowan, all in said county, farmers, the executors. Effects £724. 11s. 5d.]

DALLVAY
See CLEMENTS

DAVIDSON

[Sandstone.] Erected to the memory of James Davidson, Clementshill, who departed this life December 23rd 1828 aged 42 years. Also his beloved wife Jennet Davidson who died September 18th 1846 aged 62 years. Likewise their son James Davidson who died June 4th 1844 aged 27 years. And also their son John Davidson who died July 11th 1847 aged 27 years.

DAVIS

[Sandstone of c.1850.] Erected by James Davis in memory of his beloved parents William & Ann Davis. Also his brothers & sisters.

DAVIS

Erected by Robert Davis in memory of his beloved wife Eliza Davis who departed this life 8th Jany. 1875 aged 47 years. Also his son Robert who died 15th Feb. 1880 aged 27 years.

DEMPSIE

Erected by James Demspie of Ballygowan in memory of his beloved mother Agnes Dempsie who departed this life 24th March 1863 aged 70 years. Also his father Robert Dempsie who died 10th Sept. 1872 aged 84 years.

DICKEY
See WILSON

DOBBS

[Oval sandstone tablet on side of vault.] Erected by Margaret BRENAN to the memory of her cousin Elizabeth Dobbs who departed this life 18th July 1825 aged 63 years.

DOBBS
See PHILLIPS

DONALDSON
[Lead lettering on white marble.] Erected by Hugh Donaldson in memory of his grand-father Robert Donaldson who died 9th April 1887. His grand-mother Rose Donaldson who died 21st Feby. 1894. His mother Elizabeth Donaldson who died 23rd June 1894. His two sisters who died young. His aunt Margaret Donaldson who died 21st Decr. 1910 aged 73 years. His father John Donaldson who died 14th June 1922 aged 77 years. His aunt Anne Donaldson who died 12th Jany. 1924 aged 84 years. The above-named Hugh Donaldson who died 27th Dec. 1924 aged 37 years. His son James, "wee Bim", who died 23rd July 1925 aged 15 months. His uncle James Donaldson who died 15th Dec. 1932 aged 84 years. Jenny, Jean, wife of Hugh, died 23rd Dec. 1978.

DORMAN
[Sandstone.] Erected by William Dorman of Ballylagan in grateful & affectionate remembrance of his father Ezekiel Dorman aged 50 years. He departed this life 12th January 1839.

DOUGLAS
[Sandstone. The original inscription has been chiselled off.] Erected by James Douglas, Straid.

DUNDEE
See WILSON

DUNLOP
See McCREARY

ELLIS
See CLEMENTS

FALLOON
[Polished granite in S.W. corner of graveyard.] In memory of the Rev. Charles Falloon who died 11th April 1872 aged 74 years, rector of this parish for 18 years. "I have fought a good fight, I have finished my course, I have kept the faith". 2 Tim. 4, 7. Also his wife Eliza Matilda WOLSELEY who died 8th January 1873 aged 90 years. Also their adopted daughter Louisa, last surviving child of Richard BELL, Green House, Ballyclare, who died 2nd June 1897 aged 76 years. Also Jane Maria Nixon Falloon their daughter who died 17th February 1917 aged 94 years. "This woman was full of good works and alms-deeds which she did." Acts IX. 36.

[The Rev. Charles Falloon was born in Donegal in 1798, son of the Rev. Daniel Falloon, and entered Trinity College, Dublin in 1814, though he did not graduate. He was curate of Annahilt 1826-41 and of Shankill 1841-52, vicar of Magheragall 1852-3 and prebend of Kilroot and rector of Ballynure 1853-72. He married on 12 April 1823 at Drumbo Parish Church, Eliza Matilda, 6th daughter of the Rev. William Wolseley, prebend of Tullycorbet (Diocese of Clogher). He died at 72 Main Street, Larne, and his widow also died at Larne. See Leslie: *Clergy of Connor* (1993); Burtchaell and Sadleir; *Alumni Dublinenses* (1924); Leslie: *Clogher Clergy and Parishes* (1929).]

FERGUSSON
[Within Park enclosure.] Erected by Sarah Fergusson to the memory of her dear husband George Fergusson, born at Girvan, Scotland, on the 31st March 1825, died 9th Sept. 1876 at Ballynure House aged 52 years. He was an honest man, a sincere friend, and a loving husband. Also to the memory of her niece & nephew, children of Richard D. & Eliza J. PARK. Mary F. Park, born 20th September 1863, died three months after birth. William J. H. Park, born 27th June 1871, died the 24th May 1876, beloved by all who knew him. Eliza J. Park died 23rd June

1887. The above-named Sarah G. Fergusson died August 1901 aged 74 years. Ella T. Park died 22nd July 1906. Richard Dobbs Park died 28th Septr. 1911 aged 81 years. Elizabeth Forsythe Park died 21st September 1943 aged 76 years.

[The will of George Fergusson, late of Ballynure, county Antrim, gentleman, who died 9 September 1876 at same place, was proved at Belfast 8 January 1877 by the oaths of Sarah Ferguson of Ballynure, same county, widow, and John Ferguson of 13 Dixon Street, Glasgow, county Lanark in Scotland, merchant, the executors. Effects under £200.]

FORSYTH

[Facing western hedge.] Here lieth the body of William Forsyth who departed this life June 19th 1778 aged 76 years.

FORSYTH

[Sandstone beside Hugh Forsythe who died in 1926. Face split from body of stone. Arms: a chevron engrailed between three griffins rampant. Motto: Instaurater Ruinae.] Here lyeth the body of Agnes (B)AROLY who departed this life 8th May 1792 aged 74 years, wife to John Forsyth.

FORSYTHE

[Within a wall of basalt.] Erected in memory of John Forsythe, formerly of Ballynure, who died at Holywood 22nd June 1862 aged 80 years. And of Hester his wife who died 15th February 1861 aged 81 years. Also of their daughters: Matilda died May 1830 aged 22 years and Hessy died January 1839 aged 16 years. And of their son William died 22nd April 1847 aged 30 years.

[The will of John Forsythe, late of Ballykeel, Holywood, in the county of Down, (formerly of Belfast) Esquire, who died 22 June 1862 at same place, was proved at Belfast 9 September 1862 by the oaths of Henry Shaw Ferguson of Donegall Square, Belfast, doctor of medicine, and Andrew Forsythe of Scoutbush, town of Carrickfergus, Esquire, (and Robert Forsythe, late of Charlestown South Carolina) the executors. Effects under £8,000.] [words in brackets are MS annotations in the National Archives, Dublin.]

FORSYTHE

[Sandstone against western hedge.] Sacred to the memory of Elizabeth, wife of Samuel Forsythe, who departed this life 8th April 1846 aged 39 years. She made home happy. Also their son Samuel who died 22nd October 1857 aged 21 years. Also their grandson George died October 31st 1874 aged 6 years. And their daughter in law Mary WILSON, wife of their son Alexander, died Feb. 10th 1875 aged 30 yrs. And the above-named Samuel Forsythe died July 21st 1877 aged 82 years. And their son Robert J. died March 21st 1878 aged 47 years.

[Letters of administration of the personal estate of Samuel Forsythe, late of Bryantang, county Antrim, farmer, who died 21 July 1877 at same place, were granted at Belfast 16 June 1879 to Alexander Woodside Forsythe of Bryantang, farmer, a child of said deceased. Effects under £300.

Letters of administration, with the will annexed, of the personal estate of Robert John Forsythe, formerly of Mount Pottinger, county Down, and late of Woodlawn, Carrickfergus, merchant, who died 21 March 1878 at latter place, were granted at the Principal Registry 21 November 1879 to Annie Forsythe of Woodlawn, widow, one of the residuary legatees of said deceased. Effects under £450.]

FORSYTHE

[Narrow railed plot in the west of the graveyard. Marble set into sandstone.] Erected by Andrew Forsythe Esq. to the memory of his grand uncle James Forsythe Esq. M.D. who departed this life at Holywood in the County of Down on the 12th day of June 1849 in the 94th year of his age.

FORSYTHE

[Fallen stone, with lead lettering on decorated panels of white marble set in sandstone.] In loving memory of Robert J. Forsythe, late of Charleston, who died 21st

March 1878 aged 47 years. And of his wife Annie Forsythe who died at Carrickfergus 28th October 1884 aged 42 years.

[The will of Annie Forsythe, late of Carrickfergus, widow, who died 23 October 1884 at same place, was proved at Belfast 17 November 1884 by the Reverend Ribton McCracken of Carrickfergus, clerk, and David Legg Wilson of Ballylaggan, Carrickfergus, farmer, the executors. Effects £231. 9s. 9d.]

FULERTON
[Arms: on a chevron between three boars' heads a crescent and two mullets. Crest: a ? horse's head couped. Motto: Lux in Tenebris. The style of the stone suggests a date c.1800.] Here lyeth the body of Samuel Fulerton who departed this life Novr. 18th .... aged 67 years. Also 4 (of) his children viz. William, John, Hugh & Agness.

FULLARTON
[14 pieces found and assembled.] Erected in memory of Hugh Fullarton who died on 19th March 1858 AE 82 years. And his wife Agnes who died 16th Oct. 1829 aged 43 years. Elizabeth their daughter .... aged 27 years .... son John .... years.
[And a stump in the grave yard which may or may not be part of the same stone.] ... Fullarton .... aged 32 yrs. Also of James Fullarton who died at Dublin 19th January 1870 AE 62 ys. Also the said John Fullarton who died 12th December 1875 aged 69 years. Also his son Thomas Fullarton died 15th February 1896 aged 78 years. Elizabeth Fullarton died May 1904 aged 76.

FULLERTON
Erected by Agnes Fullerton in memory of her beloved husband Samuel Fullerton, late of Lelias, who died on the 9th November 1873 aged 60 years. Agnes Fullerton died 8th May 1889 aged 74 years. "Blessed are the dead which die in the Lord from henceforth: Yea, saith the Spirit, that they may rest from their labours; and their works do follow them." Rev XIV, 13. [Mason:-] A. Jenkins, Larne.

[The will of Samuel Fullerton, late of Kilwaughter, county Antrim, farmer, who died 10 November 1873 at same place, was proved at Belfast 5 December 1873 by the oaths of Alexander Nelson of Ballysnodd, Larne, farmer, and John McDowell of Larne, merchant, both in county Antrim, the executors. Effects under £600.]

FULTON
[Weathered sandstone next to the following.] Erected (to the) memory of John Fulton who departed this life 21(st) Nov(r). 182(5) aged 9(4 yrs). Also his wife Jane Fulton who departed this life 18th April 18(.7) aged 83 years. His s(on) James (died) 2(oth J)a(n) 18(44).

FULTON
[Painted grey stone with black lettering.] Erected by John & James Fulton to the memory of their beloved father John Fulton of Windyhill who died 24th March 1849 aged 79 years. Also their mother Rebecca Fulton who departed this life November 21st 1868 aged 89 years. Also the above-named James Fulton who died 20th October 1890 aged 78 years. In loving memory of my dear wife Mary A. Fulton who died 26th January 1955. Also her dear husband John Fulton who died 21st September 1957.

[The will of James Fulton, late of 10 Olive Terrace, Old Park Road, Belfast, gentleman, who died 20 October 1890 at same place, was proved at Belfast 19 November 1890 by James Mairs of 1 Strangemore Terrace, Crumlin Road, Belfast, provision merchant, and Samuel Stewart Walker of Shaneshill, county Antrim, farmer, the executors. Effects £1,542. 6s. 11d.]

FUTT
See WOODSIDE

GAMBLE

Erected by Jane Gamble of Castletown to the memory of her beloved husband John Gamble who died on the 27th December 1862 aged 66 years. Also his wife Jane Gamble who died March 21st 1869 aged 65 yrs.

[The will of John Gamble, late of Castletown, Ballynure, in the county of Antrim, farmer, who died 27 December 1862 at same place, was proved at Belfast 9 March 1863 by the oaths of Jane Gamble of Castletown, Ballynure, widow, Thomas Fleming of Muckamore, farmer, and William James Harson of Dunturkey, Ballynure, farmer, all in the county of Antrim, the executors. Effects under £600.

The will of Jane Gamble, late of Castletown, county Antrim, widow, who died 21 March 1869 at same place, was proved at Belfast 13 August 1869 by the oaths of William James Harson of Dunturkey, Ballynure, farmer, and Samuel Kirk of Clementshill, Ballyclare, carpenter, both in said county, the executors. Effects under £300.]

GAMBLE

Erected by John Gamble of Straid Hill. The above John Gamble who died 25th October 1893 aged 64 years. Also his wife Matilda Gamble who died 3rd August 1916 aged 81 years. Also his daughter Martha who died 27th November 1865 aged 6 years. Also his daughter Annie who died 6th June 1903 aged 47 years. Also his daughter Matilda who died 23rd November 1915 aged 44 years.

[The will, with one codicil, of John Gamble, late of Straidland, Irishhill, county Antrim, farmer, who died 25 October 1893 at same place, was proved at Belfast 28 March 1894 by John Bell of Ballynarry, carpenter, and James Jenkin of Little Ballymena, farmer, both in said county, the executors. Effects £868.]

GAMBLE

[Sandstone, fallen and broken.] Erected by Robert Hugh Gamble, Straid, in memory of his mother Margaret Gamble, who died 16th June 1884 aged 78 years. Also his father John Gamble who died 9th Decr. 1887 aged 88 years.

GETTINBY

[Sandstone, next to the following in east of graveyard.] Erected by Mary Gettinby, Lismaneary, in memory of her son W.J. Gettinby died 10th February 1864 aged 17 years. Also her husband William Gettinby died 2nd March 1864 aged 45 years. Also her daughter Sarah J. Gettinby died 12th May 1877 aged 20 years. Also her son Thomas Gettinby died 13th July 1884 aged 33 years. The above-named M. Gettinby died 7th July 1891 aged 73 years. John Gettinby died 17th April 1927 aged 84 years. His wife Matilda died 6th June 1927 aged 86 years.

Not gone from memory, or from love,
But to our Father's home above.

[The will of Mary Gettinby, late of Lismenary, county Antrim, widow, who died 7 July 1891 at same place was proved at Belfast 12 August 1891 by John Wilson of Dunturkey, said county, farmer, one of the executors. Effects £287. 10s.]

GETTINBY

[Lead lettering on white marble.] Erected by M. Gettinby in memory of his beloved wife Mary E. Gettinby who died 3rd July 1895 aged 37 years. Also the above-named M. Gettinby who died 9th Sept. 1916 aged 65 years. [Mason:-] Holden, Larne.

GILMORE

[Lead lettering on white marble enclosed by railings beside church ruin.] Erected by James Gilmore of Legaloy, in memory of his sons:
Thomas M. died 18th Feb. 1868 aged 4 years.
John " 12th March 1886 " 28 "
William " 12th May 1886 " 36 "
Also the above James Gilmore died 26th March 1893 aged 80 years. Also his wife Jane McROBERT died 12th April 1912 aged 92 years.

[The will of James Gilmore, late of Legaloy, county Antrim, retired farmer, who died 26 March 1893 at same place, was proved at Belfast 24 September 1894 by Robert McCreary of Straidland, said county, farmer, and James Gilmore of 2 Kathleen Street, Ballymacarrett, Belfast, county Down, merchant, the executors. Effects £579. 10s.]

GILMORE
See McCREARY

GILMOUR
See LOVE

GIRVAN
[White marble.] Erected by Sittlington Girvan of Ballybracken to the memory of his father William Girvan who died 15th Feby. 1857 aged 82 years. Also his wife Rose Girvan who died 11th May 1860 aged 94 years. And their beloved son Samuel Girvan who died 22nd Octr. 1875 aged 27 years. Also his beloved wife Ann Girvan, who died 16th June 1891 aged 67 years.

GIRVAN
[This panel of white marble from composite stone - the rest is missing.] Erected by Mary Ann Girvan in memory of her beloved husband William Girvan who departed this life Septr. 18th 1872 aged 37 years. Respected by all who knew him.

GIRVAN
[White marble with lead lettering.] Erected by Thomas Girvan, Ballynure, in memory of his son Samuel Girvan who died 8th April 1884 aged 10 years. The above-named Thomas Girvan died 15th Octr. 1906 aged 65 years. Also his son Patrick who died 11th Decr. 1907 aged 27 years. Also his wife Jane Girvan who died 11th Sept. 1911 aged 63 years. James Boyd Girvan died 22nd August 1959. Also his wife Hester Girvan died 2nd June 1952.
Also their son Robert Ingram Girvan, died 8th March 1993.

GIRVAN
See McELWINIAN

GORDON
[Sandstone decorated with flower head and stalk with two pairs of opposite leaves. Enclosed with McComb ledger.] Here lyeth ye body of Jane Gordon who died March ye 6 1722 aged 66 years.

GORMAN
Here lie the remains of Patrick Gorman who departed this life Novr. 14th 1793 aged 80 years. Also his grandson Barry Gorman who died 2nd April 1908 aged 85 years. William Gorman died 20th May 1925 aged 78 years. William John, son of above, died 14th February 1962.

GREENFIELD
[Lead lettering in white marble in gothic frame placed next to Dobbs tablet.] Erected by William Greenfield in memory of his mother Ann Greenfield who died 20th July 1863 in her 80th year. Also in loving memory of Jane Greenfield, daughter of the above, who died 9th August 1893 aged 72 years. This tablet is inscribed by her loving niece Theus BATES.
[The will of Jane Greenfield, late of 7 Botanic Avenue, County Antrim, spinster, who died 9 August 1893 at Harrogate, county York, was proved at the Principal Registry 7 September 1893 by Edward Bates of Queen's Buildings, Royal Avenue, Belfast, solicitor, one of the executors. Effects £3,969. 9s. 11d.]

GREENLEES
Erected by Edwd. & Henry Greenlees of Ballyboley to the memory of their beloved mother Jane Greenless who died on 23rd March 1848 aged 65 years. Also their beloved father James Greenlees who died on the 6th of February 1857 aged 69 years.

GREENLES
See BELL

GWYNN
[Cast iron plaque attached to railings.] This enclosure is the family burying ground of the Revd. John Gwynn having been 51 years rector of this parish.

[Letters of administration of the personal estate of the Reverend John Gwynn, late of Rosebrook, Carrickfergus, clerk, who died 13 February 1852 at same place (left unadministered by William James Gwynn, his son), were granted at the Principal Registry 22 December 1881 to William Evans Gwynn, esquire, and Mary Gwynn, spinster, both of Antrim, the administrators of said William James Gwynn (former grant 20 April 1852). Effects unadministered £500.

The Rev. John Gwynn was born in county Tyrone in 1760/1, son of David Gwynn, farmer. He entered Trinity College, Dublin, in 1780 and graduated B.A. in 1784. He was curate of Castlane (Ossory) 1784-7 and of Fethard (Cashel) 1787-1800. He was prebend of Kilroot and rector of Ballynure 1800-52. He married in 1789 Catherine Rolleston and was father of the Rev. Stephen Gwynn, Treasurer of Connor. Stephen was father of the Rev. John Gwynn, Dean of Derry and Regius Professor of Divinity at T.C.D., who had an eldest son Stephen Gwynne, author of *Highways and Byeways in Donegal and Antrim* (1899), etc. See Leslie: *Clergy of Connor* (1993); Burtchaell and Sadleir: *Alumni Dublinenses* (1924); Leslie: *Ossory Clergy and Parishes* (1933), *Burke's Irish Family Records* (1976).

HAGAN
[Sandstone beside following.] Erected by James Hagan of Ballymena in memory of his son John who departed this life on the 18th of February 1835 aged 20 years.

HAGAN
[Lead lettering on white marble, with a roundel and a flying dove with laurel sprig and spandrels of ivy. Beside Higgen stone.] Erected by Eliza Hagan in loving memory of her husband James Hagan, born June 1836, died 17 April 1897. Also their children: James, born 3 Sep. 1862, died 11 Jan. 1864; William, born 6 April 1870, died 2 July 1892; Francis, born 3 Aug. 1868, died 8 April 1897; James, born 6 Sept. 1864, died 17 Feby. 1935. His wife Minnie McNAIR, born 4 Feby. 1864, died 9 Feby. 1933. Above named Eliza Hagan, died 9 March 1908.

Trust in Jesus
Then when the tears and trials
Of this vain life are o'er,
In that bright land of Promise,
We'll meet to part no more.

James Hagan, son of above James & Minnie, died 28 April 1979. His wife Elizabeth Ann (Lillie) died 14 Aug. 1982. [Mason:-] Robinson, Belfast.

[Probate of the will of James Hagan, late of Little Ballymena, county Antrim, farmer, who died 17 April 1897, granted at Belfast 26 July 1897 to Samuel Stewart of Irish Hill, farmer, George Hagan of Lisglass and James Hagan of Little Ballymena, farmers. Effects £716. 15s. Re-sworn £1,036. 15s.]

HALL
See BEATTIE and BEATTY

HARPER
Erected by Margaret Harper of Dunturkey in memory of her husband John Harper who died the 1st June 1841 aged 78 years. Also John Harper their son who died the 11th May 1840 aged 22 years. Also the said Margaret Harper who died 7th Feb. 1863 aged 87 years.

HAWTHORN
Erected by Samuel & Ellen Hawthorn in memory of their son James who died 13th Feby. 1903 aged 25 years. Also their daughters Ellen and Elizabeth who died young. The above-named Ellen Hawthorn died 12th Feby. 1912 aged 65 years.

The above-named Samuel Hawthorn died 25th October 1920 aged 74 years. [Mason:-] T. Holden, Larne.

HAY

[Arms: invected bordure, three escutcheons. Crest: a ?deer's head erased. Motto: Malum Bono Vince.] Here lyeth the body of John Hay who died Augt. the 20th 1717 aged 36 years. Also Margaret Hay who died Jan. 21st 1767 aged 17 years. Near this lyeth Janet WITHERSPOON, wife to John Hay, who died Apr. 29th 1759 aged 67 years. Also Alexander Hay who died Nov. 4th 1776 aged 62 years. Also Elizth. HUDSON, wife to the above named Alexr. Hay, who died Oct. 25th 1800 aged 78 years.

HAY

See BARKLIE

HENDERSON

[Pink granite.] Erected by Reid Henderson, Dunturkey, in memory of his father Samuel Henderson who died 1st August 1859 aged 50 years. And his mother Ellen Henderson who died 29th January 1879 aged 62 years. Also his wife Jane Henderson who died 6th November 1904 aged 39 years. Also John Henderson, Ballyfore, who died 13th Sep. 1877 aged 72 years. And his wife Rebecca Jane who died 24th Sep. 1886 aged 70 years. Also their son Robert who died 7th April 1910. The above-named Reid Henderson died 26th Aug. 1913 aged 73 years.

[The will of Ellen Henderson, late of Dunturkey, county Antrim, widow, who died 29 January 1879 at same place, was proved at Belfast 9 February 1880 by the oaths fo Robert Henderson of Calhame and James Henderson of Dunturkey, both in same county, farmers, the executors. Effects under £300.

The will of John Henderson, late of Ballyfore, county Antrim, farmer, who died 13 September 1877 at same place, was proved at Belfast 5 April 1880 by the oath of Rebecca Jane Henderson of Ballyfore, widow, one of the executors. Effects under £100.]

HENDERSON

[Lead lettering in white marble.] Erected by James Henderson of New York as a last tribute to the memory of his parents James Henderson who died 9th Sept. 1903 aged 68 years. Mary Ann Boyd Henderson who died 21st Novr. 1896 aged 61 years. Also their son Samuel Henderson who died 15th October 1924 aged 69 years.

HETHERINGTON

[Small stone in west of grave yard.] Here lieth the body of John Hetherington who departed this life the 30th of May 1801 aged 54 years. Also his wife who departed this life the 6th July 1820 aged 62 years.

HIGGEN

[Sandstone incorporated with Hagan enclosure.] Erected by James Higgen in memory of his beloved wife Jane who departed this life 21st March 1877 aged 83 years.

HILDITCH

[Sandstone. A roundel contains a square and compass.] Erected by Robert Hilditch. This stone claims 3 graves west.

HILL

[Enclosed with Hugh Hill d.1810.] To the memory of Elizh. BEGGS alias Hill who departed this life October 1785 aged 33. Also Thos. Hill who departed March 1795 aged 62. Also his wife.

HILL

[Top right corner of a small red sandstone. The year is probably 1801.] .....Hill ......el who .... this life ....01 & his ....

HILL
[Red sandstone splitting badly and attached to railings surrounding Rev. Adam Hill.] (T)o the memory of William Rogers Hill (wh)o died in Demerary the 11th (F)ebruary 1809 in the 20th yea(r) of his age. The body of Bankhead Hill l(ieth) here: he died the 25th March 181(2) in the 12th year of his age. And also the bodies of 3 of his brothers who died in infancy.

HILL
Erected in memory of Hugh Hill, surgeon of Newtownards, died 23d. Feby. 1810 aged 33 years.

(HILL)
[Very low stone next to Hugh Hill, d.1905.] Errected to the memory of Robt. (Hill) late of Ballycorr who departed this live Septr. 5th 1811 aged 79. Also his 2 wives.

HILL
[Sandstone ledger within railings.] Underneath are deposited the remains of the Rev. Adam Hill, Presbyterian minister of Ballynure, who departed this life on the 21st of July 1827 in the seventieth year of his age and the fortysecond of his ministry. Like Nathaniel of old he was [Greek inscription]. Also those of hi(s) wife Helena who died on the 24th of November 182(5) aged 6(3) years. Also their son Adam who died 14th April 1832 in the 27th year of his age. And Sarah Ann BANKHEAD who died 27th of December 1838 aged 2 years & 9 months. And William John Bankhead who died 26th July 1849 in the 10th year of his age. Children of Doctor Joseph Bankhead. Also P(e)nelope Anne, his widow, who died 28th April 1853.

[The Rev. Adam Hill was born near Randalstown in 1757 and educated in Scotland. He was licensed by the Route Presbytery in 1782 and ordained for America in 1783, but did not go there. He was instituted in Ballynure on 16 April 1785. He married in 1786 the daughter of a minister. He was accused of rebellion and found partly guilty in 1798. He subsequently accompanied William Orr, as chaplain, from Carrickfergus gaol to the scaffold on 14 October 1798. He retired in 1826 and died at Bankhead Hill on 21 July 1827. See McConnell: *Fasti of the Irish Presbyterian Church, 1613-1840* (1951).]

HILL
Erected by John Hill to the memory of his father Robert Hill of Ballyboley who departed this life on the 18th January 1831 aged 63 years. Also his brother Robert who departed this life on the 13th June 1830 aged 24 years.

HILL
[Tall white marble stone with lead lettering.] Sacred to the memory of Samuel Hill who died 24th April 1831 aged 78 years and of his son John Hill who died 27th Dec. 1890 aged 77 years and of Margaret Hill, wife of above John Hill, who died 16th Sep. 1897 aged 80 years and of Martha Hill the beloved wife of William Hugh Hill of Belfast who died 19th November 1900 aged 42 years. William H. Hill died 30th December 1905. John H. Hill died 30th April 1926. [Mason:-] G. M'Cann, Belfast.

[The will of John Hill, late of Ballyboley, county Antrim, farmer, who died 27th December 1890 at same place, was proved at Belfast 4 March 1891 by Robert Junkin of Toreagh, said county, farmer, one of the executors. Effects £50.]

HILL
[Sandstone next to the following.] Erected by David Hill on the 1st January 1832. Also David Hill the erector who departed this life on the 1st of March 1834 aged 54 years. And his son Robert Hill who departed this life on the 9th of November 1831 aged 22 years. And his son David Hill who departed this life 5th April 1883 aged 68 years. David Wilson Hill, 4th May 1914-26th October 1987.

[The will of David Hill, late of Toberdowney, county Antrim, farmer, who died 5th April 1883 at same place, was proved at Belfast 4 May 1883 by John Gilmer Hill of Toberdowney, Ballynure, Thomas Wilson of Straid and John Gilmer of Dunnamoy, all in said county, farmers, the executors. Effects £2,075 14s. 7d.]

HILL
[Large sandstone.] Erected by Mary Hill of Ballynure in memory of her husband David Hill who died on the 1st of March 1834 aged 54 years. Also her son Alexander Hay Hill who died on the 8th of June 1846 aged 19 years. Also her son Samuel Hay Hill M.D. who died on the 26th Sept. 1850 aged 21 years. Likewise the said Mary Hill who died 15th January 1859 aged 64 years. Hugh Hay Hill departed this life the 15th March 1866 aged 34 years.

[The will of Hugh Hay Hill, late of Ballynure in the county of Antrim, farmer, who died 15 March 1866 at same place, was proved at Belfast 6 April 1866 by oaths of Robert Beatty and William McMurty, late of Ballynure aforesaid and James Barklie of Lismenary, Ballynure, all in said county, farmers, the executors. Effects under £1,000.]

HILL
['Bridge End' is inscribed in a variant style and on a hollowed strip suggestive of a later alteration.] Erected by David Hill, Bridge End, in memory of his beloved sons, viz. Robert who departed this life on the 21st of January 1854 aged 13 years & Alexander who died in infancy. Also his son Hugh who departed this life 14th September 1859 aged 24 years. Also the said David Hill who died on 5th December 1872 aged 70 years. Also his grand daughter Agnes Hill, B.Boley, who died 23rd February 1873 aged 9 years. Also his daughter-in-law Mary Hill who died 29th Augt. 1879 aged 44 years. Also her husband David Hill who died 27th Jany. 1904 aged 65 years.

[The will of David Hill, late of Bridge End, Ballycor, county Antrim, farmer, who died 5 December 1872 at same place, was proved at Belfast 24 January 1873 by the oaths of William John Hill of Ballyboley, Ballynure, and Thomas Hill of Tildarg, Doagh, both in said county, farmers, the executors. Effects £2,000.

Letters of administration of the personal estate of Mary Hill of Ballycor, county Antrim, who died 29 August 1879 at same place, were granted at Belfast 13 April 1888 to David Hill of Ballycorr, farmer, the husband. Effects £194 7s.]

HILL
[White marble with lead lettering near gate.] Erected by James Hill, Ballynure, in memory of his daughter Maggie Lorimer died 11th Oct. 1871 aged 1 year & 8 months. The above-named James Hill died 1st Sep. 1914 aged 70 years. Also his wife Jenny WHITEFORD who died 15th October 1919 aged 74 years. Gone, but not forgotten. Their son James Whiteford Hill died 15th September 1957 at Alhambra, California.

HILL
[Sandstone.] Erected by David Hill in memory of his mother who died in the year 1872. Also his father who died in the year 1894.

HILL
[Polished granite next to David Hill d.1834.] Erected in memory of John Hill of Ballyboley who died on the 11th February 1897 aged 78 years. And of his wife Eliza C. Hill who died on the 10th August 1899 aged 80 years. Also their daughter Jane who died on the 25th December 1872 aged 26 years. And their son Samuel Alexander who died in India on the 23rd September 1890 aged 39 years.

[Probate of the will of John Hill of Ballyboley, Ballycor, county Antrim, farmer, who died 11 February 1897, granted at Belfast 14 April 1897 to David Hill of Ballyboley, Ballynure, farmer, and John Millar of Skilganaban, shoemaker, both of county Antrim. Effects £366.]

HILL
[Grey limestone inside railings.] Erected in memory of Thomas Hill, Tildarg, who died 21st Dec. 1908 aged 76 years. Also his wife Henrietta Hill who died 17th Jan.

1893 aged 56 years. Also his mother Eliza Hill who died 9th Sept. 1877 aged 67 years. Also his son Robert Hugh Hill who died 22nd Nov. 1927. Also his daughter Margaret Hill who died 5th January 1929. Also his son Thomas Wilson Hill who died 30th June 1933. "Gone but not forgotton". Walshe, B'mena.

HILL
[Lead lettering in white marble.] In memory of Marianne Hill died 23rd June 1906 aged 58 years. Mary Parkhill Wilson Hill died 15th April 1890 aged 13 years. Mary Parkhill Hill died 3rd Jany. 1893 aged 8 months. James Houston Hill died 26th Nov. 1911. James Hill, Sen., died 2nd Oct. 1919. Hugh Hill died 5th March 1920.

HILL
See THOMSON and WILSON

HOLDEN
[Flaking sandstone decorated with fan and two quatrefoils.] Erected by Martha Holden of Ballygowan in memory of her beloved husband Samuel Holden who departed this life the 3rd April 187(9) aged 70 years. Also their son John Holden who died the 22nd August 1873 aged 31 years. Her son Robert died 22nd Novr. 1885 aged 46 years. The above Martha Holden died 21st Novr. 1887 aged 72 years.
[The will of Samuel Holden, late of Ballygowan, county Antrim, farmer, who died 3 April 1879 at same place, was proved at Belfast 9 February 1880 by the oaths of John Holden of Straid, William Adamson of Castletown and Robert Holden of Ballygowan, all in said county, farmers, the executors. Effects under £450.]

HOUSTON
[Fallen sandstone propped against railing of Barklimore.] Erected to the memory of Andrew Houston of Ballyearl who departed this life on the 8th day of October 1808 aged 73 years. Also his wife Margaret who departed this life on the 24th of June 1787 aged 41 years. And their son John who died young.

HOUSTON/HUSTON
[Sandstone.] Erected in memory of Hugh Houston, Larne, who departed this life on the 21st April 1849 aged 78 years. Also his daughter Margaret who died on the 21st May 1850 aged 37 years. His son William who died on the 22nd August 1837 aged 18 years. And two sons who died in infancy. Also his daughter Jane who died on the 12th Feb. 1860 aged 43 years. Also Jane Huston [sic], wife of the above Hugh Huston, who died 6th March 1865 aged 89 years.
[Letters of administration of the personal estate of Jane Houston, late of Larne in the county of Antrim, spinster, who died 12 February 1860 at same place, were granted at Belfast 2 March 1860 to Jane Houston of Larne aforesaid, widow, the mother, next of kin of said deceased. Effects under £100.]

HOWIE
[Sandstone.] Erected by William Howie, B. Laggan, in memory of his beloved mother who departed this life A.D. 1842 and his beloved father who died in the year 1855. Also his beloved sister who died in the year 1859. Also Robert Howie, Mounthill, Raloo, who died 16th June 1940. 2 graves south.

HUDSON
See HAY

HUGHES
See KIRK

HUME
[Lead lettering in white marble.] Erected by Thomas Hume in memory of his father James Hume died 6th Sep. 1873 aged 42 years. Also his sister Jane died 12th April 1864 aged 6 years. And his brother Robert died 8th Dec. 1884 aged 28

years. Also Jane who died in infancy. And his brother James died 4th March 1907 aged 33 years. The above-named Thomas Hume died 24th Sep. 1908 aged 48 years. Interred in Letterkenny. Also his mother Eliza Hume who died 14th March 1916 aged 84 years.

HUME
   See BEATTIE

HUNTER
   [Sandstone ledger within iron railings.] Erected by Elizabeth Hunter to the memory of her late husband Anthony Hunter of Ballyclare who died on the 13th of February 1813 aged 56 years. And of four of her children who died during infancy. Also to the memory of her three sons namely Wm. John died on the 19th of January 1822 aged 30 years. Samuel who died at Abbeville in France on the 15th of December 1834 aged 30 years. Sinclair who died at Belturbet in the County of Cavan on the 28th of March 1836 aged 34 years. And likewise of her daughter Eliza, wife of Andrew SPARROWHAWK, who died on the 11th of March 1837 aged 29 years. Also of the erector Elizabeth Hunter who died 20th November 1840 aged 72 years.

HUNTER
   [Sandstone next to James Davidson d.1828.] Here lieth the body of James Hunter of Clements Hill who departed this life 23rd February 1818 aged 80 years.

HUNTER
   [Sandstone beginning to flake, enclosed with Anthony Hunter.] Erected by James Hunter of Skilganaban in memory of his father Anthony Hunter who departed this life 29th January 1866 aged 95 years.

HUSTON
   Erected by Hugh Huston in memory of his father John Huston of Ballyboly who departed this life the 9th of June 1789 aged 88 years. Also his wife Jennet MAC-BROOM who departed this life the 4th of February 1790 aged 85 years.

JACKSON
   [Lead lettering in white marble, flying dove with laurel in roundel, grapevine and ivy in spandrels.] Erected by Thomas Jackson in loving memory of his mother Rosanna Jackson who died 18th April 1887 aged 43 years. And his brother William Stewart Jackson who died 11th Sept. 1897 aged 25 years. And his father Thomas Jackson who died 26th July 1903 aged 61 years. Also his son wee Willie who died 29th Sept. 1914 aged 7 years & 11 months. [Mason:] Holden, Larne.

JAMFREY
   See BARKLIE

JAMISON
   [White marble with lead lettering, a roundel contains a flying dove with a sprig, spandrels of ivy.] Erected by Agnes Jamison, Ballybracken, in memory of her husband David Jamison who died 23rd Augt. 1894 aged 64 years. And her son David Jamison who died 5th March 1905 aged 37 years. Also Lizzie and Matthew who died young. The above-named Agnes Jamison died 10th March 1912 aged 78 years. Also her daughter Martha Jamison who died 26th Feby. 1931 aged 73 years. Also her son William Jamison who died 2nd Jany. 1937 aged 72 years. Also Margaret, wife of the above William, died 4th November 1972. [Mason:-] T. Holden, Larne.

   [The will of David Jamison, late of Ballybracken, Ballynure, county Antrim, farmer, who died 23 August 1894 at same place, was proved at Belfast 28 June 1895 by David Curran of Ballynery and Samuel Jamison of Ballybracken, both in said county, farmers, the executors. Effects £1,052 6s. 0d.]

JENKINS
[Concrete.] Erected by William Jenkins of Browndod in memory of his father who died the 2nd July 1862 aged 61 years. Also his mother who died the 23rd May 1867 aged 59 years. Also his son Robert who died in infancy.

JENKINS
In memory of John Jenkins, Straid, who departed this life 13th October 1871 aged 84 years. Also his beloved wife Ann Jenkins who departed this life 20th June 1865 aged 77 years. Their daughter Jane Jenkins who departed this life 31st July 1869 aged 54 years.
    Ye mourning friends; dry up your tears
    We will arise when Christ appears.

JENKINS
[Sandstone within a railed enclosure. A dove in flight holding a leaf is surrounded by a laurel wreath.] 1868. The family burying place of Francis Jenkins, Straid.

JENKINS
[Beside John Jenkins, d.1871.] Erected by Sushanna Jenkins in memory of her beloved husband Samuel Jenkins who died 27th Feby. 1886 aged 60 years. Also their son John who died 22nd April 1876 aged 13 years. Also the above-named Sushanna Jenkins who died 18th June 1908. Also their son David Jenkins who died 16th January 1924 aged 58 years. Their son Robert Jenkins died 10th Aug. 1936 aged 73 years.

[Letters of administration of the personal estate of Samuel Jenkins, late of Dairyland, county Antrim, farmer, who died 27 February 1886 at same place, were granted at Belfast 17 March 1886 to Susanna Jenkins of Dairyland. Effects £294 18s. 4d.]

JOHNSTON
R. Johnston 1844.

(JU)NKIN
[Low sandstone near the following.] Here lyeth the (body) of William (Ju)nkin who departed this life December the (14) aged (2)4 years 17(09).

JUNKIN
[Low stone next to south boundary.] Here lieth the body of Samuel Junkin who departed this life the 29th of March 1786 aged 5(5) years.

KANE
[White marble with lead lettering.] "My saviour calls me home." Erected by David Kane, Straid, in memory of his beloved mother Mary Kane who died 9th Jany. 1881 aged 61 years. Also his father Eneas Kane who died 27th Sep. 1886 aged 72 years. The above named David Kane died 18th April 1927 aged 73 years.

KENNEDY
Erected by William Kennedy of Dunturkey in memory of his brother David who died 8th Septr. 1851 aged 42 years. Also his father David Kennedy who died 20th Feby. 1852 aged 83 years. And of his mother Margaret who died 13th June 1810 aged 35 years. And also of his sister Jane Kennedy who died 1st of July 1854 aged 48 years. Likewise the said William Kennedy who died 22nd Septm. 1870 aged 70 years. And also his wife Margaret who died 25th Feby. 1888 aged 69 years.

[The will of William Kennedy late of Dunturkey, county Antrim, farmer, who died 22 September 1870 at same place, was proved at Belfast 23 December 1870 by the oaths of William James Harson, farmer and Margaret Kennedy, widow, late of Dunturkey, Ballynure, aforesaid, the executors. Effects under £450.]

KENNEDY
[Broken sandstone.] Erected to the memory of Thomas Kennedy of Strade Land who departed this life August 20th 1834 agd. 79 years. Also his wife Mary Kennedy who departed this life Decr. 29th 1844 aged 75 years.

KENNEDY
[Lead lettering on polished granite, enclosed with Robert Todd's stone.] In memory of Robert Kennedy, Irish Hill House, who died 5th April 1885. His grandson George William died 4th Feby. 1919 aged 3 years. Also his wife Letitia who died 17th March 1925. Also his grand-daughter Robina Letitia (Ruby) died 29th December 1952. His daughter-in-law Elizabeth Sophia Augusta died 23rd March 1955. Also his dear son William James died 1st April 1967.

[The will of Robert Kennedy, late of Irish Hill, Straid, county Antrim, farmer, who died 3 April 1885 at same place, was proved at Belfast 16 September 1885 by William McMaster of Duff's Hill, Carrickfergus, farmer, and William James Kennedy of Irish Hill, Straid, farmer, the executors. Effects £909 16s. 3d.]

KENNEDY
[White marble next to David Kennedy, d.1851.] Castletown. Erected by Eliza Kennedy in memory of her husband John Kennedy who died 26th Novr. 1887 aged 60 years. Also their two daughters Annie Lyle & Minnie who died in infancy. Also her brother-in-law David Kennedy who died 24th July 1891 aged 74 years. Also her son William Kennedy who died 7th February 1900 aged 32 years. Also her son Samuel who died 12th January 1906 aged 19 years. Also her daughter Minnie who died 30th November 1921 aged 39 years. Also her son David who died 1st November 1922 aged 53 years. The above named Eliza Kennedy died 21st April 1937 aged 89 years. And Minnie, wife of John Kennedy, died 28th January 1948 aged 36 years. Jennie, wife of the late David Kennedy, Castletown, Ballynure, died 8th March 1964. "Absent in the body but present with the Lord."

[The will of John Kennedy, late of Castletown, county Antrim, farmer, who died 28 November 1887 at same place, was proved at Belfast 4 February 1889 by Eliza Kennedy, widow, of Castletown, James Blair of Whitepark, farmer, and Thomas Girvan of Ballynure, publican, all in said county, the executors. Effects £441.

Administration of the estate of William Kennedy, late of Ballynure, county Antrim, spirit merchant, who died 7 February 1900, granted at Belfast 26 March 1900 to Janie Kennedy, the widow. Effects £114 10s.]

KENNEDY
See KNOX

KERR
[Sandstone next to Samuel Kerr, d.1890.] 1863. This is the family burying ground of John Kerr, Straid.

KERR
[Square and compass in roundel.] In memory of William Kerr, Seskin, born 12th July 1816, died 8th April 1879. Also his wife Mary MILLEN, died December 1868 aged 51 years. Also his brother Samuel Kerr who died 30th July 1894 aged 63 years. And his wife Mary Ann Kerr who died 23rd May 1918 aged 83 years.

[The will of William Kerr, late of Seskin, in the county of the town of Carrickfergus, farmer, who died 8 April 1879 at same place, was proved at Belfast 28 April 1879 by the oaths of Samuel Kerr and Thomas McAlister, both of Carrickfergus, farmers, the executors. Effects under £300.

Letters of administration of the personal estate of Samuel Kerr, late of Altivaddy, Carrickfergus, farmer, who died 30 July 1894 at same place, were granted at Belfast 9 November 1894 to Mary Anne Kerr of Altivaddy, the widow. Effects £556 15s.]

KERR

[Sandstone, later heightened by a cap of cement-rendered brick.] Erected by John Kerr in memory of his son Alexander who died 22nd March 1879 aged 23 years. And his son John who died young. Also his beloved wife Sarah Jane Kerr who died 27th October 1900 aged 78 years. "Blessed are the dead which die in the Lord". The above-named John Kerr died 4th Augt. 1905 aged 84 years. "These are they which came out of great tribulation and have washed their robes and made them white in the blood of the Lamb."
If the cross we meekly bear
Then the crown we shall wear.
Reader, prepare to meet thy God.

KERR

[White marble.] Erected by James Kerr, Dairyland, in memory of his son Samuel who died 5th Decr. 1890 aged 33 years.
Lost to sight, to memory dear;
An honest heart lies mouldering here.
The above-named James Kerr, P.M., P.K., H.K.T. who departed this life 12th Octr. 1903 in the 77th year of his age, and who for 58 years took an active and intelligent part in the working of Masonic Lodge 276 and of masonry in this district. Deeply regretted. Also his wife Jane Kerr who died 21st Feby. 1911 aged 85 years. And his cousin Mary E. RODGERS died 18th May 1954.

KIRK

[Sandstone.] Erected by Andrew and James Kirk of Ballynure as a small tribute of regard to the memory of an affectionate mother who departed this life the 31st of July 1824 aged 50 years. Also of their sister Ann Kirk who died the 9th of January 1809 aged 11 years. Likewise to the memory of their father William Kirk who died on the 28th December 1841 aged 69 years. The remains of the above named James Kirk also lies here. He died the 23rd of October 1844 aged 42 years.

KIRK

[Sandstone next to Alexander Kirk, d. 1895.] Erected by John Kirk of Legaloy to the memory of his beloved wife Elizabeth Kirk who departed this life 2nd January 1853 aged 62 years. Also the erector, John Kirk, who departed this life 26th September 1857 aged 77 years.
[The will of John Kirk, late of Legaloy in the county of Antrim, farmer, who died 26 September 1857 at same place, was proved at Belfast 19 August 1858 by the oaths of John Park of Legaloy, Samuel McMinn of Dunturkey and John Kirk of Legaloy aforesaid, all in the county of Antrim aforesaid, farmers, the executors. Effects under £450.]

KIRK

Erected by William Kirk of Clements Hill in memory of his son John who died on the 26th April 1854 aged 27 years. Also his son James who died in Mobile, U.S. 1853 aged 23 years. Also their father William Kirk who died 14th July 1858 aged 67 yrs. Also his wife Elizabeth Kirk who died November 3rd 1868 aged 70 yrs.
[Letters of administration of the personal estate of William Kirk, late of Clements Hill near Ballyclare in the county of Antrim, farmer, who died 13 July 1858 at same place, were granted at Belfast 8 June 1859 to Elizabeth Kirk of Clement's Hill aforesaid, the widow of said deceased. Effects under £100.]

KIRK

[With lead lettering on white marble and foliage in roundel and spandrels.] Erected by Robert HUGHES, Larne, in memory of his wife Mary Hughes who died 16th July 1899 aged 70 years. Also her mother Agnes Kirk who died 20th November 1864 aged 80 years.

KIRK

[White marble panel set into heavy sandstone.] Erected by Jane Kirk of Hydepark in affectionate remembrance of her husband Thomas Kirk who died 15th Dec.

1870 aged 45 years. Their daughter Sarah died 20th June 1865 aged 17 years. Their son William died 10th Aug. 1865 aged 19 years. Also their infant children: John, Robert, and Mary Jane.

KIRK

[Polished granite.] Erected in memory of Andrew Kirk, Marsden Villa, Belfast, who died 11th May 1875 aged 75 years. Also of Sarah, wife of the above Andrew Kirk, who died 5th July 1889 aged 65 years. J. Robinson & Son, Belfast.

[The will of Sarah Kirk, late of Marsden Villa, Antrim Road, Belfast, widow, who died 5 July 1889 at same place, was proved at Belfast 29 July 1889 by Anna Molyneaux of Marsden Villa, Antrim Road, Belfast, spinster, and Ellen McCleary, wife of James Caughey McCleary, of 6 May Street, Belfast, the executrixes. Effects £8,249 4s. 11d.]

KIRK

[Sandstone of same design as William Kirk's, d. 1854.] Erected by Samuel & Jane Kirk of Clementshill in memory of their children: William Kirk died 24th April 1882 aged 15 years. Elizabeth Park Kirk died 2nd August 1884 aged 11 years. Jane Kirk died 24th August 1885 aged 15 years. James Kirk died June 1892 aged 27 years.

Parents, for us let fall no tears;
We early loved God's blessed Son,
He took us home, and hushed our fears,
And said, our earthly race is run.

Also their son David John died 10th Oct. 1907. The above Jane Kirk died 16th Feb. 1916. The above Samuel Kirk died 24th April 1916.

KIRK

[Polished granite, similar to and beside Samuel Henderson's stone.] Erected to the memory of Alexander Kirk, Legaloy, who died 25th February 1896 aged 66 years. Also his wife Margaret A. Kirk who died 7th January 1900 aged 66 years. And their son James Kirk who died 8th May 1889 aged 24 years. And their son Thomas Kirk who died 1st May 1933 aged 70 years. Also Elizabeth, wife of above Thomas Kirk, died 11th April 1955. I know that my Redeemer liveth.

[The will of Alexander Kirk, late of Legaloy, county Antrim, farmer, who died 25 February 1896 was proved at Belfast 10 June 1896 by John Kirk of Legaloy and John McRoberts of Dunturkey in said county, farmers, executors. Effects £309 4s.]

KIRK

See LORIMER and McGOOKIN

KNOX

[Next to following stone.] The burying ground of Joseph Knox. Erected by Jenny & Maggie ROBINSON. Here lyeth the body of our dear mother Elizabeth Wylie (Knox) who died 10th Sept. 1881 aged 69 years. 3 graves south.

KNOX

[White marble with lead lettering.] Erected by James Knox in memory of his daughter Jenny Knox who died 26th March 1897 aged 13 years. Also his son Joseph Knox who died 25th March 1907 aged 26 years. Also his wife Agnes Knox who died 22nd December 1925 aged 73 years. Also his grandson James KENNEDY who died 25th May 1923 aged 2 years. Also the above named James Knox who died 6th August 1932 aged 77 years. Also his grandson Wesley Knox who died 7th Febry. 1938 aged 3½ years. Also his son Robert James Knox who died 30th March 1971. Also Ann Isabel, wife of Robert James Knox who died 14th January 1988. [Mason:-] Holden, Larne.

KNOX

See CURRAN

LENNON

[Sandstone against western hedge.] Erected to the memory of Robert Lennon who departed this life on the 11th day of February 1811 aged 71 years. His wife Margt. WILSON who died 29th March 1844 aged 91 years. Their son Henry who died 7th May 1859 aged 77 years. And his wife Agnes Wilson who died 28th March 1863 aged 81 years. William Lennon died 19th May 1900 aged 78 years. His wife Catherine died 8th June 1884 aged 59 years. And their daughter Martha died 24th Sept. 1873 aged 21 years.

[Probate of the will of William Lennon, late of Ballylagan, Ballynure, county Antrim, farmer, who died 19 May 1900, granted at Dublin 25 June 1900 to Nathaniel Lennon, draper, and Charles Lennon, farmer. Effects £477 6s.]

LENNON

See WILSON

LOGAN

Erected in memory of Thomas Logan of Dunturkey who died in December 1837 aged 75 years. And his wife Mary MURPHY who died in October 1855 aged 89 years. Also of their son James who died in March 1837 aged 28 years. Also John Logan died May 1879 aged 83 years. And his beloved wife Maryann died August 13th 1887 aged 77 years. Also their son John who died 25th Decr. 1909 aged 59 years.

[The will of John Logan, late of Dunturkey, county Antrim, farmer, who died 19 May 1879 at same place, was proved at Belfast 24 September 1879 by the oath of Andrew Boyd of Straid in said county, farmer, the surviving executor. Effects under £600.]

LOGAN

[Facing west.] Erected by Thomas Logan of Straidnahanna in memory of his beloved wife Mary Ellen MADDEN who died in June 1870 aged 75 years. And of their sons John & Thomas who died, the former in March 1851 aged 21 years, the latter in October 1852 aged 26 years. They were adorned by many virtues, few failings, and no crimes.

[Thomas Logan of Loganstown, Straidnahanna, died on 11 January 1875 aged 85 and was buried with his wife and children - Dr John Logan, personal communication.]

LOGAN

[Loose red sandstone propped against vault.] Erected in memory of Mary, the loved wife of Samuel Logan, who died at Ballyhackamore, Belfast, on 17th January 1886 aged 38 years. Also the above named Samuel Logan who died May 9th 1889 aged 53 years.

[The will of Mary Logan, wife of Samuel Logan, late of Ballyhackamore, county Down, who died 17 January 1886 at same place, was proved at Belfast 6 August 1886 by Samuel Logan of Ballyhackamore, spirit merchant, the sole executor (limited). Effects £388 8s.

Letters of administration, with the will annexed, of the personal estate of Mary Logan, wife of Samuel Logan, late of Ballyhackamore, county Down, who died 17 January 1886 at same place, left unadministered by Samuel Logan, the sole executrix, were granted at Belfast 8 July 1889 to John Logan of Dunturkey, under administration granted 7 June 1889. Effects unadministered £388 8s.

Letters of administration of the personal estate of Samuel Logan, late of Ballyhackamore near Belfast, county Down, pensioner and grocer, who died 9 May 1889 at same place, were granted at Belfast 7 June 1889 to John Logan of Dunturkey, county Antrim, farmer, the guardian of the minor and infant children (limited). Effect 413 5s. 1d.]

LOGAN

[Lead lettering on polished granite.] In memory of our mother Mary Jane Logan, died April 1908. And father Hugh Logan, died July 1929. And sister Ann Jane

Thomas Logan of Loganstown, Straidnahanna (1789-1875), reproduced by permission of Dr John Logan

Francey died in the year 1894. Also John, husband of Agnes Logan, died 19th March 1964. Agnes, wife of above John Logan, died 22nd October 1975. Christ died for our sins. 1 Cor. 15,3.

LOGAN
See BOYD

LOREMR
See WEIR

LORIMER
[Low sandstone divided into two panels in the west of the graveyard.] Here lieth the body of Andrew Lorimer who departed this life Sept. 20th 1744 aged 52 years. Also his wife Mary SCOTT who depd. this life March 15th 1791 AE 90 years.
Here lieth the body of Andrew Lorimer who departed this life July 13th 1790 aged 90 years. Also his wife Jane KIRK aged 65 years.

LOVE
[Very thick sandstone, within iron railings. Arms: A fess upon three piles. Crest: a rose. Motto: (Vir) ....] Here lyeth ye body of Robert Love who died June 8th 1743 aged 70 years. Also William his son who died April 4th 1749 aged 45 years. Also Sarah CALHOON wife to Robt. Love aforesd. who died May 12th 1760 aged 8(8) years.

LOVE
[Sandstone beside foregoing.] 1989. Joseph Love, 1806-1894. Joseph 1842-1896. Margaret, nee GILMOUR, 1854-1945. John, 1877-1953, Canada. William, 1878-1949, Canada. Barry, 1879-1955. Mary Berry, 1882-1945, New York. Jenny, 1885-1893. Dorothea, 1887-1970. Joseph, 1890-1973. Thomas, 1893-1973. Robert James, 1895-1968, Carnmoney. Annie, 1910-1953, Carnmoney.

McALISTER
[Low rough stone next to another with initials A.M.] A. McAlister.

McALISTER
[A small boulder with smoothed face.] J. McA. 1857. [It is enclosed by iron railings to which is attached a cast iron plaque.] The family burying ground of James McAlister, Carrickfergus. 1907. 5 graves. [Cast by:-] The Millfield Foundry, Belfast, 1908.

McALISTER
See SCOTT

McBRIDE
Erected by J. & J. McBride in memory of their father Malcom McBride who died 13th Sept. 1887 aged 79 years. [Mason:-] Rankin. 2 graves each side.

MACBROOM
See HOUSTON

McCALMONT
[White marble.] Erected by Mary Jane McCalmont in loving memory of her husband James McCalmont who died 16th October 1902 aged 67 years. Also their son Robert Thomas who died 17th January 1890 aged 24 years. Mary Jane McCalmont died 31st January 1931.
[Letters of administration of the personal estate of Robert Thomas McCalmont, late of Ballyhackamore, county Down, publican, who died 16 January 1890 at same place, were granted at Belfast 18 April 1890 to James McCalmont of Skilganaban, county Antrim, farmer, the father. Effects £36.]

McCAMON
[White marble with lead lettering, enclosed with stone of Eally Boyd, d. 1826.] Erected by Alexander McCamon, Skilganaban, in memory of his father Thomas

McCamon died 11th July 1877 aged 77 years. Also his mother Annie died 13th Sep. 1885 aged 81 years. Also his brother John died 8th July 1870 aged 31 years. Also his uncle Samuel BOYD died 6th Sep. 1871 aged 73 years. Also his uncle John Boyd died 26th Jan. 1881 aged 84 years. Also the above Alexander McCamon who died 27th July 1911 aged 76 years. Also his sister Jane McCamon who died 25th March 1913 aged 80 years. [Mason:-] J. F. Pirie, Belfast.

[Letters of administered of the personal estate of Thomas McCamon, late of Skilganaban, county Antrim, farmer, who died 12 July 1877 at same place, were granted at Belfast 27 February 1878 to Alexander McCammon of Skilganaban, Ballyclare, same county, farmer, a son of said deceased. Effects under £450.]

McCAY

[White marble set into sandstone with railed enclosure.] Sacred to the memory of the Reverend J.W. McCay who died sincerely and deeply lamented on the 16th of October 1847 at the early age of 47 years, after a faithful and not unfruitful ministry of 21 years in the Presbyterian Church of Ballynure, during which his amiable character and Christian deportment commended him to the love and esteem of all. Also of his beloved daughters, Jane Houston Boyd who died on the 5th of April 1841 aged 2 years and 3 months, and Jane Houston Boyd who die on the 14th of September 1851 in her 9th year. 'Blessed are the dead who die in the Lord'. Rev. XIV, 13. Also his wife Margaret BOYD (widow of the late J. A. ALEXANDER M.D.) died 9th Augt. 1890 aged 70 years. 'Rest after weariness - peace after pain'.

[The Rev. James Whiteside McCay was born near Dervock in 1800. He was educated at the Belfast Academical Institution where he obtained the General Certificate in 1820. He was licensed by the Route Presbytery in 1822 and ordained at Ballynure on 21 December 1826. He married in 1836 Margaret Boyd, daughter of Andrew Boyd, of Bruslee, Ballyclare and, as well as the 2 daughters mentioned above, had 1 son, the Rev. Andrew Ross Boyd McCay, B.A., minister of Ballynure 1859-65. See McConnell: *Fasti of the Irish Presbyterian Church 1613-1840*, (1951); Barkley: *Fasti of the Irish Presbyterian Church, 1840-1870* (1986).]

McCLEAN/McLEAN

[Slate.] In memory of Margaret McClean, beloved wife of William McClean, who died October 28th 1873 aged 57 yrs. Erected by Robert McLean. 6 graves. 3 north.

McCOMB

[Ledger of Castle Espie limestone under several inches of soil and enclosed with Sarah Boyd, d.1878.] Here lyeth the body of William McComb of (B)ellyh(o)ne who departed this life ...th of (J)aniy 1726 aged (30) years. Here lyeth ye body of Mary McComb alias WALLACE who dyed ye 29th of (Decr.) 172(6) aged 26 years. Also to the memory of their son John M(cCo)mb who died in Belfast February ....)

McCONKEY

[Sandstone.] Erected by George McConkey of Ballygowan in memory of his father John McConkey who died 1st April 1871 aged 48 years. Also his mother Jeanie Elizabeth who died 8th May 1873 aged 48 years.

[Letters of administration of the personal estate of John McConkey, late of Ballygowan, county Antrim, farmer, who died 1 April 1871, were granted at the Principal Registry 25 March 1886 to George McConkey of same place, farmer, the son. Effects £99.]

McCONKY

[Red sandstone near north boundary.] Here lyeth the body of Jas. McConky who departed this life the 25th Decr. 1811 aged 63 years. Also Jane MAYNE his wife who died 31st Octr. 1816 aged 62 yrs.

McCONOC(H)

[Shattered slate. Fifteen inscribed pieces have been recovered but neither arms nor text is entire. Arms: In chief a sailing ship flying the saltire, in base a saltire, all impaling a (chevron or saltire), in the base a griffin rampant.] Here years. Also Malc(o)m Mc..no....ho died April ye 4.. 1769 ...... years. A.......n............ 4 years.

McCREARY
[With others inside iron railings.] Erected by James McCreary of Callhame to the memory of his wife Eleanor who departed this life 8th August 1827 aged 67 years. Also the said James McCreary who died 20th December 1841 aged 84 years.

McCREARY
[Within same enclosure as James McCreary, 1827.] Erected by William McCreary in me(mory of his beloved wife) Jane GILMORE wh.... (22).... (ch 1849 aged 31) ..... (Also) the (said) William McCreary who died 1st (September 18)77 aged 7... ....ter Jane McCreary who died 22nd March 1878 aged 41 years.

McCREARY
[White marble, lead lettering enclosed with foregoing.] Erected by Robert McCreary of Straidland in memory of his beloved wife Sarah DUNLOP who died 23rd August 1881 aged 23 years.

McCRONE
[Sandstone decorated with fan and quatrefoils.] Erected by Hugh McCrone in memory of his beloved daughter Sarah who died 7th July 1880 aged 50 years.

Parents dear weep not for me,
Nor wish me back again,
I have gained a heavenly home,
No more to suffer pain.

Also his wife Jane McCrone who died 12th Feby. 1882 aged 82 years. The above named Hugh McCrone died 3rd Feby. 1891 aged 94 years. Also his daughter Mary who died 5th Feby. 1900 aged 66 years.

[Letters of administration of the personal estate of Hugh McCrone, late of Lismenary, Ballynure, county Antrim, farmer, who died 2 February 1891 at same place, were granted at Belfast 18 March 1891 to David McCrone of Bryantang, Ballynure, farmer, a child. Effects £767 11s.]

McCRONE
[Lead lettering on white marble next to foregoing.] Erected by Hugh McCrone in memory of his beloved wife Jenny McCrone who died 21st October 1894 aged 41 years. Also the above-named Hugh McCrone who died 8th Nov. 1917 aged 78 years.

McCURDY
See CLEMENTS

McDERMOTT
[Small slate, cracked by a yew tree growing beside it.] W. McDermott. 2 graves.

McELWINIAN
[Last name added much later.] Here lyeth the body of John McElwinian who died July 30th 1769 aged 60 years. Samuel GIRVAN.

McFALL
[Lead lettering in white marble, in a roundel a flying dove bearing a laurel branch, spandrels of ivy.] Erected by Matilda McILWAINE in memory of her father John McFall who died 19th Dec. 1883 aged 76 years. And her mother Martha McFall who died 15th Aug. 1883 aged 79 years. The above-named Matilda McIlwaine died 18th April 1919 aged 80 years. Also her son Henry McIlwaine died 12th June 1948. T. Holden, Larne.

[The will of John McFall, late of Ballygowan, county Antrim, farmer, who died 18 December 1883 at same place, was proved at Belfast 28 April 1884 by Samuel McConkey and John Greer, late of Ballygowan, farmers, the executors. Effects £40 10s.]

McFERRAN
The burying grownd of William McFerran. In memory of his daughter Susana who died 23rd September 1896 aged 4 years. Also his daughter-in-law Annie died 28th Oct. 1908. Also his daughter Maggie Ellen died 9th Jan. 1914 aged 23 years. Also his wife Sarah McFerran who died 28th Feb. 1917 aged 68 years. Also his grandson James who died 29th Sep. 1926 aged 10 years. Also his granddaughter Susana who died 13th July 1931 aged 30 years. The above William McFerran died 17th January 1945 aged 98 years. Also his son Robert John died 19th Oct. 1958 aged 76 years.

McGOOKIN
[Composite sandstone with inset tablet of white marble.] Erected by James McGookin in memory of his beloved sons: John who died 16th March 1882 aged 20 years, and Arthur who died 29th Octr. 1882 aged 28 years. The above-named James McGookin died 6th Augt. 1894 aged 85 years. [Mason:-] (A). Jenkins, Larne.

[The will of James McGookin, late in Lismenary, county Antrim, farmer who died 6 August 1894 at same place, was proved at Belfast 21 December 1894 by James McGookin of Lismenary, Houston McGookin of Ballyrickmore and William McGookin of Lismenary, all in said county, farmers, the executors. Effects £1,344 10s.]

McGOOKIN
[Polished black granite enclosed with foregoing.] Erected by Minnie McGookin, Lismenary, in loving memory of her father William McGookin who died 3rd March 1929 aged 86 years. Also her mother Grace McGookin who died 29th October 1884 aged 37 years. Also all other deceased members of the family. Minnie KIRK died 6th May 1964 aged 86 years. [Mason:-] T. Holden, Larne.

McGOOKIN
[Loose blue slate.] In memory of Thomas McGookin who died 1895.

McGOOKIN
[Cast iron marker, cracked.] James McGookin. 3 graves.

McILROY
See WOODS

McILWAIN
Erected by John McIlwain in memory of his beloved wife Agnes McIlwain who died June the 26th 1858 aged 62 years. The above-named John McIlwain died 1873 aged 80 years.

McILWAINE
[Sandstone fragment lying beyond western perimeter of graveyard.] 4th February 1839 a(g........) Also of Jane McIlw.............. the erector who .... 1861 age ....

McILWAINE
[White marble fallen on face beside Agnes McIlwaine.] Erected by Matilda McIlwaine in memory of her beloved husband Henry McIlwaine who died 26th February 1897 aged 64 years. Also her infant daughter Agnes who died 1879. Also her son John who died 14th April 1883 aged 19 years. Also her daughter Martha (Jane) who died 11th August 1891 aged 17 years. Also her son Arthur who died 8th July 1942.

[Administration of the estate of Henry McIlwaine, late of Headwood, Kilwaughter, county Antrim, farmer, who died 27 February 1897, granted at Belfast 1 October 1897 to Edward McIlwaine and Arthur McIlwaine, both of Headwood, farmers, the sons. Effects £472 6s. 8d.]

McILWAINE
See McFALL

McKAY
: See WILSON

McKEE
: [Sandstone.] The burying ground of Thomas McKee. 2 graves north.

McKEE
: [Sandstone.] Erected by John McKee in memory of his father John McKee who died 16th May 1888 aged 80 years.

McKEE
: [Polished granite next to foregoing.] Erected by Jane McKee in loving memory of her husband James McKee who died 23rd February 1895 aged 74 years. Also their son William who died in infancy. James McKee died 18th July 1912. Ellen McKee died 30th May 1960.

McLATCHIE
: See BELL

McLEAN
: See McCLEAN

MACKEY
: [White marble stone.] Erected by Rachel Mackey in memory of her beloved husband Andrew Mackey who died 13th June 1889 aged 64 years. Also his father John Mackey who died 2nd Aug. 1864 aged 72 years. And his wife Agnes MacKey who died 12th May 1897 aged 92 years. Also her daughter-in-law Margaret Mackey who died 8th Feby. 1908 aged 26 years. Also her daughter-in-law Jane Mackey who died 10th August 1911 aged 30 years. And the above named Rachel Mackey who died 6th June 1924 aged 87 years. And her son Andrew Mackey who died 18th Sept. 1958 aged 77 years. Also her son John died 31st May 1966 aged 88 years. Also her son Robert died 19th Feb. 1971 aged 91 years.

  [The will of John Mackey, late of Ballygowan, Ballynure, in the county of Antrim, farmer, who died 2 August 1864 at same place, was proved at Belfast 11 September 1865 by the oaths of Andrew Mackey of Ballygowan and John Mackey of Carkerman, both in Ballynure in the said county, farmers, and Robert Mackey of Carrickfergus, currier, the executors. Effects under £200.

  Letters of administration of the personal estate of Andrew Mackey, late of Ballygowan, county Antrim, farmer, who died 13 June 1889 at same place, were granted at Belfast 24 July 1889 to Rachel Mackey of Ballygowan, the widow. Effects £873 15s.]

MACKEY
: See WILSON

McMILLEN
: [Red sandstone.] Here lieth the body of Robert McMillen who departed this life 12th December 1807 aged 63 years. Also his nephew Robert McNAIR of Castletown who died the 6th Nov. 1840 aged 74 years. Also Susanna, wife of Robert McNair, who departed this life 8th Feb. 1879 aged 74 years. Also their granddaughter Mary McNair who departed this life 14th Dec. 1885 aged 32 years.

McMINN
: Erected by John & James McMinn of Ballylaggan in memory of their father Robert McMinn who died 15th Aug. 1859 aged 74 years. Their mother Martha died 27th Aug. 1860 aged 68 years. Their brother William died in 1866. Also Mary, wife of the above John McMinn, died 17th Octr. 1880 aged 34 years. Ann Wilson, wife of above James McMinn, died at Ballylaggan 18th December 1913 aged 80 years. James McMinn died at Ballylaggan 20th March 1917 aged 83 years.

  Not lost to memory, not lost to love,
  But gone to a father's home above.

McMINN

[Lead lettering on white marble, in a roundel a flying dove with a leaf, ivy in spandrels.] Erected by William McMinn, Dairyland, in memory of his father Robert McMinn who died 14th Decr. 1887 aged 66 years. Also his wife Eliza McMinn who died 6th Octr. 1906 aged 50 years. The above named William McMinn died 30th August 1922 aged 75 years.

McMINN

[Polished granite.] In memory of Samuel McMinn, Dunturkey, died 18th May 1905. His wife Eliza died 23rd Sept. 1888. Their daughter Agnes died 6th Jan. 1905. Also their son Andrew died 2nd Feb. 1949. His wife Ellen died 23rd Dec. 1953. And their children: Bella died in infancy, William A. died 27th Aug. 1930, Samuel died 16th July 1949, daughter Nellie died 27th April 1985. Who soweth good seed shall surely reap.

McNAIR

[White marble panel set into heavy sandstone.] Erected by Susanna McNair, Ballylagan, in memory of her beloved brother James who died 26th June 1887 aged 56 years. The above-named Susanna McNair died 16th June 1911 aged 72 years.

[The will of James McNair, late of Ballylaggan, county Antrim, farmer, who died 26 June 1887 at same place, was proved at Belfast 10 August 1887 by William James Harson of Dunturkey in said county, farmer, and Susanna McNair of Ballylaggan, spinster, the executors. Effects £354 1s.]

McNAIR

See HAGAN, McMILLEN and SCOTT

McROBERT

See GILMORE

McSHANNON

[Arms: two halberts in saltire, in chief the crown imperial. Crest: a demi-lion rampant. Motto: ne pereas nec spernas.] Here lyeth the body of Hugh MccShannon of Castle-Town who departed this life the 28 day of October 1754 aged 67 years.

My wife and children dear grief not for me
My debts is pyed my grave you sie
Therefore prepare to follow me.

MADDEN

See LOGAN

MAPHETT

See WILSON

MARTIN

[Sandstone.] Erected by Agnes MURPHY of Dunturkey in memory of her father William Martin who departed this life 8th Oct. 1812 aged 72 years. Also her mother Agnes Martin who departed this life 31st Aug. 1823 aged 84 years. Also the above-named Agnes Murphy who departed this life 12th July 1869 aged 85 years.

MARTIN

Erected by George Martin, Carnmoney, in memory of his wife Isabella who died the 13th of June 1833 aged 30 years.

MARTIN

[Tall stone of polished granite within low railings.] Erected by Sarah NEILL in memory of her beloved mother Ann Martin who died 15th October 1850 aged 44 years. And her father Archibald Martin who died 28th April 1889 aged 68 years. Also the above Sarah Neill who died 26th February 1896 aged 47 years.

[The will of Archibald Martin, late of Ballymoney, county Antrim, spirit merchant, who died 28 April 1889 at same place, was proved at Belfast 27 May 1889 by Sarah Neill of Ballymoney, wife of James Neill, the sole executrix. Effects £956 2s. 7d.

Administration of the estate of Sarah Neill, late of Church Street, Ballymoney, county Antrim, who died 26 February 1896, granted at Dublin 28 May 1896 to James Neill of Church Street, merchant, the husband. Effects £408 3s. 8d.]

MARTIN
[Lead lettering in white marble within iron railings.] In memory of our beloved brother John Boyd Martin, White Park, who died 10th Oct. 1891 aged 38 years. Also loved ones gone before. 'I am the resurrection and the life' John. XI. 25. [Mason:-] A. McBain.

MAWHINNEY
[Lead lettering in white marble, frieze of ivy.] Erected by Arthur Mawhinney in memory of his mother Ann SEMPLE who died 22nd June 1870 aged 85 years. His daughter Agnes died 1st September 1879 aged 28 years. Also his wife Easther BLAIR who died 17th June 1894 aged 69 years. The above-named Arthur Mawhinney died 3rd Jany. 1905 in his 82nd year. His grandchild Arthur Mawhinney who died in infancy. Nellie E. Mawhinney died 5th April 1923 aged 21 years. Also Maud Mawhinney died 8th July 1929 aged 24 years. Mary Mawhinney died 3rd Dec. 1949, wife of David Mawhinney died 19th Feb. 1950. Also Margaret Hume Mawhinney, daughter of the above David and Mary Mawhinney, died 19th April 1965. [Mason:-] T. Holden, Larne.

MAWHINNEY
[Lead lettering on white marble.] Erected by William Mawhinney in memory of his father William J. Mawhinney who died 11th Sept. 1889 aged 63 years. Also his mother Ellen Mawhinney who died 18th Augt. 1910 aged 82 years. Also his grandfather William Mawhinney who died 27th Novr. 1870 aged 88 years. The above William Mawhinney died 17th Decr. 1944 aged 83 years. And his wife Agnes Mawhinney died 21st June 1977 aged 82 years.
[Mason:-] T. Holden, Larne.

[The will of William John Mawhinney, late of Ballybracken, county Antrim, who died 11 September 1889 at same place, was proved at Belfast 3 March 1890 by William Mawhinney of Ballybracken and Hugh McCrone, junior, of Lismenary in said county, farmers, the executors. Effects £191.]

MAYNE
[Sandstone.] Erected by Robert Mayne of Ballybracken in memory of his father Joseph Mayne who died 1st December 1861 aged 65 years. Also his sister Jane who died 9th January 1866 aged 26 years. Also his mother Ellen who died 1st September 1871 aged 75 years.

MAYNE
See McCONKY

MILLEN
[Roughly shaped local stone next to following.] Here lieth the body of Thomas Millen.

MILLEN
[Cast iron plaque attached to low railings.] The family burying ground of Wm. Millen, Belfast. 1886. [Cast by:-] James Moore, Millfield Foundry, Belfast.

[The will of William Millen, late of Belfast, gentleman, who died 20 February 1886 at same place, was proved at Belfast 25 June 1886 by Eliza Jane Millen of Lansdowne Terrace, Belfast, spinster, one of the executors. Effects £88 16s. 9d.]

MILLEN
See KERR

MILLER
See ROBINSON

MISSKIMMIN
See RICHEY

MOFFETT
[Sandstone close to south boundary.] Erected by Mary Moffett of Belfast in memory of her husband and children. Ellen died J.....
7th 18(3)9 (AE 2)6 John died (Nov) 2(.)th 1859 (AE .)2
Anna (H.D..................)6
James M. died Nov..............
Also her husband John Moffett who died March (1)8th 18( )8 aged 59.
David M. (S.O.U. -) died ......th 1869 ....

MULLAN
[Lead lettering on white marble, roundel has a dove with a leaf in its beak.] Erected by his mother in loving memory of John Mullen who was drowned at Dublin, 13th April 1892 aged 28 years. His remains were here interred 12th May 1892. Though lost from sight, to memory dear. Also his youngest brother Captain Thomas Mullan who was lost at sea on a voyage from Brazil in the storms of January 1895 aged 23 years. Emma J. Fullarton Mullan died 23rd June 1909 aged 71. Capt. Samuel Mullan died 15th Dec. 1912 aged 80 yrs. [Mason:-] Robinson, Belfast.

MULLHOLAN
[Arms: on a saltire, a mullet each in the base points, a stag's head overall. Crest: a castle.] Here lye(th) the body of John Mullholan who departed this life the 9th Oct. 1789 aged 73 years.

MURDOCH
Erected to the memory of John Murdoch who departed this life 15th April 1809 aged 72 years. Also his wife Mary Murdoch who died Decr. 1771 aged 40 years. Likewise their son James Murdoch who deceased Septr. 1782 aged 19 years.

MUR(D)OCH
[Cast iron plaque attached to railings.] Erected in memory of my beloved husband Revd. John Mur(d)och, pastor of Islip, U.S., born 26th Augt. 1840, fell asleep in Jesus 2nd Feby. 1881.

MURDOCK
Erected to the memory of John Murdock who died on the 1st of May 1829 aged 59 years. Also his beloved wife Elizabeth who departed this life the 5th of January 1839 aged 59 years. Both in Ballyclare. Likewise their son Robert who died on the 30th day of January 1840 aged 19 years. Also their son William who died on the 27th Decr. 1840 aged 29 years. Erected in memory of my beloved husband Revd. John Murdock, Pastor of Islip, N.Y. born 26th Augt. 1840, fell asleep in Jesus 2nd Feby. 1881.

[The will, with one codicil, of the Reverend John Murdock, late of Thorndale Avenue, Belfast, Presbyterian Minister, who died 2 February 1881 at same place, was proved at Belfast 9 May 1881 by Margaret Murdock of Thorndale Avenue, Belfast, widow, the sole executrix. Effects under £200.]

MURPHY
See LOGAN and MARTIN

NEESON
[Small concrete marker.] 1894. Erected by John Neeson. 2 graves.

NEILL
See MARTIN

NICOLEY
  See CLEMENTS

OLIVER
  [Incised on a roughly shaped local stone.] J. Oliver. 6 graves south.

OLIVER
  [Ornate cement - on a border at the top "God is love".] Erected by John Oliver, Straid, in memory of his son Hugh Oliver who fell asleep in Jesus March 3rd 1893 aged 32 years. The above-named John Oliver died 24th July 1899 aged 72 years. Also his wife Matilda Oliver who died 3rd June 1912 aged 84 years. [Mason:-] John Creeth, B'clare.

PARK
  [Red sandstone with cherub, set into wall of vault under Dobbs tablet.] Here lyeth the body of Anna WOODSIDE, wife to William Park, who depd. this life May 4th 1759 aged 54 years. Also the above named William Park who died May 27th 178(8) (aged ..) years.

PARK
  [One of four stones to Park and Fergusson, within a railed enclosure.] Here lyeth the body of William Park who departed this life April 20th 1786 aged 40 years. Also his mother Jane Park who departed this life June 1st 1786 aged 67 yrs. Also his father & her husband Alexander Park departed this life June 22d 1786 aged 77 years. Also Andrew Park who departed this life in Octr. 1796 aged 39 years. Also Mary F. SMYTH who died September 1893 aged 72 years.

PARK
  [Grey limestone tablet set into wall of vault next to Dobbs tablet.] Erected by James Park in memory of Elizabeth his wife who departed this life on the 24th of February 1823 aged 81 years. Also the above named James Park who departed this life on the 28th of September 1837 aged 89 years.

PARK
  [Sandstone insert on heavy cast iron frame, attached to railings of Park enclosure.] Erected to the memory of John Park and Mary Park his wife who died in December 1832. Also James Park who died 18th May 1839. Also Andrew Park & Ellen COYNE who died abroad.

PARK
  [In railed enclosure.] Erected by Alexander Park in memory of his beloved wife Jane who died 27th Augt. 1852 aged 43 yrs. Also the said Alexr. Park who died 8th May 1854 aged 38 years. Also Eliza PEDEN died 23rd February 1852. Also William F. Park died 12th March 1857.

PARK
  See CINNAMOND and FERGUSON

PARKHILL
  See WILSON

PEDEN
  See PARK

PHILLIPS
  [Reversed against Clements vault, reused by Crowe.] Erected by Mary DOLLAR of Dekalb, State of New York, in memory of her father John Phillips who died in May 1832 aged 80 years. In this enclosed spot rest the remains of her mother Ann CLEMENTS, her sister Jannet, and her brothers, viz. William, John, Henry, James, Samuel & David.

PORTER
[Sandstone.] Erected by John and William Porter in memory of their father John Porter who died 4th of June 1800 aged 67 years. Also their brother and sister who died in infancy.

PORTER
Here lies the body of Andrew Porter who died 5th Feb. 1829 aged 69. And his wife Agnes who died 21st Nov. 1836 aged 84. Andrew Porter Junr. died 31st Decr. 1857 aged 63 years.
[The will of Andrew Porter, late of Middle Division, county of the town of Carrickfergus, farmer, who died 2 January 1858 at same place, was proved at Belfast 20 May 1858 by the oaths of William Lockhart and John Lockhart, late of the same place, farmers, the executors. Effects under £100.]

PORTER
[Late Victorian stone beside vault.] Erected by John Porter, Ballyboley, in memory of his brother James. Blessed are the dead who die in the Lord.

REA
See BILSHER

REID
[Flaking sandstone.] Erected by Eliza Reid in memory of her beloved husband James Reid who departed this life 4th January 1870 aged 55 years.
Eliza dea(r w)eep not for me,
I am not dead but sleepeth here,
In hopes in Heaven we will meet;
When all our joys shall be complete.
[The will of James Reid, late of Ballyvallagh, county Antrim, farmer, who died 3 January 1870 at same place, was proved at Belfast 28 January 1870 by the oaths of John Cross and Andrew Baird, senior, both of Ballyfore, Carrickfergus, in said county, farmers, the executors. Effects under £100.]

RENTOUL
See WYLIE

RICHEY
[Sandstone. Arms: a chevron between three crosses crosslet. Crest: a garb.] Here lyeth the body of John Richey who died Oct. 27th 1779 aged 86 years. Also his wife Anne MISSKIMMIN who died June 2d 1784 aged 89 years.

RICHEY
See SCOTT

ROBINSON
[Red sandstone.] Samuel Robinson of Castletown died 29th July 1813 aged 58 years. His wife Janet MILLER died the 1st August 1807 aged 50 years. Also his daughter Frances Robinson died August 7th 1808 aged 18 years. Also his daughter Grace an infant child.

ROBINSON
[Lead lettering in white marble.] Erected by Thomas Robinson in memory of his daughter Elizabeth who died 17th Feb. 1887 aged 9 years. [Mason:-] Rankin.

ROBINSON
See KNOX

RODGERS
See KERR

ROSS
[Within iron railings.] Erected to the memory of William Ross, Ballynure, who died 16th June 1847 aged 58 years. Also his beloved wife Sarah who died 26th May 1859 aged 62 years.

ROSS
[Sandstone, fallen and broken.] Erected by Patrick Ross, Ballynure, in memory of his father Andrew Ross who died 8th Novr. 1881 aged 82 years. Also his mother Jane who died 4th Novr. 1880 aged 77 years. The above-named Patrick Ross died 14th May 1914 aged 70 years.

ROWNEY
[White marble.] In memory of James Rowney, Ballybracken, who died 8th July 1873 aged 81 years. Also his wife Margaret Rowney, who died 26th March 1872 aged 81 years. Their daughter, Jane, who died 6th March 1848 aged 30 years. Their son William, who died 19th Novr. 1879 aged 40 years. Their daughter Mary Ann, who died 14th Oct. 1899 aged 70 years. Their grand-daughter Ellen Rowney. Their son James Rowney who died 23rd Novr. 1909 aged 87 years. Also Jane Rowney, wife of the above William, who died 25th April 1921 aged 83 years. Their great grand-daughter Mary who died 7th Novr. 1925 aged 3½ year. Their grand-son Hugh, who died 10th May 1926 aged 53 years. Their grand-son William who died 25th April 1948. Also Mary Rowney, wife of the above William, died 23rd Jan. 1959. Their grand-daughter Ellen died 15th July 1970.

[The will of James Rowney, late of Ballybracken, county Antrim, farmer, who died 8 July 1873 at same place, was proved at the Principal Registry 24 August 1874 by the oaths of James Rowney of same place and Nathaniel Agnew of Ballygowan, county Antrim, farmer, the executors. Effects under £450.]

SCOT
[Sandstone.] Here lyeth the body of William Scot who departed this life 12th Jan. 1788 aged 21 years. Also his mother Jane RICHEY who died June 30th 1791 aged 61 years. And also William Scott his father who died May (.)th ..(07) aged 79 years.

SCOTT
[Black polished granite.] In memory of William Scott, Crossroads, Bryantang, born 1820, died 1907. His wife Ann McNAIR born 1834, died 1876. His father Adam Scott born 1762, died 1848. His mother Ann McALISTER born 1778, died 1864. His son Hugh born 1862, died 1928. His daughter Mary born 1860, died 1939. Annie CLARKE, wife of his son James, born 1875, died 1945. His brother Hugh born 1805, accidently drowned 1834, His daughter Elizabeth Jane born 1866, died 1948. His son James born 1872, died 1949. His son Robert born 1864, died 1950. His son Adam born 1870, died 1959. Evelyn Isabella Mary, wife of his son Adam, born 1887, born 1960. Interred in Rashee New Cemetery.

SCOTT
[Cast iron plaque.] James B. Scott. Four graves. Two each way. [Cast by:-] James Moore & Sons Ltd., Ironfounders & Engineers, Belfast, Millfield Foundry.

SCOTT
See ADAMSON and LORIMER

SEMPLE
See BARKLIMORE and MAWHINNEY

SHANNON
[Ledger next to MccShannon stone.] To the memory of Hugh Shannon of Castletown. He died the 3d. of August 1805 in the 47th year of his age.

SIMM
[Arms: a chevron, in chief two mullets, in base a halberd. Crest: a sword in pale.] Here lyeth the body of William Simm who died Sep. 15th 1734 aged 72 years.

Also Janet CAIRNS his wife who died Feb. 21st 1744 aged 68 years. Also their grand-son Samuel Simm who died April 9th 1766 aged 16 years.

SIMM
See CLEMENTS

SIMMS
See ADAMSON

SMILEY
[White marble next to Maggie Boyd Beatty.] In loving memory of the Rev. Wm. Smiley, LL.D., Methodist minister, son-in-law of Robert Beatty, who died at Ballynure on the 9th Jan. 1886 aged 35 years. Ever loyal and devoted to his king, he has been thus early promoted to higher service. "Blessed are the pure in heart for they shall see God". Also his wife Mary Hay Hill Smiley, fourth daughter of Robert BEATTY, who, loving and dearly loved, entered into life eternal on 15th February 1914 aged 62 years. Also Rev. Thomas KNOX, son-in-law of Robert Beatty who after 50 years of devoted work in the Methodist ministry went home to God 10th Feby. 1919 aged 82. And of his wife Sarah Jane Boyd Beatty, whose gentle spirit passed away 6th October 1921 aged 73. And Sarah Robina Beatty Smiley, M.A., daughter of Rev. William Smiley, LL.D., whose kind and loving spirit entered into rest 4th December 1930 aged 50. [See also WALLACE.]

[Letters of administration of the personal estate of Reverend William Smiley, late of Ballynure, county Antrim, Wesleyan Minister, who died 9 January 1886 at same place, were granted at Belfast 26 February 1886 to Mary Hay Hill Smiley of Ballynure, the widow. Effects £380 12s.]

SMYTH
See PARK

SNODDY
[Lead lettering in white marble next to following.] Erected by Patrick Snoddy in loving memory of his sister Ellen died 29th May 1900 aged 24 years and 11 months. Also his father Patrick died 5th June 1900 aged 65 years. Also his mother Mary Jane died 12th April 1930 aged 89 years. Also his sister Margaret died 11th December 1938 aged 75 years. Also his infant son Ernest died 24th January 1892 aged 5 weeks. Also his beloved wife Agnes died 9th July 1940 aged 78 years.

SNODDY
[Facing south in railed enclosure.] In loving memory of my dear brother Ernest Snoddy, passed away 24th January 1892 aged 5 weeks. Also my dear mother Agnes Snoddy passed away 9th July 1940 aged 78 years. Also my dear father Patrick Snoddy passed away 5th January 1951 aged 92 years. Erected by their loving daughter Rebecca Snoddy. Loves last gift - remembrance.

SPARROWHAWK
See HUNTER

STEEL/STEELE
[Red sandstone.] Erected in memory of James Steel, Ballynerry, who departed this life 7th July 1867 aged 87 years. Also of his beloved wife Jane Steel who died 25th July 1868 aged 82 years. Also of their son William John who died in infancy. Also their son James Steel who died 4th November 1914 aged 88 years. Also his great grand children James & Mary Steel who died in infancy in 1907. Elizabeth Steele died 3 June 1920. James Steele died 27th May 1935.

STEWART
[Flaking sandstone next to John Stewart of Ballyeaston, d. 1849. The year might have been 1824 as 1 and 2 occupy the same space.] To the memory of May Stewart who died Feby. 4 1814 aged (4)8 years.

STEWART

Erected by Thomas Stewart in memory of his father Walter Stewart of Ballyearl who departed this life the 8th of August 1822 aged 84 years. Also his mother Ann who died 21st November 1838 aged 85 years. Also Mary Anne daughter of the above who departed this life 12th August 1805 aged 21 years. Likewise their daughter Jane Stewart who died 25th Nov. 1857 aged 81 yrs. Their son Thomas Stewart died 2nd July 1858 aged 78 years.

[The will of Thomas Stewart, late of Ballyearl, in the county of Antrim, farmer, who died 2 July 1858 at same place, was proved at Belfast 30 November 1858 by the oaths of John Wilson of Straid, John Houston of Ballyearl and Thomas Bigger of Mallusk, all in said county of Antrim, farmers, the executors. Effects under £300.]

STEWART

[Next to foregoing.] Sacred to the memory of William Stewart of Ballyearl who departed this life 12th Septr. 1831 aged 74 years. Also William Stewart of Ballycorr who departed this life 23rd March 1865 AE 77 years.

STEWART

[Low iron railings enclose this stone with the following.] Erected by Samuel Alexander Stewart of Belfast. John Stewart of Ballyeaston died 4th June 1849 aged 64 years. Samuel Stewart of Belfast died 18th May 1855 aged 64 years. William Stewart of Belfast died 24th Nov. 1872 aged 75 years.

STEWART

1875. The burial place of Hugh Stewart, Belfast. The above-named Hugh Stewart was lost at sea 8th Feby. 1876 aged 45 years. Also his beloved daughter Martha who died 18th May 1888 aged 25 years.

We shall sleep, but not for ever,
There will be a glorious dawn.
We shall meet to part no never,
On the resurrection morn.

STEWART

[White marble.] In memory of Thomas B. Stewart, Ballycorr, who died 24th Sept. 1884 aged 63 years. Also his son Robert who died 23rd Octr. 1882 aged 17 years. Also his daughter Agnes who died 24th Octr. 1892 aged 24 years. And his wife Rachel Stewart who died 30th April 1893 aged 56 years. Also their son James who died 8th Jan. 1904 aged 33 years. Also his son William who died 4th October 1931 aged 68 years. Also the above-named William's son John who died in infancy. Also their daughter Rachel who died 29th January 1934. Also his son John H. Stewart died 19th April 1936. And Margaret, wife of the above William Stewart, died 13th Feb. 1955.

[The will of Thomas Beggs Stewart, late of Ballycor, county Antrim, farmer, who died 25 September 1884 at same place was proved at Belfast 5 December 1884 by Rachel Stewart, widow, John Stewart, farmer, and Robert Allen of Ballyboley, farmer, all in said county, the executors. Effects £978 8s. 9d.

Letters of administration of the personal estate of Rachel Stewart, late of Ballycor, county Antrim, widow, who died 29 April 1893 at same place, were granted at Belfast 18 September 1893 to William Stewart of Ballycor, farmer, a son. Effects £5.]

STEWART
See ADRAIN

STRAIGHT
See BAIRD

TATE

[White marble with lead lettering and panels of foliage.] Erected by Francis Tate in loving memory of his wife Margaret Tate who died 23rd May 1891 aged 67 years. Also her grand-child Maggie, daughter of Robert Tate, who died 5th November 1879 aged 5 months. The above named Francis Tate who died 20th June 1900.

We loved her, yes, no tongue can tell
How dearly, deeply, and how well:
Christ loved her, too, and though it best
To take her home with him to rest.
[Mason:-] Gemmell, Belfast.

[Probate of the will of Francis Tate, late of 45 Penrith Street, Belfast, gentleman, who died 22 June 1900, granted at Belfast 22 August 1900 to James Tate, merchant tailor. Effects £459 14s. 6d.]

THOMPSON
[Sandstone.] Erected by Thomas Thompson of Ardboley in memory of his daughter Matilda who died in infancy. 4 graves.

THOMPSON
[Sandstone.] Erected by Robert & Andrew Thompson in memory of their parents: Thomas Thompson who departed this life April 1843 aged 67 years; Agnes, his wife who departed this life June 1864 aged 88 years.

THOMPSON
[Concrete.] Erected by Jane Thompson, Ballyclare, in memory of her beloved husband Thomas Thompson who died 28th February 1877 aged 51 years. Also her son Wm. Thompson who died 31st October 1884 aged 11 years. Also the above named Jane Thompson who died 23rd July 1908 aged 77 years. Also her son James Thompson who died 1st December 1923 aged 62 years. Also her daughter Sarah Thompson who died 17th March 1926 aged 65 years. Also Mary Jane Thompson who died 19th March 1947.

THOMSON
[Low stone.] Saml. Thomson died Nov. 1794.

THOMSON
[Sandstone beside foregoing.] Erected by Samuel Thomson of Dunturkey in memory of his wife Eliza HILL who died (1st) September 1845 aged 34 years. This stone also marks the grave (where) rests the remains of his father and mother, his sister, and brother, and his daughter Mary who died in childhood.

TODD
[Within iron railings.] Erected by David Todd of Straid-Land in memory of his beloved father Robert Todd who departed this life on the 20th. Nov. 1845 aged 91 ye's. Also his beloved mother Jane Todd who departed this life on the 14th Aug. 1859 aged 91 years. The above David Todd departed this life on the 13th March 1890 aged 91 years.

[The will of David Todd, late of Irish Hill, county Antrim, farmer, who died 13 March 1890 at same place, was proved at Belfast 16 March 1891 by Thomas Kennedy of Irish Hill, farmer, one of the executors. Effects £125 10s.]

TODD
The family burying place of Hamilton Todd. 1877.

WALLACE
[Sandstone.] Erected by John Wallace in memory of his two sons, viz. William who died 28th Feb. 1848 aged 11 years & Francis Wallace who died 8th Novr. 1860 aged 27 years. Prepare to meet thy God. 8 feet north.

WALLACE
[White marble next to Rev. Wm. Smiley.] (In) memory of Rev. Robert Wallace, Wesleyan minister, Ireland, who when on a deputation to the M.E. Church America died of cholera at Cincinnati, Ohio, U.S., Sept. 2nd 186(6) in the (54)th

year of his age and 31st of his ministry. His remains are interred in the C(umm)insville Cemetery, Cincina(ti). Also Caroline Hill Wallace who died at Lisburn May 13th 1852 aged 5 years and 7 months. Her remains are buried at Lisburn. Also Alexander Beatty Wallace who died at Belfast March 26th 1862 aged 6 years and 10 months. Also Jane Caroline Hill Wallace who died at Belfast July 26th 1869 aged 9 years and 2 months. Rev. John Beattie Wallace, LL.B., Wesleyan minister, died 3rd April 1872 aged 27 years.

[The will of Robert Wallace, late of Lower Abbey Street [Dublin], Wesleyan Minister, who died 2 September 1866 at Cincinati, Ohio, North America, was proved at the Principal Registry 28 February 1867 by the oaths of Mary Wallace, the widow, and Anna Beatty Wallace, spinster, the daughter, both of lower Abbey Street aforesaid, the executrixes. Effects under £1,500.

Letters of administration of the personal estate of the Rev. John Wallace, late of Longwood Avenue, Dublin, Wesleyan Minister, who died 3 April 1872 at Charlemont Place, Dublin were granted at the Principal Registry 4 June 1872 to Catherine Louisa Wallace of No. 138 Leinster Road, Rathmines, County Dublin, the widow of the said deceased. Effects under £600.]

WALLACE
See McCOMB

WEATHERUP
[Sandstone near obelisk.] Erected by James Weatherup in memory of his father Thomas Weatherup who died 18th January 1864 aged 75 years. Also his mother Mary who died 15th October 1869 aged 75 years.

[The will of Thomas Weatherup, late of the Middle Division of the county of the town of Carrickfergus, farmer, who died 18 January 1864 at same place, was proved at Belfast 29 February 1864 by the oaths of James McAlister of Ballyfore, Carrickfergus, in the county of Antrim, farmer, and William McAlister of Slievetrue, Carrickfergus, in the county of the town of Carrickfergus, farmer, the executors. Effects under £100.]

WEATHERUP
[Granite obelisk decorated with square and compass enclosing 'V' and a triangle that has WLBTTPT BONTLOI BAOSIOG along the sides and HTGMGF at the centre.] I.N.R.I. Erected by Straid Masonic Lodge NO. 276 in grateful & affectionate remembrance of Samuel Weatherup who died 27th January 1873 aged 73 years.

> He died as a Christian dieth,
> A calm and a peaceful death,
> He boasted not of his talent of worth,
> But Christ was his last drawn breath.

[Mason:-] A. McBain.

[The will of Samuel Weatherup, late of Slievetrue, Carrickfergus, farmer, who died 25 January 1873 at same place, was proved at Belfast 19 February 1873 by the oath of James Weatherup of Ardbooley, Carrickfergus, farmer, one of the executors. Effects under £200.]

WEATHERUP
[Scratched on a small blue slate near Thomas Weatherup's stone.] In memory of T. Weatherup died in the year of our Lord 1901 aged 54 years. And his son Robert in the year 1892 aged 15 years.

WEATHERUP
See WILSON

WEIR
[Stone broken at bottom.] George Weir departed March ye 26th & Elizabeth LOREMR his wife Novr. ye 5th, both in 1765. Said George aged 80 years. Sd. Eliz aged 70. Also their children Anne & Mary & their grandchildren Archibald Wil-

son Weir (And Elizabeth Weir) ......

WHITEFORD
[Arms: on a bend bordured between two garbs three crosses patee. Crest: a garb. Motto: Ubique aut nusquam.] Here lyeth the body of Hugh Whiteford who died March 1st 1780 aged 50 years. Also his son Willoughby who died April 17th 1788 aged 21 years. Also in memory of James Whiteford, M. Inst. C.E. died 25th Aug. 1904. Jane WILSON his wife died 3rd March 1900. Their children: James Henry Price Whiteford died 18th Nov. 1883, John Wilson Whiteford B.E. died 20th Aug. 1921, David Gray Whiteford died 11th July 1930. Mary M. Whiteford died 15th Nov. 1938.

WHITEFORD
[White marble inset to gothic sandstone, next to foregoing.] Erected by James Whiteford, Woodford, C'fergus, 1876, in memory of his mother Jane who died 23rd March 1845 AE 82 years. His father Hugh who died 28th Sept. 1845 AE 83 years. His son John who died 20th Feby. 1839 AE 2 years. His son John who died 15th May 1851 AE 12 years. Also the above James Whiteford born Feby. 1800, died 1st June 1878. Mary, relict of above James Whiteford, died 10th Novr. 1892 aged 84 years. Also their son Hugh Whiteford who died 21st May 1919 aged 87 years. And his wife Jane Whiteford who died 25th Aug. 1885 aged 33 years.

[The will of James Whiteford, late of Woodford, Carrickfergus, farmer, who died 1 June 1878 at same place, was proved at Belfast 10 July 1878 by the oaths of Hugh Whiteford of Ballylaggan, Straid, and James Whiteford of Woodlawn, Woodburn, both in said county, farmers, and James Ritchie of Lisnataylor, Ligoniel, county Antrim, farmer, the executors. Effects under £600.]

WHITEFORD
See HILL

WILEY
[Within railings of Wm. A. Wylie, 1881.] Erected by Jane Wiley in memory of her beloved sister Eliza Simms Wiley who departed this life 29th May 1860 aged 61 years. Also the above Jane Wiley who died Nov. 1886.

WILSON
[Sandstone with face (cherub) at apex, near James Wilson, Fern Hollow.] Here lyeth the body of Ephram Wilson who departed December 24 1717 & age 24. & H.W.

WILSON
[Sandstone near above.] Here lyeth the body of John Wilson who died 1st Jany. 1764 aged 52 years. Also his son George who died 24th June 1766 aged 18 years. Also Henry Wilson who died 15th April 1793 aged 79 years.

WILSON
[Sandstone beginning to flake, within iron railings in front of foregoing.] Erected to the memory of William Wilson of Bryantang who died 15th Feb. 1833 aged 80 years. Also Mary his wife who died 18th Feb. 1825 aged 60. And of John their son who died 22nd Jan. 1816 aged 28 years. Also their son William who died 13th May 1844 aged 41 years. Malcolm M. Wilson died 20th September 1879 aged 84 years. His son John died 6th March 1879 aged 35 years. Also his wife Elizabeth DICKEY who died 6th Jany. 1890 aged 77 years. Also his son David who died 17th Dec. 1923 aged 82 years.

[Letters of administration of the personal estate of John Wilson, late of Bryantang, county Antrim, farmer, a bachelor, who died 6 March 1879 at same place, were granted at Belfast 9 April 1879 to Malcolm McConachey Wilson of Bryantang, Ballynure, farmer, the father of said deceased. Effects under £600.

The will, with one codicil, of Malcolm McConachie Wilson, late of Bryantang, county Antrim, farmer, who died 20 September 1879 at same place, was proved at Belfast by the oaths of David Wilson and William Wilson, both of Bryantang, farmers and James Dickey of Ballyeaston, teacher, all in Ballynure, said county, three of the executors. Effects under £1,500.

The will of Elizabeth Wilson, late of Bryantang, county Antrim, widow, who died 6 January 1890 at same place, was proved at Belfast 7 March 1890 by William Wilson and David Wilson, both of Bryantang, and James Dickey of Saint John's Place, Larne, retired school teacher, all in said county, the executors. Effects £526 10s. 6d.]

WILSON
[Sandstone near John Wilson, Ballylagan, d.1896.] Erected in memory of Agness Wilson who died 23rd Jany. 1832 AE 25 years. Also her daughter Ann Wilson who died in infancy. Also George Wilson, the erector of this stone, died at Milebush 25th Sept. 1884 aged 84 years. And his wife Janie who died 19th Feb. 1877 aged 70 years. His daughter Ellen who died 19th Feb. 1879 aged 38 years. His two grand-daughters Maggie Wilson died 13th Aug. 1879 aged 8 years and Annie Wilson died 24th Dec. 1897 aged 18 years. Also his daughter-in-law Anna Maria Wilson who died 1st Dec. 1916 aged 69 years. And her husband David Legg Wilson who died 11th April 1922 aged 84 years.

[The will of George Wilson, late of Castleview, near St. Catherine's, Carrickfergus, farmer, who died 25 September 1884 at same place, was proved at Belfast 17 October 1884 by David Legg Wilson of Ballylaggan, county Antrim, farmer, one of the executors. Effects £285.]

WILSON
[Flaking sandstone, next to Samuel Wilson, d.1897.] Interred here .... the body of (Thomas) Wilson of Ballylaggan who departed this life 30th Jany. 1847 aged 67 years. Likewise Henrietta his wife who died 7th Septr. 1848 aged 71 years. Also his son Henry who died 27th March 1833 aged 14 years. Also his sister Margaret who died 4th Dec. 1884 aged 81 years.

WILSON
[Sandstone next to south boundary of graveyard.] Erected to the memory of John Wilson, Ballylaggan, who died 5th December 1873 aged 88 years. Also his wife Jane LENNON who died 19th December 1843 aged 51 years.

[The will of John Wilson, late of Ballylaggan, Middle Division of Carrickfergus, farmer, who died 5 December 1873 at same place, was proved at Belfast 4 March 1874 by the oaths of John Wilson of Ballylaggan, Ballyclare, county Antrim, farmer, and Robert Wilson of Upper Ballylaggan, Carrickfergus, farmer, the surviving executors. Effects under £600.]

WILSON
[Low sandstone.] Erected by Hugh Wilson in memory of his brother John who died 20th May 1847 aged 25 years.

WILSON
[Sandstone.] 1849. The family burying ground of James Wilson, Legaloy, who died 24th May 18(54) aged 42 years. 8 feet north.

WILSON
[White marble. Crest: an open palm scattering seed. Motto on encircling buckle: Ut sementem feceris ita et metes.] Erected by James Forsythe Wilson, Belfast, in memory of his father William Wilson who departed this life 12th Dec. 1852 aged 50 years. [Mason:-] A. Jenkins, Larne.

WILSON
[Polished granite.] Sacred to the memory of Willoughby Wilson, Ballylagan, who died 3rd Dec. 1872 aged 56 years. His wife Mary who died 18th Feb. 1860 aged 37 years. Also their sons: Samuel who died 10th May 1855 aged 3 years, Robert who died 27th May 1868 aged 22 years, David who died 17th Dec. 1886 aged 27 years.

Also Elizabeth Jane, wife of Thomas Wilson, who died 19th Feb. 1890 aged 33 years. Thomas Wilson who died 11th March 1923 aged 78 years. Jeannie Agnes, daughter of the above Thomas and Elizabeth Jane Wilson, died 26th October 1976.

[The will of Willoughby Wilson, late of Lower Ballylaggan, county Antrim, farmer, who died 3 December 1872 at same place, was proved at Belfast 20 June 1873 by the oaths of Thomas Wilson of Lower Ballylaggan, Straid aforesaid, farmer, and Robert Wilson of Ballylaggan, Straid, Carrickfergus, farmer, and Thomas Wilson of Straid, county Antrim, farmer, the executors. Effects under £2,000.

Letters of administration of the personal estate of Elizabeth Jane Wilson, late of Ballylaggan, Ballymore, county Antrim, who died 19 February 1890 at same place, were granted at Belfast 27 June 1894 to Thomas Wilson of Ballylaggan, farmer, the husband. Effects £252 7s. 8d.]

WILSON
[Slate panel in composite frame of sandstone.] Sacred to the memory of Thomas Wilson of Straid who died 3rd October 1855 aged 48 years. Also his beloved wife Mary PARKHILL who died 4th Aug. 1869 aged 56 years. Also Mary HILL, the beloved wife of Thomas Wilson Junr., who died 15th Octr. 1894 aged 53 years. And their eldest son David Hill who died 4th Decr. 1902 aged 35 years. Also John Wilson M.A., M.D., Fleet Surgeon R.N., who died 22nd Jany. 1897 aged 50 years, interred at Fareham. Also Robert Henry Wilson who died 5th Feby. 1904 aged 59 years. Also the above-named Thomas Wilson Junr., J.P. who died 17th February 1915 aged 73 years.

[Administration of the estate of Mary Wilson, late of Straid, county Antrim, who died 15 October 1894, granted at Belfast 23 June 1897 to Thomas Wilson of Straid, merchant, the husband. Effects £807 15s. 3d.]

WILSON
[Attached to railings of the following.] The family burying ground of John Wilson, Straid. 1859.

WILSON
Erected by John Wilson of Straid in memory of his wife Jenny MAPHETT who died April 8th 1868 aged 56 years. Also Ellen their daughter who died Octr. 16th 1859 aged 24 years. Also Thomas who died Octr. 10th 1879 aged 31 years. Also the above John Wilson who died Sept. 6th 1883 aged 82 years. Also John Dundee Wilson, son of the above Thos. Wilson, who died 25th April 1890 aged 16 years. Also Elizabeth DUNDEE, wife of the above Thomas Wilson, who died 17th November 1933 aged 81 years.

[Letters of administration of the personal estate of Thomas Wilson, late of Straidmills, Straidlands, county Antrim, farmer, who died 10 October 1879 at same place, were granted at Belfast 5 December 1879 to Eliza Wilson of same place, the widow of said deceased. Effects under £800.]

WILSON
[White marble set into sandstone.] Sacred to the memory of James Wilson of Dunturkey who departed this life on 17th Feby. 1867 aged 61 years. Also his daughter Mary who died 20 March 1878 aged 23 years. Also his son John who died 4th Feby. 1897 aged 59 years. And his wife Mary Wilson who died 29th May 1917 aged 72 years. Also their daughter Jane Harper Wilson who died 19th Feby. 1893 aged 22 years. Also their son James Dixon Wilson who died 11th November 1921.

[The will of James Wilson, late of Drumahoe, county Antrim, farmer, who deceased 17 February 1867 at same place, was proved at Belfast 4 March 1867 by the oaths of John Wilson of Dunturkey, Ballynure, and Hugh Wilson of Drumahoe, Larne, both in said county, farmers, two of the executors. Effects under £1,500.

Administration of the estate of John Wilson, late of Dunturkey, Ballynure, county Antrim, farmer, who died 4 February 1897, granted at Belfast 9 April 1897 to Mary Wilson of Dunturkey, the widow. Effects £2,066 17s. 6d. Re-sworn 2,654 13s. 7d.]

WILSON
[Lead lettering in white marble.] Erected by James Wilson, Fern Hollow, in memory of his children. Martha died 8th March 1872 aged 4 years. James died 12th March 1872 aged 2 years. Samuel died 14th Sep. 1874 aged 3 years. Alice died 1st Oct. 1885 aged 20 years.

WILSON
[Lead lettering in white marble, next to John Wilson, d.1764.] Erected by Eliza Ann Wilson, Antrim, in memory of her mother Margaret Wilson who died in 1874. Also her sister Margaret. The above-named Eliza Ann Wilson died 16th Feby. 1899. "Asleep in Jesus". Also her uncle Joseph MACKEY who died December 1890. Also her sister Martha Wilson who died December 1913. [Mason:-] A. Jenkins.
[Administration of the estate of Eliza Wilson, late of Larne, county Antrim, spinster, who died 16 February 1899, granted at Belfast 12 May 1899 to Martha Wilson of Larne, spinster. Effects £237 2s. 11d.]

WILSON
[Polished granite, collapsed within same enclosure as Thomas Wilson d.1855. Crest: a demi lion rampant. Motto: semper vigilans.] Sacred to the memory of Robert Wilson of Legaloy born 12th Nov. 1805, died 24th Jan. 1878. And of Mary Ann his wife who died 31st December 1891 aged 83 years. Erected by their nephew and adopted son Brigade-Surgeon W.J. Wilson M.D., late 28th Regt. and Army Medical Staff, who died 8th February 1918 aged 79 years and is interred at Fareham, Hants., England.
[The will, with one codicil, of Mary Anne Wilson, late of Legaloy, county Antrim, widow, who died 31 December 1891 at same place, was proved at Belfast 5 February 1892 by William Mann of Marshaltown, county Carrickfergus, and Thomas Wilson of Straid, county Antrim, farmers, the executors. Effects £1,127 13s. 6d.]

WILSON
[Modern granite with lead lettering.] In loving memory of Betsy Wilson who died 28th August 1885. And her husband John Wilson who died 12th April 1912. Their daughter Martha Ann, beloved wife of James WEATHERUP, who died 12th January 1944. [Mason:-] Hastings, Larne.

WILSON
[Lead lettering on white marble.] Erected by George BARTON, Larne, in memory of William Wilson, Ballysnodd, who died 20th April 1888 aged 59 years. Also his two children Sarah & Mary Ellen Wilson who died in infancy. Ruthven Wilson Barton died 26th July 1897 aged 5 months. Ruth Wilson Barton died 15th March 1899 aged 9 months. Also Ruth, wife of the above George Barton, who died 3rd May 1903 aged 39 years. Also his daughter Maggie C. Barton who died 4th July 1905 aged 14 years. Also Agnes, wife of the above William Wilson, who died 1st July 1914 aged 81 years. T. Holden.

WILSON
[Polished granite beside John Wilson, Ballylaggan, d. 1873.] In memory of John Wilson, Ballylagan, died 2nd November 1896 aged 82 years. Janet Wilson died 6th July 1898 aged 78 years. Their son James died 9th May 1901 aged 56 years. Their son Robert died 20th April 1902 aged 44 years. Their son John died 25th May 1907. Their daughter Jane died 25th Dec. 1908. Their son William Graham died Oct. 1921. Their daughter Marianne died 11th Feb. 1932. And their daughter-in-law Mary, wife of Joseph Graham Wilson, died 23rd September 1911. And their grand-daughter Margaret Elizabeth who in infancy. The above Joseph Graham Wilson died 28th February 1937 aged 86 years.

WILSON
[Polished granite in front of John Wilson, Ballylaggan, d.1873.] Erected by John Wilson, Larne, in memory of his brother Samuel Wilson M.D. who died at Bass, Australia, 24th June 1897 aged 41 years. His brother James Wilson who died at Sydney, 4th Jany, 1898 aged 45 years. His daughter Gertrude Elizabeth who died 8th July 1898 aged 3 years & 8 months. His sister Mary Jane Wilson who died 20th Jan. 1906 aged 57 years. The above named John Wilson died 5th March 1935 aged 79 years. [Mason:-] A. Jenkins.

WILSON
See BAIRD, FORSYTHE, LENNON and WHITEFORD

WITHERSPOON
See HAY

WOLSELEY
See FALLOON

WOODS
[Lead lettering on white marble.] 1896. In loving memory of James Woods who died 4th Dec. 1893 aged 74 years. Also his wife Anne died 14th January 1883 aged 61 years. Also his infant Ellen aged 9 months. Also his son Samuel died 4th Sept. 1887 aged 28 years. Also his daughter Ellen died 9th Dec. 1895 aged 27 years. And his daughter Jane McKAY died 13th February 1917. His sons, Andrew died 1st November 1918, William died 1st December 1928. And daughters, Margaret McILROY died 2nd February 1933, Mary Ann Woods died 28th March 1933. This stone claims 4 graves.

WOODSIDE
Erected by Alexander Woodside of Skillganaban in memory of his uncle Robert Woodside who died 14th Febry. 1791 aged 59 years. Also his brother Robert Woodside who died 19th Septr. 1796 aged 19 years. Also his son Alexander Woodside, who died 24th Augt. 1823 aged 6 years. Also Martha, wife of Alexander Woodside, who died 16th April 1824 aged 77 years. Also her husband, 10th Decr. 1835 aged 89 years. Also Martha Woodside who died 24th Decr. 1825 aged 14 weeks and John her brother 23rd Decr. 1833 aged 12 years. Also their brother William Futt 24th March 1836 aged 20 years.

WOODSIDE
[Sandstone.] Erected by Robert Woodside, Ballyvoy, in memory of his wife Sarah Woodside, who died 28th November 1860 aged 64. Also his daughter Mary, who died 2d September 1849 aged 22. Also the above Robert Woodside who died 26th June 1886 aged 84 yrs. His son Robert Woodside. Also his daughters Sarah and Eliza.
    [The will of Robert Woodside, late of Duncansland, Ballyvoy, county Antrim, farmer, who died 26th June 1886 at same place, was proved at Belfast 25 May 1888 by Sarah Woodside of Duncansland, Ballyvoy, spinster, one of the executors. Effects £398 7s. 3d.]

WOODSIDE
[Enclosed with Robert Woodside, d.1791.] Erected by Alexander Woodside in memory of his son John who died 26th Decr. 1854 aged 18 years. Also Margaret Ellen daughter of his son Robert who died 19th April 1854 aged 2 years. Likewise his daughter Martha who died 30th January 1860 aged 25 years. Also the said Alexander Woodside of Skilganaban who died 10th March 1875 aged 94 years. Also his wife Charlotte who died 8th February 1877 aged 83 years. Also his son Alexander Woodside M.D., Ballyclare, who died 3rd February 1878 aged 50 years. Also his son James Woodside who died 19th March 1886 at his residence Quincy, Ill., U.S.A. aged 63 years. Also his daughter Eliza Woodside who died 12th April 1909 aged 90 years.

WOODSIDE
Erected by John Woodside of Ballyneery in memory of his father James Woodside who died 18th July 1856 aged 96 years. Also his mother Martha Woodside died 5th February 1856 aged 80 years.

WOODSIDE
Erected by Alexander Woodside, Headwood, in memory of his daughter Sarah Jane who died 20th Feby. 1885 aged 18 years. Also his son Abraham who died 6th Octr. 1885 aged 15 years. Also his daughter Margaret who died 8th Augt. 1886 aged 22 years. The above Alexander Woodside who died 5th March 1897 aged 84 years.

Also his wife Jenny Woodside who died 31st Jany. 1903 aged 73 years. Also his son Andrew who died 17th Nov. 1910 aged 56 years. Also his son Robert who died 2nd Feb. 1913 aged 55 years.

WOODSIDE
See PARK

WYLIE
[Railed off with the following.] Erected by William & John Wylie in memory of John Wylie their father who died 24th July 1829 AE 70 and Martha their mother died 16th May 1832 AE 74 years.

WYLIE
[Tall stone of polished granite, enclosed.] In memory of Wm. A. Wylie, Rushvale, b. 1800, d.1881. Jane BEATTY his wife b.1812, d.1884. Samuel B. Wylie, their third son, b. 1842, d. 1864. Janie W. RENTOUL granddaughter, b.1883, d.1900. A. Smyth Wylie, their sixth son, b.1847, d. 1924. Mary Wylie, their last surviving child, b. 1855, d. 1940.

[The will, with one codicil, of William Andrew Wylie, late of Rushvale, Ballyclare, county Antrim, who died 14 August 1881 at same place, was proved at Belfast 9 January 1882 by the Reverend William Wylie of Larne and the Reverend John B. Wylie of Belfast, Presbyterian ministers, and James Moore of Cogry, Doagh, merchant, all in said county, the executors. Effects £4,537 8s. 10d.]

WYLIE
See KNOX

[Small loose sandstone.] The top is badly damaged. On the reverse are skull, hourglass, and saltire (crossbones).] .....
[Sandstone fragment c.1840.] ....John ... of St(raid) above Jo.. died 2(5)t(h ....)
[Some pieces of a shattered stone were found to interlock to give:] ....
Robe(r....lo...) who died (.)th June .... aged (34 ....)o his mother .... October (18)46 (........d) his daughter .... 20th May 1841 ....
[Sandstone fragment. .... (depart)ed (t)his such ....(n)ie .... 7 (years).

BALLYNURE CHURCH OF IRELAND CHURCH

O.S. 45 Grid Ref. J 315936

When the present parish church was built in 1856 a fresh site was chosen across the road from the old graveyard, and so responsibility for the older site passed from the Church at disestablishment. Like the older church it is in the townland of Toberdowney, parish of Ballynure, and barony of Lower Belfast, but unlike its predecessor, is dedicated Christ Church.

Since then only one grave has been opened in the grounds of the church, but inside are a number of memorial tablets and stained glass windows. All have been copied.

ANDERSON

[White marble tablet in form of a scroll.] In affectionate memory of Thomas Anderson, of Hemingford Abbots in the County of Huntingdon, who was for 58 years the faithful and valued friend and servant of Conway R. DOBBS of Castle Dobbs Esq., D.L. and who departed this life at Ballynure Sept. 17, 1883 aged 75 in sure and certain hope of his resurrection to eternal life through Jesus Christ. This memorial is erected by the members of the family he served so long. "He that believeth in me though he were dead yet shall he live". St. John XI. 25.

[Letters of administration, with the will annexed, of the personal estate of Thomas Anderson, late of Bryantang, county Antrim, farmer, who died 17 September 1883 at same place, were granted at Belfast 18 August 1884 to Jane Anderson of Bryantang, the widow and residuary legatee. Effects £227.]

ARMSTRONG

[Brass cross of Calvary placed on ledge of east window.] To the glory of God and in loving memory of William Armstrong died 9th February 1980. Presented by his wife Ruth, October 1980.

ARMSTRONG

[Below window on north side, with a picture of a house and this church.] To the Glory of God and in loving memory of Samuel and Eileen Armstrong and their grand-daughter Helen, this window is the gift of their family. Dedicated 7th September 1986 by the Bishop of Tuam.

BAILIE
See NESBITT

DOBBS

[Four of the five leaded lights in the east window have memorials as follows.]
Charlotte Maria, the beloved wife of Conway Rd. Dobbs, died June 22nd 1870.
Richard Archibald Conway, born October 2nd 1842, died Feby. 24th 1853.
Nichola Susan, born June 30th 1836, died June 19th 1857.
Charlotte Louisa Mary, born June 10th 1830, died March 28th 1860.

DOBBS

[Tablet of white marble surmounted by urn.] In memory of Richard Archibald Conway, eldest son of Conway Richard Dobbs of Castle Dobbs who slept in Jesus on 24th February 1853 aged 10 years. "I am the Resurrection and the Life. He that believeth in Me though he were dead yet shall he live". John 11th, 25th. [Memorial by:-] T. & W. Fitzpatrick, Belfast.

DOBBS

[White marble scroll hanging from cornice. Open bible.] In memory of Nichola Susan, 6th daughter of Conway Richard Dobbs of Castle Dobbs who, washed in the blood of the lamb, entered into life eternal on the 19th June 1857 aged 20 years. "Behold the Lamb of God which taketh away the sin of the world". John 1st, 29th. [Memorial by:-] T & W Fitzpatrick, Belfast.

[The Dobbs family was established here by John Dobbs who came to Ulster in 1596 with Sir Henry Dockwra. In 1603 he married Margaret, only child of John Dalway of Ballyhill, Kilroot. When Dalway died in 1618 a bitter dispute on the title to his estates divided the Dalway and the Dobbs families. By judgement of Chancery in 1625, Hercules, son of John Dobbs was awarded the lands of Ballynure and the townland of Castle Dobbs, where the family still lives. The family included amongst its members Richard Dobbs, who, as mayor with Williamite sympathies was committed to the 'common gaole' during the siege of 1689; Arthur (1689-1765) who became Governor of North Carolina; Richard (d.1802), Dean of Connor; and William Cary (1806-1869), judge of the Landed Estates Court in Ireland. The present representative, Sir Richard A.C., is the first resident of Castle Dobbs to be knighted.

Conway Richard Dobbs of Castle Dobbs (1795-1886) married (1) Charlotte Maria Sinclair, daughter and co-heiress of William Sinclair of Fort William, county Antrim. They had 2 sons and 7 daughters:

1. Olivia Nichola Dobbs (1827-1906) married Sir James Macaulay Higginson
2. Frances Millicent Dobbs (b.1828) married Major-General Hugh Boyd and was present at the siege of Lucknow.
3. Louisa Charlotte Mary Dobbs (1830-1860) (vide supra).
4. Alicia Hester Caroline Dobbs (1831-1907) married Sir Gerald George Aylmer, 9th Bart., of Donadea Castle, county Kildare.
5. Harriet Sydney Dobbs (1834-1907) married (1) the 6th Duke of Manchester and (2) Sir Arthur Stevenson Blackwood, K.C.B.
6. Nichola Susan Dobbs (1836-1857) (vide supra).
7. Millicent Georgina Montagu Dobbs (1840-1926) married George William Bulkeley Hughes of Carreg Bran, Anglesey.
8. Richard Archibald Conway Dobbs (1842-1853) (vide supra).
9. Montagu William Edward Dobbs (1844-1906) died unmarried.

Conway Richard Dobbs married (2) Winifred Susannah Morris. See McCrum ed. of McSkimin: *History and Antiquities of Carrickfergus* (1909); Clarke: *Arthur Dobbs, Esquire, 1689-1765* (1957); *Burke's Irish Family Records* (1976); Rankin and Nelson: *Curious in Everything, The Career of Arthur Dobbs of Carrickfergus, 1689-1765* (1990). See also Dobbs entry under Carrickfergus Old Graveyard.]

DOBBS

[Plain tablet of white marble.] In memory of William Cary Dobbs of Ashurst, Killiney, Co. Dublin, judge of the Landed Estates Court, born August 17th 1806, died April 17th 1869. [Mason:-] Coates, Dublin.

[William Cary Dobbs (1806-1869) of Ashurst, Killiney was a first cousin of Conway Richard Dobbs, above. He married Eleanor Jones Westropp and had many descendants scattered throughout Ireland. See *Burke's Irish Family Records* (1976).]

DOBBS
See ANDERSON

FALLOON

[Mural tablet of white marble with arms: two greyhounds rampant supporting a sword in pale between them. Crest: a hawk rising. Motto: Fortiter et fideliter.] In affectionate remembrance of Rev. Charles Falloon A. M. Trinity College, Dublin, for twenty years rector of Ballynure Parish, died 11th April 1872 aged 74 years. [See his entry in the old graveyard.]

HALL

[Brass plate on nave wall.] To the glory of God and in loving memory of the Rev. William Hall, M.A., B.D., incumbent 1931-1971. Erected by the parishioners in gratitude and thanksgiving 12th December 1976.

KELLY
[Below window on north side.] The Kelly memorial window, to the Glory of God, the gift of their family circle, dedicated by the Rev. J. F. A. Bond, B.A., 5th April 1987.

LEITCH
[Below window on the south side.] To the Glory of God and in loving memory of Mary, the gift of her parents Crawford and Sarah Leitch, 26th October 1986.

MORROW
[Below window on the north side.] The Morrow window, to the Glory of God, the gift of the family circle at home and in Canada. [Window by:-] Caldermac Studios, 1984.

NESBITT
[Brass plate on transom of pipe case on the organ, Evans & Barr, Belfast.] Dedicated to the Glory of God and in loving memory of Rev. Samuel Nesbitt who was rector of this parish from 10th January 1896 till 15th June 1926. He departed this life 20th September 1931. Erected by parishioners, friends and brethren of the Orange Institution as a token of affection and esteem 3rd Dec. 1933.

NESBITT
[Polished granite headstone and surround.] In loving memory of the Rev. Samuel Thomas Nesbitt for 30 years rector of this parish, born 2nd May 1863, died 20th September 1931. Also his beloved wife Agnes BAILIE born 23rd October 1873, died 11th August 1966. In heavenly love abiding.

SCOTT
[Two-light window on the south side of nave.] "I am the Good Shepherd". To the glory of God and in loving memory of Carrie Scott died 3rd November 1981, the gift of the Scott family. [Window by:-] McManus Design, Belfast 1984.

SCOTT
[Below window on the south side.] To the Glory of God and in loving memory of Carrie Scott, died 3rd November 1981, the gift of the Scott family.

SCOTT
[Below window on the south side.] To the Glory of God and in loving memory of James and Ellen Scott, the gift of their family.

CARRICKFERGUS OLD GRAVEYARD (ST. NICHOLAS')

O.S. 52 Grid Ref. J412874

The church spire is a prominent landmark at the centre of the old town. The graveyard may be entered from Market Place or Lancasterian Street. Within the church itself, some Norman pillars survive, as do features from many of the architectural periods down the centuries. It therefore comes as a disappointment to find that relatively few gravestones predate 1800. The earliest memorials are inside the church. As this was the old parish graveyard it was used for interment by all religions. When the pressure of accommodating all the deceased became too great a new cemetery came into use on the North Road. As burials here are becoming progressively fewer, the proportion of twentieth century headstones is small and so all memorials were copied.

In April 1830 Thomas Fagan listed the surnames he saw in the churchyard. Some of these names are no longer found on gravestones: some have reappeared on more recent stones. Those which have been lost are: Addison, Barkley, Bashford, Baxter, Benn, Bigger, Blair, Booth, Bowden, Breaden, Brown, Chaplin, Creight, Crig, Doyle, Ferrell, Flinter, Glass, Grant, Hanna, Hendren, Hil, Hudson, Jack, Jafrey, Jamison, Jordan, Keilty, Ker, Lewis, Lynch, Lynchy, McBride, McCarn, McClewarty, McCullough, McFerran, McGill, McGown, McIlherron, McIlwrath, McSkimin, Martin, Mean, Montgomery, Moore, Murphy, Nelson, Nisbet, O'Donnell, Parkhill, Pogue, Reid, Robertson, Rowan, Sanderson, Seeds, Sheilds, Sherer, Singleton, Strain, Stephens, Weatherup, Wiliamson, Wisoncraft, Wright and Wood.

ADAIR
see SIMMS

ADAMS
[Cement surround] Paul Adams

ADAMSON
[Cast iron plaque on railed enclosure of 20th century] The burying place of W. A. Adamson.

[On vase] Adamson, Seaside Farm, Kilroot. Agnes died 13-7-52. Edward died 1-1-71.

AGNEW
Erected by Daniel Agnew in memory of his two children Robert & Lizzie who died in infancy. The above Daniel Agnew died 5th June 1895 aged 76 years. Also his wife Elizabeth DONALD who died 20th Jany. 1904 aged 77 years.

AGNEW
See DONALD

AICKIN
Burying place of P.B. Aickin, Surgeon R.N., Jane Aickin his wife, Patrick B. Aickin son, Elizabeth Aickin, Jane Aickin, Sarah A(ickin), daughters.... Mar(tha) RONEY (ser)ved the above faithfully for 40 years.

ALEXANDER
[Badly flaking sandstone between Legg and Agnew]....(Alex) and... (Eliz)a(be)th (Al...) his (...ght)er died 3rd May ..(4)0 in infancy. Samuel Alexan(der) his ... died 16th April 184(.) in i(nfancy). Also his son Robert James born Augt. 15th 1847 died Jany. 2(4th) 1849. His beloved wife Elizabeth died 5th December 1856 aged 40 years. Also the above Robert Alexander died 20th August 1887 aged 77 years. Also his wife Lydia McKIBBIN died 22nd Sep. 1889 aged 67 years.

ALEXANDER
[Brass plate on small table.] To the glory of God in loving memory of Jim Alexander, died 2nd September 1976. The gift of his grandparents William and Annie BLACK, June 1977.

ALLAN
See STEWART

ALLEN
Erected by William All(en) in memory of his son (Ge)orge Allen who died 5th March 1855 aged 11 years. His son Will(iam) John All(en) died 27th December 1866 aged 16 years. His daughter Ma(r)y Allen died 23rd May 1867 aged 19 years. Also the a(bove) William Allen who departed this life 24 O(ctr.) 1877 aged 57.

[The will of William Allen, late of the Middle Division, County of the Town of Carrickfergus, farmer, who died 24 October 1877 at same place, was proved at Belfast 5 December 1877 by the oaths of George Patterson of the Middle Division, Carrickfergus, County of the Town of Carrickfergus, farmer, and George Allen of 33 Belmore Street, Belfast, County Antrim, bricklayer, the executors. Effects under £200.]

ALLEN
See LUNDY and STEWART

ANDERSON
[Near the west door] Here lieth the body of Forbes Anderson who departed this life the 31st day of May 1817 aged 42 years. He was an affectionate husband, a tender parent and a sincere friend. Also Robert his son aged 1 year.

ANDERSON
[Sandstone with white marble inset of clasped hands and legend "we part to meet again"] (Erected by) Agnes (Anderson) in memory of her beloved husband Captain Samuel Anderson who departed this life on the 27th Feb. 1854 aged 63 years. Also the above named Agnes who died Aug. 1860 aged 53 years and their son Robert aged 18 years who was lost at sea. Also their daughter Mary who died June 1869 aged 18 years.

[Letters of administration of the personal estate of Samuel Anderson, late of Carrickfergus of the county of the town of Carrickfergus, sailor, who died March 1854 at same place, were granted at Belfast 8 August 1861 to Samuel Anderson junior, of Carrickfergus aforesaid, sailor, the son, one of the next of kin of said deceased. Effects under £600.

Letters of administration of the personal estate of Agnes Anderson, late of Carrickfergus in the county of the town of Carrickfergus, widow, who died September 1860 at same place, were granted at Belfast 9 August 1861 to Samuel Anderson of Carrickfergus aforesaid, the son, one of the next of kin of said deceased. Effects under £200.]

ANDERSON
[White marble to south of chancel]. In memory of Jane Eccleston Anderson, died 1877. Also child Henry William 1866. Whose husband William Anderson 1891, with Louisa, 1897 and John, 1904 had burial at Belfast. "Thanks be to God".

ANDERSON
[Recumbent on HAGGAN plot] Erected by Jam(es) (And)erson in memory of (his bel)oved wife ...y..., who departed (this life) 17th March 1868, aged ..years. Also their granddaughter Eliza Jane McKEEN who departed this life 23 March 1871 age(d...) years. Also their grandson James McKeen who died March 29th 1871 aged 15 months and their granddaughter ....McKeen who died 6th April (18)71 aged 3 years, Esther McKeen who died 26th February 1891, Thomas McKeen who died 18th July 1909.

ANDERSON
See HAGGAN and JENKINS

ANGUS
See GARDNER

ANSELL
[Recumbent] Sacred to the memory of Francis Thomas Ansell, son of Capt. Augustus (F) Ansell 74th Regt., obiit 6th July 1831 aged 5 years & 2 months. Suffer little children to come unto me and forbid them not for of such is the kingdom of God. Mark chap. 10, ver. 14.

APSLEY
[Mid nineteenth century sandstone, broken and laid flat in front of that of John Apsley d.1934] Erected by............f(K......... NM.......................wh(o de)parted..................7............................aged.........years. ...John Apsley who departed .... life 27th) May 19(3. aged 89) years. Also his wife Margaret Apsley who departed this life 2nd Dec. 1955 aged 82 years.

APSLEY
In loving memory of Robert Apsley who died 25th December 1895. Also his wife Martha died 26th April 1921. Their daughters: Agnes died 22nd January 1904; Ellen died 8th July 1917. Sons: Robert died 25th Oct. 1944; William John died 19th September 1952; James died 27th May 1955.

[The will of Robert Apsley, late of Carrickfergus, farmer, who died 25 December 1895, was proved at Belfast, 28 February 1896 by Martha Apsley, widow, and Robert Apsley, farmer, both of Carrickfergus, the executors. Effects £1,080.]

APSLEY
[Polished black granite] Erected by Andrew Apsley in loving memory of his son Andrew who entered into rest 19th Ferbuary 1908 aged 32 years. Also his daughter Mary who died in infancy. The above-named Andrew Apsley died 14th Decr. 1910 aged 77 years. Also his wife Jennie Apsley, died 29th April 1920 aged 87 years. His son William Apsley died 17th May 1924 aged 62 years. And Catherine DONALDSON, daughter of William Apsley, who died in infancy. Also his grand-son Willie LARKIN who died 16th Novr. 1930 aged 5 years. "God is Love". Margaret, wife of Wm. Apsley, died 30th July 1934. [Mason:-] T. Holden, Larne.

APSLEY
In fond memory of George loved husband of Agnes Apsley, died 18th November 1961. And their children:- Eileen died 4th May 1926, David George died 19th October 1931, William James died 12th January 1941, Jeanie died 27th June 1950. Agnes, wife of the above named George, died 29th Sept. 1971.

APSLEY
[Beside Andrew Apsley, d. 1908] In loving memory of John Apsley who died 8th May 1934 aged 59 years. Also his wife Margaret Apsley who died 2nd December 1955 aged 82 years.

ARDIS
[Polished granite] Erected by James Ardis in memory of his parents: William Ardis who died 21st March 1898. Sarah Ardis who died 26th April 1879. Also the above James Ardis who died 6th April 1937. "Thou has the better part".

[Administration of the estate of William Adair Ardis, late of 72 Broadway, Belfast, engineer, who died 21 March 1898, granted at Belfast 13 April 1898, to James Ardis of 72 Broadway, the son. Effects £2,737. 6s. 6d.]

AS...
[Badly weathered sandstone in front of Kirk monument] Erected in memory of William As... who died on (2)1.. November 1850 aged 77 years. Also his beloved wife Jane who died 7..(Ma)y 1872 aged 9(5) years.

(ASLIN)
Erected to the memory of Robert (A)... who died 31st Decr. 1(84. aged..) years. A(lso hi)s daughter Elizabeth who .... 16th J.... aged 25 years ....er ....thy God. (Also) his son Joh(n Aslin) who died ....ptember .... aged ......

(AT...)
[Possibly about 1800]. The burying ground of Edward (At....)

ATKIN
[Granite cross against eastern boundary wall]. In loving memory of Margaret CARLETON, the dearly loved wife of Walton Thomas Roberts Atkin, died 5th February 1885 aged 33 years. "For ever with the Lord". 1 Thess. iv. 17.

BAILEY
Erected by Robert Bailey in memory of his beloved wife Jane who departed this life at Belfast June 15th 1847 aged 64 years. Also three sons who died in infancy.

BAILEY
[Next to foregoing] In loving memory of my dear mother Mary died 28th February 1919. Also my dear father Thomas died 22nd September 1923. Also my dear wife Annie died 27th February 1961. Also Thomas Walker Bailey died 7th March 1978 aged 87 yrs. And Elizabeth Wilson Bailey died 1st December 1979 aged 78 yrs. [Mason:-] Hart.

BAIN
See VINT

BAIRD
[Cut on modern sandstone lintel over doorway to baptistry.] The structural alterations in converting this old porch into the present baptistry were enabled to be carried out through the generosity of Major Sir William Baird D.L., Glynn Park, Carrickfergus, who defrayed the entire cost, 1952.

BAIRD
See KERR

BARBOUR
See BELL

BARKLEY
[Behind Matthew & Eleanor Barkley, Greenisland].............. th........................ Barkley who died ....1818 aged 6(6 years). Also Elizabeth Barkley his ... who departed this life the 1st of July 1837 aged 92 years.

BARKLEY
Erected by Wm. M. Barkley in memory of his affectionate wife Margaret THOMPSON who departed this life 15th March 1850 aged 39 years. Also his daughters; Grace Thompson who died 26th June 1851 aged 16 years and Annie SPENCE who died 28th March 1847 aged 10 months. Also the above named William M. Barkley who died 12th Feby. 1883 aged 68 years. Also his second wife Mary ROWAN who died 10th Sept. 1900 aged 80 years.
[The will, with two codicils, of William Morrow Barkley, late of Queen's Square, Belfast, and of Cooleen House, Strandtown, county Down, ship owner and coal merchant, who died 12 February 1883 at latter place, was proved at Belfast, 20 April 1883 by James Morgan Barkley of Queen's Square, Belfast, ship owner and coal merchant, one of the executors. Effects £8,671 8s. 11d.]

BARKLEY
[Polished granite] Erected by Matthew & Eleanor Barkley, Greenisland, in memory of their dearly beloved son William Morrow, who departed this life 13th June 1893 aged 22 years. Psalm XXIII. Also their dearly beloved daughter Margaret THOMPSON who died 19th Feby. 1911 aged 41 years.

BARKLEY
[Mid nineteenth century sandstone between the two preceding stones] (Erected) to ......M(att)h............. (who departed (who) died 18th September 1919 in his (8.......)

BARKLEY
[Nineteenth century sandstone with surface planed off and a fresh inscription cut.] Barkley, Greenisland. Matthew 1831-1914 and his wife Eleanor 1843-1914, their son Thomas Johnstone 1873-1951 and his wife Wilhelmina Seeds 1880-1975.

BARNETT
See LYNN

(BAR)RY
[Attached to north boundary wall and enclosed with Robert Barry d.1869] Erected by R(obert Barr)y in memory (of his father and) mother William (& Mary Barry), the former of whom departed this life the 1st Feby. 18.. aged .. years .... h Decr. 1821 aged (8...... (Also the rem)ains of the above .... R(obert Bar)ry who departed this life the 23rd ... November 1830 aged 52 years. Also his wife Sarah who departed this life on the 9th Feby. 1846 aged 6(5) years. And their daughter Deborah died 14th February 1893 aged 80 years.

[Robert Barry's will was proved at Down and Connor on 14 January 1832. See National Archives, Dublin, T.19224.]

BARRY
Erected by his widow in memory of her husband Robert Barry died 7th July 1869 aged 42 years. Also their son John died 21st Jany. 1870 aged 4 years. Also their son Robert died 25th Feby. 1870 aged 11 years. Also their son William died 17th Jany. 1886 aged 29 years. Also his wife Mary Ann Barry died 15th May 1903 aged 73 years. Also their granddaughter Margaret McKINSTRY died 8th Octr. 1930 aged 34 years. Also their daughter Agnes BRYSON died 24th December 1940 aged 77 years. Also Robena Bryson died 9th March 1946 aged 43 years. "And there shall be no light there; and they need no candle neither light of the sun; for the Lord God giveth them light: and they shall reign for ever and ever". Rev. XXII c,5 v. [Mason:-] A. McBain, Belfast.

[The will of William Barry, late of Knockagh, Carrickfergus, farmer, who died 17 January 1886 at same place, was proved at Belfast 17 March 1886 by Mary Ann Barry of Knockagh, widow, the sole executrix. Effects £705.]

BARRY
[Brass plate on prayer desk] Presented by St. Nicholas' Mothers' Union in memory of the following past members: Isabella Barry (April 1964) Elizabeth TURNER (June 1964), Helena MASTERMAN (August 1964), Jane PATTERSON (January 1965), Margaret MONEYPENNY (June 1965), Elizabeth McCUNE (June 1965), Eliza POWERS (July 1965), Martha Houston McQUITTY (November 1965), Mary Jane McQUITTY (November 1965). December 1966.

BASHFORD
[Between vestry and north transept]. Erected by Thos. Bashford to the memory of his wife Agnes Bashford who died .... June [continued below ground level].

BASHFORD
Erected by David Bashford to the memory of his father Robert Bashford who died 5th Jany. 1845 aged 66 years. Also his mother Susan Bashford who died 12th Feby. 1849 aged 76 years.

BASHFORD
[Recumbent slate in very poor condition]......................... anna Bas(h).. their daughter (di)ed 7th July 18...............ine their eldest d........ died 12th July 185(.) .....Anna Eliza Peyt........ 24th May 1861............hford died............ arle...c........186(.)

BATES
See YOUNG

BATT
Erected to the memory of Sarah, the beloved wife of Samuel H. Batt of Belfast, who departed this life at Glynn near Larne on the 17th November 1864 aged 38 years.

BEATTIE
See PATTERSON

BELL
[Black granite against east boundary wall] "Until the day break". In memory of Jeanie Nicholas Bell, daughter of James and Annie Bell, born 11th June 1882, died 31st Augt. 1882. The above-named James Bell died 30th August 1920. His wife Annie Bell died 23rd January 1924. Elizabeth BARBOUR died 27th November 1937. David Samuel Milliken Bell, son of James and Annie Bell, died 20th March 1952. His wife Mary died 1st February 1969. Grace KELLY, daughter of Robert G. and Margaret Kelly, Rantalard, Whitehouse, died 1st August 1980. Erected by James Bell, Carrickfergus.

BELL
See POLLIN

BENSON
[Recorded in McCrum ed of McSkimin: *History and Antiquities of Carrickfergus* (1909), p. 188 as a slab against wall of Donegall aisle. Not mentioned in the 1811 ed. Now in floor beside pulpit.] Here lieth the body of the Revd. Hill Benson, Dean of Connor. He was born the 3rd of October 1704 and departed this life the 21st of April 1775. "They that be wise shall shine as the brightness of the firmament and they that turn many to righteousness as the stars for ever and ever".
[The Rev. Hill Benson was born near Belfast on 3 October 1704, eldest son of the Rev. Edward Hill Benson, Prebend of St. Andrews (Down) by Jane Winder. He was educated at Lisburn by Mr Clark and at Trinity College, Dublin, 1720-24, graduating B.A. He was curate of Crumlin 1733-45, rector of Kilmoon and Macetown (Meath), vicar of Piercetown Landy 1745-75 and Dean of Connor 1753-75. He married on 24 November 1757 Margaret Leslie, daughter of the Rev. Peter Leslie, rector of Ahoghill, by Jane Dopping and had a son Henry Hobart Benson who was born at Carrickfergus on 6 March 1760. He died at Carrickfergus 21 April 1775 and his widow died at Tandragee on 21 April 1786. See Leslie: *Clergy of Connor* (1893); Burtchaell and Sadleir: *Alumni Dublinenses* (1924).]

BIRD
[Brass plate beside Bull window to north of communion rail]. The exterior stonework of this ancient window was restored by Edwin Darley HILL and Deborah his wife of Ballynascreen, Greenisland, in the year of our Lord 1932 to the glory of God and in loving memory of their daughter Georgina Darley; Ina, wife of the Rev. Richard Bird, D.S.O., M.A. died 18th January 1931.
[The Rev. Richard Bird was educated at Trinity College, Dublin and graduated B.A. in 1904 and later M.A. He was curate of Clonenagh (Leighlin) 1905-7, of Ballyfin 1907-19, rector of St Kevin's, Dublin 1919-39, of Delgany (Glendalough) 1939-, canon of Christ Church, Dublin 1945. He was awarded the D.S.O. during World War I. He died c.1956. See Irish Church Directories.
Edwin Barley Hill was chairman of the Northern Bank. He retired in 1928, died 25 July 1935 and was buried in Belfast City Cemetery. He wrote a guide book to St. Nicholas' Church.]

BLACK
See ALEXANDER

BLACKBURNE
Erected by William Blackburne in memory of his son James Blackburne who died 5th January 1867 aged 9 years. Also his daughter Mary who fell asleep in Jesus

18th November 1884. Also the above-named William Blackburne who died 19th June 1895 aged 87 years. Also his wife Martha died 23rd October 1908 aged 92 years.

BLACKBURNE

[Brass plate in baptistry beneath triple light window depicting St. Nicholas.] To the glory of God and in loving memory of Henry Blackburne, churchwarden and hon. solicitor to select vestry, born 1851, died 1924. This window designed and made by his granddaughter, Mary E. (Mollie) Blackburne is erected by his daughter Margaret G. WARREN 1952.

[Henry Blackburne married Agnes Graham, daughter of Capt. William and Agnes Graham, see Graham stone, below.]

BORTHWICK
See McGOWAN

BOWDEN

[Slate] Here lieth the remains of Sarah Bowden, February 3rd 1818. Also her sister Jane SIMMS, born 12th August 1765, died 8th April 1843.

BOWMAN

[Beside McGOWAN d. 1(837)]...(a)re (int)erred....mem....(Whit)ney Bo(w)... who died the 2...January 18.... years. Eleanor Bowman who ... the 1(3)th January 1.. aged (36 years) Eleanor VE(ACOCK) who died the (3)1 May 1812 aged (26) years. Robert McG(OWAN) who died the 1(6)th (Septr.) 181(.. aged ..) years. Letitia McGowan who died the 27th February 1830 aged 71 years.

[Whitney Bowman was an attorney of the Town and was made a Freeman in 1787. There is a pedigree of Bowman and associated families in the P.R.O.N.I., Malcolm Papers D3165.]

BOWMAN

[Against north boundary wall]. In memory of Samuel Bowman who died 30th Decr. 1831 aged 40 years. Isabella his relict died 27th Jany. 1863 aged 67 years. Margaret his sister died 29th Novr. 1834 aged 49 years. His son James died 21st Decr. 1851 aged 28 years. Thomas his brother died 1st Augt. 1857 aged 78 years. His grand-children: Isabella Bowman DOBSON died 12th Septr. 1872 aged 17 years and John James DOBSON died 21st Augt. 1886 aged 22 years. Walter Bowman THACKERAY died 18th Feby. 1892 aged 19 years. Jane Bowman Dobson died 6th March 1909 aged 78 years. Susan Kearsley Bowman died 21st February 1917 aged 82 years.

Oft as the bell, with solemn toll,
Speaks the departure of a soul:
Let each one ask himself am I
Prepared, should I be called to die?

[On the other side which was originally the front.] 1832. Samuel Bowman. Reader, prepare to meet thy God.

BOWMAN

Erected by Johnston & Catherine Bowman in memory of their dearly loved children, Mary R. Bowman, born 8th June 1855, died 22nd May 1856. Samuel B. Bowman, born 28th June 1859, died 13th Jan. 1875. The above-named Catherine Bowman died 12th April 1899. The above-named Johnston Bowman died 12th September 1903 aged 82 years. Also his sister-in-law Mary Rowan NESBITT who died 3rd October 1904.

BOWMAN

[Recorded in McCrum ed. of McSkimin: *History and Antiquities of Carrickfergus* (1909), p. 193. Mural tablet behind pulpit.] In loving memory of Davys Bowman who died 2nd February 1904 aged 44 years. "He asked life of Thee and Thou gavest him a long life: even for ever and ever".

BOWMAN
In loving memory of Margaret A. B. Bowman who entered into rest 20th December 1914 aged 64 years.

BOWMAN
[Bronze lettering on coffin-shaped concrete enclosure]. Daniel Bowman 4 March 1920.

BOYD
(In) m(emory of..)a.... Boyd... d.... March 1883 .... 77 years. (Also Eli)zabeth THOMPSON (who died) 20th September 1860 aged 53 years. Also their children: William lost at sea 1858 aged 26 years, John & Joseph who died in infancy, and Anne who died 27th Novr. 1904 aged 74 years. Mary Jane who died 5th October 1917 aged 68 years.

BOYD
[Cast-iron plaque on low railings.] The burying place of David Boyd, Carrickfergus, 1896.

BOYD
See CRAIG and EVERARD

BRABAZON
[Cast iron plaque.] The family burying ground of H. G. Brabazon Belfast, 1888. [Cast by:-] D. & W. Grant, York St. Foundry, Belfast.

BRAVINGTON
Erected by Mary Bravington to the memory of her husband William Bravingston who departed this life 24th (June) 184(5) aged (40) years. Also her mother Ann JOHNSTON who departed this life the (6)th May 1847 aged (63 years). Also Mary MILLS who departed this life 20th April 1875 aged 63 years. Also Benjamin MILLS, formerly of H.M. 13th P.A.O.L.I., who died 17th July 1891 aged 68 years and 3 months. Deeply and deservedly regretted.

[The will of Benjamin Mills, late of Davys Street, Carrickfergus, publican, who died 17 July 1891 at same place, was proved at Belfast, 14 August 1891 by Susan Mills of Davys Street, widow, the sole executrix. Effects £89. 10s.]

BRIDGEMAN
See WILLIAMS

BRUTON
See CLARKE

BRYSON
See BARRY

BULL
[Recorded in McCrum ed. of McSkimin: *History and Antiquities of Carrickfergus* (1909), p. 189. Brass plate on sill of three light window in north wall of chancel. Window depicts feeding of the five thousand]. To the glory of God and in loving memory of Anne Bull, born A.D. 30 Jan. 1823, died A.D. 16 Nov. 1881. This window is erected by her husband the Very Rev. George Bull, D.D., Dean of Connor, Rector of Carrickfergus and Raloo. "He that cometh unto me shall never hunger and he that believeth in me shall never thirst." John VI, 35. [Both were buried in North Road Graveyard, q.v.]

BULL
[Three-light window in chancel opposite the organ.] Follow me and I will make you fishers of men. To the glory of God and in loving memory of George Bull D.D., Dean of Connor.

BULWORTHY
See LANG

BURLEIGH

[Table stone.] Here lieth in the hope of a happy resurrection the body of Henry Burleigh who departed this life in the year of our Lord 1801 of his age (32). Neither virtue nor piety, neither strength nor youth could avert the arrow of death. But (he) will revive. Also the body of Ann Burleigh, wife of Wm. (D). Burleigh, who died May 1827 aged (5)1 years. Also the body of Wm. D. Burleigh who died August 18(2)9 aged 6(5) years. Charlotte Louisa, daughter of William Burleigh, who died 8th March 1851 aged 16 years. Also the body of Lucretia, wife of William Burleigh, who died the 31st December 1856 aged 49 years. William Burleigh died January 18th 1871 aged 73. William Robert Burleigh April 18th 1872 aged 41.

[The first of the Burleigh family, William Burleigh, came to Ireland as a captain in Sir John Clotworthy's Regiment of Horse and was wounded in the defence of Lisburn against O'Neill in 1641. The family built two houses in the eighteenth century, Burleigh Hill and St Catherine's. The former is a sober Georgian house which still stands to the north-west of the town and not far from it is a burial vault (without inscription) erected by John Robinson (vide infra).

William Dobbs Burleigh (1764-1829) was a barrister of the Middle Division who was made a freeman in 1807.

William Burleigh (1797-1871) married in 1828 Lucretia Wills, daughter of James Wills of Plas Bellin, county Flint and had 6 sons and 6 daughters. The last of these surviving were Rebecca Mary Burleigh (d. March 1929) and Lucy Close (d. July 1929), wife of Samuel Patrick Close (vid. inf.). Charlotte Louisa, the youngest daughter, was born in December 1852 and married on 15 October 1885, in Beckenham, Samuel Forster Freyer, M.D., second son of S. Freyer of Clifden, county Galway.

See McCrum ed. of McSkimin, *History and Antiquities of Carrickfergus* (1909) p. 503; Burke: *Dictionary of the Landed Gentry of Great Britain and Ireland* (1866).]

BURLEIGH

Here is deposited the rema(ins of) George Burleigh Esq., late of Burleigh Hill, obit the 16th of M.. 1822 aged 78 years. Also M(rs) R. Burleigh, relict of the above, obit the 20th of January (1824) aged 82 years.

[George Burleigh was the son of a Henry Burleigh (not the above). He presented the Church with its sixteenth century Flemish window depicting John the Baptist and Christ in the River Jordan. He was sheriff in 1818 and died at Burleigh Hill. Having no children he bequeathed his estate to his nephew John Robinson (q.v.). His widow died in Dublin but was interred in Carrickfergus. See McCrum ed. of McSkimin: *History and Antiquities of Carrickfergus* (1909) pp. 175 and 429; Mitchell: *A Guide to St. Nicholas' Church* (1962).]

BURLEIGH

[Window in south transept.] To the glory of God and to the dear memory of William Robert Burleigh who died April 12th A.D. 1872.

BURLEIGH

[Small white marble headstone enclosed with Henry Burleigh d. 1801.] Olivia Burleigh born 4th Aug. 1847, died 16th Decr. 1885.

[Letters of administration of the personal estate of Olivia Isabella Anne Burleigh, late of Carrickfergus, spinster, who died 16 December 1885 at same place, were granted at Belfast, 6 January 1886 to Lucy Close of Carrickfergus, wife of Samuel Patrick Close, a sister. Effects £419. 17s. 2d.]

BURLEIGH

See MONTGOMERY

BURNS

[To south of south transept.] Erected by James Burns in memory of his daughter Margaret Burns, obiit 4th May 1849 aged 13 years.

BURROWS
    See HILDIGE

BUSBY
    [Granite, to south of chancel.] Erected by Joseph F. Busby, Eden, in loving memory of his sister Annie who died 26th April 1882, also his father George Busby, who died 5th June 1884, his brother George, who died 29th Decr. 1886, his brother Robert John who died 13th Sept. 1890, his sister Hannah who died 17th Augt. 1903, and his mother Fanny Anne Busby who died 19th March 1910. Also his sister Catherine H. Busby who died 22nd March 1940. Jane Catherwood Busby, born 24th November 1866, died 4th October 1943. Joseph Fulton Busby, born 24 March 1874, died 20th November 1947.

    [Letters of administration, with the will annexed, of the personal estate of George Busby, late of Eden, near Carrickfergus, merchant, who died 5 June 1884 at same place, were ganted at Belfast 7 July 1884 to Fanny Anne Busby of same place, the widow and the residuary legatee. Effects £304. 7s. 6d.]

BUTCHER
[A small brass plate attached to wooden chair which has "R B 1659" carved on the back.] This chair (1659) of Robert Butcher, West Street, Carrickfergus, was presented by Mrs. W.H. TURNER, Irish Quarter West, Carrickfergus, May 1948.

BUTLER
    See SPEAR

BYRTT
    [Polished granite surround south of chancel - no details.] [Mason:-] Robinson.

CAIN
    The burying ground of William C. and Benjamin Cain. In loving memory of Charles Cain, beloved husband of Margaret Cain, who was killed in action at sea on 29th February 1916. Also his daughter Mary Elizabeth who died 15th July 1916 aged 4 years. And William C. Cain, beloved husband of Abby Cain, who died 18th October 1920.

CAIRN
    See WILLIAMS

CAMPBELL
    [Recumbent slab] In memory of John Campbell of this town, sur(ge)on, who departed this life the (2)5(th) of................ 8(4)th year of his .... wife who d................ of M................ Also Stuart Campbell grand nep(hew of the a)bove who died Sep. 1(0..) 18.. aged (77 yrs). A few days before this death he composed the following lines which he addressed to his children.

        O (mourn not ....)d ha... of Death
        E...ing shall mak(e..resign) my last breath
        But open the Bible and read the bl..d story
        Emmanuel's death and a(ssension to glor)y
        Then know that the (monster's depriv'd of his sting)
        And to his meek victor triumphantly sing
        Then think of the day when again we shall meet
        Emmanuels p(raise..... joys to rep)eat.
        Oh think with what rapture and love we shall si(ng)
        The anthem in praise of our saviour and king.

CAMPBELL
    See CHARLESSON and HAMILTON

CANNING
    See CARREY

CARLETON
    See ATKIN

CARNAGHAN

[An "L" is carved on top edge of stone.] Here lieth the body of John Carnaghan who departed this life the 16 of Nov. 1815 aged 68 years. Also his wife Agns Carnaghan who died 10. Feb. 1816 aged 5(6) years. Also their son John Carnaghan died the (3) of Sep. 181(6) aged 27 years.

[John Carnaghan, farmer, of West Division was made a freeman in 1787.

John Carnaghan died intestate and administration was granted to his eldest son Samuel Kernaghan on 27 April 1819. Effects £131.19s.8d. See Connor *Will and Grant Book 1818-20*, p.296, National Archives, Dublin.]

CARNEHAN

[Split and uprooted slate.] Erected by Arthur Carnehan in memory of his deceaced children: Arthur and Ellen who died in infancy 1844.

CARREY

[Within railings.] The family burying place of John Carrey. In memory of the above John Carrey of Meadowbank 1790-1859. And his wife Agnes POAGUE 1800-1859. Their children: Mary 1821-1910, William 1823-1849, Anthony 1826-1855 died at Elba, Jane 1828-1851, Elizabeth 1832-1907, John 1830-1866 and his wife Elizabeth THOMPSON 1832-1871. And their children: William Poague 1854-1868, lost at sea, Agnes 1856-1861, John 1858-1859, John Canning 1860-1875 lost at sea, Anthony 1862-1942, Wilhelmina Colquhoun 1864-1943, Alexander 1866-1911 died in N. Zealand. John Carrey, Lieut. Col. Indian Medical Service, only son of Anthony Carrey, born 1894, died at Worcester 6th March 1949. His ashes were interred here October 1949. And Mabel, his beloved wife, died at Worcester January 1967. Her ashes interred here July 1968. John 14, 1-4. Robert Carrey, born 12 9 1929, died 26 2 1977. [Also a tablet in front of the stone.] In memory also of Marjory Carrey 1897-1973, daughter of Anthony Carrey, the last of the family to live at Meadowbank.

[John Carry, mariner, of the town, was made a freeman in 1811.

The will of John Carrey, late of Meadow Bank in the West Division of the County of the Town of Carrickfergus, master mariner, who died 22 July 1866 at same place, was proved at Belfast, 13 September 1866 by the oaths of William Larmour of Joymount Bank, teacher, and Elizabeth Millar Carrey of Meadow Bank aforesaid, widow, both in Carrickfergus, the executors. Effects under £1,000.]

CARREY

Erected by Thomas Carrey in memory of his beloved wife Letitia who departed this life the 22nd Septr. 1856 aged 41 years. Also his undernamed children: Mary who died the 14th of February 1845 aged 5 years. William Thomas who died the 9th of July 1852 aged 7 years. James who died the 9th November 1855 aged 14 years. Letitia Elizabeth who died on 10th September 1856 aged 7 months. Mary who died the 22nd November 1856 aged 9 years. The above Thomas Carrey died 1st May 1876 aged 61 years. His son Robert McKinlay Carrey died 29th May 1902.

CARREY

In loving memory of Sarah Carrey, died 7th June 1882, and her sister Margaret HIND, died 26th Nov. 1914, aunts of William T. Carrey. Also his youngest son Douglas Carrey died 10th July 1915. Margaret Carrey, daughter of Thomas Carrey, died 26th Feb. 1869, interred at Torquay. Wm. McKinlay Carrey died 2nd Nov. 1918, second son of Wm. T. Carrey. Sarah J. Carrey died 8th Nov. 1919, beloved wife of Wm. T. Carrey. And of the above named William T. Carrey, died 30th July 1925. Letitia Jane (Leta) their daughter died 4th May 1968 and her sister Margaret died 8th December 1975.

[The will of Sarah Carrey, late of Carrickfergus, spinster, who died 7 June 1882 at same place, was proved at Belfast 23 June 1882 by William Thomas Carrey of Carrickfergus, mercantile clerk, one of the executors. Effects of £354. 10s.]

CARREY
[Next to Letitia Carrey d.1856.] In loving memory of Thomas, beloved husband of Elizabeth Carrey, who died 12th August 1954. Also the above named Elizabeth Carrey who died 1st January 1970.

CARSON
[Next to following stone] Erected by Jas. Alexander Carson in loving memory of his mother Eliza Carson who died 14th June 1887 aged 58 years. Also his father Hugh Carson who died 14th Nov. 1889 aged 64 years. Also their daughter Lizzie WILSON who died 5th July 1894 aged 26 years. Also their son Paul Carson who died 10th July 1921 aged 60 years. Also their daughter Sarah Carson who died 19th March 1926 aged 71 years. Also Martha, wife of the above Paul Carson, died 31st July 1932.

CARSON
[Within low railings.] Erected by J.A. & M. Carson in memory of our eldest and dearly beloved daughter Maggie A. Carson, died 15th July 1918 aged 20 years. Also the above named J.A. Carson, the beloved husband of Margaret Carson, died 10th April 1928 aged 63 years. Also the above named Margaret Carson who fell asleep 21st September 1934.

(CATERS)
[Loose sandstone south of south transept.] (............i)
a(n Caters to the mem... o)f (her husb)and Nathan(ie)l (C.....)
who departed this life 7th (Fe.....) 18(3)1 aged 50 years. Also of his children who died in infancy.

CATERS
In memoriam, Catherine Caters died 4th Feby. 1848 aged 55 years. Also her son Nathaniel Caters died at Carlisle 21st May 1862 aged 39 years. His wife Ellen Caters died 1st Novr. 1897 aged 77 years. Their infant son Francis John died 6th March 1856. Also Samuel, son of Ezkl. Caters died 23rd Aug. 1897 aged 4 months. Ezekiel Caters died 9th May 1916 aged 65 years. Ellen N. died 28th March 1939. Nathaniel died 23rd Novr. 1945. F.J. Nelson died 8th Decr. 1954. William James L. died 6th Jan. 1955. Alexander died 14th Decr. 1955. Arthur L. died in Australia 13th June 1959. Mary died 25th Jan. 1929, wife of the above Ezekiel. [Mason:-] A. Jenkins.

CATERS
[Polished granite headstone.] In loving memory of Nathaniel Francis, died 21st February 1940; his wife Margaret Mary died 13th February 1969; his father Nathaniel Francis Nelson 1862-1929; his wife Mary Ann 1869-1895 and infant son William Moore, 1894.

CATHERWOOD
Erected by Samuel Catherwood in memory of his father, Samuel Catherwood who died 21st Octr. 1874 aged 64 years. His mother Jane Catherwood who died 13th Feby. 1869 aged 59 years. His sister Jane who died 20th Octr. 1855 aged 11 years. His sister Sarah who died 15th April 1857 aged 17 years. His brother John who died 15th May 1884 aged 36 years. His brother Robert who died 14th March 1888 aged 45 years. His wife McClaverty MITCHELL who died 4th Sept. 1909 aged 53 years. Also the said Samuel Catherwood who died 5th Sept. 1919 aged 64 years. Annie Catherwood died 21st March 1980 aged 90 years. [Mason:-] Rankin.

[The will of Samuel Catherwood, late of Knockagh, West Division, Carrickfergus, farmer, who died 22 October 1873 at same place, was proved at Belfast 7 September 1881 by Elizabeth Jones, wife of Alexander Jones of the Knockagh, mariner, and William Charles Todd of Belfast, book-keeper, the executors. Effects £379.

The will of John Catherwood, late of Carrickerfergus, farmer, who died 15 May 1884 at same place, was proved at Belfast 16 June 1884 by William Logan, farmer, and Elizabeth Jones, wife of Alexander Jones, mariner, both of Carrickfergus, the executors. Effects £291.

McCleverty ("Clevy") Hamilton Mitchell was the youngest daughter of Capt. John Mitchell of Joymount Bank. She married Samuel Catherwood on 3 August 1886. Samuel, their infant son, died at Joymount Bank on 12 July 1893. See *Carrickfergus Advertiser*, 14 July 1893.]

CATHERWOOD
See GARDNER and McSKIMIN

CHAINE
[Inscription on white marble framed with sandstone, fallen and broken next north boundary wall.] Sacred to the memory of Mary, the beloved daughter of the Very Revd. John Chaine, Dean of Connor, and Julia his wife who departed this life 1(3)th May 18(5)2 aged 18 years. "In the midst of life we are in death". Also to the memory of the above John Chaine who died 21st June 1861 aged 60 years. Also to the memory of the above Julia Chaine who fell asleep 22nd July 1891 aged 83 years.

CHAINE
[Recorded in McCrum ed. of McSkimin: *History and Antiquities of Carrickfergus* (1909), p. 189. Brass tablet under window in north wall of nave.] To the glory of God and in loving memory of John Chaine M.A., sometime Dean of Connor, and Julia his wife, also of Mary their daughter, this window is placed by Rebecca, William and Margarette Chaine. A.D. 1892.

[The Rev. John Chaine was born in county Antrim, son of William Chaine, merchant, entered Trinity College, Dublin in 1818 and graduated B.A. in 1822 and M.A. in 1832. He was Dean of Connor 1839-55, exchanged with his successor George Bull 1855-8, rector of Claughton in Lonsdale, Lancashire 1858-62. He married in Antrim Church, 1 February 1831 Julia Hyndman, daughter of Hugh Hyndman of Eglantine Hill, county Antrim and died on 20 June 1862. See *Clergy of Connor* (1993); Burtchaell and Sadleir: *Alumni Dublinenses* (1924).]

CHAMBERLAIN
[Window in east wall of south transept depicting the parables of the good Samaritan, the lost sheep, and the prodigal son.] In affectionate memory of Reverend George Chamberlain M.A., for 22 years the faithful and honoured rector of this parish 1886-1908. Erected by parishioners and friends.

[The Rev. George Chamberlain was son of Richard Chamberlain of Castletown, county Limerick. He was educated at Trinity College, Dublin and graduated B.A. in 1875 and M.A. in 1894. He was curate of Tullylish 1876, of Ballywillan 1877-81, rector of Drumbo 1881-4, of Christ Church, Lisburn 1884-6, of Carrickfergus 1886-1908. He married at Rathmines Church on 29 April 1880 Dilliana Mary Brereton, daughter of Hugh Westropp Brereton of Limerick and had 4 sons and 1 daughter:-

1. Rev. George Ashton Chamberlain, Canon of St. Patrick's, Dublin and rector of the Mariners' Church, Kingstown
2. Rev. Arthur Percival Chamberlain, rector of Castlerock (Derry) (vid. inf.)
3. Ralph Brereton Chamberlain, M.A. Edinburgh, died 21 November 1909 (vid. inf.)
4. Lieut. Henry Neville Chamberlain, R.N.R., killed in action 16 July 1916.
5. Dilliana Mary Violet Chamberlain married on 3 July 1901 the Rev. C.C. Manning, Archdeacon of Down.

See Leslie: *Clergy of Connor* (1993); Burtchaell and Sadleir: *Alumni Dublinenses* (1924).]

CHAMBERLAIN
[Carved on oak panelling that lines the sanctuary.] We laud and magnify thy glorious name with thanksgiving for the services in this church to this day 21st September 1928 during the ministries of George Chamberlain, M.A., 1886-1908,

and John Frederick MACNEICE B.D., Archdeacon of Connor, Rectors of this parish.

CHAMBERLAIN

[Rude granite cross beside campanile.] Here rest George Chamberlain M.A., 22 years rector of this parish, born 19th Dec. 1852, died 4th Sept. 1910, and his wife Dilliana Mary born 20th Sept. 1850 died 16th Feb. 1935. Ralph Brereton Chamberlain M.B. born 31st Jan. 1885, died 21st Nov. 1909. Canon Arthur Percivale Chamberlain M.A., born 18th May 1890, died 8th July 1980. Charles George Campbell MANNING, grandson of Revd. George Chamberlain, died 22nd May 1919 aged 16 years.

CHAMBERLAIN

[White marble tablet on the west wall of the south transept with enamelled arms:- sable, on a bordure gules eight martlets of the first. Crest:- on a mural crown of the second a demi lion rampant holding a key both of the second. Motto on a scroll vert:- Je garde la foi. The sable is given by the exposed surface of metal.] To the glory of God and in loving memory of Ralph Brereton Chamberlain, M.B. Edin., third son of the late Rev. George Chamberlain M.A., who passed into eternal life 21st Nov. 1909 aged 24. "To be with Christ which is far better".

CHARLESSON

Erected by Richard W. Charlesson in memory of his father Captain Montague Grahame Charlesson died 24th April 1856 aged 29 years, interred at Shanghai, China. His sister Jessie Jemima died 17th May 1861 aged 5 years. His daughter Emma Jessie died 8th March 1888 aged 9 years. His mother Emma Johns CAMPBELL died 27th November 1907 aged 86 years. His wife Caroline S. Charlesson died 29th October 1931 aged 75 years. The above named Richard W. Charlesson died 1st December 1941 aged 88 years.

CHICHESTER
See OPENSHAWE

CLARKE

[The inscription lacks punctuation towards the end.] Sacred to the memory of Agnes Clarke obiit 1826 AE 56 years. And her husband Hill Benson Clarke, died 26th Decr. 1830 AE 62 years, with their children viz Henry, Samuel, Catherine & Agnes, and grand-children, viz. Reilly CUMMINS Reilly BRUTON & Agnes CRAIG

[Hill B. Clarke, cordwainer of the town was made a freeman in 1787.]

CLEMENTS

[Recorded in McSkimin: *History and Antiquities of Carrickfergus* (1811) p. 43 as "slab on the floor near pulpit" but it was lost by 1909.] Here lyeth the body of Henry Clements of Strade Esq. aged 52 years who departed this life the 2d. day of November 1696 being then Mayor of Carrickfergus.

[The Clements family, who settled locally in the early seventeenth century, held a modest estate at Straid acquired from John Dalway of Bellahill in 1609 (P.R.O.N.I. D1905/2/153B). In the late eighteenth century the estate passed to Henry Clements Ellis of Prospect, Carrickfergus and subsequently to his daughter Jane Anne Clements Nicholay. The Clements and Ellis families were prominent in the corporate life of Carrickfergus throughout the later seventeenth and eighteenth centuries. See P.R.O.N.I., Adair Papers D3860; McCrum ed. of McSkimin: *History and Antiquities of Carrickfergus* (1909) pp. 418-9 (Clements family) and 478-82 (Ellis family). See also Ballynure Old Graveyard.]

CLEMENTS

[Next to Henry Eccleston d. 1829. The style of this stone would place it in the second quarter of the nineteenth century.] (Er)ec(ted) by George ECCLESTON in memory of his grandmother Agnes Clements. Also her son James and his wife Isabella Clements.

CLOSE
Erected by Jane Close in memory of her parents. Jane Close died 10th Aug. 1825 aged 43 years. Hugh Close died 11th Nov. 1835 aged 84 years. Also her brothers William died 23rd Feby. 1841 aged 44 years. Edward died 18th Feby. 1842 aged 26 years.
   [Hugh Close, mason, was made a freeman in 1811.]

CLOSE
[Slate next to path.] Errected [sic] by Alexr. Close in memory of his beloved father who died Feby. 18 1869 aged 54.

CLOSE
[Concrete surround next to foregoing.] J. Close.

CLOSE
[Brass plate near Dobbs window.] The adjoining window was restored in the year 1932 by the Right Rev. J. F. MACNEICE D.D., Bishop of Cashel and afterwards of Down and Connor and Dromore, a former Rector of Carrickfergus, in memory of Samuel Patrick Close A.R.H.A., architect, 1843-1925, a devoted member of this church, a churchwarden, and who as honorary architect gave of his worthy professional skill during many years. [Memorial by:-] Purdy & Millard, Belfast.
[S.P. Close was born in 1843 at Kilmaine, county Mayo, where his father, the Rev. Robert Shaw Close, was rector. After an education in Dublin he joined the Belfast firm of architects, Lanyon, Lynn and Lanyon, and came to Carrickfergus to work on the Shiels Institute. The same year saw the publication of his measured drawings of Holy Cross Abbey (county Tipperary) which won him the Fitzgerald Medal. Close's name was associated with Magheramorne, Drumalis, and Runkerry Houses, the McGarel Buildings in Larne, St. Patrick's, Ballymacarrett; and St. Columba's Knock; and the Methodist churches in Larne and Carrickfergus. F.J. Bigger described him as a big rugged man who shunned publicity, but who was gentle and kind. His wife was a daughter of William Burleigh (q.v.) and Lucretia Wills. His son, Mills Close, married firstly (1918) Emily Elizabeth Rowan-Legg (d. July 1929) and secondly Kathleen who continued to live at Cooleen, Larne Road, until 1974 when she returned to Wales, where she died in 1975. There were no children. See McCrum ed. of McSkimin: *History and Antiquities of Carrickfergus* (1909); Young and Pike: *Belfast and the Province of Ulster in the Twentieth Century* (1909): Brett: *The Buildings of Belfast* (2nd ed. 1985); *The Corran*, no 35, 1985, pp. 20-21.]

CLOSE
[Plain tablet on south wall of nave.] This tablet is erected by his fellow church members in grateful remembrance of Richard Mills Close, M.R.I.A.I., 1880-1949, who as Honorary Architect gave of his professional skill for many years in the service of this church as his father Samuel Patrick Close, A.R.H.A. had done.

CLOSE
See MILLS and WILSON

CONNOR
Erected by Alexander Connor in loving memory of his daughter Eliza Jane who died 15th Decr. 1885 aged 13 months and his wife Eliza Jane Connor who died 27th Jany. 1888 aged 45 years. his grandson Samuel WILSON died 11th May 1899 aged 6 months. His daughter Maggie ROSS, died 9th Decr. 1900 aged 24 years. His daughter Joanna Wilson died 22nd Jany. 1904 aged 35 years. His granddaughter Maggie Wilson died 4th March, 1904 aged 7 months. The above-named Alexander Connor died 23rd May 1928 aged 88 years. [Mason:-] T. Holden, Larne.

CONNOR
[Inscription on plinth. The stone is missing.] The above named William Connor died 1st May 1922 aged 83 years. His daughter Isabella Connor died 11th Aug. 1923 aged 51 years.

CONOLLY
See HOLMES

COOPER
[Recorded in McSkimin: *History and Antiquities of Carrickfergus* (1811), p. 47 as "Above the arch, at the entrance of the aisle" (south transept). In the 1909 edition it was "now at the west end of the south wall of nave".] This work was begune 161(0). Mr Cooper then maior and wrought by Thomas PAPS freemason: Mr OPENSHAWE being parson: Vivat Rex Jacobus.

COUPER
[Mounted on the south wall of the chancel. The arms are carved in stone but the epitaph is only painted. McCrum in her *History and Antiquities of Carrickfergus* (1909), pp.181-182 "Couper and Ratcliffe impaled". Arms:- per pale: argent, three martlets gules, on a chief invected of the second three annulets or, in the fess point a crescent azure; impaling argent a bend invected sable, in the chief a scallop shell gules. Crest:- a unicorn's head erased gorged.] Thomas Couper Mayor of Carrickfergus obiit 16(.)7. [McCrum gives a longer text:- Here lieth the body of Thomas Couper Alderman and twis maire of Carickfergus desesed the 20th of Augt. 1625.]

COX
[Recumbent.] Mary Anna M. K. Cox died 12th May 183(5). Also her infant son who died 8th May 183(5). This stone is erected as a mark of love and esteem by her afflicted husband Capt. D. Cox R.N.

CRAIG
[Ornamental stone sarcophagus surmounting stone pillar.] [(i) Sarcophagus]The family burying place of James Craig Esq., late of Glen Park. [(ii) Pillar, west face:-] This monument was erected by Thomas Craig of Glen Park in commemoration of his father James Craig Esq. M.P. late of Glen Park and formerly of Scoutbush who was twice returned the representative in the Imperial Parliament for the county of the town of Carrickfergus. He died at Glen Park on the 1st June 1833 aged 62 years. He was a true patriot and sincere friend of Civil and Religious Liberty. Also the remains of Janetta who died at Scoutbush on the 3rd April 1813 aged 31 years and Jane who died in 1822 aged 30 years, wives of James Craig Esq., late of Glen Park. Likewise are interred here the remains of James Craig Esq. and his wife Jane, daughter of A. BOYD Esq. of Prospect, County Antrim, parents of the aforesaid James Craig Esq. [East face:-] The following are the children of James Craig, Esq., late of Glen Park. Helena B. Craig died in infancy, Emily Craig died in infancy, James Craig died in 1826, Edward Craig died in 1832, Robert Craig his eldest son drowned in the Gulf of St. Lawrence, Thomas Craig died 18th Decr. 1836, Anne PENNELL died in 1840, and Rachel Craig died in 1862. Also in loving memory of Mary, wife of above Thomas Craig of Glen Park, who died in 1874. [South face:-] In loving memory of Cecil De Vere Craig, only son of Colonel James Craig, 2nd Brigade N.I.D. Royal Artillery, who died at Carlton Hall, Carlton on Trent, Nottinghamshire, on the 4th Octr. 1887. Also the above-named James Craig J.P. who departed this life 15th October 1910. "I am the resurrection and the life, he that believeth in me, though he were dead, yet shall he live." S. John XI, 25. "The Lord gave and the Lord hath taken away; blessed be the name of the Lord".

[James Craig who lived in the Scotch Quarter was born in 1691. He was a linen bleacher and merchant and died in 1767 leaving his property to his son James. The latter married Jane, daughter of Andrew Boyd, Prospect. Their one son James Craig of Scoutbush was elected to represent the borough in Parliament twice in the single year of 1807. Their daughters were: Sarah who married Admiral Rapier, R.N.; Jane who married Captain Ellis (q.v. Ballynure); and Mary who married Rev. Richard Dobbs, son of the Dean of Connor (q.v.). James' son Robert, was the father of Col. James Craig J.P., who married the Hon. Margaret Clementia Skeffington nee Dennistoun in 1885. Though resident in Nottinghamshire, Col. and Mrs Craig were considerable benefactors to the town. "Carlton House" in Market Place was presented to the Y.M.C.A. in 1900. Three years later ten iron seats were placed on the sea front and the town was given its first fire engine.

See McCrum ed. of McSkimin: *History and Antiquities of Carrickfergus* (1909); Burke: *Dictionary of the Landed Gentry of Great Britain and Ireland* (1866); Young and Pike: *Belfast and the Province of Ulster* (1909); P.R.O.N.I. D639/49, LPC 98 99].

CRAIG
Erected by James Craig of G(len)field in memory of his beloved wife Agnes Craig (who departed this life 26th Ju..) 186(.) aged (68) years (A...... daughter Agnes .... Sep. 187(5) aged
Augt.) 1886 aged ......

CRAIG
[Probably a re-used stone.] Erected...David Craig (in mem)ory of his (dear wife) Jane Craig died 10th Ju(ne 1895) aged 53 years.

CRAIG
Erected by John Craig in loving memory of his mother Jane Craig who died 10 January 1898, and his father David L. Craig who died 3rd June 1912. Also his brother James Craig who died 3rd October 1914. And his sister Elizabeth Craig who died 18th October 1932. The above John Craig died 31st August 1960. Also his wife Anna, died 12th December 1970.

CRAIG
See CLARKE and KANE

CRANMER
[Flaking sandstone between Wales and Harrison.] E(recte)d by John Cranmer to the memo(ry) of his daughter Betsy who departed this life on the 15th day of February 1825 aged 16 months.

CRAWFORD
[Cast iron plaque. There may be a date below ground level.] The family burying ground of John Crawford.

CRISPIN
[In floor of chancel.] William Crispin was buried in this church on Wednesday the 9th April 1645 by William PENN, father of William Penn founder of Pennsylania.

CRISPIN
[Window depicting St. Andrew in east wall of north transept.] To the memory of William Crispin 1602-1645. [Brass plate attached to wall beneath window. Arms:- ermine three lions rampant azure armed gules. Crest:- a demi griffin azure langued gules. Motto:- Dum clavum rectum teneam.] 1645 "8th Aprill A Bout 3 a clocke in the morningh our master William Crispin departed out off this World. 9th Wednesdaye A Bout 2 a Clocke in the afternoone, wee carried our master ashoare & gave him 10 peeces off ordinance, & wee buried him in the Chansel in the Church off Carickffergus" - From the journal of the Fellowship commanded by Captain, afterwards Admiral Sir, William PENN. The above window was erected by M. Jackson Crispin of Berwick, Pennsylvania, and New York City, to the honour of his ancestor, A.D. 1929.

CROMWELL
See ROBINSON

CROOKS
[Laid flat in enclosure of Christian Porter 1870.] Here lieth the body of Abigal Crooks who departed this life the 30th day of May 1783 in the 87th year of her age. Also her son Andrew Crooks who departed this life March 13th 181(3) aged 88 years. Also Agnes PORTER his daughter who departed this life 23rd Septr. 1844 aged 84 years.

[Andrew Crooks, linen merchant, was made a freeman in 1785. He is mentioned in the diary of his friend John Moore of Carrickfergus, P.R.O.N.I., Malcolm Papers D3165. Probate of the will of Andrew Crooks, late of Carrickfergus, was granted on 12 January 1820. See Connor Will and Grant Books 1818-20, p. 434.]

CRYMBLE
[White marble with lead lettering.] Erected by Carrickfergus District L.O.L. No. 19 to the memory of Bro. John Crymble who died 5th August 1904 aged 70 years. He was W.M. of L.O.L. No 508 for 30 years and filled the office of D.D.M. for over 20 years. A brother of sterling worth and a man revered and respected by all who knew him. [Mason:-] Hamilton, B.mena.

CUMMINS
See CLARKE

CUNNINGHAM
[Against Legg vault.] Sacred to the memory of Hugh B. Cunningham, obit Sept. 28th 1830 aged 58 years and Arminella his wife obiit Decr. 24th 1837 aged 46 years.

CUNNINGHAM
[Beside foregoing.] In memory of S.D. Stuart Cunningham died 2nd December 1879.

[The will (with one codicil) of Samuel Davys Cunningham, late of Carrickfergus, merchant, died 2 December 1879 at same place, was proved at Belfast 16 February 1880 by Eleanor Harriet Huggins Cunningham of Carrickfergus, widow, one of the executors. Effects under £8,000.]

CUNNINGHAM
[Black granite.] Erected by Ellen Cunningham in memory of her parents, James and Ellen Cunningham, also her brothers and sisters. "God is love".

CUNNINGHAM
[White marble attached to cast iron enclosure.] In loving rememberance.

CUPPLES
[Near path between west door and south transept.] Erected by Arthur Cupples in memory of his father Art(hur Cu)pples who died

CUPPLES
See LEGG

CURRAN
In loving memory of my dear wife Martha died 30th November 1963. The Lord is my shepherd. 23rd Psalm. [Mason:-] Hamilton, Belfast.

DARBY
[Recorded in McCrum ed. of McSkimin: *History and Antiquities of Carrickfergus* (1909), p.193. Brass tablet in black marble on north wall of chancel.] To the glory of God and in memory of Anne C. Darby, widow of the Rev. Jonthan Lovett Darby, rector of Poyntzpass, died January 5th 1888 aged 68 years. [Cast by:-] Jones & Willis.

[The will, with four codicils, of Anne Catherine Darby, late of Carrickfergus, who died 5 January 1888 at same place, was proved at Belfast 18 April 1888 by William Johns and Alexander Johns, late of Belfast, esquires, the executors.

Effects £1,190. 7s. 6d.

The Rev. Jonathan Lovett Darby, only son of William Lovett Darby and Elizabeth Hawkshaw, was born in 1799/1800 and entered Trinity College, Dublin in 1816. He graduated B.A.in 1820 and M.A. in 1832 and was curate of Collon 1821-31, of Creggan 1831-33 and perpetual curate of Acton (Poyntzpass) 1833-58, all in the diocese of Armagh. He married on 1 April 1846 Anne Catherine Johns, eldest daughter of Alexander Johns of Carrickfergus. He died on 1 March 1858, being buried in Acton and his will was proved in the same year. His widow returned to Alton, Carrickfergus. See *Burke's Landed Gentry of Ireland* (1912); Leslie: *Armagh Clergy and Parishes* (1911) and *Supplement* (1948); Burtchaell and Sadleir: *Alumni Dublinenses* (1924).]

DARRAH
[Slate to west of north transept, now removed to the vestry.] Erected to the memory of John Darrah who died 20th of Dec. 1819.

DAVEY
[To the south of the chancel.] Erected by Ann Davey in memory of her husband Edward Da(ve)y who died January (11) 181(5) aged 57 years.

[There were two Edward Davys, both weavers, made freemen in 1785 and 1787.]

DAVEY
Erected by James Davey to the memory of Agnes S. Davey who died 16 October 1880 aged 17 years. The above-named James Davey died 28th Novr. 1900 aged 89 years and his wife Margaret Davey who died 16th Jany. 1909 aged 86 years.

DAVEY
[Cast iron plaque to south of chancel.] The burying ground of Samuel Davey one grave. [Cast by:-] The Millfield Foundry, 1913.

DAVIDSON
Erected by James Davidson in memory of his daughter Bella who died 6th Aug. 1866 aged 1 year. Also his son John who died 16th Oct. 1875 aged 2 years. Also his mother Bella who died 11th Aug. 1880 aged 69 years. Also his daughter Isabella who died 3rd Oct. 1888 aged 21 years. Also his son Thomas who died 30th Aug. 1889 aged 23 years. Also his wife Margaret who died 26th Jany. 1899 aged 63 years. Also the above-named James Davidson who died 28th Nov. 1902 aged 70 years. Also William John Davidson who died 4th July 1928 aged 52 years. Also James Davidson who died 4th March 1934 aged 62 years. Also Ellen Davidson who died 8th August 1941 aged 72 years.

DAVIDSON
[Cast iron plaque.] The family burying ground of John Davidson, Belfast, 1872. [Cast by:-] Victor C. Taylor, Atlas Foundry, Belfast.

DAVISON
Erected by Mary Davison in memory of her beloved husband Thomas Davison who departed this life 9th February 1861 aged 31 years. Also her son William who departed this life 14th September 1861 aged 15 months. Mary MACKINTOSH died 24th April 1914 aged 87 years.

DAVISON
Erected by John Davison in memory of his wife Sarah who died 15th August 1868 aged 62 years.

DAVYS
[Recorded in McSkimin: *History and Antiquities of Carrickfergus* as "on a slab on the floor", but it is "now beside the Chichester monument" in the 1909 ed.] Here lyeth the body of Edmond Davys, Alderman, twice mayor of Carrickfergus who departed this life the 6th day of July anno dom. 1696 in the 73rd year of his

age. Here also lyeth Mary his wife, Katherine, Ann and Martha, Edmond Ezekiel and Nathaniel, sons and daughters of ye said Edmond and Mary, being descended of a branch of the ancient family of GUSANNA in North Wales.

[The Davys were one of the leading corporate families in seventeenth century Carrickfergus. A number of family portraits, including a likeness of Edmond Davys are in the possession of Carrickfergus Borough Council. Members of the senior branch of the family frequently represented the borough in parliament between 1639 and 1713 and equally frequently married into the aristocracy. They removed from the district in the early eighteenth century and their property in and around the town eventually passed to Arthur Thomas, Lord Blaney. When Alderman Samuel Davys (son of Edmond) died in 1719 his property passed to his nephew Ezekiel Davys Wilson. Throughout the eighteenth century the Davys Wilsons were active in corporate affairs. Ezekiel Davys Wilson, the last of the line, was M.P. for the borough from 1785-1797. His heir was his cousin Robert Duncan who subsequently took the name Davys-Wilson. See McCrum ed. of McSkimin: *History and Antiquities of Carrickfergus* (1909), pp.471-474. P.R.O.N.I. T467 p. 362A and T1021/6 p. 36.]

DAVYS
[Tablet on wall of nave opposite baptistry, but the reference would be to the font now placed at the crossing. The plaque was in the same position in 1811 and 1909.] This font, a silver flagon, the tables of the comandments, Lords Prayer & creed were given to this church by Samuel Davys, alderman, ano Dom. 1714.

DAVYS
See MALCOLM

DAWSON
[Slate, now laid flat.] Here lieth ye body of Ann Dawson who died Novr. ye 24 1775 aged 74 years.

DICKSON
[Near south boundary wall.] The family burying ground of M. Dickson, 1919.

DIXON
In memory of Crow, beloved little daughter of William and Mary Vickers Dixon, born July 27th 1894, died February 26th 1905.

DOBBIN
[No memorial or inscription now mentions this ancient Carrickfergus family, but Samuel McSkimin, while describing the church interior mentions "a flag with the name of James Dobbin engraven on it, who died 1757, aged 75 years; with the other names of that family." See McCrum ed. of McSkimin: *History and Antiquities of Carrickfergus* (1909) p. 180.]

DOBBS
This vestry room was erected at the expence of the Rev. Richd. Dobbs, Dean of Connor, Anno 1787.

DOBBS
[Recorded in first (p.42) and in McCrum ed. of McSkimin: *History and Antiquities of Carrickfergus* (1909), p. 179. Tablet with urn in low relief on the south wall of the chancel. Sacred to the memory of the Revd. Richard Dobbs A.M., Dean of Connor, whose life was devoted to a faithful & zealous discharge of pastoral duties thro' a period of near forty years. Possessed of a temper calm and deliberate his calmness was the result of firmness of mind; and his deliberation, wisdom. His piety was unaffected and sincere. The affections of his heart strong and permanent. He was called to receive the everlasting reward of his pious & charitable labours on the IVth day of Febry. MDCCCII in the LXIst year of his age. Multis ille bonis flebilis occidit.

[The will of the Rev. Richard Dobbs, dated 23 March 1798 was proved in the

Prerogative Court in 1802. See Vicars: *Index to the Prerogative Wills of Ireland, 1536-1810* (1897); Ellis and Eustace: *Registry of Deeds, Dublin, Abstracts of Wills, Vol. III 1785-1832* (1984).

The Rev. Richard Dobbs was born in Lisburn in 1740/1, the son of the Rev. Richard Dobbs, rector of Lisburn and a brother of Arthur Dobbs of Castle Dobbs d.1765. He was educated at Eton and entered Trinity College, Dublin, in 1757, graduating B.A. in 1761 and M.A. in 1764. He was curate of Loughinisland 1762-3, of Lisburn 1763-6, Vicar-Choral of Lismore 1766-8, Prebend of Kilroot 1768-75, Dean of Connor and Rector of Carrickfergus 1775-1802. He was a J.P. for county Antrim. He was responsible for the transcription of the early Town Books of Carrickfergus (P.R.O.N.I. T707) which were of such value when the originals were lost in the early nineteenth century. He married Harriet, widow of Ralph Lambert and daughter of John Walsh, Dean of Connor. She died on 25 March 1784 aged 45. They had 4 sons:-

1. Rev. Richard Dobbs, Rector of Layd.
2. Rev. John Dobbs, Vicar of Glynn.
3. William Ryder Dobbs died in August 1814.
4. Conway Edward Dobbs (1773-1870) married in 1806 Maria Sophia Dobbs and had 3 sons and 5 daughters (vide infra)

See Leslie: *Clergy of Connor* (1993); Burtchaell and Sadleir: *Alumni Dublinenses* (1924); Carmody: *Lisburn Cathedral* (1926); *Burke's Landed Gentry of Ireland* (1958 ed.).]

DOBBS

[Recorded in McCrum ed. of McSkimin: *History and Antiquities of Carrickfergus* (1909), p. 189. Three light window depicting hope, charity and faith. Brass plate on sill south of communion rail.] To the glory of God and in memory of Conway Edward Dobbs, fourth son of Revd. Richard Dobbs formerly Dean of Connor, born 29 August 1773, died 18 March 1870. Also of Maria, his wife, born 1 May 1778, died 29 April 1869. This window is placed by their surviving children who in them reverenced examples of faith, hope and charity.

[The will (with 2 codicils) of Conway Edward Dobbs, late of Glendum Lodge, county Antrim, esquire, was proved at the Principal Registry 22 April 1870 by Conway Edward Dobbs of 41 Leeson Street, Dublin, esquire, barrister and sole executor. Effects under £2,000.]

DOBBS

[Tablet on north wall of chancel with crest:- a unicorn's head. Motto:- Amor Dei et [sic] beatitude proximi summa.] To the glory of God and in loving memory of Senator Major Arthur Frederick Dobbs, D.L. of Castle Dobbs, born 31st March 1876, died 16th Feb. 1955. And of his wife Hylda Louisa, died 20th Oct. 1957. Peace perfect peace.

DONALD

[Slate.] Erected by Isabella Donald in memory of her husband William Donald died 7th March 1839 aged 40 years. Also 3 of her children John, Jane & William.

DONALD

Erected by William Donald in memory of his brother Robert Donald who died April 1852 aged 4 years. Also his brother Robert John who died 30th Decr. 1861 aged 3 months. Also his sister Ellen who died August 14th 1862 aged 4 years. And his son Robert John Donald who died 30th June 1870 aged (8) years.

DONALD

[Slate beside AGNEW.] Erected by Thomas Donald in memory of his beloved wife Margaret who departed this life 2nd Sept. 1856 aged 65 years. She was a most affectionate wife and mother, and has left her husband five sons & one daughter to lament their loss. The above Thomas Donald died 15th Oct. 1862 aged 72 years.

[Thomas Donald, servant, of the Town, was made a freeman in 1813.]

DONALD
Erected by Alexander Donald to the memory of his son John who died on the 12th of May 1871 aged 29 years.

DONALD
[Cast iron plaque lying close to the preceding.] The family burying place of Robert Donald, Carrickfergus, 1903. [Cast by:-] James Moore & sons Ltd., ironfounders, engineers, Belfast, Millfield Foundry.

DONALD
See AGNEW

DONALDSON
See APSLEY

DOUGLAS
See MARSH

DORMAN
[Recumbent stone.] Erected to the memory of John Dorman who departed this life on the 21st December 1840, aged 75 years. Also to his son Edward Dorman who died at sea on 8th March, 1857 aged 25 years. Also to his grandson Edward son of Wm. Dorman who died on the 12th September 1866 aged 3 years and 11 months. Also to his beloved wife Leonora Dorman who died 2nd November 1867 aged 75 years. Also in memory of Robert Dorman, son of the above-named John and Lenora [sic] Dorman, who died 4th April 1898 aged 8(.) years, also of his wife Sarah (.........t) September, 1906 aged 80 ......

[John Dorman, weaver, of the Middle Division, was made a freeman in 1787.

Probate of the will of Robert Dorman, late of Oakfield, Carrickfergus, farmer, who died 4 April 1898, granted at Belfast 6 June 1898 to Robert Dorman of Oakfield, Carrickfergus, merchant. Effects £287.]

DRENNING
Erected by John & Charles (D)renning in memory of their mother Susanna Drenning who departed this life the 23rd of December 1828 aged 48 years. Encomiums to the sleeping dust are vain. But when alive she was possessed of virtue, charity and love.

DUFF
Erected by Margaret Duff in memory of her daughter Jane Duff who departed this life December 17th 1856 aged 22 years.

DUFF
See GREEN and JACK

DUNBAR
See LATTIMORE

DUNCAN
See WILSON

ECCLESTON
Sacred to the memory of Henry Eccleston, obiit 1829 aged 60 years. Also his wife Mary Ann who died 1850 aged 74 years. Also their son James Eccleston who died at Hobart Town, Van-Diemens-Land, 3rd March 1850. And their grandson Ezekiel James McCANN who died at sea 3rd September 1853.

[The *Northern Whig* of 8th August 1850 contains the following:- *The Hobart*

Town Courier of March 13, conveys to us the sad intelligence of the death, in the 34th year of his age of J. Eccleston Esq. brother of Mr. John Eccleston, Carrickfergus, and himself a native of that town. Mr. Eccleston had but recently arrived at Hobart Town, to undertake the duties of Rector and Head Classical Master of the High School of that colony, to which he had been appointed about a year ago by the Council of the Institution in London, out of a very numerous list of candidates. The opening of the school took place on the 21st January last, with great eclat, under the auspices of Sir W. Denison, the Governor; and, on the 8th of the following March, the newly appointed Rector was no more. He was the author of several works, including one on English antiquities.

Henry Eccleston, chandler, of the Town, was made a freeman in 1787.]

ECCLESTON

[Recorded in McCrum ed. of McSkimin: *History and Antiquities of Carrickfergus* (1909), p.190. Marble plaque in splay of window on south of nave.] Sacred to the memory of Henry Eccleston who in the 38th year of his age was drowned off the Island of Barbuda in the West Indies. His barque the "Lancashire Witch" having been wrecked in a hurricane on the 18th August 1851. This tablet is erected by his widow Jane Eccleston in remembrance of a beloved husband and affectionate father.

Far, far he lies from holy ground,
Deep in his coral bed;
The sea weeds wrap his corse around,
The waves roll o'er his head.

"And the sea gave up the dead which were in it". Rev. XX, 13. Also his daughter Georgina who died 10th May 1845 aged 3 years.

ECCLESTON
See CLEMENTS

EDGAR

I am the resurrection and the life. Erected by Elizabeth Edgar in memory of her father Robert Edgar who died 24th December 1820. Also her mother Ann Edgar who died 1st May 1854 aged 81 years. And her grandfather Michael McALLEN who died 2nd June 1823.

[Robert Edgar weaver, of the North-East Division, was made a freeman in 1811.]

EDGAR
See STUART

EDMONDSON
See McKIBBIN

ERSKINE

[Railed enclosure near baptistry.] "Blessed are the dead which die in the Lord". This stone is erected in memory of James Erskine who departed this life 22nd December 1852 aged 71 years, by his sorrowing widow and affectionate children as a lasting tribute of their love and a memorial of their loss. They mourn not without hope for their trust is that he sleeps in Jesus. Also his beloved wife Mary who died 28th April 1870 aged 70 years. Also Mary, the beloved wife of Pakenham Erskine, who died 23rd January 1884 aged 61 years. And Pakenham Erskine, son of James Erskine, who died 6th January 1889 aged 61 years. "Come unto me, all ye that labour and are heavy laden, and I will give you rest". - Matt. XI, 28. Pakenham Erksine, son of Pakenham Erskine, who died 9th October 1934 aged 74 years. And his beloved wife Barbara Rodgers Erksine died 29th June 1946 aged 82 years. William Rodgers Erskine, son of last named Pakenham Erskine, killed in action in France 30th December (1916) aged 23 years. [Continues on plaque on grave] Grace Magill PIM died 30th Nov. 1961 aged 60 years, youngest daughter of Pakenham and Barbara Erskine and wife of Lieut Col. Gerald Robert

Pim M.C.R.E. killed in action near Dunkirk 3rd June 1940. Pakenham Erskine died 28th May 1967 aged 78 years. Animo et Fortitudino.

[Mary Erskine, formerly of Carrickfergus and late of 3 Lansdowne Crescent, Glasgow, widow, died 29 April 1870. Confirmation from the Commissariat of Lanarkshire dated 10 November 1870. Resealed at Principal Registry, 17 November 1870. Effects £in Ireland 327. 7s. 5d.

James Erskine had been Governor of the County Antrim Jail in Carrickfergus for 28 years when he retired in May 1849 and was succeeded by his nephew Robert Forbes, Deputy Governor. He left 3 sons:- 1) James Erskine, solicitor; 2) Pakenham Erskine, grain merchant in Belfast; and 3) John Erskine, Rector of Wycliffe, England; and 3 daughters. See McCrum ed. of McSkimin: *History and Antiquities of Carrickfergus* (1909) pp. 512-513.]

EVANS

Elizabeth Martin Evans died 24th August 1859 aged 9 months. Samuel Evans died 16th August 1862 aged 18 months. Margaret Evans died 7th August 1867 aged 4. Patrick Evans, died 21st May 1914 aged 85. Margaret Evans his wife died 2nd January 1918 aged 87. John McAuley Evans died 18th August 1921 aged 66. William Beck Evans died 9th March 1946 aged 79. Robert Evans, late of Slate House, Carrickfergus, died 11th April 1951 aged 94. Samuel Evans born 1865 - died 1955. Ellen, wife of Samuel Evans, died 7th December 1963 aged 79 years.

EVANS
See HAMILTON

EVERARD

[Recorded in McCrum ed. of McSkimin: *History and Antiquities of Carrickfergus* (1909) p.191. A white marble tablet surmounted by naval trophies, on the south wall of chancel.] Sacred to the memory of Lieutenant James Everard. Also of William TODD, Robert HENDERSON, and John BOYD, seamen of this place; late belonging to His Majesty's Sloop "Nimrod", who were drowned in Belfast Lough by the upsetting of a boat August 15th 1825. As a tribute of respect for an amiable young man and highly meritorious officer and for three worthy good seamen the captain, officers and ship's company of the Nimrod have erected this tablet. [Carved by:-] Crake, London.

FAIR(F)OO(T)

[Laid flat in front of modern Harvey stone.] Here lieth the body of (John) Fair(f)oo(t) who departed this life December the seventh 1791 aged sixtyseven years. In loving memory of Ruth, wife of Archibald HARVEY, who died 15th June 1933 aged 47. And her mother Letitia WATSON who died 5th August 1930 aged 86. Also their four children: Ernest died 12th March 1920, Letitia died 29th May 1912, James and John died in infancy.

[John Fairfoot, senior, farmer, of the Middle Division, was made a freeman in 1785.]

FEENEY
See THOMPSON

FINL(E)Y

Here lyeth the body of Thomas Finl(e)y (who) departed this life the 1... day of October 1700.

FISKEN

[Granite against east boundary wall.] In loving memory of Margaret STOCKMAN, dearly beloved wife of Alexander Fisken died 24th September 1912 aged 79 years. Also Alexander Fisken died 23rd September 1915 aged 83 years. "Blessed are the dead which die in the Lord".

FLECK
See WILLIAMSON

GARDNER

[Recorded with the photograph in McCrum ed. of McSkimin: *History and Antiquities of Carrickfergus* (1909) p. 184; also in 1811 ed., pp. 149-150 and M.D., Vol. III, p. 5. White marble with finely carved cherub heads mounted on wall of south transept, rusting of internal pins causing spalling. Arms:- argent, upon a chevron sable between three griffins' heads erased of the second langued gules, two lions passant confronte of the third. Crest:-a demi griffin sable.] M:S: Prope hoc Marmor jacet Honesta stirpe Andreas Gardner Assiduus Dei Cultor, Amantissimus Patriae, In adversis Strenuus Deo fidens Omnibus Charus. Superstitibus duobus relictis filijs Iohanne (viz.) elte Roberto, et Quatuor filiabus Margareta, Sara, Anna, et Elizabetha, Et uxore maestissima Quam aequo studio amplectentem, Castissimo animi ardore Unice coluit. Qui diu cum gravi valetudine Conflictatus, Omne terrestre negotium dereliquit, Ut coelestia intueretur. Cumque sexagesimum sextum aetatis suae Annum peregisset: Mortem piam placidam, ac tranqillam 40to Februarij, 1682, Obijt. Hoc Marmor in piam Patris Memoriam, Robertus filius minor natu, Londini Armiger, Anno Christianae salutis 1713. Erigendum Curavit. [Translation:- In sacred memory: Near this monument lies Andrew Gardner of honourable lineage, an unremitting worshipper of God, a fervent lover of his country, strong amid troubles, trusting in God and beloved by all. He was survived by two sons, John and Robert, and four daughters, Margaret, Sara, Anna and Elizabeth, and by his deeply sorrowing wife to whom he was equally attached and for whom he cared with warm and faithful affection before all others. At length, having been afflicted with grave illness, he laid aside all earthly business so that he might contemplate heavenly things and when he had completed his 66th year he met a holy, peaceful and calm death on 4th February 1682. His younger son Robert of London, esquire, caused this monument to the pious memory of his father to be erected in the years of Christian salvation 1713.

Andrew Gardner was sheriff in 1657. Robert Gardner was the younger brother of John and grandson of John Bullworthy, a High Street carpenter, who was mayor in 1654 and 1655. He was an agent in London and acquired a very great fortune but was ruined in the South Sea Bubble. The ceremonial sword and mace of the borough were presented by Col. Robert Gardner in 1712. The Gardners acquired land at lower Greenisland in the West Division (formerly called Bullworthystown, later Gardnerstown) as a result of the marriage of Andrew Gardner and Joan Bullworthy, daughter and heiress of John Bullworthy, mayor of Carrickfergus 1654-55. See McCrum ed. of McSkimin: *History and Antiquities of Carrickfergus* (1909), pp. 265, 415.]

GARDNER

[Ledger of Castle Espie limestone, recorded in McSkimin: *History and Antiquities of Carrickfergus* (1811), p.47 as "lying in the passage" of south transept. In McCrum's ed., p.186, it was beside the Chichester monument. Now it has been returned to the floor of the south transept.] Here lyeth the body of Andrew Gardner, burges, who departed this life ye 4th of Febuary 1682. Allso here, lieth ye body of Joan his wife who was buried ye 18th of March 1694.

GARDNER

[Ledger of Castle Espie limestone matching the above. It has also been moved round the church and is recorded in both editions of McSkimin's *History and Antiquities of Carrickfergus*.] Here lyeth the body of Margret CATHERWOOD and Sara A(N)G(U)S, daughters to An(dr)ew Gardner. Margret O'BRIEN departed this life ye 28 of Janry. 1728-9 aged 50 years.

GARDNER/GARDINER

Erected by Mary Gardner in memory of her beloved husband Isaac Gardner who departed this life 20th Jan. 1859 aged 52 years. Also her beloved daughters: Isabella who departed this life 3rd Dec. 1863 aged 18 years; Agnes MINNIECE who departed this life 17th May 1875 aged 42 years. Also the above Mary Gardner who departed this life 21st Dec. 1883 aged 73 years. Thomas Poag Gardner who departed this life 4th Feb. 1931 aged 82 years. Also his wife Margaret Gardiner died 23rd Dec. 1937 aged 89 years. "Blessed are the dead who die in the Lord".

[Robina, youngest daughter of Isaac Gardiner, married Augustus T. Johnstone on 7 October 1885, both of Greenisland. See *Carrickfergus Advertiser*, 16 October 1885.]

GARRELL
See MACONKEY

GEORGE
See MARTIN

GETTY
In loving memory of William Getty who departed this life 11th Septr. 1898 aged 56 years. Also of his son Arthur C. Getty who departed this life 8th July 1899 aged 24 years. And his wife Martha SAYERS who died 1st December 1924. Also his grandson William Getty who died 3rd November 1910. "Blessed are the dead which die in the Lord". Erected by the employees of the B. & N. C. Ry. in memory of their esteemed colleague William Getty, 1899. [Mason:-] Robinson, Belfast.

[Probate of the will of William Getty, late of Greenisland, county Antrim, railway official who died 11 September 1898, granted at Belfast 12 December 1898 to Martha S Getty of Greenisland, widow. Effects £957. 11s.]

GIFFEN
Erected by Mary Giffen in memory of her husband James Giffen obiit 7th March 1849 aged 41 years. Also her daughter Annie who died 3rd July 1882 aged 36 years. Also the above Mary Giffen died 11th February 1883 aged 72 years. Her son Captain Nathaniel Giffen who was lost in the S.S. City of Glasgow on her voyage from Glasgow to Oporto in the year 1883 aged 44 years. Her daughter Isabella Giffen who died 22nd June 1903. Her daughter Mary DUFF who died 8th February 1906.

[The will of Mary Giffen, late of Carrickfergus, widow, who died 11 February 1883 at same place, was proved at Belfast, 2 April 1884 by David Pasley of Carrickfergus, bank manager, the surviving executor. Effects £554. 12s. 6d.

Letters of administration of the personal estate of Nathaniel Giffen, late of Belfast, master mariner, who died 1 September 1883 at sea, were granted at Belfast 5 September 1884 to Emma Giffen of 35 Bentwick Street, Belfast, the widow. Effects £233.]

GILL
[Henry Gill was buried in the church, as recorded in both 1811 and 1909 editions of McSkimin's *History and Antiquities of Carrickfergus*. The present inscribed stone is modern.] The grave of that great benefactor of the poor, Henry Gill, who died September 16, 1761.

[Henry Gill was the son of a sergeant in the army and kept a stall in Carrickfergus market. This prospered and he was made a freeman of the town in 1712, a burgess in 1720, a sheriff in 1729, alderman and mayor in 1739 and treasurer in 1740. He left a manuscript history of Carrickfergus which has been valuable to later historians. He died unmarried and his will, dated 23 March 1761, was proved in the Prerogative Court in Dublin later in the year. He left his fortune between the poor of Carrickfergus and St. Patrick's Hospital in Dublin. See Vicars: *Index to the Prerogative Wills of Ireland* (1897); McCrum's ed. of McSkimin *History and Antiquities of Carrickfergus* (1909) pp. 180, 234-5, 398-9 and 440-1.]

GILLIAM
[Small headstone against the west boundary wall; the inscription is repeated on polished granite 18 metres to the east.]

Family burying ground of William Gillick [sic.]. John Gilliam died 1907 aged 50 years. Annie, daughter of the above named John, died 21st April 1942.

His wife Janey died 5th May 1954. Their son William died 4th Nov. 1955. Frances L.C. Gilliam & Lena McC. Gilliam died in infancy. Until the day break.

[John Gilliam placed a notice in the *Carrickfergus Advertiser* of 11 January 1895 recording the death of William Gilliam on 10th aged 94 years, at his residence, Slievetone, W. Division, burial to be at St Nicholas.]

GILLILAND

Erected to the memory of John Gilliland who died the (10)..... aged .. years. Also his mother M..... Gilliland who died (January th....18..) a(ged....)s. Likewise Thomas A (the above's) father (who) died.....M....... (aged)...... And (his wife) Mary who (died .. of April ..18 aged .... And their son G..r.. who died 31 .... aged 56 years).

GILLINGTON
See WILLSON

GILMORE

[Recorded in McCrum ed. of McSkimin: *History and Antiquities of Carrickfergus* (1909), p. 189. Window on south side of chancel depicting the transfiguration.] In loving memory of John Boyd Gilmore who died 27th November 1859 and of Barbara his wife who died 22nd May 1865.

[The will with one codicil of John Boyd Gilmore, late of Ravenhill, in the county of the town of Carrickfergus, esquire, Q.C., who died 27 November 1859 at Ravenhill aforesaid, was proved at Belfast, 6 January 1860 by the oath of John Gilmore of same place, esquire, barrister-at-law, one of the executors. Effects under £12,000.]

GIRVAN/GIRVIN

Erected by Annie Girvan in memory of her beloved son Johnston Girvan who died 21st April 1870 aged 4 years and 8 months. Also her husband Francis Girvin who died 19th March 1892 aged 77 years. Also her son Francis Girvin who died 15th May 1894 aged 25 years. The above Annie Girvin who died 16th March 1924. And her son Johnston Girvin died 31st January 1932. Eliza WELSH died 6th March 1947. Andrew Girvin died 21st March 1954.

GIRVAN

[Black granite against east boundary wall.] In memory of Thomas Girvan who died 4th December 1902 aged 82 years. Also his wife Agnes who died 16th December 1914 aged 89 years. His son John who died in Mildura [Australia], 25th May 1927 aged 77 years. Also his son David who died 12th January 1931 aged 79 years. His daughter Mary died 29th Nov. 1933 aged 80 years. His grandson Thomas HAMILTON died 10th Oct. 1949 aged 62 years. And his wife Henrietta died 26th Oct. 1953 aged 62 years.

GIRVIN
See GORMAN

GORDON

[Against north perimeter wall. Divided into two panels.] In loving memory of John, only son of the late James W. Gordon of Sheepbridge, Newry, who died 23rd Nov. 1891 aged 19 years. Also of Anne Augusta, younger daughter of the aforesaid James W. Gordon, who died July 14th 1906. "Blessed are the pure in heart".

Second panel:- Jane YOUNG, widow of John HORSBOROUGH of Seamount and Carrickfergus, whose remains rest here.

GORMAN

[Laid flat.] Erected (in) memory of Samuel Gorman who departed this life 10th September 1839 aged (6) years. "Be ye also ready for in such an hour as ye think not". Also his brother John Gorman who departed this life 17th September 1859 aged 48 years. Also their father Thomas Gorman who died 28th August 1866 aged

82 years. Also their mother Mary Gorman who died 27th Feby. 1877 aged 86 years. Also Jane, the beloved wife of Edward Gorman, who died 2nd September 1882. And their brother the said Edward Gorman who died 3rd April 1903. And his daughter Mary GRANT who died 2nd Jany. 1910 aged 53 years. Also her son Edward who died 13th Octr. 1909 aged 29 years.

[The will of Thomas Gorman, late of Carrickfergus, farmer, who died 28 August 1866 at same place, was proved at the Principal Registry, 2 August 1867 by the oaths of Edward Gorman, farmer and William Gorman, merchant, late of Carrickfergus aforesaid, the executors. Effects under £20.]

GORMAN

[Broken into several pieces.] Erected by Jane Gorman in memory of her beloved husband Francis Gorman who died 14th April 1887 aged 70 years. Also the above Jane Gorman who died 14th October 1893 aged 76 years.

[Francis Gorman of Albert Road had been a guard on the Northern Counties Railway.]

GORMAN

[Square pillar topped by draped urn.] In loving memory of Dr. Thomas Gorman died 9th March 1893 aged 29 years. His mother Margaret, beloved wife of Wm. Gorman, J.P., died 25th May 1907 aged 70 years. Alexander J. Gorman, second son of the above Wm. Gorman, beloved husband of Maud WOODS, died 29th Jany. 1910 aged 43 years. Wm. Gorman J.P. died 10th Nov.1911 aged 81 years. James Charles Gorman, third son of above Wm. Gorman, J.P., died 7th Sept. 1925 aged 59 years. John Pearson Gorman, fifth son of Wm. Gorman, J.P., died 30th January 1935 aged 64 years. And Mary Ellen, wife of John Pearson Gorman, died 20th December 1941 aged 72 years. William Gorman of Sandycove, Co. Dublin, fourth son of Wm. Gorman, J.P., died 3rd November 1955 aged 88 years.

[Letters of administration of the personal estate of Thomas Gorman, late of Carrickfergus, M.D., who died 9 March 1893 at same place, were granted at Belfast 26 April 1893 to William Gorman of Carrickfergus, merchant, the father. Effects £313. 11s.]

GORMAN

[Polished granite with gold lettering.] In loving memory of Richard Gorman died 5th May 1899 aged 86 years. His wife Sarah GIRVIN died 17th Feb. 1907 aged 87 years. Their son Samuel died 17th Feb. 1900 aged 47 years. Their daughter Sarah Jane died 13th Nov. 1932 aged 67 years. Their daughter Mary died 16th Dec. 1951 aged 90 years.

GORMAN

[Three light window in east wall of south transept showing Saints Columba, Patrick, and Aidan. The inscription is in the stone below.] To the glory of God and in loving memory of William Gorman J.P., sometime churchwarden of this parish, born 3rd May 1830, died 10th Nov. 1911. Also of Margaret his wife, born 22nd Feb. 1837, died 25th May 1907. This window is placed here by their surviving children, 1912.

GORMAN

In affectionate remembrance of Annie HOLMES, beloved wife of John Gorman, who died 10th Septr. 1911 aged 46 years. Also the above named John Gorman who died 25th December 1932 aged 78 years, son of the late Richard Gorman, Carrickfergus. For ever with the Lord.

GORMAN

[Brass plate on organ.] To the glory of God and in memory of Thomas Gorman, a life long member of this church who served in the choir for over seventy years, and in the sunday school as teacher and superintendent for sixty years, died 8th May 1935. This organ screen and console panelling are presented by his daughter Jessie

BIRNEY
Dedicated 16th May 1976. "Let everything that hath breath praise the Lord".

GORMAN
[White marble.] In loving memory of Thomas Gorman died 26th September 1957.

GORMAN
See McCANN

GRAHAM
[Tall slate facing west door.] Erected in memory of Elenor [sic.] Graham who departed this life 28th January 1851 aged 85 years. Also her son Richard Graham who departed this life in 1833 aged 18 years. Also her grand children James & Martha Graham in 1848 aged 4 & 2 years. Also her grand-daughter Eleanor died 1860 aged 18 years. Also her son William lost at sea 1869. Also his wife Agnes died 4th March 1894 aged 79 years.

[Letters of administration of the personal estate of Agnes Graham, late of Lancasterian Street in the county of the town of Carrickfergus, widow, who died 4 March 1894 at 2 Copeland Terrace, Carrickfergus, were granted at Belfast 18 April 1894 to Agnes Blackburn of 2 Copeland Terrace, wife of Henry Blackburn, a child. Effects £10.]

GRAHAM
[Brass plate on oak bookstall in porch.] To the glory of God and in memory of William John Graham obit May 1969.

GRANT
In loving memory of our dear father William Grant called home 18th Oct 1945. Also our dear mother Jane called home 14th Oct. 1973. Worthy of everlasting remembrance.

GRANT
[Could be a nineteenth century stone.] This stone claims 2 graves on each side. The burying ground of James Grant. In remembrance of James Grant who died 23rd July 1950. Also his sister Martha Grant who died 5th February 1955. And his wife Joyce who died 29th April 1959.

GRAY
[Polished granite.] In memory of William Gray, died December 12th 1857 aged 18 years. Hugh Gray died March 31st 1864 aged 26 years. Also James Gray who died in South Carolina November 26th 1855 aged 24 years. Martha Gray who died 12th July 1883 aged 79 years. John Gray died 30th April 1896 aged 67 years. Asleep in Jesus. George Gray died 5th June 1900 aged 69 years. Also Mary Jane, wife of above John Gray, died 27th Sep. 1931 aged 89 years.

[Probate of the will of John Gray, late of Duncrue, Carrickfergus, county of the town of Carrickfergus, farmer, who died 30 April 1896, granted at Belfast, 21 September 1896 to Mary Jane Gray, widow and George Gray, farmer, both of Duncrue. Effects £2,405. 6s. 6d.]

GRAY
Erected by David Gray of Carrickfergus in affectionate remembrance of his son David George who died 28th April 1874 aged 12 months. His son Thomas Wilson who died 6th Sept. 1876 aged 7 years & 11 months. His daughter Margaretta "Ettie" Gray who died 30th October 1887 aged 9 years. Also in loving memory of the above David Gray who died 23rd April 1895 aged 68 years, deeply and deservedly regretted. Jenny Gray, wife of the above David Gray, who died 24th Aug. 1900 aged 60 years. His daughter Janeie Gray who died 12th February 1929 aged 61 years. "She is not dead, but sleepeth". His daughter Ina RUDDELL, who died 22nd April 1930 aged 53 years interred at Winnipeg, Canada. His son, Dr.

David George Gray, who died 24th December 1934 aged 60 years. Interred at Childwall, Liverpool.

[The will of David Gray, late of Rhanbuoy Park, Carrickfergus, county Antrim, retired merchant, who died 23 April 1895 at same place, was proved at Belfast 26 July 1895 by Jenny Gray, widow, and George Gray, retired borough treasurer, both of Carrickfergus and Thomas Wilson of Straid, said county, merchant, the executors. Effects £3,964. 17s. 4d.]

GREER
[Polished granite with lead lettering.] In loving memory of our dear parents. Joseph died 17th November 1939. Elizabeth died 7th March 1966. [Mason:-] Wilton.

GUNNING
[Ledger between Kain and Isaac Gardner.] To the memory of Alice Gunning who departed this life on the 8th day of Octr. 1782 in the 24th year of her age - her husband Alexr. Gunning pays this last tribute of his affection to the best of wives, a tender parent, and sincere friend. She lived beloved and died lamented by all her acquaintances. Alexr. Gunning Esqr., Alderman, departed this life 15th Octr. 1823 aged 83 years. Jane Gunning, relict of the above Alexr. Gunning, departed this life the 11th of Septr. 1831 aged 42 years. A woman in whom was combined extraordinary talents, benevolence of heart and true religion. His daughter Jane Gunning who departed this life 3rd January 1906, beloved by all who knew her.

GUSANNA
See DAVYS

GYLE
[Small stone in front of Legg vault.] Hear lieth the body of Rachel Gyle died June the 10th 1810 aged 28 yrs.

GYLE
[White marble, fallen.] Erected by Annie WHARRY in memory of her father Alexander Gyle who died 30th June 1902 aged 65 and her mother Mary Logan Gyle, who died 4th September 1897 aged 51 years. Also her son Alexander Wharry who died in infancy.

HAGAN
[Cast iron plaque.] James Hagan 1885.
[James Hagan of Irish Quarter West died 6th October 1885 aged 71 years. See *Carrickfergus Advertiser*, 9 October 1885.]

HAGAN
[Polished granite against south boundary wall.] In loving memory of Agnes Hagan, died 1954. William Hagan died 1946. His wife Agnes died 1982. Ross KENNEDY died 1959. His wife Janet Hagan Kennedy died 1964. Blessed are the dead which die in the Lord. [Mason:-] Davidson.

HAGGAN
[Recumbent on Haggan plot.] Here (li)eth the body (of) Esther Hagg(an who) departed (this) life April 25th 1815 aged 17 years. Also her mother Margaret Haggan who died 1st March 1832 aged 61 years. Also Reev(es) ANDERSON who died 28th Augt. 1909 aged 66 years. Also his wife Elizabeth who died 3rd July 1919 aged 73 years.

HAGGAN
[Granite with surround, lead lettering.] In loving memory of John Haggan died 2nd March 1935. And his wife Sarah Haggan died 10th May 1943. Also Stanley, youngest son of the above named and dearly loved husband of May, died 1st February 1972. Margaret May Haggan died 27th April 1979. [Mason:-] Kirkwood.

HAGGAN
See ANDERSON and KAIN

HALE
See POAGUE

HALL
See STEWART

HAMILTON
..............who......... 1801 a..................................... Also the above Alexan.......(a)m....n who departed this life th..2th Augut. 1810 aged 82 year.. Also his wife Martha Hamilton who departed this life the 21st of Decemr. 1810 aged 72 years.

[Alexander Hamilton, shoemaker, of the Town/Bank, was made a freeman in 1807.]

HAMILTON
[Celtic cross of portland stone.] 1883. In memory of Revd. George Hamilton died 8th November 1817 aged 49 years. Ann CAMPBELL, his widow, died 11th May 1853 aged 71 years. James Hamilton, Knt. their son, born 26th August 1815, died 26th October 1882.

[The will of Sir James Hamilton, late of Bangor, county Down, Knight, who died 26 October 1882 at same place, was proved at Belfast 17 January 1883 by William Stark Hamilton, James Napier Hamilton and Thomas Sinclair, all of Belfast, merchants, three of the executors. Effects £104,267 13s. 8d.]

HAMILT(ON)
[Next to William Hamilton d. 1857.] Sacred (to the) memory (of J)ohn Hamilt(on) ...departed .... October 18(5. aged 75 years.) Erected (by his ...i.ing) w(idow Rose (Hamilton who died ....6 years. Mark(the perfect man and behold the up)right: for the end of that man is pea(ce. Psalm X)XXVII, 37.

HAMILTON
Erected by William Hamilton in memory of two of his children Henry & Ellen who died in infancy. Also his daughter Isabella who died 2nd April 1853 aged 17 months. Also his daughter Ellen who died 18th February 1857 aged 8 years. Also his son Richard Ware who died 27th Febry. 1861 aged 4 months. Also his son Henry who was drowned 2nd June 1871 at Darien, South America, on his way home aged 28 years. Also his grandson Henry Hamilton who died 22nd March 1872 aged 6 months. Also his beloved wife Isabella who died 30th March 1880 aged 61 years. Also the above William Hamilton who died on the 25 September 1880 aged 65 years. [Continued on reverse of stone] Also the burying place of W(ill...) H....... w........ in memory of (his w....) N.....y Mary who .... on .... (Mar) ....6....(s) Henry who (died on) 1(6th) Janry. 187(.) ..d 1....... (3 months) Elizabeth (who died 1(6th) Oct(ober 18)77 aged 3 months.

[The will of William Hamilton, late of Carrickfergus, merchant, who died 25 September 1880 at same place, was proved at Belfast 5 November 1880 by the oaths of Catherine Gillespie (wife of Robert Gillespie of Market Place, Carrickfergus, merchant) and David Taggart, M.D., of Governor's Place, the executors. Effects under £1,000.]

HAMILTON
Erected by Mary Ann Hamilton in memory of her husband, William Hamilton, who departed this life 6th May 1857 aged 41 years. Here also lie the remains of her daughter Jane wife of James DAVISON who died 8th Decr. 1871 aged 25 years. Also the above-named M.A. Hamilton who died 31st Decr. 1871 aged 54 years. Susan Hamilton who died 29th Sept. 1922 aged 79 years.

HAMILTON
[Slate in sandstone frame now laid flat.] Erected by William Hamilton in memory of his wife Catherine Jane who departed this life 18th January ..... aged 26 years.

The a(bove n)amed William Hamilton died at Luberlady, Carrickfergus 28th May 1872. Here lies also Ellen Antonia McBRINN who died 8th June 1903 aged 18 years, daughter of Mrs Annie McBrinn, widow of the above. Also Alexander Kirk Hamilton, only son of above, died 23rd Sep. 1932 aged 66 years: interred at Brighton.

[The will of William Hamilton, late of Lubberlady, Carrickfergus, merchant, who died 28 May 1872 at same place, was proved at Belfast 26 July 1872 by the oaths of Anne Hamilton, widow and David Pasley, bank manager, both of Carrickfergus aforesaid, two of the executors. Effects under £2,000.]

HAMILTON
[Cast iron plaque.] The family burying ground of James Hamilton, 1894.

HAMILTON
[Loose and cracked iron plaque.] The family burying ground of John Hamilt(on) 1902.

HAMILTON
[Polished granite pillar.] Erected in memory of Joseph Hamilton. Loughview, who died 15th January 1906. [Mason:-] McNally, Belfast.

HAMILTON
See GIRVAN, JUNKIN and MILLAR

(HANLY)
[Next to stone erected by Archibald Magee.] H(ere) lies the body of Jo(hn Hanly) who departed this life March (2)0 180(7) aged children) (R)obert, Ann, William .... John & Hugh .... abovenamed John .... Ma... 1775 died Sept. 4 ....

[John Hanly, linen weaver, of the West Division, was made a freeman in 1787.]

HANLY
[Recorded in McCrum ed. of McSkimin: *History and Antiquities of Carrickfergus* (1909), p. 187. Mural tablet of white marble in black frame mounted on east wall of south transept.] Sacred to the memory of Robert Hanly who lived esteemed and died regretted May 1t. 1831. This monument was erected by Lord George A. HILL, representative for Carrickfergus, as a memorial of his respect and regard.

[Robert Hanly, linen weaver, of the West Division was made a freeman in 1787. At the time of his death he was election agent for Lord George Hill (chosen to represent the borough of Carrickfergus in 1830 and 1831).]

HANLY
See WILSON

HANNA
[Polished marble with surround, lead lettering.] Erected in loving memory of James G. Hanna, Armagh, beloved husband of Mary Dorman Hanna, died 21st March 1941 aged 77 years. Also the above Mary Dorman Hanna died 11th May 1954 aged 91 years. [Mason:-] Hart, Carnmoney.

HARRISON
Erected by Sara Hawthorn in loving memory of her mother Sally Harrison died 20th Feby. 1874 aged 65 years. Her father George Harrison died 20th Feby. 1880 aged 72 years. Also her husband James Hawthorn died 10th June 1898 aged 56 years. And their infant son George H. Hawthorn died 26th Jany. 1882. Also Sara H. COE (nee LAIRD) died 24th January 1963, beloved mother of Barbara and Mollye. [Mason:-] Jenkins.

[The will, with three codicils, of George Harrison, late of Carrickfergus, builder, who died 27 February 1880 at same place, was proved at Belfast 5 May 1880 by the oath of Sarah Hawthorne, wife of James Hawthorne of Carrickfergus, gentleman, one of the executors. Effects under £1,000.]

HARVEY
[Laid flat.] Erected by Ann Harvey in memory of her husband James Harvey who died 1st April 1848 aged 42 years. Also their son Joseph who died 12th Dec. 1857 aged 23 years. Also the above-named Ann Harvey who died 29th Decr. 1869 aged 62 years.

HARVEY
[Polished granite.] Harvey. Until the day break.

HARVEY
See FAIRFOOT and MILLIKEN

HAWTHORN
See HARRISON

HAY
[Facing west door.] Erected by E(li)zabeth (Ha)y in (memory of S)amu(el) H(ay) who d(eparted t(his (life) Febru(ry) the 10th 18.. in th(e .... year of his age). Also 6 of his children. Also Samuel Hay Junr. died Novr. 28th 1833 AE 24 years.
[Samuel Hay, weighmaster, of the Town, was made a freeman in 1807.]

HAY
[Badly worn sandstone near south perimeter wall, south-east of south transept.]
.... Samuel (&) Eleanor Hay W..............................
s...........11.........ch..(an)..................................Ann Jane Hay.......... June (187)9. [On back of stone.] Be ye also ready, for in such an hour as you think not ......

HAY
See VINT

HAYS
Erected by Samuel & Wm. Hays in memory of their father Samuel Hays who died 14th January 1855 aged 40 years. Also their sister Isabella who died 4th February 1855 aged 2 years and 4 months. And their aunt Margaret Hays who died 12th November 1871 aged 64 years. Also their aunt Maryann Hays who died 11th March 1872 aged 67 years.

HENDERSON
See EVERARD

HERDMAN
[White marble facing west beside north boundary wall.] In memory of Thomas Herdman, West Division, Carrickfergus, died April 1848 aged 95 years. Also his grand-daughter Agnes Hunter STUART died 15 June 1886 aged 65 years.
[Thomas Herdman, farmer, of West Division, was made a freeman in 1787.]

HERDMAN
Erected by William Herdman in memory of his beloved wife Esther who departed this life the .... April 1866 aged 69 years.

HIGGINSON
[Inside Legg vault.] In this vault have been interred the remains of Captain Philip Higginson and Eleanor TALBOT his wife, the latter died in 1783 aged 96 years. Anthony HULL died the 23rd June 1789 aged 70 years. Alice his wife, daughter of Philip Higginson and Eleanor Talbot aforesaid, died the 2nd November 1791 aged 62 years. Henry Hull their son died 15th January 1821 aged 53 years. John LEGG died 23rd June 1831 aged 84 years. Mary Hull, relict of Thomas Legg and daughter of Anthony Hull and Alice Higginson, died 18 January 1832 aged 68 years. Alice Hull, relict of the above named John Legg and also daughter of Anthony Hull and Alice Higginson, died 6th July 1860 aged 92 years.
[Anthony Hull, gentleman, of the Town, was made a freeman in 1787. John Legg, farmer, of Scotch Quarter, was made a freeman in 1785.]

Letters of administration with the will annexed, of the personal estate of Alice Legg, late of Carrickfergus, widow, who died 6 July 1860 at same place, were granted at Belfast, 11 September 1868 to Elizabeth Rowan, wife of Edward Rowan of Carrickfergus, Esquire, the daughter and one of the next of kin. Effects under £300.]

HILDIGE
Sacred to the memory of Mary Hildige, who died 5th Nov. 1886 "Blessed is he that considereth the poor". Also her grand-son James BURROWS, who died in infancy.

[The will of Mary Hildige, late of Carrickfergus, county of the town of Carrickfergus, widow, who died 5 November 1886 at same place, was proved at Belfast 17 January 1887 by Harriett Jane Hildige of Edenderry, Portadown, county Armagh, spinster, the sole executrix. Effects £4,807. 14s. 1d.

Mary Hildige was the daughter of James Graham, a Dublin architect, and widow of William Hildige.]

HILDITCH
[Sandstone laid flat.] (Erected) to the memory of (Th)omas (Hilditch who de)par(ted t)his life t(he 17th ....) aged 53 y(ear)s. Also (his daughter) Maryanne Hilditch w(ho depart)ed this life the 29th June 1824 aged 19 years. Also William Hilditch, son to the abovenamed Thomas Hilditch, died Augt. 1 1847 aged 42 years. Also William Hilditch junr., son to the last named William Hilditch, died June 8 1856 aged 23 years. Also Thomas Hilditch, son of the .... Thomas Hilditch, died ....d (4)9 years. Also Mary ....
first named Thomas .... Augt. 6 1859 aged 82 years. Also Janet, daughter of the first named Thomas Hilditch, died at Larne April 22nd 1871 aged 61 years.

[Letters of administration with the will annexed of the personal estate of Janet Hilditch, late of Larne, county Antrim, spinster, who died 22 April 1871 at same place, were granted at the Principal Registry 17 November 1871 to Maria Alexander, wife of Thomas Alexander of Killester near Raheny, county Dublin, M.D., one of the residuary legatees. Effects under £500.]

HILDITCH
[White marble with lead lettering in the same plot as foregoing.] Erected to the memory of Thomas Hilditch who died 17th May 1821 aged 53 years. His daughter Mary Ann died 29th June 1824 aged 19 years. His son William died 1st August 1847 aged 42 years. His grandson William Hilditch Junr., son of William, died 8th June 1856 aged 23 years. His son Thomas died 3rd August 1857 aged 49 years. His wife Mary died 6th August 1859 aged 82 years. His daughter Janet died at Larne 22nd April 1871 aged 61 years.

HILL
[Recorded in McCrum ed. of McSkimin: *History and Antiquities of Carrickfergus* (1909), p. 186, but the tablet was lost before this.] Here lyeth ye body of Elizabeth Hill who departed this life ye 9th of Decb. 1726 aged 50 years. Here also lyeth ye body of Ann her daughter who departed ye 10th of Novb. 1720 aged 22 years.

HILL
[Brass plate on display cabinet containing Book of Kells facsimile.] To the glory of God and in memory of Arthur Hill, diocesan lay reader, select vestry man and choir member, died 8th July 1980. The gift of his family.

HILL
See BIRD, HANLY and JACK

HILTON
[Cast iron plaque, loose, against perimeter wall.] Erected by Robert Hilton in memory of his father, mother, brother & sisters whose remains are interred here 1873. [Cast by:-] Millfield Foundry, Belfast.

HIND
See CARREY

HOLMES
[Soft grey stone with shallow lettering.] Erected (by) John Holmes of Carrickfergus .... of his wife Mar(g....t who died the 24..) of (April 1828) aged (51 years ....) his d(aughter A..) M(ary...) died (1st) May 18(..) aged 2(.) y(ears. Margaret) who died 2 (of Aug. 18.8 ...)d 1(8) years. And Elizabeth died on the 20 April 1829 (a)e 2(5) years.

HOLMES
Here lies the body (of) Elizabeth Holmes who died .... March 1810 aged 19 years. Also her grandson William John (CON)OLLY who died 20th June 1837 aged 6 years. Edward McMAW died 21st June 1872 aged 74 years. Also his grandson Edward James McMaw died 21st April 1877 aged 8 months.

HOLMES
Erected to the memory of John Holmes who departed this life on the 9th (day) of June 1855 aged 50 years. Also his wife Mary and daughter Sarah.

HOLMES
See PENNY

HOPPER
See ROWAN

HORSBOROUGH
See GORDON and GORMAN

HOUARD
Erected by Ellen JINKINS in memory of her father Jeremiah Houard who died 15th March 1824. Also her mother Ellen Houard who died 22nd March 1824. Also her sister Elenor Houard who died 15th April 1809 aged 2 years. Also her brother Jeremiah Houard who died 22nd May 1809 aged 7 years.
[Jeremiah Howard, labourer, of the Town, was made a freeman in 1813.]

HULL
[Thin white marble, probably of mid-twentieth century.] H. Hull.

HULL
See HIGGINSON

HUMPHRY
[Decorated with compass and square.] Erected by David Humphry in memory of his beloved brother John who departed this life 11th June 1858 aged 24 years.

HUNTER
[Slate.] Erected by Samuel Hunter in memory of his beloved wife Elizabeth Hunter who died Feby. 1st 1875 aged 65 years. Also the above named Samuel Hunter who died Feby. 14th 1883 aged 83 years. Also Thomas Hunter who died 18th May 1920 aged 71 years.

HUNTER
[Cast iron plaque near south perimeter wall.] The family burying ground of Jane Hunter. 408

HUNTER
[Polished granite next to foregoing.] In memory of our parents. William Alexander died 22nd June 1948. His wife Jane nee SIMMS died 5th February 1984. Samuel Simms, father of above Jane nee Simms, died 23rd October 1931 aged 89 years. At rest.

HUSTON
[Polished granite against west perimeter wall.] The burying place of John Huston, formerly LOGAN. Here lie the remains of William Huston who died 1st March

1881 aged 9 years. The above-named John Huston who died 30th July 1887 aged 75 years. His brother James Huston who died 11th July 1895 aged 79 years. Mary, wife of above John Huston, who died 4th Sepr. 1912 aged 80 years. John Huston, eldest son of John and Mary Huston, who died 9th April 1941 aged 78 years. His wife Margaret "Maggie" died 17th August 1949.

[The will of John Huston, late of Carrickfergus, farmer, who died 30 July 1887 at same place, was proved at Belfast 23 September 1887 by John Huston of Middle Division and Robert Hart of Bellahill, county Antrim, farmers, the executors. Effects £421. 4s. 0d.

In 1878 this grave was sold by Hugh Logan to John Huston complete with the headstone erected by his father, William Logan, in 1828. As a condition of the sale John Huston agreed to perpetuate the name of Logan on the plot. He left his farm in the Middle Division to his eldest son John and his farm in N.E. Division to Samuel. The other surviving children were Jane, Mary, James, Hugh and Thomas.]

INGRAM

Erected by James Ingram in memory of his father Percival Ingram who departed this life on the 23rd of February 1848 aged 57 years. Also his mother Elizabeth Ingram who departed this life on the 3rd August 1849 aged 55 years. Also Martha Ingram who died 3rd June 1858 aged 25 years. Also the above James Ingram who died 12th July 1869 aged 53 years. Also his brother Captain Percival Ingram who died at sea 19th February 18(..) aged 43 years.

[The will of James Ingram, late of Joymount Bank, Carrickfergus, racket court and billiard room proprietor, who died 28 July 1869 at Carrickfergus, was proved at Belfast 20 September 1869 by the oath of Percival Ingram of Carrickfergus, master mariner, the sole executor. Effects under £1,000.

The will of Percival Ingram, late of Carrickfergus, master mariner, who died 19 February 1871 at sea, was proved at Belfast 19 April 1871 by the oaths of James Miscampbell, tailor, and Charles Stewart, pawnbroker, both of Carrickfergus, the executors. Deceased died domiciled in Ireland. Effects in the U.K. under £1,000.]

IRWIN

Sacred to conjugal and parental affection. Below repose in kindred dust the ashes of Ann Irwin, wife of James Irwin, who died December 12th 1832 aged 48 years. Also the remains of their much lamented daughter Eliza who died March 12th 1833 aged 17 years. Here also are deposited the remains of the above named James Irwin who departed this life the 23rd June 1836 aged 65 years.

[James Irwin, carman, of the Town, was made a freeman in 1813.]

JACK

Erected by John Jack of this town in memory of his mother Ann Jack who departed this life August 24th 1864 aged 64 years. Also his father John and brother Robert P. Jack who were drowned near the harbour of Portrush on Decr. 3rd 1863, the former aged 65 and the latter 33 years. Also are interred in this graveyard his 3 sons who died infants. Also the above named John Jack, master mariner, died 13th Oct. 1886. Also his daughter Agnes DUFF died 27th May 1925.

JACK

In loving memory of John Jack died 7th July 1896 aged 82 years. Also his sons: William died at Calcutta aged 20 years. Robert died at New York aged 48 years. David died at C.fergus aged 1 year. David died at Rio De Janeiro aged 33 years. Alexander died at Rio De Janeiro aged 22 years. James died at C.fergus aged 4 years. Agnes Jack died 10th July 1899 aged 79 years. John drowned in Belfast Lough 25th Feby. 1910 aged 60 years. Thomas SHAW died 9th May 1911 aged 51 years. Ellen Jack, died 16th May 1929 aged 72 years. "Blessed are the dead that die in the Lord"

[Thomas Shaw, blacksmith, of the North East Division, was made a freeman in 1807.]

JACK
[Slate.] The burying ground of John Jack Millicent HILL his wife who died March 15th 1904 aged 74 years. Marianne Gordon Jack died 23rd May 1918.

JACK
See McFERRAN and McGIFFIN

JENKINS
[Polished pink granite.] In memoriam Peter Jenkins who died 1858 aged 52 years. His son Robert who died 1860 aged 19 years. His wife Margaret who died 1877 aged 74 years. Their daughter Margaret who died 1879 aged 40 years. Their son William who died 1895 aged 59 years. Their daughter Lydia ANDERSON who died 1907 aged 78 years.

[The will of Peter Jenkins, late of Carrickfergus in the county of the town of Carrickfergus, publican, painter and glazier, who died 5 May 1858 at Carrickfergus, was proved at Belfast 30 June 1858 by the oath of Margaret Jenkins of same place, widow, the sole executrix. Effects under £200.]

JENKINS
See JUNKIN

JINKINS
See HOUARD

JOHNS
Erected by Alexander Johns in memory of an infant son who died 25th March 1814. His daughter Margaret who died 24th July 1819 aged 4 months. His son Henry (In)cledon who died 27th January 1825 aged 6 months and Henry C. Ellis Johns who died 13th April 1837 aged 6 months. And his beloved wife Emma who died 9th March 18(5)7 aged 63 years. Here also was buried the abovenamed Alexander Johns who died 13th May 1866 aged 81 years.

[The will of Alexander Johns, late of Carrickfergus, in the county of the town of Carrickfergus, bank manager, who died 13 May 1866, was proved at Belfast 11 June 1866 by the oaths of William Johns, solicitor, and Alexander Johns, bank director, both of Belfast in the county of Antrim, the executors. Effects under £800.

Alexander Johns (1784/5-1866) was storekeeper in the Castle and must also lived for some time in Dublin but was superannuated in 1834. He became the first manager of the Carrickfergus branch of the Northern Bank. His drawings of antiquities were used to illustrate McSkimin's *History*. He married Emma French and had at least 6 sons and 5 daughters:-

1. Infant, died in 1814.
2. The Rev. Bennett William Johns (or Jones) was born in Dublin in 1815/6, entered T.C.D. in 1831 and granted B.A. in 1837. He was curate of Carrickfergus 1840-41.
3. William Johns (1817/8-1898), barrister and solicitor, of Joymount Court. This large town house with extensive gardens was later used for the Technical College but was demolished after it was vacated in 1967. He served as chairman of the Municipal Commissioners. He married firstly Mary Catherine Goddard (d.1863), daughter of Robert Goddard of Joymount Court. He remarried and had at least 4 sons and 2 daughters:-
    1. Henry Incledon Johns, J.P., of Ardeen, Antrim Road, Belfast was born on 19th April 1860, B.A., T.C.D., solicitor, Director of Belfast Banking Company, Treasurer of the City of Belfast.
    2. Bennett William Johns (1861/2-1899), civil service in Sydney, N.S.W.
    3. Tyndall Stuart Johns (1868-1947), solicitor.
    4. Christopher Johns, practised medicine in Assam, India
    5. Emma Louise married George Henry Bayly C.E., son of Richard Uniacke Bayly of Ballyre, Co. Cork in 1885.

Marble bust of Alexander Johns, J.P. (1784-1866) by Albert Bruce Joy, photograph reproduced by kind permission of the Trustees of the Ulster Museum

4. Margaret Johns (1819-1819)
5. Anne Catherine (1820-1888) married Rev. J.L. Darby, Acton.
6. Alexander Johns (b.1822/3), B.A., T.C.D. 1842, solicitor, director of the Belfast Banking Company from 1860, President of the Belfast Chamber of Commerce 1872 and 1878. He had at least 2 sons:-

   1. Alexander John was born in 1853.
   2. Sir William Arthur Johns was born in 1858, educated at Uppingham and the R.I.E. College, Cooper's Hill, and entered the Indian Public Works Department in 1880. He was a very successful railway engineer in India and shortly after his retirement in 1914 was knighted and later created C.B. He died while visiting the Andrews family in Comber.
   3. Emma Margaret married Edward Leslie Pooler M.D. of Newtownards on 26 April 1886
   4. Harriet Anne Frances (1870-1871)

7. Henry Incledon Johns (1824-1825)
8. Harriett French Johns (1824/5-1888)
9. Maria Noy Johns (1828-1916)
10. Marianne Stuart Johns (1829/30-1894)
11. Henry C Ellis Johns (1836-1837)
12. Thomas Digby Johns, solicitor, of Rosebrook, town clerk of Carrickfergus 1865-85, died in 1893 leaving 4 children:-

    1. Alexander Digby Johns (1865/6-1894)
    2. Bessie French Johns (1869/70-1895)
    3. Mary Catherine married William Edward Head of Derrylahan Park, Co Tipperary, on 17 Aug. 1886
    4. Edward H. Johns, B.L.

See McCrum ed. of McSkimin: *History and Antiquities of Carrickfergus* (1909); Young and Pike: *Belfast and the Province of Ulster* (1909); *Carrickfergus Advertiser*, 24 Nov. 1893 and 7 June 1918; Burtchaell and Sadleir: *Alumni Dublinenses* (1924); Chambers: *Faces of Change*; Leslie: *Clergy of Connor* (1993).]

JOHNS

[Recorded in McCrum ed. of McSkimin: *History and Antiquities of Carrickfergus* (1909), p.193. Tablet on chancel wall in form of sarcophagus with funeral urn in niche above.] In memory of the Revd. Bennett W. Johns, curate of Carrickfergus, through divine grace a shining model of a Christian pastor and a meek and lowly servant of the Lord Jesus Christ. This monument is raised by his brethern in the ministry and a sorrowing flock to record for a perpetual example the faith and integrity of a man of God whose animated zeal was not less powerful to win souls than his gentleness and loving kindness to retain them. In the inscrutable Providence of the Most High His Faithful servant was called from His blessed labours whilst his usefulness was full of promise. Attacked by malignant fever in Dublin, he died 27th May 1841 in the second year of his honoured ministry and 25th of his age. The will of God be done.

JOHNS

[Recorded in McCrum ed. of McSkimin: *History and Antiquities of Carrickfergus* (1909), p.189. Window in north wall of chancel with floral and geometric design.] In memory of Alexander Johns who died 13th May 1866. And of Emma his wife who died 9th March 1857. [Window by:-] Mayer & Co. of Munich and London, 70 Grosvenor St.

JOHNS

[Recorded in McCrum ed. of McSkimin: *History and Antiquities of Carrickfergus* (1909), p.193. Brass plaque on north wall of chancel with arms:- per pale: ermine, a chevron engrailed between three castles impaling on a chevron between three garbs, a naval crown and two anchors, in the chief point a medal of the Nile.

Crest:- a centaur regardant. Motto:- Carpe diem.] To the glory of God and in loving memory of William Johns of Joymount Court, Carrickfergus, who died March 26th 1898 aged 80 years. [Engraved by:-] Jones & Willis.

[Probate of the will of William Johns, late of Joymount Court, Carrickfergus, solicitor, who died 26 March 1898, granted at Belfast 20 February 1899 to Mary C. Johns of Joymount Court, Carrickfergus, widow. Effects £9,294 15s. 10d.]

JOHNS
[Recorded with the above, p.193.] To the glory of God and in loving memory of Bennett Wm. Johns, second son of the late William Johns of Joymount Court, Carrickfergus, died at Sydney, N.S.W., 25th July 1899 aged 37 years.

JOHNS
[Above foregoing and below Rev. B.W. Johns.] To the glory of God and in loving memory of Tyndall Stuart Johns, son of William Johns of Joymount Court, born 13th March 1868, died 7th February 1947.

JOHNSTON
[Beside Legg vault.] Erected by Elizabeth Johnston to the memory of her affectionate husband Robert Johnston, Gunner R.N., who departed this life 1804 aged 60 years. The said Elizabeth Johnston died April 1847 aged 89 years. Also Charles, son of the above parents, died June 1837 aged 45 years.

JOHNSTON
See BRAVINGTON

JOHNSTONE
[Polished granite stone in old sandstone plinth.] In loving memory of Robert Johnstone who died 21st January 1869 aged 82 years. And his wife Mary, who died 28th August 1868 aged 76 years. Erected by their sons R. and C. Johnstone. Also Margaret, wife of R. Johnstone, who died 1st January 1905 aged 86 years. Robert Johnstone who died 11th April 1916 aged 96 years.

[The will of Robert Johnston, late of Silverstream, Carrickfergus, farmer, who died 19 January 1869 at same place, was proved at Belfast 5 February 1869 by the oath of Charles Johnston of Silverstream, farmer, the sole executor. Effects under £1,500.]

JOHNSTONE
[Gothic stone fallen face downward beside Legg vault.] In memory of Thomas Johnstone died 14th October 1872 aged 72 years. Also his wife Eleanor who died 30th September 1879 aged 70 years. And Robert, eldest son of above, who died 5th June 1895 aged 63 years. And their daughter Isabella died 9th Decr. 1920. [Mason:-] Geo. Rankin, 108 York St., Belfast.

[Letters of administration of the personal estate of Robert Johnstone, late of Whinfield, Greenisland, county of the town of Carrickfergus, farmer, who died 3 June 1895 at same place, were granted at Belfast 10 July 1895 to Francis Johnstone of Greenisland, stockbroker, the brother. Effects £443. 15s. 9d.]

JOHNSTONE
See LYNN and McCREVEY

JONES
In loving memory of Mary Ann Jones who died 29th Sep. 1875 aged 58 years. Her husband Alexander Jones who died 5th May 1885 aged 84 years. Their daughter Ellen KING who died 15th March 1903 aged 62 years. Their daughter Mary Ann Jones who died 26th Jany. 1933 aged 80 years.

JONES
[Next to foregoing.] Erected by Alexander Jones in loving memory of his son Alexander died June 14th 1888 aged 5 years. His daughter Mary Ann Pearson died March 15th 1890 aged 4 months. His step-daughter Sarah Jane (Janie) RODGERS

died August 13th 1913 aged 36 years. The above-named Alexander Jones died 8th May 1919 aged 71 years. His wife Elizabeth died 12th November 1924 aged 74 years.

[Robert, eldest son of Alexander Jones, died 19 March 1886 at 456 West 27th Street, New York. See *Carrickfergus Advertiser*, 9 April 1886.]

JUNKIN
[Beside Craig, Glen Park.] Here lyeth the body of William Junkin who died Janry. ye 7th 1776 aged 63 yrs.

JUNKIN
[Original inscription was plastered and stone reversed for re-use.] Erected by George Junkin in memory of his deceased parents viz (Ann) Junkin who died 30d. July 17(92) AE 42 years. And David Junkin who died 1(4th Novr.) 1808 aged (.3) years. Also said (George Junkin died 1(5)th A(ugt.) 1823 aged (3)6 years. Also (C....ia) McCONNELL who died (4th) F(eb. 1834) aged 70 years. [And inscribed on the other side of the stone:-] In memory of Samuel McConnell died Augt. 1845 aged 40 years. And his wife Annie MILLIKEN died April 1871 aged 68 years. And their nephew John Milliken son of Samuel and Jane Milliken died 16th March 1931 aged 84 years.

JUNKIN/JENKINS
[Flaking badly.] Erected (by) William (Jun)kin (in memory of his dau)g(hte)r Mary .... (t)cy in 1826. (Al.........) son William (who departed this) li(fe) 10th March 1854 aged 2(6) years. ..... his daughter Ellen who (died) 27th June 1863 aged 40 years. (Also) his wife Mary Junkin who died 6th May 1875 aged 77 years. The above-named William Junkin died 26th Sept. 1878 aged 88 years. Also his grand-son William Junkin who died 6th Sept. 1885 aged 6 years. Also his daughter Mary who died 27th Sept. 1885 aged 53 years. Also his daughter-in-law Mary Jenkins who died 7th Sept. 1916 aged 71 years. [A bronze plaque continues:-] William 1887-1969. Jane HAMILTON 1898-1975. For ever in our thoughts.

KAIN
[Sandstone laid flat in front of James McFerran d. 1863] Here lyeth ... body of Ellean.. Kain who depart.. this life 2d Feby. 178(.) aged 65 years. Als(o) Elleanor HAGGAN who departed this life 1st Augt. 1800 aged 17 years.

KANE
[Twin stones with railings, one has no legible inscription.] Erected by William CRAIG in memory of his uncle John Kane, Turf Lodge, Mayor of Belfast, died 8th May 1807. Also above named William Craig died 15th December 1865. Also his wife Agnes died 15th November 1885. Also their sons: Robert died 22nd September 1912, interred in Bristol; James, died 18th September 1913, interred in Portland U.S.A. Also his son-in-law William GAW died 5th June 1917. Also his daughter Margaret Ann, wife of above named William Gaw, died 14th May 1937. Anna daughter of the above William and Margaret Ann Gaw, died 9th January 1945.

[The will of William Craig, late of Carrickfergus, spirit dealer, who died 13 December 1865 at same place, was proved at Belfast 18 January 1866 by the oaths of David Gray, merchant, and Alexander Hart, farmer, both of Carrickfergus, the executors. Effects under £300.]

KARR
[Slate.] Erected by John Karr.

KELLY
See BELL

KENNEDY
[Behind Skelton stone.] Erected to the memory of Roger Kennedy who departed this life the 21st February 182(3) aged 66 years. He was a loving husband and indulgent father.

KENNEDY
   See HAGAN

KERR
   Erected to the memory of Robert Kerr who died 11th Decr. 1861 aged 61 years. Also his wife Margaret Kerr, who died 10th Feby. 1837 aged 35 years. And his daughter Jane Kerr who died 17th April 1831 aged 14 months.

KERR
   [Polished granite.] In memoriam David Kerr, born 2nd Feb. 1836, died 2nd Feb. 1896. His wife Sarah BAIRD died 19th April 1927. Their children: Thomas Wheeler died 28th July 1873. Sarah died 27th November 1886. James Thomas lost at sea off Cape Horn 14th July 1898. William died 2nd February 1907. Mary Catherine died 23rd June 1957. Agnes died 27th February 1962.

   [The will of David Kerr, late of West Street, Carrickfergus, county of the town of Carrickfergus, grocer, who died 2 February 1896, was proved at Belfast 24 April 1896 by Sarah Kerr of West Street, Carrickfergus, widow, the sole executrix. Effects £472.]

KERR
   In loving memory of my dear husband Wilson Kerr, Lamorna, Greenisland, born 27th July 1879, died 23rd March 1955. Margaret, his wife, born 12th May 1889, died 24th May 1973. David Kerr their son, born 28th Sept. 1926, died London 14th Dec. 1979. Until the day break.

KIDLEY
   In memory of Edward A. Kidley died 29th March 1834 aged 16 years. Reader if thou mournest the extinction of those endearing qualities which entwine themselves round the heart, if thou sorrowest for the untimely death of the child of genius, weep here. Also in memory of Penelope Eliza Kidley died 24th May 1887 and Jane Kidley died 3rd April 1888.

   [Letters of administration of the personal estate of Penelope Eliza Kidley, late of Rocklands, who died 24 May 1887 at same place were granted at Belfast 13 June 1887 to Jane Kidley of Rocklands, Carrickfergus, the sister. Effects £680. 4s. 4d.

   The will of Jane Kidley, late of Rocklands, Carrickfergus, spinster, who died 3 April 1888 at same place, was proved at Belfast 20 June 1888 by Thomas Kidley of Springfield House, Sheffield, county York, M.D., the sole executor. Effects £6,092. 6s. 5d.]

KIDLEY
   [Recorded in McCrum ed. of McSkimin: *History and Antiquities of Carrickfergus* (1909), p.191. Plain marble tablet mounted on south wall of chancel.] Sacred to the memory of John Edward Kidley M.D. who departed this life 6th April 1852 and Frances Anne Kidley who departed this life 17th June 1852, son and daughter of John Kidley of Fownhope, Herefordshire, England. Also Jane MAXWELL, relict of Surgeon Maxwell, who departed this life 27th December 1844. Also of Sarah Eliza Kidley, relict of John Kidley, Esq. of Fownhope, Herefordshire who departed this life 1st January 1855.

KING
   See JONES

KINKAID
   Here ly(eth th)e remains of Na(nc)....min who depart.........ife May 23rd 1820 a...... years. Also the remains of Elizabeth Kinkaid, daughter of John Kinkaid, who departed this life November 15th 1820 aged 9 years. We make the grave our bed and then are gone.

KIRK
   Here li(et)h the body of Elizabeth K(ir)k who d(ep)art(ed this l)ife Nov....... 17.. aged (8 years). [Vase in front:-] McCOY 1974.

KIRK
[A stele of white marble surmounted by a wheeled cross. Ornaments in high relief contrast with the shallow lettering only read with difficulty. The west side has arms:- a crosier and sword saltireways, on a chief a thistle (the fine vertical lines on the field probably indicate the conventional hatching to represent red.) Crest:- a crosier and sword saltireways. Motto:- Optimum quod primum.] Sacred to the memory of Sir William Kirk (of Thornfield,) Carrickfergus, who died 1st June 18(19) aged (77 years) [The supposed Biblical text that follows is unreadable. The east side also has arms:- quarterly, in the first and fourth, a crosier and sword saltireways, on a chief a thistle; second and third, three lions statant guardant. Crest: a crosier and sword saltireways. Motto: Optimum quod primum.] Sacred to the memory and the affectionate remembrance of Ellen Kirk of Thornfield, Carrickfergus, who died 7th November 1853 aged 51 years and of her husband Peter Kirk, esquire, D.L., son of Sir William Kirk and for many years Member of Parliament for the Borough of Carrickfergus, who died 15(th) November 1856 aged 56 years. "Her children arise up and call her blessed" (Prov. XXXI, 28v.) "He that believeth in me though he were dead yet shall he live" St. John XI, 25 v. [North side decorated with a laurel wreath] Sacred to the memory of William, eldest son of Peter and Ellen Kirk who died 1(3th) May 1855 aged 26 years. "Be thou faithful unto death and I will give thee a crown of life." (Rev. 2. XX.) [South side decorated with sword and two military flags.] Sacred to the memory (of Charles) Edmonston Kirk, late captain (1st) Royal Regt., last surviving son of Peter and Ellen Kirk. He served throughout the Crimean Campaign and died 29th July 1857 aged 26 years.

[The will of Eleanor Kirk of Carrickfergus was proved in the Connor Diocesan Court on 11 March 1857. (See Down and Connor Will Book No. 8935).

The will of Charles Edmonston Kirk was proved in the Connor Diocesan Court on 27 November 1857. (See Down and Connor Will Book No. 9093).

Sir William Kirk (1742-1819) was a linen bleacher at Sullatober, Carrickfergus. His parentage is unknown but he may have been a son of Daniel Kirk who owned a brewery in the town in the mid-eighteenth century. Under the patronage of the Donegall family, whose political interest in the constituency he managed for forty years, Kirk entered the ranks of the local gentry. He acquired a sizeable

Kirk arms from the railings round the Celtic cross

estate in the district, built (or improved) the house known as Thornfield which became the family seat (now the site of Carrickfergus Grammar School). He was Port Surveyor and a leading member of the corporation. As mayor for the time being he was knighted when the Lord Lieutenant of Ireland visited the town in 1787. The arms appearing on the Kirk monument were presumably granted at ths time.

Kirk's 'gentrification' was achieved in spite of the open scandal of his private life. In c. 1776 he married well, to Ann Ker, daughter of William Ker, a wealthy Ballymena linen merchant and bleacher, who brought her husband a substantial dowry. It seems likely that she died within a few years of the marriage. Subsequently Kirk established a relationship with Elizabeth Johnstone who was probably a servant at Thornfield. The four children she bore him, Daniel, Eleanor, Elizabeth and Sally, were all acknowledged in his will but nothing more is known of them. Peter Kirk, who inherited the estate, his brother Charles and sisters, Susanna and Frances were the children of another liaison. Their mother, Susanna Edmonstone Gint, was clearly the elderly Sir William's darling. In an election squib of 1808 she was described as 'his faithful Sookey' and Kirk made every effort to ensure post-mortem fidelity. His will stated that she would cease to be a beneficiary 'in case that [she] shall marry or misbehave after my decease'.

Peter Kirk, who was M.P. for Carrickfergus from 1835-47, married Ellen Dalway, daughter of Noah Dalway of Bellahill. Both their sons, William and Charles, died young, two daughters remained unmarried and the third, Anne, became the wife of the Very Rev. George Bull, Dean of Connor and Rector of Carrickfergus. Their descendants took the name Kirk and continued to live at Thornfield until the 1920s. See P.R.O.N.I. Kirk Papers D1255 and D2121; *MOPIA KPATEOMENH ... being a collection of all the addresses, squibs and songs, which appeared before, and at the Carrickfergus midsummer election, 1808.* (Carrickfergus, 1808). See also under North Road Cemetery under BULL and KIRK.]

KIRK
[Celtic cross of pink granite within railings to which is attached a plaque bearing arms:- engrailed, a crosier and sword in saltire, on a chief a Scottish thistle. Crest:- crozier and sword in saltire. Motto:- optimum quod primum.] A.D. 1890. Entrance to vault under footway. Ethel Margaret, wife of George Edmonstone Kirk of Thornfield, youngest twin daughter of James and Sarah Elizabeth SEARIGHT, born April 6: 1862, fell asleep Jan. 21: 1890. Also Agnes Beatrice his second wife died June 24: 1935 aged 64. George Edmonstone Kirk D.L. died and was buried at sea March 23: 1909 aged 50. The Lord is my Shepherd. I shall not want. In peace.

KIRK
[Three light window in west wall of south transept illustrating Christ walking on the water.] Be of good cheer. It is I. Be not afraid. To the glory of God and in loving memory of George Edmonstone Kirk, D.L., of Thornfield, Carrickfergus, who died March 23rd 1909 aged 50 years, while on a voyage home from China & was buried at sea. This window is dedicated by his wife Agnes Beatrice Kirk.

KIRKBRIDE
See LOWE

KIRKPATRICK
[Slate behind vestry]... lyeth ye body ...... Kirkpatrick Qr. master .... of ye 31st Regt. who died No(vr.) the 19th in ye year 1774 aged 37 years.

KIRKWOOD
See SMYTH

LAIRD
[In north-west of graveyard against boundary wall.] Erected by Walter MILLER in memory of his grand mother Martha Laird who died 16th July 1834 aged 70 years. His grand father Samuel Laird who died 1st August 1837 aged 73 years. Also his mother Letitia Miller who died 12th July 1850 aged 58 years.

LAIRD
See HARRISON

LANG
[McSkimin: *History and Antiquities of Carrickfergus* (1811), p.47 - "west end of the church, south wall". McCrum ed., p.182 gives similiar position. Now in floor beneath gallery.] Here lyeth ye body of Richard Lang who departed this life ye 20th of May 1620. Here also lyeth ye body of James Lang who departed ye 7th of October anno 1687. Here also lyeth Letitia his wife who was interrd ye 4th of June 1705, a daughter of John BULWORTHY alderman and twice Mayor of Carrickfergus. Mary 10.

LANG(FO..
[Laid flat outside east window.] Judith ...... daughter... Henry Lang(fo.......) Esqr. obi(it..........)

LARKIN
See APSLEY

LARMOUR
Sacred to the venerable dead. John Larmour who died 4th February 1829 aged 87 years. Ann his wife died 14th December 1825 aged 77 years. Also Jane Larmour, their daughter-in-law, died 11th December 1825 aged 51 years. And her daughter Jane, who died 11th April 1830 aged 16 years. E. WILLIAMSON died 1839.
[John Larmour, baker, of the Town/Bank, was made a freeman in 1785.]

LATIMORE
[Sandstone, possibly of eighteenth century.] The burying ground of Edward (L)at(imor)e.

LATTIMER
[Polished granite.] In memory of Robert Lattimer died 11th August 1846. Margaret Lattimer died 23rd December 1867. Mary Jane their daughter died 20th September 1884.
[Robert Lattimore of the Middle Division, was made a freeman in 1807.]

LATTIMOR
See MARSH

LATTIMORE
In memoriam. John Lattimore, Carrickfergus, died 23rd December 1893 aged 60 years. His son John died 20th June 1878 aged 17 years. His wife Jane SCOTT died 12th September 1905 aged 68 years. His daughter Annie died 12th July 1924 aged 60 years. Also Elizabeth DUNBAR, daughter of Joseph Lattimore, died 2nd June 1922 aged 19 years. Joseph Lattimore, son of the above John Lattimore, died 14th November 1943 aged 77 years. Elizabeth McKEOWN, wife of Joseph Lattimore, died 30th April 1952 aged 81 years.
[Letters of administration of the personal estate of John Lattimore, late of Stoneyford, county Antrim, manager of waterworks, who died 23 December 1893 at same place, were granted at Belfast 8 February 1894 to Jane Lattimore of Cavehill Road, Belfast, the widow. Effects £169. 10s.
John Lattimore had been a stonemason in his younger days like his father William before him. In turn John's eldest son William also trained as a stonemason. John was employed by the Belfast Water Commissioners at Carrickfergus, Stoneyford, and Leathemstown, becoming clerk of works and dying at his residence The Lodge, Stoneyford Waterworks, from where he had attended Magheragall Presbyterian Church. His son Joseph became superintendent at Stoneyford and later (1924-1935) at Woodburn. A brother was Captain Ralph Lattimore. See *Carrickfergus Advertiser*, 30 December 1893; Cameron: Carrick's Pacific Colony in *Carrickfergus and District Historical Journal* 1985; 1:35.]

John Lattimore (1833-1893), reproduced by permission of Robin Cameron

LAVERTY
This stone was erected by John L...... in memory of his m............. who departed this life on .... 1818 aged 50 years. Also his father Felix Laverty who died on the 28th of September 1827 aged 6(4) years. Likewise th(eir) grand son aged (.4).

LAVERTY
[Sandstone beside path.] Erected to the memory of John Laverty, who died 9th Sept. 1862 aged 65 years.

LAVERTY
[Slate next to the above; the painted letters have almost disappeared.] The family burying place of Wm. Laverty.

LAVERTY
[Sandstone north of North transept.] Erected by John Laverty in memory of his mother Ellen Laverty who departed this life 26th October 1879 aged 94 years. The above named John Laverty died 14th December 1894 aged 76 years. (And t)o his daughter Ellen Laverty (wh)o died 10th Octr. 1905 aged 65 years.

LAVERTY
[Celtic cross. Each arm bears one of the symbols of the four gospels. In the centre is the agnus dei. St. Patrick stands with snakes on the shaft.] In memory of Henry Laverty who departed this life 24th Feb. 1896 in the 69th year of his age. Also of his wife Jane Laverty who departed this life 1st June 1898 in the 67th year of her age. This monument has been erected by the sorrowing family in loving memory of their father and mother.
[The will of Henry Laverty, late of 58 Brougham Street and Cambridge Street, Belfast, builder, who died 24 February 1896 at Brougham Street, was proved at Belfast 1 April 1896 by John Laverty and James Laverty, both of Brougham Street, Belfast, builders, two of the executors. Effects £6,827. 15s.]

LAVERTY
[Granite column next to following.] Erected by William Laverty in memory of his son William Henry Laverty, born 18th August 1906, died 5th February 1909. Also the above named William Laverty, born 9th Feb. 1864, died 26th March 1926. Maria, wife of Wm. Laverty, born 27th May 1877, died 17th September 1934. Johnston MONTGOMERY, born 25th August 1889, died 26th October 1945. "For if we believe that Jesus died and rose again even so them also which sleep in Jesus will God bring with him". 1st Thessalonians, 4th chapter, verse 14. Marie Byrtt ROSS, Farmhill, Carrickfergus, died suddenly 24th April 1968, wife of John F. Ross.

LAVERTY
[Granite obelisk.] Erected to the memory of John Laverty, builder, son of the late Henry Laverty, builder, of Carrickfergus and Belfast, who departed this life July 5th 1909 in his 53rd year. Also his daughter Sarah E. Laverty died 29th March 1955. In loving memory of Hannah Margaret, beloved wife of John Laverty, born 10th October 1888, died 12th March 1963. Her husband John died 17th December 1968.

LAVERTY
[Decorated Celtic cross.] Erected in loving memory of James Laverty, born 25th December 1857, died 26th October 1923. And Martha Laverty, born 7th November 1873, died 8th June 1924. Emily F. Laverty, born 14th Feb. 1869, died 7th Feb. 1938. Robert Laverty, born 29th June 1871, died 30th October 1934.

LAVERTY
[Cast iron plaque on railed enclosure outside baptistry.] The family burying place of Henry Laverty [Sandstone plaque laid in enclosure.] The burial ground of Henry Laverty. Closed 1926.

Pillar and Celtic cross to Laverty family

LAWRENCE

[In Legg vault.] Sacred to the memory of Edward Lawrence who departed this life 23rd July 1865 aged 62 years. Also of Catherine Maria, his wife, who died 14th January 1878 aged 77 years. And of James Henry, their son, who died 15th July 1867 aged 25 years. And of Charlotte TURPIN, their daughter, who died 1st Sep. 1903 aged 66 years.

LEE

[On back of McILWRATH stone.] (Er)ec(ted) by Jean Lee in the Scotch Qua(rter) to the memory of her parents: viz Clements Lee, shoemaker, who departed this life 10th Sept. 1780 aged 7(0) years and Mary Lee her mother who departed this life 1(3)th March 1788 aged 80 years. Also Thomas Lee her brother who departed this life 8th April 1764 aged 16 years and ..... [continued below ground level.]

LEE

Here lieth the body of Isaac Lee who departed this life the 29th day of January 1793 aged 39 years. Also John Lee, nephew to said Isaac Lee, who departed this life the 31st day of August 1793 aged 3 years.

LEE

See McILWRATH

LEGG

[Ornamented slate set into western boundary wall.] Sacred to the memory of the children of John and Eliza Legg of this town. Joseph died 17th Septr. 1846 aged 3 years. Eliza [died] 3rd March 1848 [aged] 2 years. "They died for Adam sinned, they live for Jesus died". John Legg, born 18th Feby. 1816, died 3rd Feby. 1884 aged 68 years. Eliza Legg, born 1816, died 1898. And their daughter Jane, born 1844, died 1906. Also their son Matthew, born 18th May 1849, died 6th April 1919. And their daughter Margaret, born 9th June 1847, died 10th May 1929.

[The will of Eliza Legg, late of Minorca, Carrickfergus, widow, who died 5 September 1898, was proved at Belfast 20 January 1899 by Matthew Legg, gentleman, and Charles Legg, merchant, both of Carrickfergus. Effects £36 6s. 6d.

The Leggs are said to be descended from the Lugg family who filled various offices in the Corporation in the sixteenth and seventeenth centuries and owned property including Castle Lugg, the tower house beside the Silver Stream. Thomas Legg began a new tradition of public office, serving as sheriff from 1786 to 1791. By the late nineteenth century the Leggs were shipowners and coal merchants. After attending the Model School and Belfast Royal Academical Institution, Matthew Legg (d.1919) entered the linen spinning trade and managed several large mills before his quiet retirement. His youngest brother, Charles M. Legg J.P. of Bayview bequeathed Legg Park (tennis courts and children's playground) to the public in memory of his only son. One feature still stands: the structure of rough hewn granite which housed the drinking fountain. On its north face is a slate panel with the inscription 'This Park was given in memory of Charles Legg 2nd Lieutenant, born Carrickfergus 1893, served 1915-1918, died in France. He loved his country and his God.'

See McCrum ed. of McSkimin: *History and Antiquities of Carrickfergus* (1909); *Carrickfergus Advertiser*, 11 April 1919; Town Brochure c.1960; Speers: 'A Note on Castle Lugg, West Division' in *Carrickfergus and District Historical Journal* 1986, 2:56.]

LEGG

[In Legg vault.] Sacred to the memory of John Legg Esq. of Glynnpark who died 26th of August 1861. And Margaret, his wife, who died 6th of December 1852. Also Alice Legg, mother of the above John Legg, who died 6th of July 1860. And Antonia CUPPLES, her daughter, who died 18th of April 1863. And also Henry Legg, her youngest son, who died 6th June 1881.

[Letters of administration of the personal estate of Henry Legg, late of Carrickfergus, gentleman, who died 6 June 1881 at same place, were granted at Belfast 24 August 1881 to Elizabeth Maria Rowan of Carrickfergus, widow, a sister. Effects £768. 6s.]

LEGG

[Inside Legg vault.] Erected to the memory of David Legg who died 20th March 1854 aged 51 years. Also his wife Ann Legg who departed this life 5th February 1873 aged 63 years. "And God shall wipe away all tears from their eyes".

[David Legg, eldest son of John Legg, merchant, and Alicia Hull, was educated at Loughmorne and became a solicitor. He was elected Town Clerk of Carrickfergus in January 1838 and continued in office until his death. See Keane, E., Phair, P.B. and Sadleir, T.U. *King's Inns Admission Papers, 1607-1867* (1982); McCrum ed. of McSkimin: *History and Antiquities of Carrickfergus* (1909), p.272.]

LEGG

Erected by Captn. Wm. Miller Legg in memory of his mother Martha Millar, wife of Joseph Legg, who died 22nd Feb. 1881 aged 68 years. His brother Andrew Legg died 21st Nov. 1852 aged 8 years. And his uncle Hugh Gordon Legg lost at sea 21st Nov. 1852 aged 39 years. Also his father Joseph Legg who died 1st Jan. 1890 aged 79 years. His sister Martha, beloved wife of George F. NEWTON, died 4th March 1895. Also the said George F. Newton died 13th June 1906. And his son Wm. Legg Newton died 7th June 1914. Capt. Wm. STRAHAN, son-in-law of George F. Newton, died 29th Dec. 1945. Agnes MISCAMPBELL, wife of above Wm. Strahan, died 5th January 1951. [Mason:-] Gemmell, Belfast.

LEGG

[Recorded in McCrum ed. of McSkimin: *History and Antiquities of Carrickfergus* (1909), p.187. White marble tablet mounted on black, on west wall of south transept. Arms above:- azure a stag's head cabossed argent. Crest:- five ostrich plumes of the second and first rising from a coronet or. Motto:- gaudet tentamine virtus.] In memory of David Legg, solicitor and town clerk of Carrickfergus, who died 20th March 1854 aged 51 years. A few attached friends erected this tablet as a mark of their regard. [Mason:-] T. & W. Fitzpatrick, Belfast.

LEGG

See HIGGINSON and ROWAN

LIVINGSTONE

[Polished granite headstone.] In loving memory of a devoted husband and father, Douglas, born 4th September 1916, died 17th September 1987. [Mason:-] Mulholland, C'fergus.

LOCKHART

[Sandstone.] Sacred to the memory of Robert Lockhart who died 10th Sept. 1834 aged 73 years.

[Robert Lockhart, labourer or farmer, of the Middle Division, was made a freeman in 1787.]

LOCKHART

[Slate set in concrete surround.] The burying-ground of Robert Lockhart. In loving memory of William MALONE who died 7th May 1957. Also his dear wife Anna who died 4th January 1977. Redeemed.

LOGAN

[Castle-espie limestone.] Here lyeth ye body of Robert Logan who departed this life March ye 22 1716 aged 42 years. David his son died ye 24 of August 1707 aged 18 moeths [sic.].

LOGAN

[Broken in two.] Erected by his family to the memory of William Logan who died 4th February 1900 aged 59 years and to his daughter Annie who died 9th September 1900 aged 31 years. Also his little grand-daughter Susan who died 13th May 1906 aged 5 months.

[The will of William Logan, late of Knockagh, Greenisland, county Antrim, farmer, who died 4 February 1900, was proved at Belfast 30 March 1900 by Susan Logan, widow, and Paul Logan, farmer. Effects £297.]

LOGAN
See HUSTON, McGRIFFIN and STEPHENS

LOWE
Sacred to the memory of Stephen WALKER, died 24th March 1891 aged 60 years. Also James Lowe, died 1846 aged 74 years. Mary Lowe, relict of the above, died 1st August 1860 aged 84 years. Prov. IV, 18. Also Sarah Walker, wife of the above Stephen Walker, died 16th January 1909 aged 60 years. Also Sarah KIRKBRIDE, wife of Albert Kirkbride and daughter of the above Stephen Walker, who died 6th September 1925 aged 48 years. Also Stephen Walker, son of the above Stephen Walker, died 21st April 1941 aged 68 years. And Mary Walker, daughter of the above Stephen Walker, died 3rd Nov. 1949 aged 82 years. Also George M.L. Walker, son of above Stephen Walker, died 15th June 1950 aged 80 years.

[Letters of administration of the personal estate of Stephen Walker, late of West Street, Carrickfergus, grocer, who died 24 March 1891 at same place, were granted at Belfast 28 October 1891 to Sarah Walker of West Street, Carrickfergus, the widow. Effects £393. 11s. 7d.]

LOWRY
See McGIFFIN

LUFF
See WALLACE

LUNDY
[Polished granite with surround.] In loving memory of Joseph W. Lundy who died 24th Jany. 1906 aged 16 years. Also Robert M. Lundy who was accidentally killed at Workman & Clark's 30th June 1909 aged 21 years. William Lundy died 29th Oct. 1928 aged 75 years. John Lundy died 13th Nov. 1934 aged 48 years. Elizabeth Lundy died 26th Oct. 1935 aged 81 years. David ALLEN died 14th July 1942 aged 53 years. Margaret Heron Allen died 3rd Dec. 1956 aged 64 years. "Gone but not forgotten". [Mason:-] T. Holden, Larne.

LYNN
[Beside north boundary wall.] Sacred to the memory of Henry Lynn who died 31st Decr. 1851 aged 40 years. His infant daughter Jane Singleton who died 2nd Feby. 1851 aged 2 years. His son John who died 15th Octr. 1859 aged 19 years. His daughter Elizabeth Jane BARNETT who died 20th Septr. 1879 aged 28 years. His son Henry who died 1st Jany. 1931 in this 85th year. Also Mary JOHNSTONE, wife of the last named Henry Lynn, died 23rd February 1949 aged 92 years. [Mason:-] Geo. Rankin, 108 York St. Belfast.

LYNN
[Polished granite with lead lettering.] In loving memory of Harry, second son of Henry & Mary Johnstone Lynn, died 12th Feb. 1957 aged 70 years.

LYNN
See MACONKEY and RODGERS

McALISTER
Erected by Margaret McAlister in memory of her beloved husband Robert McAlister who died (4)th June (18)67 aged 2(.) years. And their son who (died) in infancy.

McALISTER
[Cast iron plaque.] The family burying ground of Js. McAlister 1887. [Cast by:-] R.J. Boyd, Henry St., Belfast.

McALISTER
See WISNOM

McALLEN
See EDGAR

McALLISTER
See WISNOM

MACASSEY
[Box tomb to south of chancel.] Erected by Mary Macassey in memory of her beloved husband the Rev. John Macassey of Carrickfergus, who died on the 13th January 1847 after a long illness brought on in the faithful discharge of his ministerial duties aged 36 years. May my last end be like his. Also in memory of the Rev. John Wm. Livingston Macassey, the eldest son of the above, who died at Armagh 28th October 1862 aged 23 years, after giving bright promise of a glorious future. Also in affectionate remembrance of Mary Macassey, wife and mother of the above who, after a life of exemplary piety chastened by many trials and much suffering, was called to her eternal rest on 10th April 1871 aged 59 years. May we meet in heaven, mother dear. Also Luke Livingston Macassey, born 7th April 1843, died 9th May 1908, youngest son of the above and interred in City Cemetery, Belfast. "Blessed are the dead which die in the Lord."

[The Rev. John Macassey was minister of the Carrickfergus Congregational Church from 1834. His son the Rev. J.W.L. Macassey followed the same vocation and ministered to a congregation in Tralee. Luke Livingston Macassey set up a civil engineering practice in Chichester Street, Belfast about 1864. He was also a barrister and is probably best remembered for his work with Belfast Water Commissioners. He married a daughter of the Rev. James White of First Carrickfergus Presbyterian Church. Their eldest son Sir Lynden Livingston Macassey, b. 14 June 1876, d. 23 February 1963, also combined engineering with law and served on several cabinet committees in London. Their third son Rev. Ernest Livingston D.D. was ordained in 1910 and served as an army chaplain and later became Vicar of Mapledurham in England, dying on 28 August 1947. See McCrum ed. of McSkimin: *History and Antiquities of Carrickfergus* (1909), p.213 and *Who Was Who*.]

McAUGHTRY
Erected by Marriot McAughtry in memory of his father Thomas McAughtry who departed this life 28th July 1842 aged 42 years. Also his daughter Isabella McAughtry who died in infancy in 1855. Also his son Marriot McAughtry who died 4th December 1863 aged 1 year & 6 months.

McAULEY
Erected by Henry McAuley in memory of his wife Jane McAuley who departed this life 24th June 1847 aged 86 years.

McAULEY
Wm. McAuleys burying ground. Erected by John McAuley in memory of Ellen his wife, obiit 30th Jany. 1848 aged 43 years.

McAULIFFE
In loving memory of George McAuliffe who died 25th July 1910 aged 84 years. And his daughter Kathleen McAuliffe who died 16th June 1913. Also Edith McAuliffe third daughter who died 3rd June 1925. His daughter Ellen McAuliffe who died 20th December 1954.

Luke Livingston Macassey (1843-1908) (from Loudan, Jack: In Search of Water)

McBRINN
Erected ... Char(les) M(cBrinn) in mem.......... who died 1.............
Also......................... who(o)................. A........(Z) M(cBrin)n W(illiam) M(cBr)inn died (1.... April) 18(.)1 aged 81 years.

McBRINN
Erected (to) the memory (of Henry Mc)Br(inn who departed) ...... 2(8)th .... (years.) Also his daughter Mary who died 2... July 184(.) aged 15 months. Also his son Charles died 13th July 1854 aged 11 years. Also his daughter .....e died .....(h) 1871 aged 28 years. Also his granddaughter Margaret M.... died on 10 September 18(7)6 aged 9 years. Also Mary, the beloved wife of the above named Henry McBrinn, who died Feby. 8th 1891 aged 74 years.

[Henry McBrin, tailor, of the Irish Quarter, was made a freeman in 1803 and another Henry O'Brien, farmer, of the Middle Division, was made a freeman in 1807.]

McBRINN
[South of chancel.] Erected by Henry McBrinn to the memory of his father Henry McBrinn who departed this life 13th August 1841 aged 57 years. Also his mother Agnes McBrinn who departed this life 27th April 1847 aged 58 years. Also his son John died 10th August 1862 aged 1 year. And his daughter Agnes died 5th October 1865 aged 2 years.

McBRINN
[Beside path south of church.] Erected by Anthony McBrinn in memory of his son William who died in America 3rd March 1877 aged 24 years. Also his daughter Martha who died 26th Feb. 1879 aged 21 years. His wife Ellen who died 23rd Dec. 1876 aged 55 years. His son Anthony who died 6th Dec. 1882 aged 15 years. The above Anthony McBrinn died 11th Feby. 1898 aged 79 years. Also Sarah beloved wife of James McBrinn, who died 4th May 1912 aged 51 years. Also her son Anthony McBrinn died 26th Dec. 1971 aged 87 years. Also James Thomas Vance McBrinn died 8th July 1973 aged 38 yrs., in Canada, dear son of Christina and the above Anthony McBrinn.

[The will of Anthony McBrin, late of West Division, Carrickfergus, farmer, who died 11 February 1898, was proved at Belfast 1 April 1898 by James McBrinn, farmer, and Robert Cambridge, merchant, both of Carrickfergus. Effects £459.5s. 11d.]

McBRINN
See HAMILTON

McCALPIN
[Blue slate] Erected by Robert McCalpin in memory of his wife Agness McCalpin who died on the 25th May 1847 aged 50 years. Their daughter Mary McCalpin, born 30th May 1817, died 27th February 1826. Also 3 of their children who died in infancy.

McCAMLEY
[Cement] Burying ground of W. McCamley.

McCANDLESS
In memory of Matilda McCandless, the beloved daughter of Saml. and E.J. McCandless, died 24th Oct. 1856 aged 10 yrs.

McCANN
Erected by the descendants of Catharine McCann who departed this life 20th February 1817 aged 77 years. Also her husband (E)d(ward) McCann who departed this life 30th of May 1822 aged (8.)years. Also Elizabeth McCann, wife of George McCann, who departed this life 22nd November 1827 aged 65 years.

[Edward McCann, carman, of the Town was made a freeman in 1785 and George McCann, clothier, of the Middle Division, was made a freeman in 1787.]

McCANN
Erected by Patr.........ann................ Also his daughter Jane who departed this life on the 24th of March 1837 aged 7 years. Also Margar(et), his daughter, who departed this life (1st) September 1837 aged 8 years. And his daughter Mary Also the above named Patrick McCann who departed this life 5th June 1844 aged 56 years. And of his wife Ann McCann who departed this life 15th June 1844 aged 45 years.

McCANN
[Enclosed with Dr. Thomas Gorman, d. 1893.] In loving memory of Mary, the beloved wife of Henry M.J. McCann and daughter of Wm. GORMAN J.P., died 22nd August 1927 aged 58 years. The above Henry M.J. McCann died 16th November 1953 aged 90 years. The parents of Will, Terence, and Denis.

McCANN
See ECCLESTON

McCLURE
[Decorated with wheeled cross motif] In loving memory of a dear husband and father, Ernest, died 17th January 1981. At rest. [Mason:-] J. Wilton 38.39.

McCOMBE
[White marble with lead lettering against south boundary wall] Erected 1898 in memory of Samuel McCombe died 9th April 1898. Samuel A. McCombe died 18th July 1892. Agnes P. McCombe died 1st May 1856. Jane, wife of Samuel McCombe, died 11th December 1908. Mary E. McCombe died 25th April 1915. Margaret M. McKELVEY died 22nd November 1921. John McCombe died 10th September 1930. David McKelvey J.P. died 22nd February 1935 aged 92 years. William J.P. McCombe died 2nd October 1937 aged 80 years. Father, I will that they also, whom thou hast given me, be with me where I am, John 17 & 24.

[Probate of the will of Samuel McCombe, late of Jordanstown, county Antrim, gentleman, who died 9 April 1898, granted at Belfast 6 May 1898 to William J. McCombe, George McCombe and David McKelvey, all of Belfast, rent agents. Effects £3,623. 10s. 3d.]

McCONKEY
[White marble against west boundary wall.] Erected by William McConkey in memory of his parents: Samuel McConkey died 2nd July 1873 aged 64 years. Jane McConkey died 5th July 1859 aged 45 years. Also his sisters Ellen McConkey died 27th Sept. 1844 aged 5 months. Margaret McConkey died 28th Jan. 1860 aged 5 years. Also his brother-in-law Samuel ROSS who died 3rd Aug. 1893 aged 53 years. Elizabeth Ross died 13th March 1897 aged 55 years. Alexander McConkey died 12th Feb. 1900 aged 51 years. Rachel McConkey died 14th Feb. 1909 aged 70 years. [Mason:-] Gemmell, Belfast.

[Probate of the will of Elizabeth Ross, late of Market Place, Carrickfergus, county Antrim, widow, who died 12 March 1897, granted at Belfast 9 June 1897 to William McConkey of 69 South Parade, merchant tailor, and Thomas S. Hogg of 6 Cooke Terrace, M.D., both of Belfast. Effects £64. 1s. 9d.]

McCONNELL
[Slate outside baptistry.] Erected by Charles McConnell in memory of Margaret STRAIN died 11th Septr. 1903. William Strain died 1st July 1906. Mary Strain died 23rd Novr. 1906. Jane Logan died 23rd February 1910. Also Elizabeth McConnell, wife of the above named Charles McConnell, died 5th December 1925.

McCONNELL
See JUNKIN

McCOY
See KIRK

McCRACK(E)N
........(ng place) of William McCrack(e)n.

McCREVEY
[Granite stone and surround with lead lettering south of chancel.] McCrevey. In memory of Robert McCrevey died Sept. 30 1876 aged 78. And his wife Elizabeth died Oct. 14 1853 aged 56. Their daughter Mary Eliza died Oct. 11 1903 aged 69. And her husband Charles JOHNSTONE died Nov. 26 1918 aged 86. Their son James, died at Hyderabad June 11 1870 aged 38. Their daughter Ellen, died Oct. 15 1885 aged 46. [Mason:-] Gemmell, Belfast.

[The will of Ellen McCrevey, late of Silverstream Cottage, Greenisland, Carrickfergus, spinster, who died 15 October 1885 at same place, was proved at Belfast 15 January 1886 by Mary Eliza Johnstone, wife of Charles Johnstone, and said Charles Johnstone, farmer, late of Laurel Lodge, Greenisland, the executors. Effects £80.]

McCUNE
[Wooden panel imbedded in concrete to west of south transept.] Erected by Joseph McCune in loving memory of his dear father Joseph McCune who died 1st June 1908 aged 60 years. Also his dear mother Matilda McCune who died 25th February 1921 aged 73 years.

McCUNE
See BARRY

McDONNELL
[Recorded in McCrum ed. of McSkimin: *History and Antiquities of Carrickfergus* (1909), p.179. This was evidently the inscription on the Marchioness's lead coffin, but has now been carved on a flag on the floor.] The most honourable the Lady Marchioness of Antrim, relict of the Most Honourable Randall McDonnell, Marquis & Earl of Antrim, Viscount Dunluce and sole daughter and heir of Sir Henry O'NEILL of Edenduffcarrick, in the county of Antrim, who departed this life at Edenduffcarrick aforesaid on the 27th day of April anno Domini 1695 in the 64 year of her age.

McDOWELL
He(ir) liet(h the body of M.... M................................ Ap... 17.1 a............... (Also) Mary McDowell who departed this life April 6th 180(2) his (wif)e aged 62 years.

McDOWELL
[Slate.] Erected by David McDowell.

McDOWELL
[Severely eroded sandstone of mid nineteenth century.] (E)rected by ....(l)l, in memory............h McDowell w................. aged 33 years.

McDOWELL
[Small slate.] Edward McDowell died 10 April 1866 AE 46 yrs. Also James died 1 August 1864 AE 6 years.

McDOWELL
[Slate.] Erected by James McDowell in memory of his daughter Agness who departed this life January 8th 1867 aged 18 months. Also his daughter Ellen, who departed this life December 18th 1868 aged 14 months. Also his daughter Lizzie who departed this life October 6th 1873 aged 3 months. Also his son Gorge[sic,] who departed this life July 19th 1899 aged 16 years.

McDOWELL
[Black granite against east boundary wall.] Erected by W.J. McDowell in memory of his beloved wife Mary Anne who died 1st Jany. 1909 aged 60 years. The abovenamed W.J. McDowell died 9th Jany. 1918 aged 74 years. "Asleep in Jesus". [Mason:-] T. Holden, Larne.

McDOWELL
[Loose cast iron plaque.] In memory of Elizebeth [sic.] McDowell died 26 Dec. 1923.

McDOWELL
[On prayer desk.] Given to St. Nicholas' Church by a parishoner in gratitude for God's blessing and in loving memory of Stuart and Edith McDowell, June 1977.

McDOWELL
See MARTIN

McDOWL
[Sandstone laid flat behind McGookin.] This is in remembrance of Marya(nn) McDowl, doughter to Matthew McDowl, who departed this life in the first year of her age March 2 1798.
[Matthew McDowell, carpenter, of Irish Quarter, was made a freeman in 1785.]

McFERRAN
[Cast iron plaque; the forename was on a metal strip which was screwed into place.] The family burying ground of ..... McFerran NO.97.

McFERRAN
[Wheeled cross of white marble.] Until the day breaks and the shadows flee away. In loving memory of Susannah McFerran who departed this life on the 15th day of June 1890 and whose remains are here interred and of her husband John McFerran who died on August 21st 1862 [sic] and was buried at sea. Also of their children: John, born October 15th 1850, died in infancy; Matilda, born September 18th 1855, died February 14th 1860. Both of whom also lie here. "Through the gates of death we enter into everlasting life".
[Letters of administration of the personal estate of John McFerran, late of Scotch Quarter, Carrickfergus, master mariner, who died 21 August 1861 at sea, were granted at Belfast 10 January 1862 to Susan McFerran of Scotch Quarter, Carrickfergus, the widow of said deceased. Effects under £450.]

McFERRAN
Erected by Robert McFerran in memory of his brother James who departed this life 8th April 1863 aged 38 years. Mary, the beloved wife of Robert McFerran, died 3rd Feb. 1882 aged 64 years. Also her sister Rachel WEATHERUP died 31st March 1865 aged 61 years. Also the above-named Robert McFerran, the beloved husband of Margaret McFerran, died 31st March 1900 aged 79 years. "Gone but not forgotten". Margaret McFerran died 21st Nov. 1914 in her 71st year.
[Probate of the will of Robert McFerran, late of Whitehead, county Antrim, retired ship owner, who died 30 March 1900, granted at Belfast 16 May 1900 to Margaret McFerran, widow. Effects £1,000. 4s. 7d.
On the 17th January 1851 Captain Robert McFerran was a passenger in a train from Belfast to Carrickfergus. At Carrickfergus Junction (now Greenisland) the engine was detached during shunting operations. The storm that was blowing set the carriages into motion. They accelerated on the incline to Carrickfergus. Captain McFerran mounted the roof of his carriage and made his way to the brake van, from where he guided the runaway carriages safely into Carrickfergus Station. The directors of the Northern Counties Railways presented the captain with a free pass for life and a silver medal. He lived at Castle Chester, Whitehead, for 25 years. The free pass was extended until his wife's death in 1914. See McCrum ed. of McSkimin: *History and Antiquities of Carrickfergus* (1909), p.110-111.]

McFERRAN
Sacred to the memory of Marianne JACK, wife of the late John McFerran, who died 7th September 1872 aged 49 years. Also in loving memory of her eldest son

George McFerran who died 9th October 1919 aged 70 years. And Annabella, wife of George McFerran, died 21st Dec. 1933 aged 82 years. Her son Blair McFerran died 8th Feby. 1941 aged 79 years.

McFERRAN
[White marble cross above east boundary wall.] In memory of Ellen wife of John McFerran, The Barn, Carrickfergus, died 27th Sept. 1901. Also John McFerran, born 13th April 1832, died 21st August 1904. James Love McFerran, Oakfield, born 1st May 1867, died 5th February 1936. And of Helen STEWART, his devoted wife, born 10th August 1880, died 24th April 1948.

McFERRAN
[Brass on wood, south wall of chancel.] In ever dear remembrance of Maurice Anderdon McFerran, M.C., Lieutenant 4th Battalion Royal Irish Rifles, killed in action near St. Quentin on the 21st March 1918 aged 20.

McFERRAN
[Brass plate on reading desk used to support roll of honour for 1914-1918 War.] In remembrance of James Love McFerran, by the employees of the Barn Mills died 5th February 1936.

McGIFFIN
[Large blue slate.] McGiffin. Eliza JACK, wife of Wm. McGiffin, born 1831, died 1860. William McGiffin, born 1815, died 1900. Martha LOWRY, also wife of Wm. McGiffin, born 1816, died 1905. 3 graves.

McGIFFIN
[A stone which has been used twice.] Erected by Charles McCONNELL in memory of Margaret STRAIN died 11th Septr. 1903. William Strain died 1st July 1906. Mary Strain died 23rd Novr. 1906. Jane LOGAN died 23rd February 1910. Also Elizabeth McConnell, wife of the above-named Charles McConnell, died 5th December 1925. This stone claims 4 graves. [The inscription on the back is almost certainly earlier:-] Wm. McGiffin's burying place.

McGIFFIN
[Polished granite.] In loving memory of William Archibald McGiffin, died 26th November 1918 aged 19 years.

McGLADDERY
[Cast iron plaque.] The burying-place of John McGladdery, 1896.

McGOLPIN
Sacred to the memory of William Mc(G)olpin (who was lost at sea) 24th Decr. 18(.)0. Also his w............lpin who died .... 18(56). Erected (by) ....
[There are two McGolpins on the freeman's list. The first without Christian name was a resident of the North East Division, made a freeman in 1787. A William McGolpin, fisher, of the Town was made a freeman in 1819.]

McGOOKIN
[Polished granite.] The family burying ground of John McGookin.
[Mason:-] Jameson, Belfast.

McGOOKIN
[Slate south of chancel.] Erected by Daniel McGookin to the memory of his father Daniel McGookin who departed this life the 14th June 1871 aged 73 yrs.

McGOWAN
[White marble in sandstone frame against south boundary wall.] Sacred to the memory of John McGowan, M.D. who died (Oct.) 17th 1(837) aged (6)0. Also to the memory of John McGowan, fourth son of John (B)ORTHWICK (who died) Aug (.)th 1(84)4..... years. Michael Andrew (B)orthwick, late Lieutenant in the

Headstone to Daniel McGookin who died in 1871 aged 73

3(7)th Regt, who died 31st July 1866 aged (2)7 years. Letitia Borthwick who died 19th March 1876 aged 76 years. The above-named John Borthwick died 17th Dec. 18(8)5 aged 76 years, and was buried at [John Borthwick, formerly of Prospect, Carrickfergus in Ireland, and late of 3 Derby Villas, Dulwich, county Surrey, esquire, died 17 December 1885. Probate granted at London 8 February 1886. Resealed at the Principal Registry, Dublin 2 March 1886. Effects in Ireland £496.

John Borthwick J.P. was manager of the Belfast Savings Bank for 36 years, a partner and manager of Kilroot Bleach Works, chairman of the Carrickfergus Gas Company, Ltd. (1858-81) and an active member of the North East Agricultural Association.]

McGOWAN
[Weathered sandstone.] Er(ected by Ho)ward McGow(an) in (memory of) his (father .... Mc)Gowan who d....... this life (.)th... 1849 ag.........

McGOWAN
See BOWMAN

McILHER(NON)
Erected by Elizabeth McIlher(non) in memory of Robert M(cIlhernon) her deceased husband who died the 13th December 1... aged (5)5 years. Also their son Robert who departed this life the 2(4)th November 1(8)2(7) aged (36) years,

de(ser)vedly and universely lamented. Likewise their daughter Mary who departed this life the 15th November 1..... aged (5)6 years.

McILROY
The family burying ground of Charles McIlroy who died 15th April 1871 aged 6(.) years. Also his wife Elizabeth McIlroy who died 2nd Novr. 1899 aged 60 years.

[The will of Charles McIlroy, late of Clipperstown, Carrickfergus, gentleman, who died 15 April 1871 at same place, was proved at Belfast 12 May 1871 by the oaths of David Pasley, bank manager, and William Stephens, merchant, both of Carrickfergus, the executors. Effects under £100.]

McILWRATH
[LEE inscription on other side. Reversed for use by McIlwrath.] (..eo.... McIlwrath who) died (.....o......... aged) 7(5) years. Also his .... John McIlwrath died 20th May 18(58) aged 5 years & 7 months.

McILWRATH
See LEE

MACKAY
Erected in memory of James Mackay who departed this life 18th March 1801 aged 90 years. Also his daughter Brabazon Mackay who departed this life 22nd June 1810 aged 22 years. Also his wife Eleanor Mackay who departed this life 6th July 1818 aged 67 years.

[James Mackay, carpenter, of the Town, was made a freeman in 1787.]

MACKAY
See McKINNEY

McKEEN
[On reverse are arms:- fretty, on a fess on boar trippant. Crest:- in a dexter hand couped at the wrist a sword. Motto:-Amo Pro(b)os.] Here lyeth ye body of John McKeen who died Nov. ye 7th 1748 aged 82 years. Also his son Thomas died June ye 25th 1747 aged 42 years.

McKEEN
[White limestone with lead lettering.] "Thy will be done". In loving remembrance of William McKeen, Straid, who departed this life 24th May 1861 aged 52 years. And of his beloved wife Sarah STEWART who departed this life 4th Feby. 1887 aged 72 years. "One less tie to break on earth".

McKEEN
[Sandstone lying flat in front of Holmes, 1820.] (Erected by) Ja(m)es .....erson in (memory of his b)eloved wife Ja(net) who departed (this life) 17th March 1863 aged .. years. A(lso) their granddaughter Eliza Jane McKEEN who departed this life 3rd March 1871 ag... 8 years. Also their grandson James McKeen who (died Ma)rch 2(9)th 1871 aged 15 mo(nths). And their grand daughter (...r Mc)Keen who died 6th April 1871 aged 3 years. Esther McKeen who died 26th February 1891. Thomas McKeen who died 18th July 1909.

McKEEN
[White marble with lead lettering.] The family burying ground of Robert McKeen.

McKEEN
See ANDERSON

McKEGG
[Slate.] Erected by Amos McKegg to the memory of his father James McKegg who departed this life 17th January 1848 aged 77 years. Also his mother Martha, who departed this life 20th January 1859 aged 77 years.

[James McKeg, fisherman, of Irish Quarter, was made a freeman in 1814.]

McKELVEY
See McCOMBE

McKEOWN
See LATTIMORE

McKIBBIN
[Outside baptistry.] Never forgotten. Erected by Eliza Jane EDMONDSON in loving memory of her sister Sarah Martha McKibbin who died 27th Nov. 1890 aged 26 years. Also her mother Eliza McKibbin who died 17th April 1868. And her sister Isabella McKibbin who died 16th April 1878. Also Annie, William, Eugenie & Sarah, beloved children of William & Eliza Jane Edmondson. Also the above named Eliza Jane Edmondson who died 29th Nov. 1924 aged 75 years. "Blessed are the dead which die in the Lord".

McKINNEY
[To south of church.] Erected by John McKinney in (memory of his s)on John McKinney who departed this life 17th Feb. 1854 aged 17 years. Also his son Alexander who departed this life 23rd Sept. 1868 aged 28 years. Also his son James who died 13th Feby. 1876 aged 41 years.

McKINNEY
[A hand pointing heavenward holds a scroll inscribed "gone home". Broken in two.] Erected by David Legg McKinney in memory of his father and mother. Also his youngest son Willie MACKAY who died 4th June 1904 aged 17 years.

McKINSTRY
See BARRY

MACKINTOSH
See DAVISON

McKINTY
In loving memory of my dear husband Robert died 25th June 1954. Also my dear father and mother Hugh and Eliza BELCH. Also brother Hugh and sister Elizabeth. [Mason:-] Hart, Carnmoney.

McKNIGHT
See MILLAR

McMAHON
See STUART

McMASTER
Here lies the body of Jane McMaster who departed this life on the 14 of Decr. 181(.) aged 54 years, also ...... McMaster died 20th F....... aged 7(6) years .... wife Ellen McMaster who died Nov ..... aged 15 months. Their son Andrew who died 1(6)th Oct. 189(.) aged 1(5) years. Their daughter Mary who died 26th Dec. 191(3) aged 44 years. William McMaster who died 8th Feb. 1945 aged 78 years.

McMAW
See HOLMES

McMEEKAN
[Sandstone of mid-nineteenth century.] The burying place of James McMeekan

McMURTRY
[To south of chancel.] Erected by Mary McMurtry in (memory (35) years. Their son Jas. died (3rd) March 18.. aged (.. years). Mary, wife of Wm. McMurtry, died 27(th Decr.) 1871 AE (7)2 (yrs.)

[The will of Mary McMurtry, late of Belfast, widow, who died 27 December 1871 at same place, was proved at Belfast 9 February 1872 by the oath of William

McMurtry of Ballywalter, county Down, coast guard, one of the executors. Effects under £200.]

McMURTRY
[Sandstone of the mid-nineteenth century.] Erected by James August (18..) aged (.4) years. Also the abov(e named) James McMurtry (who) died (at) Maryport 18th Sept. 1(85.) aged (4.) years. Also his son James who died (8)th (J...) 186(5) aged .. years.

McMURTRY
Erected by Robert McMurtry in memory of his dear son John McMurtry who departed this life 22nd August 1866 aged 3 years & 5 months. Also his daughter Martha McMurtry who departed this life 19th December 1900 aged 31 years.

McNEELY
[Flower vase between north transept and vestry.] Audrey Wilma McNeely 2.9.1975.

MacNEICE
[Carved on end of a choir stall.] These oak stalls are presented to this church with thankfulness for the life and love of Elizabeth Margaret MacNeice who entered into rest 18th December 1914. Dedicated 18th December 1929.

[John Frederick MacNeice was born on 20th March 1866 and spent his early childhood in Connemara, Co. Galway, where his father William Lindsay MacNeice was a schoolmaster employed by the Society for Irish Church Missions. He was ordained in 1895, was Rector of Carrickfergus 1908-31, Bishop of Cashel and Emly, Waterford and Lismore 1931-34, and Bishop of Down and Connor and Dromore from 1934 until his death on 14th April 1942. He married Elizabeth Margaret Clesham who died Dec. 1914. They had three children: Caroline Elizabeth (later Lady Nicholson), Frederick Louis (poet, broadcaster, and playwright) and William Lindsay Bushe. He married secondly Georgina Beatrice, second daughter of Thomas Greer of Seapark, Carrickfergus, in April 1917. There were no more children. Mrs MacNeice died 7th April 1956 aged 83. See *Carrickfergus and District Historical Journal* 1993, vol. 7, passim.]

MacNEICE
See CHAMBERLAIN and CLOSE

McNEILLY
[Granite with lead lettering and surround.] In loving memory of Edward McNeilly died 27th December 1891, and his wife Annie McNeilly died 3rd January 1918. And James Gorman McNeilly, fourth son of above, died 27th February 1945. And his wife Martha McNeilly died 21st May 1945. And Samulena Jane McNeilly, infant daughter of above James Gorman and Martha McNeilly, died 20th December 1906. [Mason:-] Kirkwood.

[Edward McNeilly was a master mariner who lived at Minorca.]

MACNEVIN
[Recumbent.] Here lie the remains of Andrew Macnevin Esqr. late a captain in his Majesty's 4th R.V. Battalion who departed this life on the 28th of June 1819 aged 68 years.

MACONKEY
[Brass plate in porch.] The installation of electric lighting in this church dedicated 20th December 1936 by the Right Reverend J.F. MacNeice, D.D., Bishop of Down and Connor and Dromore, is the gift of Miss Susan Maconkey, a life-long church worker and devoted member. J.C. RUTHERFORD, Prebendary of Kilroot, Incumbent. John S. GARRELL, Henry LYNN, churchwardens.

McPHERSON
[Propped against boundary wall facing west door.] 1846. Angus McPherson's burying ground.

McQUILLAN
In loving memory of Dorothy ROBINSON, nee McQuillan, beloved wife of William J.G. Robinson died 5th May 1952 aged 23 years. Also her father Robert G. McQuillan died 10th Dec. 1942 aged 63 years. And her mother Elizabeth Laws McQuillan died 22nd Dec. 1953 aged 70 years. "Asleep in the Lord till he come". May they rest in peace and awake to a joyful resurrection.

McQUILLEN
[Slate against perimeter wall next to preceding stone.] The burying ground of John McQuillen.

McQUITTY
Erected by Ellen McQuitty in memory of her beloved father William McQuitty who departed this life 17 May 1867 aged 73 years. Also her mother Sarah McQuitty who departed this life 9th August 1877 aged 77 years. Above named Ellen McQuitty who departed this life 14th November 1908 aged 69 years. "Until the day break".

[The will of William McQuitty, late of Lower Woodburn, West Division in the county of the town of Carrickfergus, carman, who died 17 May 1867 at same place, was proved at Belfast 12 November 1867 by the oath of James Bailey of Woodburn, Carrickfergus, farmer, one of the executors. Effects under £20.]

McQUITTY
See BARRY

McSKIMIN
To the memory of Samuel McSkimin obiit 1843 aged 68 years. Nancy McSkimin died 7th May 1857 aged 77 years. Jane CATHERWOOD died 23rd April 1872 aged 29 years. Hugh Catherwood died 11th December 1882 aged 75 years. William Catherwood died 17th July 1884 aged 31 years.

[The will of Hugh Catherwood, late of Bluefield, Carrickfergus, farmer, who died 11 December 1882 at same place, was proved at Belfast 9 November 1883 by William Catherwood of Bluefield, Carrickfergus, farmer, and David Kane of Alfred Street, Belfast, foreman mechanic, the executors. Effects £598. 10s.

The will of William Catherwood, late of Bluefield, Carrickfergus, farmer, who died 17 July 1884 at same place, was proved at Belfast 8 December 1884 by Hugh Catherwood of same place, farmer, one of the executors. Effects £675.

Samuel McSkimin was born near Ballyclare in 1775 but moved to Carrickfergus in 1797 and conducted business as a grocer in the Irish Quarter. His great work was *The History and Antiquities of the County of the Town of Carrickfergus*, first published in 1811 and successively enlarged for editions in 1823, 1829, 1833, 1839 and 1909. The last was updated by his great-granddaughter Elizabeth J. McCrum. His mind embraced many subjects and he contributed to a wide selection of a periodicals. He was made a freeman in 1818.

His father, also Samuel, died in November 1808 aged 54 and his mother Nancy in May 1820 aged 80 years. He married Nancy Goodacre on 4th April 1802 and had six children, of whom James emigrated to Quebec and Elizabeth married Hugh Catherwood of Knockagh in 1837 and died 16th August 1893. Samuel McSkimin died on 21 February 1843. See McCrum edition of McSkimin as above, pp. 525-527.]

MAGEE
Erected (by) ....e(e) in memory of (his beloved) w(ife) El..a(b)e.. Magee who d.............ad.........

MAGEE
E(rec)ted .... in mem(ory of ....) Magee.

MAGEE
Erected by Archibald Magee of Ballymena in memory of Mary HANLY his beloved wife who departed this life 6th Septr. 1849 aged 29 years. Also of Mary Ann

their only daughter, who died in infancy.

MAGEE
[White marble, with a hand pointing heavenward in a roundel.] Erected by Isabella Magee, in loving memory of her father, James Magee, who died May 15th 1888, her brothers Edward and William James, who died in the bloom of youth, also John and Willie, who died in infancy. Also her sister Jane, and niece Isabella MILLIKEN. Also her gentle and loving mother Isabella Milliken Magee, who died May 28th 1904. Also the above Isabella Magee who died April 23rd 1918. Peace perfect peace. [Mason:-] G. McCance, Belfast.

MAGOWAN
[Cast iron plaque next to Davidson, south of chancel.] The burying ground of James Magowan (Carric)kferg(us). [Cast by:] The Millfield Foundry 1928.

MAJOR
[Cast iron plaque, loose.] Erected by William Major, Belfast, in memory of his mother Margaret Major died 14th Jany. 1903. Also his brother Robert died 8th Jany. 1903. [Cast by:-] James Moore & Sons Ltd. ironfounders, engineers, Belfast, Millfield Foundry.

MALCOLM
In memory of Anne Davys Malcolm, widow of the Rev. James Malcolm of Chester, died 22nd August 1906 aged 91 years. And of their son James Chester Malcolm died 9th July 1866 aged 14 years. Also their daughter Florence died 11th October 1936 aged 87 years. Also their daughter Eleanor DAVYS died 8th October 1938 aged 91 years. [Mason:-] McNally, Belfast.

[James Malcolm was minister of the Remonstrant Presbyterian Church on Joymount Bank 1835-1838 and then continued his ministry in England. For further details of the family see the biography of his brother *Andrew Malcolm of Belfast 1818-1856, Physican and Historian* by H. G. Calwell (1977).]

MALONE
[Brass plate.] To the glory of God and in memory of Charles Thomas and Margaret Spears Malone. The extension to the communion rail was given by their children December 1967.

[Charles T. Malone was an Urban Councillor. He died in February 1949 at 62 Albert Road.]

MALONE
See LOCKHART

MANNING
See CHAMBERLAIN

MARSH
[Enclosed with this is a sandstone whose inscription has completely eroded, but on its reverse side are mortuary symbols, viz:- skull, hourglass and hand holding scales.] Erected by Charles Marsh in memory of his mother and father Margaret & Robert Marsh who died 1851-1854. Also his wife Elizabeth LATTIMOR who died 1877. And his wife Susan DOUGLAS who died 1909. The above Charles Marsh died 27th June 1920 aged 86 years.

MARTIN
Erected by Nathan Martin memory of his loving wife and kind mother Lilley McDOWELL, born 6th Dec. 1817, died 28th April 1883. Their son Nathan, born 24th Dec. 1839, died 8th March 1840. Their son Samuel, born 23rd April 1846, died 28th December 1848. Their daughter Mary Jane, born 2nd Feby. 1858, died 6th April 1859. Their son William, born 8th Dec. 1843, died at New Orleans, U.S., in July 1867. Their son James, born 21st June 1853, died at sea off the American coast in July 1878. Their son Samuel, born 9th March 1851, lost at sea off the Mel-

bourne coast in October 1880. Also their two grand-children Agnes & William James who died young. Their son John, born Augt. 23rd 1848, drowned off C'fergus Sept. 30th 1884. The above named Nathan Martin, born July 11th 1817, died April 11th 1898. Nathan Martin Junr., born Jany. 1st 1842, died May 19th 1913. Janet GEORGE died 13th Nov. 1925 aged 67 years. Ellen Martin died 25th Dec. 1913. William Martin died 28th Nov. 1930.

MARTIN
[Slate.] Erected by Benjamin MILLS to the memory of Thompson Martin who departed this life 28th Sept. 1878 aged 93 years.

MASTERMAN
See BARRY

MATHEWS
[Recumbent.] Deborah Mathews died 30th June 1824 aged 71 years. This stone erected to her memory by her attached niece Mary Ann STUART. Also to the memory of Elizabeth E. MORTIME(R) who died 27th May 1878.

[The will of Eliza Emily Mortimer, late of Carrickfergus, spinster, who died 27 May 1878 at same place, was proved at Belfast 8 July 1878 by the oath of William Johns of Joymount House, Carrickfergus, solicitor, the sole executor. Effects under £600.]

MAXWELL
See KIDLEY

MAYNE
(Sacred to the memory) of (Thomas) Mayne who died (1...) May 182(3) aged (35) years. Also his son Andrew Mayne who died 24th Jan. 1868 aged 65 years. Also to Ann, wife of the above Thomas, Mayne who died on the 29th March 1876 aged 95 years.

MAYNE
(Sacred) to the memory of Thomas Mayne who departed this life 15th May 1827 aged 53 years.

MAYNE
[Slate against south perimeter wall.] Erected by Hugh Mayne in memory of his daughter Isabella who departed this life 3rd Jan. 1892 aged 23 years. The above-named Hugh Mayne departed this life 20th Aug. 1912 aged 85 years. "Not dead but gone before".

[Isabella was 4th daughter of Hugh and Anne Jane Mayne of North Street, Carrickfergus. See *Carrickfergus Advertiser*, 8 January 1892.]

MAYNE
See PICKEN

MESNEY
See STEPHENS

MILLAR
Recorded in McCrum ed. of McSkimin: *History and Antiquities of Carrickfergus* (1909), p.187. Plain white marble tablet on west wall of south transept.] To the memory of Staff Surgeon John Millar who died at Glasgow May 3rd 1850 aged 55 years. In affectionate remembrance the Officers who served with him in the 43rd Light Infantry of which regt. he was surgeon for 18 years have erected this monument. His remains rest in Lighthill Cemetery at Glasgow.

MILLAR
Erected in loving memory of Henry Millar died 21st Jany. 1913 aged 68 years. Also his wife Ellen McKNIGHT died 1st March 1877 aged 28 years. Their son

James died 30th Jany. 1898 aged 26 years. Their daughter Mary died in infancy.

MILLAR
[Loose cast iron plaque south of chancel.] The family burying ground of John Millar, 1903. [Cast by:-] Victor C. Taylor, Atlas Foundry, Townsend St., Belfast.

MILLAR
[Small loose marble tablet at foot of William HAMILTON d.1857.] Ellen Millar and her daughter Annie. Also her eldest daughter Martha Smith Millar.

MILLER
Her lieth the body of Samuel Miller, who departed this life 28th February 1810 aged 65 years.

MILLER
See LAIRD

MILLIKEN
[Next to McConnell d.1845.] Erected by Samuel Milliken in memory of his beloved wife Jane who departed this life 23rd March 1858 aged 44 years. Also their daughter Ellen Jane Milliken who departed this life 22nd July 1857 aged 13 years. The above Samuel Milliken died 3rd October 1880 aged 70 years. "Not dead but sleepeth". Also his daughter Maria H. F. Milliken who died 10th December 1887 aged 23 years. "Whiter than snow". Also Eliza Milliken, wife of the above Samuel Milliken, who died 24th December 1927. Also his daughter Ellen J. Milliken who died 1st December 1931. Also his grandson Edwin Milliken PATTON who died 4th October 1917, at Passchendaele, Belgium.

[The will of Samuel Milliken, late of Lower Woodburn, Carrickfergus, merchant, who died 3 October 1880 at same place, was proved at Belfast 5 January 1881 by Eliza Milliken of Lower Woodburn, Carrickfergus, widow, the sole executrix. Effects under £200.

Agnes Florence, youngest daughter of Samuel Milliken, married Hugh Ferguson Patton in Frederick Street Methodist Church, Belfast, on 13 July 1893.]

MILLIKEN
Erected in memory of James Milliken who departed this life 13th Novr. 1859 aged 63 years. Also his brother Robert Milliken who departed this life 28th Decr. 1865 aged 75 years. Also his son James Milliken who departed this life 1st May 1889 aged 60 years. And his wife Isabella HARVEY who departed this life 9th Octr. 1892 aged 67 years. Also their son James who departed this life 20th Novr. 1875 aged 18 years.

MILLIKEN
Erected by John Milliken in memory of his beloved wife Janet, ... departed this life (2)0th Feb. 1870 aged 6(5) years. The above named John Milliken departed this life on the ....h day of January 1874 ..... years.

MILLIKEN
[Cast iron plaque.] The family burying ground of Captain Wm. Milliken, Carrickfergus 1887.

MILLIKEN
[Polished granite.] Erected by John Milliken in loving memory of his daughter Annie Jane Milliken, born 24th April 1891, died 12th October 1914. Also his wife Ellen who died 16th April 1920 aged 63 years.

MILLIKEN
See JUNKIN and MAGEE

MILLIKIN
[Flaking sandstone.] Erected (by) Ezekiel Millikin in memory of his c(hildren) viz Agnes Mary Sem(m).. who departed this life A.D. 1829. Also his son Wm. who

died 1st May 1832 AE (9) years. Also said Ezekiel Millikin died 10th (April) 1833 AE 55 years.
[Ezekiel Milliken, painter, of 5 Scotch Quarter, was made a freeman in 1803.]

MILLIKEN
See JUNKIN and MAGEE

MILLS
[White marble against east boundary wall.] In memory of Sarah Mills who died 25th Dec. 1907 daughter of the late Michael Mills, Collinstown, Clondalkin, Co. Dublin. Also Lucinda Fanny, wife of Samuel Patrick CLOSE, died 24th November 1920. Also the above named Samuel Patrick Close, architect, died 2nd August 1925.

MILLS
See BRAVINGTON and MARTIN

MILNER
[Polished granite adorned with motif of wheeled cross.] In loving memory of William Shaw Milner J.P. 1908-1976. A devoted husband and father. [Mason:-] Hart.

MILNER
[Brass plaque mounted on west wall of nave and bearing the badge of Rotary International.] To the glory of God these doors were given by the Rotary Club of Carrickfergus in memory of William Shaw Milner, J.P. founder president who loved to enter and worship here. Dedicated 14th January 1979.

MINNIECE
See GARDNER

MISCAMPBELL
[Obelish of grey limestone with inscription on a slate tablet.]
In memory of Hugh Miscampbell died 19th June 1838 aged 24 years. James Miscampbell died 6th June 1865 aged 82 years.
Elizabeth Miscampbell died 11th February 1866 aged 82 years.
James Miscampbell died 4th July 1869 aged 25 years. William Miscampbell died 20th July 1869 aged 20 years. Agnes Miscampbell died 4th April 1872 aged 61 years. Hugh Miscampbell died 29th Octr. 1881 aged 39 years. James Miscampbell died 20th Novr. 1902 aged 86 years. James Miscampbell, eldest son of Alexander Miscampbell, died 11th December 1896 aged 16 years. [On another slate tablet.] The burying place of James Miscampbell.

MISCAMPBELL
[Polished granite with surround.] James Miscampbell, born 8 Feby. 1764, died 6 June 1865. Elizabeth Miscampbell, born 10 Decr. 1783, died 11 Feby. 1866. Alexander Miscampbell, born 20th September 1851, died 11th November 1927. Agnes, wife of Alexander Miscampbell, born 2nd July 1854, died 14th June 1937.

MISCAMPBELL
See LEGG

MISSCAMPBELL
Erected by David Misscampbell in memory of his daughter Mary who departed this life 16th June 1846 aged 9 years. The above David Misscampbell died 7th Octr. 1868. Also his wife Martha who died 7th March 1900.

MITCHELL
See CATHERWOOD

MOGEY
Erected to the memory of Daniel Mogey of Carrickfergus who died 9th March 187(5) aged (6)9 years and of his dearly beloved wife Anne PETRIE who died

19th January 1889 aged 79 years. His mother Isabella Mogey who died 25th March 182(5) aged (5)6 years. His father Alexander Mogey who died 22nd August 1837 aged 54 years. His daughter Sarah Jane who died 27th January 1841 aged (3) years. His daughter Isabella who died 7th July 1842 aged 10 years. His daughter Anne who died (29)th April 1846 aged 2 years. His son Alexander who died 1(3)th May 1846 aged (.) years. His brother Stewart who died 21st June 1878 aged 67 years. His son Daniel who died 31st January 1887 aged 50 years. Interred at Liverpool. "The righteous shall be in everlasting remembrance" - Psalm CXII.6.

[The will of Ann Mogey, late of 3 Cameron Street, Belfast, widow, who died 19 January 1889 at same place, was proved at Belfast 11 February 1889 by Joseph Edward Mogey and Alfred Mogey, late of Belfast, gentlemen, the executors. Effects £278. 10s.]

MONEYPENNY
See BARRY

MONTGOMERY
In memory of Nathaniel Montgomery died 5th Decr. 1862 aged 71 years. His wife Alice died 9th Sept. 1873 aged 83 yrs. His son Davys died 10th Oct. 1829 aged 13 yrs. His son Nathaniel died in infancy 24th Oct. 1829. Margaret, wife of his son John, died 2nd Jany. 1843 aged 21 years. His son-in-law Thomas BURLEIGH died 7th June 1853 aged 29 years. His daughter Alice died 27th June 1885 aged 57 years. Also his daughter Ann Burleigh who died at Dundonald 16th Feby. 1898 aged 72 years.

[The will of Nathaniel Montgomery, late of Carrickfergus, in the county of town of Carrickfergus, carman, who died 5 December 1862 at same place, was proved at Belfast 23 January 1864 by the oaths of Alice Montgomery and Ann Burleigh, widows, both of Carrickfergus, the executors. Effects under £300.

Administration of the estate from Ann Burleigh, late of Orrinay Villa, Dundonald, county Down, widow, who died 16 February 1898, granted at Belfast 18 March 1898 to Mary Shepherd of Orrinay Villa, Dundonald, widow, the sister. Effects £292. 18s.]

MONTGOMERY
[Polished granite.] Erected by Agnes Montgomery in loving memory of her dear husband Robert Montgomery who died 24th Dec. 1921. [Mason:-] T. Holden, Larne.

MONTGOMERY
See LAVERTY

MOORE
The family burying place of Thomas Moore who died 27th December 1900 aged 87 years. Also his wife Elizabeth who died 25th May 1908. Also their children: Annie died 1886, Ada died 4th July 1896, Agnes died 8th June 1907, Alexander died 15th July 1940, Elizabeth died 28th August 1944, Joseph and Matthew who died in infancy.

[Annie Moore died 16 June 1886 aged 10 years, daughter of Thomas and Lizzie Moore of High Street. See *Carrickfergus Advertiser*, 18 June 1886.]

M(OOR)E
[Surface dissolved - very shallow lettering.] Erected by John and Mary THOMPSON in memory of their beloved daughter Mary M(oor)e died 21st June 1901 aged 2(3) years. Also their beloved son Robert Henry died 23rd June 1901 aged 2(6) years.

MORRIS
In loving memory of Ellen Morris died 8th March 1921 aged 24 years. Agnes Morris died 17th March 1923 aged 70 years. Thomas Morris died 1st Novr. 1927

aged 47 years. David Morris died 30th July 1931 aged 82 years. John Morris died 2nd March 1962 aged 78 years.

MOORE
See POLLIN

MORRISON
[Small stone in revetting wall to south of chancel.] John & Catherine Morrison A.D. 1793.

[John Morrison, linen weaver, of Scotch Quarter, was made a freeman in 1787.]

MORRISON
[Recorded in McSkimin: *History and Antiquities of Carrickfergus* (1811), p.49 - "head stone ... on the south side of the yard". Now lost.] Set up by Elizabeth HAY in remembrance of Robert Morrison, gunner many years in the Royal Navy: he departed this life Feby. 2nd in the year of our Lord 1794 aged 87 years.

Death took away this good old man.
He was honest, true, and just;
Faithfully he served three kings;
Now his body lies in dust.

[Robert Morrison, gunner, of the Town, was made a freeman in 1785.]

MORRISON
Erected in memory of ....d (children) by William (& Ellen) Morrison. Mary .... died 1(8th) October 18(.6). (Luc)r(e)t(ia) Charlotte b(orn) 1 .... Jan)uary 1(8)64. Ellen born 2(.)th... ...)4 died 9th November 1867. Also the above Captain William Morrison who (departed) this life 9th (A)..il ...7 at H......n Cheshire aged 57 years a(nd interr)ed here. "There shall be no more sea". Also Ellen, wife of the above-named Wm. Morrison, who entered into rest on 16th November 1903 aged 73 years. (Un)ite(d). [Mason:-] J. Robinson & Son, Belfast.

MORRISON
The burying ground of William Morrison. In memory of (his) mother & father: (Ellen) Morrison died 17th (May) 1877 aged (82) years; John Morrison died 22nd January 1887 aged 91 years. This stone claims 2 graves.

MORRISON
[Small white marble tablet in Poaque enclosure.] In memory of Alister, infant son of Hugh Morrison, who died 1st December 1927.

MORRISON
See POAGUE

MORTIMER
See MATHEWS

MULHOLLAND
[Loose slate.] Erected by John Mulholland in memory of his wife Ann Mulholland who departed this life 20th Augt. 1815 aged 42 years.

MULHOLLAND
Erected to John Mulholland Jnr. in memory of his wife Mary who died the 21st Sepr. 1837 AE 28 yrs. Also her two children Maria and Susanna.

MULHOLLAND
Erected by Mat'w Mulholland in memory of his wife Ann aged 68 years, died 20th Septr. 1841.

MULHOLL(AND)
[Small sandstone.] (John) Mulholl(and).

M(UR)RA(Y)
Erected by James M(ur)ra(y) of Belfast to the memory of his wife Jane who died the 5th of September 182(5) aged 2(5) years.

MYNE
[Cast iron plaque; loose; to north of north transept.] The burying place of H. Myne, Carrickfergus, 1895. [Cast by:-] Millfield foundry.

NESBITT
See BOWMAN

NEWTON
See LEGG

NORRIS
[Cast iron plaque attached to low railed enclosure.] The family burying ground of Samuel Norris. James M... & Sons, Ltd. [Cast by:] Millfield Foundry. Iron founders & Engineers Belfast.

NORRIS
[Slate next to foregoing.] The family burying ground of Samuel Norris.

O'BRIEN
See GARDNER

OGILVIE
[Slate.] Erected by Elizabeth Ogilvie in memory of her beloved husband James Oglivie who departed this life July 15th 1883 aged 61 years. Not lost but gone before.

OGLE
[Recorded in McCrum ed. of McSkimin: *History and Antiquities of Carrickfergus* (1909), p.191. South wall of chancel. Brass on black marble decorated with the regimental and Queen's colours of the Royal Fusiliers (7th) and their badge - a rose in a garter crowned.] To the glory of God and the beloved memory of Garth Ogle, Lieutenant, Royal Fusiliers, born at Carrickfergus 1877 and accidentally drowned near Pretoria 30th Oct. 1901 whilst serving with the Mounted Infantry in the South African War. This tablet is erected by his parents Major General F. A. Ogle C.B. and Agnes his wife as a tribute of affection to a gallant young soldier, a staunch friend and a devoted son. [Memorial by:-] Singers, Frome.

[Major-General Frederick Amelius Ogle C.B. was the only son of Admiral Thomas Ogle. He was born 16th February 1841 and in 1858 joined the Royal Marine Artillery, from which he retired in 1895 to live in Hampshire and died 30th June 1931. He saw action in the Gold Coast, 1862; China, 1869; and was wounded in Egypt, 1882. From 1875 to 1880 he served as adjutant to the Antrim Artillery Militia, marrying Agnes Richmond Reid (see North Road, Taylor) in 1876. Mrs Ogle died 1926. See *Army List*; *Who Was Who*.]

O'NEILL
See McDONNELL

OPENSHAWE
[Recorded in McSkimin: *History and Antiquities of Carrickfergus* (1811), p.43 as 'near pulpit' and in McCrum ed. (1909), p. 181 as a 'slab of black marble against the north wall'. Now engraved on a modern stone in chancel floor beside the bishop's tomb.] Here lieth the body of Robert Openshawe, minister, dean of the Cathedral Church of St. Saviours of Connor in the County of Antrim, to the Towne of Cragfergus, pastor, and Chaplayne to the Right Hon'ble Lord CHICHESTER Baron of Belfaste & Lord High Treasurer of Ireland - died 1627.

[The Rev. Robert Openshawe entered St. John's College, Cambridge in 1569 where the graduated B.A. and M.A. He was ordained at Peterborough in 1575 and

Major-General Frederick Amelius Ogle (1841-1901), taken at Southsea in 1896, reproduced by permission of Miss Ann Weatherup

Mrs Agnes Ogle (nee Reid) (died in 1926), taken at Southsea in 1895, reproduced by permission of Miss Ann Weatherup

was rector of Benacre, Suffolk 1575-7. He was then rector and vicar of various parishes in counties Antrim and Down before being Dean of Clogher 1606-17 and of Connor 1615-27. See Leslie: *Clergy of Connor* (1993); Leslie: *Clogher Clergy* (1929).]

OPENSHAWE
See COOPER

OWENS
In loving memory of our dear mother Martha Owens died 26th Jan. 1931 aged 58 years. Also her sons: George H. Owens killed in action in France 1st July 1916 aged 21 years. And Willie Owens, lost at sea through the wreck of S.S. Woodburn 18th Feb. 1923 aged 21 years. Also her daughter Margaret died 9th October 1971. "Together with the Lord".

PAPS
See COOPER

PARKER
See ROBINSON

PARKHILL
Erected in memory of George Parkhill who died 22nd July 1861 aged 61 years.
[George Parkhill, carpenter, of Scotch Quarter, was made a freeman in 1818.]

PARKHILL
[Cast iron plaque behind Swede.] The family burying place of J. & A. Parkhill, 1887.

PARKS
Erected by William Parks in memory of his mother and children, 1818.

PARSONS
Sacred to the memory of Robert Parsons, preacher of the Gospel who died in Carrickfergus the 31st October 1831 aged 27 years. In early life he was brought to the knowledge of Salvation by the remission of his sins and in after character manifested an unshaken confidence in the promises of God and an ardent love for the Salvation of men. By his exit was realised that experimental Godliness alone hath the Majesty in death.
   Blame not the monumental stone we raise
   T'is to the Saviour's not the creature's praise.
[Robert Parsons was a Methodist preacher and his death is recorded in Crookshank: *History of Methodism in Ireland*, Vol. III (1888) p.172.]

PASLEY
Erected by David Pasley in loving memory of his wife Isabella who died 8th November 1898 aged 78 years and his youngest son Robert Henry of the Uitenhage Volunteer Rifles, who died at Port Elizabeth S.A. 13th May 1902. The above named David Pasley died 13th February 1903 aged 87 years. Isabella, second daughter, born 22nd January 1849, died 28th November 1919.

PATRICK
See THOMPSON

PATTERSON
Erected by George Patterson in memory of his daughter Martha, who died 9th August 1866 aged 5 years. Also his wife Margaret died 1st December 1897 aged 62 years. Also the above named George Patterson, died 28th April 1904 aged 70 years. Also his grandson George BEATTIE died 8th March 1907 aged 21 years. Also his son George died 14th May 1934. Also his daughter Margaret died 31st March 1937.

PATTERSON
> See BARRY

PATTON
> See MILLIKEN

PENN
> See CRISPIN (2)

PENNALL
> [Polished granite.] In memory of Thomas Pennall who died in Philadelphia U.S.A. 15th April 1860 aged 34 years. His wife Elizabeth Pennall who died 29th July 1902 aged 75 years. Also their son William McCann Pennall who died 30th Sept. 1915 aged 58 years.

PENNELL
> See CRAIG

PENNEY
> [Polished granite headstone.] In loving memory of our dear parents: William died 22nd December 1955; Martha died 29th June 1968. [Mason:-] Davidson, Carrickfergus.

PENNY
> [Cast iron plaque on low railings south of chancel.] The family burying ground of James Penny, 1888. [Cast by:-] Robinson.

PENNY
> [Polished granite with surround beside path.] Erected by Robert Penny in loving memory of his mother Mary Ross Penny who died 17th May 1945 aged 77 years. Also the above Robert Penny who died 8th December 1946 aged 49 years. His father Thomas Penny who died 23rd January 1948 aged 81 years. His niece Susan Quinn HOLMES died 25th March 1926 aged 5 years. His grandfather Robert Penny died 14th Dec. 1896 aged 66 years. His grandmother Mary Penny died 27th March 1914 aged 79 years. Their daughter Margaret Jane Penny died 13th Jan. 1944 aged 75 years. His aunt Elizabeth Penny died 12th Sep. 1948 aged 88 years. His aunt Mary Penny died 22nd March 1949 aged 85 years.

PETRIE
> See MOGEY

PEYT.....
> See BASHFORD

PICKEN
> Erected by George Picken in memory of his father James Picken who died December 1818 aged 34 years. Samuel MAYNE died 7th Feb. 1835 aged 73 years.
>
> [There were two James Pickens, both farmers of West Division, who were made freeman in 1807 and 1813.]

PICKEN
> Erected by David Picken in memory of his wife Agnes who died 1st May 1911 aged 54 years. Also his daughter Elizabeth McDOWELL who died 30th June 1926. Also his son Thomas who died 3rd February 1929. The above David Picken died 29th May 1936 aged 83 years. Also his son David died 12th July 1956. Also his sons: George died 30th July 1964, John S. died 27th November 1965. [Mason:-] T. Holden, Larne.

PICKEN
> See RODGERS

PIM
See ERSKINE

POAGUE
18(88) The family burying place of William Poague and his wife Agnes Poague. Isabella HALE, wife of Thomas Poague, died 28th February 1871. William Francis Poague died at Valparaiso 6th April 1872. Robert Poague died 1st September 1882. Mary Poague MORRISON, born 15th March 1884, died 4th April 1884. Mary Poague, wife of W. J. Morrison, died 12th October 1917. And her daughter Isabella Hale Morrison died 31st March 1931.

POAGUE
See CARREY

POLLIN
[Granite stone with surround south of chancel.] In loving memory of John Pollin died 14th Feb. 1893. His wife Sara MOORE. His children Mary, Stafford, George, and Henry. His widow Harriet WALSH. His grandson John BELL.

[The will of John Pollin, late of Carrickfergus, auctioneer, who died 14 February 1893 at same place, was proved at Belfast 24 March 1893 by Harriett Pollin of Irish Quarter, Carrickfergus, widow, one of the executors. Effects £331. 10s.]

PORTER
[Polished granite against south perimeter wall.] To the memory of Christian Porter died 27th July 1870 aged 71 years. William Porter died 14th April 1883 aged 90 years. Their son William Porter died 9th August 1906 aged 85 years. Also his wife Elizabeth Jane Porter died 22nd October 1906 aged 71 years. Their son William Porter died 29th January 1919 aged 63 years. Also his wife Charlotte Hester Porter died 28th February 1932 aged 79 years. Anne Porter, daughter of William and Christian Porter, died 17th December 1923 aged 100 years.

[When William Porter died at his residence of Hawthorn Villa in 1883, he was the town's second oldest inhabitant. (The oldest was Isaac Baxter aged 110). Like his grandfather he was a shipowner. When quite a young man he was pressed for the navy during the Napoleonic Wars and took an active part in the blockade of Flushing. He was made a Freeman in 1811. He was a staunch Liberal and took a very active part in the return of M.R. Dalway as member of Parliament in 1868 and 1874. As a member of the First Presbyterian Church he gave the bell for its tower as a gift. The shipping firm of "William Porter and Sons" was managed by his son, John Porter, from Waring Street, Belfast until amalgamation transferred control to Liverpool as "Peter Iredale and Porter". As a young man Captain William Porter J.P. (d.1906) had "followed the sea" in his father's ships. He supplied information to Samuel Plimsoll M.P. during the campaign to legislate on shipping safety. He was high sheriff of Carrickfergus in 1891, a member of the Shipowner's Corporation of London and a member of the Marine Board of Belfast. When he died at his home, Bayview, Greenisland, he left 7 sons and three daughters. See *Northern Whig*, 10 August 1906; McCrum ed of McSkimin: *History and Antiquities of Carrickfergus* (1909), pp.501 and 506; newspaper cutting in "Lizzie Steen's Album", in the possession of Helen Munroe of Glengormley; Anderson: *Sailing Ships of Ireland* (1984), pp. 60-63, 286.]

PORTER
[Decorated Celtic cross of granite against east boundary wall.] In memory of my beloved husband Robert Johnstone Porter, solicitor, born 21st Sept. 1857, died 25th Sept. 1918. Also his wife Georgina, born 24th Augt. 1865, died 15th Sept. 1937. And their son Robert Kerr Porter, born 26th June 1889, died 7th June 1938. Their son Major Harold William Porter died 17th September 1967. Also his dear wife Edith died 23rd December 1969. [Mason:-] Gemmell.

PORTER
See CROOKS

POWERS
See BARRY

POYNTZ
See STEWART

(PR)ICE
[Small sandstone beside Kirk monument.] Erected in memory of George M. Portis (Pr)ice who departed this life the 8th of April A.D. 1838 aged 68 years.
[George P. Price, esquire, of the Town, was made a freeman in 1818.]

RAINEY
In memory of James Rainey who died April 3rd 1836 aged 39. William his son who died 8th August 1837 aged 8. Margaret his wife who died 2nd June 1840 aged 35. Anne his mother who died 5th Jany. 1844 aged 90. James his son who died March 8th 1844 aged 13. And his sister Elizabeth Rainey who died the 14th day of January 1860 aged 72 years.

RAMSEY
Erected to the memory of William Ramsey late of Carrickfergus who departed this life Sept. 17th 1847 aged 68 years.

REID
[Blue slate.] Erected by John Reid in memory of his wife Susanna who died 10th January 1844 aged 57 years. Also her son John who died 1813 aged 5 years. Also her daughter Ann who died 1826 aged 7 years. Also the abovenamed John Reid who died on the 21st August 1855 aged 77 years.
[John Reid, weaver, of Scotch Quarter, was made a freeman in 1807.]

REID
Here (lies) the remains of William Reid of Carrickfergus who departed this life on the 26th of Feby. 1834 in the fiftieth year of his age. In him society was suddenly deprived of (an active &) useful member and his (famil)y of a kind faithful and indulgent head. His bereaved widow (has caused) this stone to be erected to the memory of a beloved & affectionate husband.
[William Reid, pawnbroker, of the Town/West Street, was made a freeman in 1829.]

ROBB
Sacred to the memory of David Robb, born 7th May 1780, died 5th May 1865. Also his wife Mary Robb born 7th November 1777 died 11th Septr. 1851. And their daughter Mary who died 16th Novr. 1887 aged 76 years.

ROBINSON
[Ledger to SE of chancel.] In memory of Elizabeth Robinson, relict of the (late) John Robinson Esq. of Burleigh (Hill) who died the 23rd February 1860 aged 82 years. And of her niece Jane SHIELDS who died the 7th April 1853 aged 62 years. Both rest in the same grave.
[The will of Elizabeth Robinson, late of North Lodge, Carrickfergus, widow, who died 23 February 1860 at North Lodge aforesaid, was proved at Belfast 28 March 1860 by the oath of William Johns of Carrickfergus, esquire, one of the executors. Effects under £2,000.]

ROBINSON
Sacred to the memory of Richard Robinson who died 19th November 1856 aged (8)9 years. Also his wife Frances who died 12th ...il 1867 aged 74 years. Also (his) ... John who died 3rd (...cember) 1848 aged (1)7 years. Also his daughter Jane died (1st ...ober) 1(86)4 aged .. years. (Also his so)n William (who di)e(d 21st D)ecem-

ber 1886 aged 73 years. Also his wife Frances who died 3rd November 1823.
[Mason:-] Geo. Rankin, 108 York St., Belfast

[The will of William Robinson, late of the West Division of Carrickfergus who died 21 December 1886 at same place, was proved at Belfast 9 May 1887 by Frances Robinson of same place, widow, one of the executors. Effects £876.]

ROBINSON

[Inscription on both sides. Robinson epitaph smoothed with plaster and the stone reversed for re-use.] Erected by Elizabeth Robinson in memory of her daughter Margt. Anne Robinson who departed this life 8th Feb. 1859 aged 20 years. In loving memory of Johanna CROMWELL aged 71 years who died 4th May 1906. Also her husband Robert Cromwell who died 26th December 1906 aged 72 years.

ROBINSON

[Gothic sandstone and white marble.] Erected by Thomas Robinson in memory of his son Thomas, who died 15th Feb. 1871 aged 28 years. Also the above named Thomas Robinson died 30th Dec. 1872 aged 71 years and his wife Jane Robinson died 29th June 1881 aged 75 years. Also his daughter Susan PARKER died 13th Aug. 1893 aged 59 years. Also his son William Robinson died 20th Jan. 1908 aged 75 years and Jane, wife of the above named William Robinson, died 28th Feb. 1926 aged 78 years. Jane died 25th March 1949 aged 74 years, Susan died 6th April 1949 aged 72 years, daughters of the above William and Jane Robinson.

[The will of Thomas Robinson, late of Carrickfergus, butcher, who died 30 December 1872 at same place, was proved at Belfast 16 May 1873 by the oath of William Robinson of Carrickfergus, butcher, one of the executors. Effects under £600.

The will of Susan Parker, late of Joymount, county of the town of Carrickfergus, widow, who died 13 August 1893 at same place, was proved at Belfast 29 September 1893 by Margaret Parker of Carrickfergus, spinster, Patrick Crawford of Larne, merchant, and Thomas W. McNinch of Ballyboley, farmer. Effects £187. 0s. 6d.

Thomas Robinson, butcher, of Joymount was made a freeman in 1839.]

ROBINSON

See McQUILLAN and YOUNG

RODGERS

[Between Lynn stones.] Erected by Paul Rodgers in affectionate remembrance of his beloved wife Janet who died Feby. 5th 1888. In loving memory of Beatrice Helena LYNN, F.R.C.S., wife of Paul Rodgers Lynn, died 5th February 1966 aged 66 years. And of the above Paul R. Lynn died 24th Feb. 1972 aged 90 years. [Mason:-] Purdy & Millard, Belfast.

[The will of Janet Rodgers, late of Maritime Cottage, Carrickfergus, wife of Paul Rodgers, who died 5 February 1888 at Albany Cottage, Carrickfergus, was proved at Belfast 24 February 1888 by Robert McCheyne Johnston, Knockagh House, Carrickfergus, farmer, and Henry Lynn of Albany Cottage, Carrickfergus, writing clerk, the executors. Effects £404.

Beatrice Helena Lynn graduated M.B., B.Ch., B.A.O. at Queen's University, Belfast in 1923 and obtained the F.R.C.S. of Edinburgh in 1928. She was an opthalmic surgeon at the Opthalmic and Ulster Hospitals, Belfast.]

RODGERS

[White marble decorated with floral panels.] Erected to the memory of John Rodgers who died 18th August 1897 aged 76 years. Also his daughter Joanna who died 1st July 1859 aged 1 year. Also his daughter Mary who died 4th December 1875 aged 17 years. And his grandson Paul PICKEN who died 12th May 1894 aged 16 years. Also his wife Sarah Rodgers who died 24th March 1902 aged 75 years. Also his daughter Joanna Rodgers who died 21st May 1923 aged 62 years. [Mason:-] T. Holden, Larne.

[Probate of the will of John Rodgers, late of Bryantang, Middle Division,

County of the Town of Carrickfergus, farmer, who died 18 August 1897, granted at Belfast 22 October 1897 to Charles McBrinn, senior, and Samuel Rodgers, both of Carrickfergus, farmer. Effects £827. 13s. 11d.]

RODGERS
[Granite obelisk with urn against east boundary wall.] In loving memory of Paul Rodgers, fell asleep in Jesus March 8th 1901. What I do thou knowest not now; but thou shalt know hereafter. John 13,7. Also Mary, wife of the above, who died 18th February 1947. [Mason:-] Purdy & Millard.

[Paul Rodgers was born at Slievetrue in 1834. He became an apprentice shipwright in Carrickfergus in 1852 and by 1868 was shipyard manager with a growing reputation for designing fast sailing vessels. Robert Johnston, whose daughter Janet married Rodgers, relinquished ownership of the yard to his son-in-law. Financial difficulties in 1892 caused him to sell to Robert Kent and Company, but in 1895 he rebought the shipyard. He was a shipowner 1876-1887 and again from 1899 to his death. Robert Johnston died 11th September 1891 at Loch Lomond aged 84 and left four sons and two daughters. David Rodgers learned his trade in the Carrickfergus shipyard. He later earned kudos as the chief director and general manager of the Skinner and Eddy Corporation, a large shipbuilding enterprise at Seattle - especially in the drive to increase tonnage during the Great War. See McCrum ed. of McSkimin: *History and Antiquities of Carrickfergus* (1909), p.128-9 and 511; *Carrickfergus Advertiser* 7 Feb. 1919; McCaughan "Paul Rodgers: an Ulster Shipbuilder and his Welsh Connections" *Maritime Wales*, 1983, No 7; Anderson: *Sailing Ships of Ireland*, 1984, pp. 271-274.]

RODGERS
See JONES

RONEY
See AICKIN

ROSS
See CONNOR, LAVERTY and McCONKEY

ROWAN
[Railed enclosure against south boundary wall.] 1842. Henry Rowan obiit 5th March 1841 aet 54 years. Mary his relict obiit 24th July 1853 aet 64 years. Also their children:- Martha obiit in infancy May 1827, Ann obiit 9th April 1839 aet 14 years, Charles obiit at Laguna, Mexico, 8th July 1843 aet 20 years, Elizabeth obiit 7th April 1867 aet 34 years, James obiit 7th December 1884 aet 55 years. Eliza, wife of their son John, obiit 15th October 1862 aet 40 years. Also the above John obiit 28th December 1884 aet 68 years. And his wife Mary Agnes obiit 3rd May 1905 aet 70 years: and their children:- William Henry Rowan, M.A. aet 33 years, Marriott Logan Rowan, B.A., M.D. obiit August 1922 aet 51 years, Medical Superintendent, Derby Co. Asylum, interred at Mickleover, Derby. Meta, Mrs M. I. HOPPER, obiit 15th October 1931 aet 50 years. John Charles Rowan, M.B., Surg-Capt. R.N. obiit 11th November 1939 aet 70 years. Mary Catherine Rowan, B.A., schoolmistress, obiit 20th July 1951 aet 78 years.

[Marble tablet added to stone.] In loving memory of John Rowan died 28th Dec. 1884 aged 68 years. Also his wife Mary Agnes born 9th March 1835, died 3rd May 1905.

[Granite cross placed in enclosure.] To the beloved memory of W. H. Rowan, M.A., H.M. Inspector of Schools, son of John and Agnes Rowan, died 12th December 1900 aged 33 years. "Blessed are the pure in heart."

[Small plaque placed in the same enclosure.] In loving memory of John Charles Rowan, M.B., Surgeon Captain, Royal Navy, died 11th November 1935.

[Henry Rowan, shoemaker, of Irish Quarter was made a freeman in 1807. James Rowan was a grocer and draper in West Street. John, a boot and shoemaker, also began trading in West Street, but moved to High Street. He was a director of the Gas Company and on the committee of the Literary and Scientific Society. His widow was a milliner.]

ROWAN
[White marble tablet on concreted area south of Craig monument.] Sacred to the memory of John Legg Rowan, second son of Commander Edward Rowan R.N. who departed this life 14th November 1855 aged 10 years. Also of the above Commander Edward Rowan R.N. who departed this life 31st January 1871 aged 83 years. And of his eldest son William Rowan LEGG who departed this life 5th November 1873 aged 30 years. And of his widow Elizabeth M. Rowan who departed this life 28th July 1888. And Alice Rowan who departed this life 20th October 1929, eldest daughter of the above Commander Edward Rowan R.N.

[The will of Edward Rowan, late of Carrickfergus, late Commander R.N., who died 31 January 1871 at same place, was proved at Belfast 17 May 1871 by the oath of Snowden Corken of Ingram near Lisburn, county Antrim, esquire, the sole executor. Effects under £600.

Edward Rowan was the fifth son of Robert Rowan of Mullans, Garry, and Bellisle, Co. Antrim. His father and eldest brother John both served as High Sheriff and Deputy Lieutenant for Co. Antrim. Two brothers were knighted: Sir Charles K.C.B. was appointed Chief Commissioner of the Metropolitan Police Force (London) on its foundation in 1829; Sir William G.C.B. was colonel of the 52nd Foot and became a field-marshal. Captain Robert (d.1863) was another brother. Edward Rowan entered the Royal Navy 28 May 1799; midshipman, February 1801; lieutenant, October 1807; retired on half pay, September 1814; Commander, April 1844. Edward was, for a time, inspector of the county gaol. He became a municipal commissioner, treasurer to the Grand Jury and a director of the Gas Company. He lived in High Street and married Elizabeth Maria Legg. William Rowan adopted the name of Legg on inheriting the property of his uncle John Legg, who was a currier and tanner in Scotch Quarter and who lived at Glynn Park. William graduated at Trinity College and was High Sheriff of Carrickfergus in 1868. On his death the property went to his brother Edward Lutwidge Rowan-Legg who joined the Canadian Pacific Railway. He married Jane, daughter of William Burleigh, J.P. Their daughter Emily Elizabeth married Mills Close in February 1918, while their 3 sons became bankers in Canada: Edward Lutwidge (born 1877) married Ann Catherine Stewart in 1904; Aubrey Burleigh (born 1879) married Bessie Herbert Perley and had 3 sons:- Edward Stewart (born 1905); Dr. Kingsley, and Allan Aubrey (born 1912), a petroleum company executive and diplomat. See Martin's *Directory* (1841); *Belfast and Ulster Directory*; McCrum's ed. of McSkimin: *History and Antiquities of Carrickfergus* (1909), p. 503; *Burke's Landed Gentry of Ireland* (1912 ed.); *Dictionary of National Biography*.]

ROWAN
[Recorded in McCrum's ed. of McSkimin: *History and Antiquities of Carrickfergus* (1909), p. 192. North wall of chancel.] In loving memory of Robert Rowan late captain 52nd Oxfordshire Light Infantry, born 17th March 1780 at Belleisle, county Antrim, died 6th January 1863 at Carrickfergus. And of Henrietta Maria his wife, born 20th November 1814 at Waterford, died 9th March 1879 at Carrickfergus. "In the world ye shall have tribulation: but be of good cheer; I have overcome the world". John, XVI.33. [Mason:-] J. Robinson & Son, Belfast.

[The will of Henrietta Maria Rowan, late of Carrickfergus, widow, who died 9 March 1879 at same place, was proved at Belfast 18 April 1879 by the oaths of Annabella Rowan of Carrickfergus, spinster, the sole executrix. Effects under £1,000.]

ROWAN
See BARKLEY

RUDDELL
See GRAY

RUTHERFORD
[Brass plate beside north door to chancel.] To the glory of God and with thankfulness for the life and ministry of James Cooper Rutherford, Prebendary of Kilroot 1932-1950, Treasurer of Connor 1950-1958, Rector of this Parish 1931-1958, during whose incumbency much was done to restore and enrich this church, died 28th November 1971. The adjoining door was given to his memory by Margaret Rutherford his widow and dedicated on 16th May 1976. The west entrance doors of the church were provided by the parishioners in affectionate memory of Canon Rutherford and dedicated on 8th September 1974.

RUTHERFORD
See MACONKEY and YOUNG

SAYERS
See GETTY

SCOTT
See LATTIMORE

SEARIGHT
See KIRK

S(HAW)
Erected to the memory of Elizabeth S(ha).. who died 22nd De(cembe)r 1864 aged 6(. ye)ars.

SHAW
[Pointed head with two fern leaves.] Sacred to the memory of Robert Shaw who died 10th Sepr. 1889 aged 76 years. His wife Jane Shaw who died 15th Jany. 1860 aged 44 years. His son Thomas who died 22nd Sepr. 1879 aged 40 years. His daughter Maggie who died in infancy. His brother John Shaw who died 18th Decr. 1880 aged 61 years. Also his daughter-in-law Maggie Shaw who died 20th March 1912 aged 58 years and her husband David Robb Shaw died 24th March 1916. Also Robert Shaw, eldest son of the above David Robb Shaw, died 25th March 1946.

SHAW
See JACK

SHERER
Erected by J(am)es Sherer to the memo(r.......fath)er Robert S(h.r)er who dep(a....) th(is lif)e the (.) of (April) 1800 aged 7(.) ye(ars).

SHIELDS
See ROBINSON

SIMM
[Slate.] Erected to the memory of James Simm who departed this life 17th January 1863 aged 69 years.
[The will of James Simm, late of Carrickfergus in the county of the town of Carrickfergus, master mariner, who died 17 January 1863 at same place, was proved at Belfast 18 December 1863 by the oath of James Stannus of Carrickfergus aforesaid, builder, one of the executors. Effects under £450.
There were two people called James Simm who were made freemen in 1811. One was a shoemaker of Irish Quarter and the other was a carman of Middle Division.]

SIMMS
Erected by Henry Simms in fond and loving memory of his father James Simms who died 18th May 1916 aged 58 years. Also his mother Millicent ADAIR who died 10th May 1926 aged 65 years. Also their youngest son Morral who died 14th

May 1908 aged 19 years. Also their eldest daughter Jane who died 14th August 1885 aged 7 years. [Mason:-] Holden, Larne.

SIMMS
Erected by John Simms in memory of his father and mother. The above-named John Simms died 7th May 1916 aged 70 years. Also his daughter Jane (Cissie) who died 6th July 1916 aged 30 years. And Mary, wife of the above named John Simms, died 14th June 1932 aged 71 years. Also his grandson James (Jim) died 5th April 1944 aged 18 years. Also his daughter-in-law Eliza died 5th May 1962 aged 73 years. Also his son Samuel died 22nd Dec. 1968 aged 85 years.

SIMMS
[Granite with lead lettering and surround next to foregoing.] In loving memory of James Lockhart Simms who died 13th Oct. 1940. His wife Jenina died 10th Oct. 1945. Their son William died March 1906 aged 14 months.

SIMMS
[Polished granite]. In loving memory of our dear father William Grant called home 18th Oct. 1945. Also our dear mother Jane called home 14th Oct. 1973. Worthy of everlasting remembrance. [Mason:-] Davidson, Carrick.

SIMMS
[White marble with lead lettering on granite plinth.] In loving memory of James died 21st November 1963 beloved husband of Margaret.

SIMMS
[Polished granite next to foregoing.] In loving memory of a devoted husband and father Robert James died 19th January 1973 and his wife our beloved mother Agnes Jane died 29th March 1982. [Mason:-] Davidson.

SIMMS
[Polished black granite.] In loving memory of Samuel, dear husband of Lilian and devoted father and grandfather, died 19th May 1992 aged 82 years. Freeman and former mayor of this borough.
 [One of a family of eleven, educated at Woodburn Public Elementary School, newsagent in Ellis Street, Borough councillor 1965-1981, mayor 1979-1981, freeman 1986, survived by wife Lilian, 4 daughters, and 2 sons. *Carrickfergus Guardian*, 27 May 1992.]

SIMMS
See BOWDEN and HUNTER

SKELLY
[Small cast iron wheeled cross.] In loving memory of J. Bell Skelly J.P. died April 16 1924 aged 64.

SKELTON
[Granite with lead lettering near west door.] In loving memory of John Skelton died 1st January 1952. His wife Jeannie died 13th June 1958. Peace.

SLOAN
[Slate and sandstone to south of chancel.] In loving memory of John Sloan died 15th January 1883. Also his wife Agnes died 20th February 1889. In loving memory of my son Thomas Sloan died 17th September 1913. Also my wife Margaret Sloan died 20th September 1917.
 [The will of John Sloan, late of Carrickfergus, farmer, who died 16 January 1883 at same place, was proved at Belfast 26 February 1883 by Daniel McGookin of Carrickfergus, farmer, the sole executor. Effects £113. 15s.]

SMITH
[Cast iron plaque.] The family burying ground of James Smith, Belfast.

SMYTH

In loving memory of Catherine Smyth who died 24th May 1914 aged 64 years. Also her beloved husband Thomas Smyth who died 5th Nov. 1917 aged 69 years. Also Mary A. Smyth KIRKWOOD died 2nd February 1929 aged 77 years.

SMYTH

Erected by Jane Smyth in loving memory of her dear husband Henry Smyth who departed this life 13th November 1916 aged 65 years. Also the above Jane Smyth who died 9th February 1920 aged 65 years. Also their dear son William, beloved husband of Elsie Smyth, died 4th November 1950. "He giveth his beloved sleep". [Mason:-] Kirkwood, Belfast.

SMYTH

[To east of south transept.] Mary Ann Smyth died 23rd July 1928.

SPEAR

[Near west wall.] Sacred to the memory of Catherine Spear daughter of George Spear, Carrickfergus, Esq., who died 8th March 1850. Here also are interred the remains of Jane Spear his wife. (And) Anna Rebecca his daughter. Also George Spear, treasurer of the (Coun)ty of the Town of Carrickfergus who departed this life 18th August 1852. Also of Eliza t(heir) daughter and the beloved wife of the Revd. Richard BUTLER of Manchester who died on the 27th May 1873 aged 73 years. Also Eleanor Spear died (5th) of December 1877. Also Margaret daughter of the above George Spear who died March 13th 1895.

[George Spear, merchant, of the Town, was made a freeman in 1807.

The will of Eleanor Spear, late of Carrickfergus, spinster, who died 5 December 1877 at same place, was proved at Belfast 1 July 1878 by the oath of Margaret Spear of Carrickfergus, same county, spinster, the sole executrix. Effects under £1,500.

Probate of the will of Margaret Spear, late of High Street, Carrickfergus, county Antrim, spinster, who died 13 March 1895 at Carrickfergus, granted at Dublin 18 April 1895 to Sarah Nolan of High Street, Carrickfergus, spinster. Effects £3,502. 17s. 2d.]

SPEAR

[Recorded in McCrum ed. of McSkimin: *History and Antiquities of Carrickfergus* (1909), p. 188. White marble on west wall of north transept.] Margaret, fourth daughter of the late George Spear of Carrickfergus, died 13th March 1895. Every good work had her kindly help and every deserving object her active sympathy and support. This tablet is erected by a few loving friends to perpetuate her memory. "She stretched out her hand to the poor: yea, she reached forth her hands to the needy". Proverbs, XXXI, 20. [Mason:-] Robinson, Belfast.

SPENCE

See BARKLEY

STANNUS

[Near west door.] Erected by James Stannus Junr. in memory of his daughter Jane obiit 12th Feby. 1835 aged 7 years. Also his mother Jane Stannus obiit 14th April 1837 aged 79 years. And his wife Margaret who died 30th March 1854. Also the above James Stannus who died 10th Septr. 1877. Also Hannah Stannus who died 4th September 1905.

[The will of James Stannus, senior, late of Irish Quarter, Carrickfergus, county of the town of Carrickfergus, builder, who died 22 August 1877 at same place, was proved at Belfast 10 September 1877 by the oath of John Knox Mitchell of 9 High Street, Belfast, county Antrim, merchant, one of the executors. Effects under £200. NOTE the discrepancy in dates of death.

James Stannus junior pursued his trade as a builder successively from High Street, Governor's Place and Irish Quarter South. He was made a freeman, as a carpenter, in 1818. In 1837 he ran unsuccessfully for the office of town clerk, but was appointed harbour master in 1842. He was 83 when he died in August 1877 (McCrum). His third son Anthony Carey Stannus became an artist and landscape painter, dividing his life between London and Belfast, with a period in Mexico exhibiting at the Royal Academy 1863-1903. See Belfast and Ulster Directories; McCrum ed. of McSkimin: *History and Antiquities of Carrickfergus* (1909), pp.115, 219, 272-3, 336, 522, 528; Hewitt: *Art in Ulster*, I, pp.184-5; Kennedy: *British Art 1900-1937* (1982), pp.134-135.]

STEPHENS
[Recorded in McCrum ed. of McSkimin: *History and Antiquities of Carrickfergus* (1909), p. 170. Gothic framed tablet of marble on north wall of nave.] This monument is erected by James Stephens in memory of his father Stratford Stephens who died 24th January 1848 aged 48 years and in affectionate remembrance of his dear mother Margaret Stephens who died 18th April 1873 aged 67 years. Deeply regretted by her children for whom her love and devotion were unbounded.

STEPHENS
[Granite with surround.] Erected by Robert Stephens in loving memory of his father Stratford Stephens died 24th January 1848 aged 47 years. His mother Margaret Stephens died 18th April 1873 aged 67 years. His brothers and sisters, Sarah Eliza Stephens died 27th November 1837 aged 1 year and 26 days, John Stratford Stephens died 3rd March 1844 aged 13 months, Stratford Stephens died 10th November 1849 aged 2 years and 7 months, William Stephens died 22nd June 1892 aged 61 years, Thomas Stephens died at Sydney, New South Wales, 27th July 1880 aged 47 years. James Stephens died 30th March 1895 aged 55 years, interred at Highgate, London, Margaret MESNEY died 2nd July 1901 aged 66 years, interred at New York, U.S.A. Fanny LOGAN died 28th February 1919. Also her son Dr. Thomas Stratford Logan died 31st October 1918. And her daughter Dr. Ellen Margaret Logan died 12th March 1926.

[The will of William Stephens, formerly of Whitehead, county Antrim, and late of Carrickfergus, commission agent, who died 22 June 1892 at latter place, was proved at Belfast 8 August 1892 by James Stephens of 44 Dartmouth Park Road, London, manufacturer, and Henry Blackbourne of Carrickfergus, press correspondent, the executors. Effects £1,246. 0s. 2d.]

STEPHENS
[Polished granite against east boundary wall.] In affectionate memory of Mary Margaret, infant daughter of Robert and Emma Stephens, who died 29 June 1873 aged 6 months. Also Emma, the beloved wife of Robert Stephens, born 7 May 1844, died 13 August 1913, interred at Rostherne, Knutsford. Also the above named Robert Stephens, J.P., born 24 March 1845, died 12 October 1927, interred 14 October 1927.

STEUART
[Recorded in McCrum ed. of McSkimin: *History and Antiquities of Carrickfergus* (1909), p. 181. White marble on south wall of chancel with funeral urn and draped figure above.] This monument is erected by a few friends of Samuel Davys Steuart of Carrickfergus M.D. who from a long and intimate knowledge of his worth offer it as a faithful tribute to his lamented memory. It is consecrated by the tears of the poor and the prisoner to heal whose bodily diseases and to improve whose moral condition his eminent professional talents, his enlightened understanding, and the feelings of his benevolent heart were applied. Died November 4th 1817 aged 36 years.

STEWART
[Recorded in McCrum ed. of McSkimin: *History and Antiquities of Carrickfergus* (1909), p. 192. Mounted on north wall of chancel. Arms:- quarterly, first and fourth or a lion rampant gules, second and third azure three garbs of the first, a bordure company of the first and second. Crest:- a severed head.] Near this place lies interred the body of Captain Charles Stewart, 5th (Lord Molesworth's) Dragoons,

son of Alexr. Stewart of Wester Cluny, Perthshire, and Isabella Stewart of Ballnakillie his wife. He died 4th June 1774 distinguished alike in his military and private career by his fidelity to the path of duty and by the display of every amiable and Christian virtue. Also to the memory of Rose his wife who died 11th Feby. 1779 aged 92 years.

She was daughter of Roger HALL, Esq. of Narrow Water, Co. Down, and grand-daughter of Sir Toby POYNTZ, Knt. of Acton and Brenock, Co. Armagh.

STEWART
[Small stone south of chancel.] Erected by John Stewart in memory of his wife Ellenor who died March the 10th 1782 aged 45 years.

STEWART
Erected by D. Stewart, Carrickfergus, in memory of his mother Mary Stewart who died the 2nd of March 1823, aged 60 years. And his two infant sons, viz. William K. Stewart who died 13th January, 1829 aged 11 months; Charles K. Stewart who died 1st June 1833 aged 2 years.

STEWART
Erected by Margaret Stewart in memory of her husband James Stewart who departed this life the 19th Novr. 1831 aged 67 years. Also the above Margaret Stewart who departed this life 25th April 1861 aged 90 years.

STEWART
Hugh Stewart obiit 24th September 1845 age 30 years.

STEWART
Erected by her daughter Eliza ALLEN in memory of her beloved mother Ann Stewart who died 2nd June 1874 aged 88 years. Also the above-named Eliza ALLAN [sic] who died on 4th Jany. 1905 aged 84 years.

Exterior of baptistry with tablet to Charles Arthur Wellesley Stewart, barrister, who died in 1899

STEWART
[Granite tablet attached to exterior wall of baptistry.]
Charles Arthur Wellesley Stewart, barrister-at-law, died 5th May 1899 aged 84 years.

[Probate of the will of Charles Arthur Wellesley Stewart, late of Scotch Quarter, Carrickfergus, county of the town of Carrickfergus, barrister, who died 5 May 1899, granted at Belfast 21 July 1899 to Henry J. Johns, Director of the Belfast Bank, Belfast. Effects £36,067. 9s.

C.A.W. Stewart was the only son of Col. Matthew Stewart of Carrickfergus and was born in January 1815. He was educated at Trinity College, Dublin where he took his B.A. in 1837, M.A. in 1840 and was called to the Irish Bar in 1839. He relinquished his practice on succeeding to the property of his aunt, Miss Duncan of Carrickfergus. He was agent for the Dobbs estate for about 35 years and also for W.D.D. Wilson. He was also high sheriff in 1881, auditor of the gas company, director of the Great Northern Railway and Ulster Spinning Co., and president of the Literary and Scientific Society and died unmarried at his residence in the Scotch Quarter. See McCrum ed. of McSkimin: *History and Antiquities of Carrickfergus* (1909), pp 114, 376, 501 and 504-5; Burtchaell and Sadleir: *Alumni Dublinenses* (1924); Belfast and Ulster Directories.]

STEWART
[Recorded in McCrum ed. of McSkimin: *History and Antiquities of Carrickfergus* (1909), p. 189. Window in south wall of chancel depicting Christ's ascension.] To the glory of God and in loving memory of Charles Arthur Wellesley Stewart who died 5th May 1899. This window is dedicated by E. WILSON A.D. 1900. [Window by:-] T.F. Curtis Ward & Hughes, London, 1900.

STEWART
[War Graves Commission stone with regimental badge: an acorn between oak leaves within a circle bearing the legend "The Cheshire Regiment", all upon a cut star of eight points.] 4130457 Private J. Stewart, The Cheshire Regiment, 8th February 1941 age 33. [Latin cross.] Ever remembered.

STEWART
[Loose iron plaque.] The family burying ground of Robert Stewart.

STEWART
See McFERRAN and McKEEN

STOCKMAN
See FISKEN

STRAHAN
See LEGG

STRAIN
See McCONNELL and McGRIFFIN

STUART
[Laid flat beside south boundary wall.] Erected by Felix Stuart to the memory of three of his children viz. Jh. Alexander who died on the 1(5)th October 1824 aged nine months. Also Mry. Jane who died on the 16th July 1826 aged eight months. Also Flx. Hugh who died on the 7th February 1827 aged four years and nine months.

STUART
[Large slate to south of chancel.] Sacred to the memory of Samuel Davys Stuart, merchant, who departed this life 29th of May 1857. Also to that of his wife Elizabeth Jane Hudson Stuart who died on the 3rd of August 1841. George Stuart died 1861. Mary Stuart died 1876. Here also is buried the body of John McMAHON who died 17th March 1898 aged 84 years. "Looking unto Jesus, the author and

finisher of our faith". And of his niece Mary EDGAR who died 13th Novr. 1904 aged 63 years. "Here we have no continuing city, but we seek one to come".

[The will of Samuel Davys Stuart, late of Carrickfergus, in the county of the town of Carrickfergus, merchant, who died 29 May 1857 at same place (left unadministered by George Stuart one of the executors), was proved at the Principal Registry, 23 October 1861 by the oath of Mary Stuart of Carrickfergus, spinster, the surviving executor. Effects under £450.

Letters of administration of the personal estate of George Stuart, late of Castle Street, Carrickfergus, in the county of the town of Carrickfergus, merchant, a bachelor, who died 6 July 1861 at same place, were granted at Belfast 16 September 1861 to Mary Stuart of Carrickfergus, spinster, the sister, sole next of kin of said deceased. Effects under £8,000.

The will of Mary Stuart, late of Carrickfergus, spinster, who died 22 January 1876 at same place, was proved at Belfast 11 February 1876 by the oaths of John Borthwick of Prospect, Carrickfergus, esquire, Justice of the Peace, and Anne Davys Malcolm of Belfast, widow, the executors. Deceased died domiciled in Ireland. Effects within U.K. of G.B. and I. under £5,000.]

STUART
See HERDMAN and MATHEWS

SWANSTON
[Small white marble.] In memory of Isabella Swanston who died 4th Feby. 1848 aged 6 years.

SWEDE
In loving memory of Elizabeth Swede who died 28th July 1928 in her 80th year. "She hath done more than they all"

TAGGART
[Recorded in McCrum ed. of McSkimin: *History and Antiquities of Carrickfergus* (1909), p. 188. Mural tablet in south transept.] Isaiah XXXV, 10. In loving memory of Surgeon Major David Redmond Taggart M.D. Royal Antrim Artillery and Coroner County Antrim and Carrickfergus, died 10th April 1886 aged 47 years. "Until the day break, and the shadows flee away".

[The will of David Redmond Taggart, late of Carrickfergus, M.D., who died 10 April 1886 at same place, was proved at Belfast 11 June 1886 by Julia Alice Taggart, widow, and Samuel McKee Shannon, both of Carrickfergus, and Campbell Taggart of Thorn Hill, Randalstown, county Antrim, esquire, the executors. Effects £2,847. 16s. 2d.

He was buried in North Road graveyard, q.v.]

TALBOT
See HIGGINSON

TAYLOR
[Slate.] In loving memory of James Taylor who died 17th August 1930. Also his mother Margaret Taylor who died 10th July 1909. And his wife Mary who died 12th Dec. 1932.

TAYLOR
[Polished granite.] In loving memory of our dear parents: John died 8th March 1933, Joseph died 3rd February 1972.

THACKERAY
See BOWMAN

THOMPSON
[Sandstone, probably erected in 1840s.] Erected by John Thomps(o)n, U.S. America, in memory of his fathe(r) John Thom(pson who dep)arted th........ 19th M(arch ....) aged 67 years. Also his .... (S)amuel who died .... aged 5 years.

THOMPSON

[Against north boundary wall.] Erected by Thomas Thompson in memory of his children:- Alexander died in infancy November 1839. John Millar died April 1853 aged 15 years. Wilhelmina died Jan. 185(.) aged 10 years. Richard died Feb. 1857 aged 7 years. Also his son Thomas Alexander, Surgeon in the Peninsular and Oriental Company's Service, who was lost in the wreck of the Steam Ship Car(n)ati(c) in the Red Sea on the 14th September 1869 aged 26 years. The above Thomas Thompson who died 28th March 1871 aged 76 years. Also his wife Wilhelmina who died 16th November 1894 aged 78 years. Also his son-in-law Dr. Josias Wilson PATRICK who died 9th January 1891. And his wife Ann Patrick who died 16th August 1916. Also Susan FEENEY, daughter of Thomas Thompson, who died 10th March 1905. [A polished granite tablet is placed in front of the gravestone:-] Also in memory of Susan Elizabeth Feeney. Ashes interred here May 1973. Last surviving grand-daughter of the above Thomas Thompson & daughter of Susan Feeney.

[The enquiry into the loss of the *Carnatic* was published by order of the House of Commons 10 Feb., 1870. She had a displacement of 1,254.06 tons, was built of iron in 1862, brig-rigged with three decks, two masts and two engines of 400 H.P. On her last voyage she carried 34 passengers, a large amount of specie, a full cargo and Government mails, besides a crew of 176 commanded by Captain Phillip Burton Jones. On 12th September 1869 at 10 a.m. she left Suez for Bombay in fine calm conditions but during the night the ship struck on the Shadwan Reef. It was not until 11 a.m. on the 14th that the decision was made to disembark the passengers. "As several of them were in the act of getting into the boats the ship suddenly slipped down stern foremost, heeling over and leaving the foremast only out of the water precipitating several of the passengers and crew into the sea. Five passengers and twenty-six of the crew unfortunately were drowned. The remainder landed on the island by means of the ship's boats" and were later picked up by the *Sumatra*. Captain Jones' master's certificate was suspended for nine months.

The will of Thomas Thompson, late of Carrickfergus, gentleman, who died 28 March 1871 at same place, was proved at Belfast 16 June 1871 by the oaths of David Pasley, bank manager and the Reverend William Graham, independent minister, both of Carrickfergus, two of the executors. Effects under £6,000.

There were two Thomas Thompsons recorded as freemem. One was a shoemaker of the north-east division who was made a freeman in 1814. The other was a baker of the Town who was made a freeman in 1818.]

THOMPSON

Erected by (J)ames Thompson in memory of his wife Martha who died 23rd Nov. 1848 aged 59 years. Also his daughter Agnes who died 12th Septr. 1855 aged 24 years. Also the above named James Thompson who died 18th Feby. 1858 aged 77 years.

[James Thompson, weaver, of the north-east division, was made a freeman in 1803.]

THOMPSON

Erected by James Thompson in memory of his beloved mother Margaret Thompson who departed this life 23rd November 1864 aged 64 years. "Come now and let us reason together, saith the Lord: though your sins be as scarlet, they shall be as white as snow: though they be red like crimson, they shall be as wool". Isaiah 1.18.

THOMPSON

[In a low railed enclosure, flaking badly.] .... March 1883.. their children. William lost at sea aged 26 years..........John and Joseph who died in infancy. And Anne who died 27th Nov. 1904 aged 74 years. Mary Jane who died 5th October 1917 aged 68 years.

THOMPSON
[Cast iron plaque laid flat near main path.] The family burying place of John Thompson 1888.

THOMPSON
[White limestone, surface dissolving.] Erected (by) Mary Thompson in memory of her beloved daughter Mary (.....) died 21st J(une 1901 aged 23 years. Also) Robert Henry died 2(3rd June 1901 aged 20 years).

THOMPSON
See BARKLEY (2), BOYD, CARREY and M(OOR)E

TODD
See EVERARD

TOWNLY
Here lyeth the body of George Townly who departed this life the 2th day of May 1791 aged 21th years.

TURNER
See BARRY and BUTCHER

TURPIN
See LAWRENCE

VEACOCK
See BOWMAN

VINT
[Granite pillar surmounted by a draped urn.] In memory of William Vint who departed this life 25th February 1879 aged 69 years. Also his wife Sarah HAY who departed this life 18th February 1902 aged 82 years. Also their son Singleton who departed this life 28th October 1893 aged 36 years. Also their daughter Jane who departed this life 20th September 1928 aged 82 years. Also their daughter Mary died 1st July 1937. Elizabeth died 19th March 1944.

[Further inscriptions are recorded on the west face:-] The burial place of John Vint J.P. His sons Hugh McMillan died 7th April 1903 aged 19 years, William died 5th Decr. 1905 aged 23 years. Margaret, wife of John Vint, died 13th Oct. 1926 aged 70 years. Also the above John Vint J.P. died 14th Sept. 1933 aged 85 years. And their elder daughter Maud Edith Vint died 26th Feby. 1965 aged 84 years.

The will of William Vint, late of Loughview, Carrickfergus, baker, general merchant and farmer, who died 25 February 1879 at same place, was proved at Belfast 2 April 1879 by the oaths of Joseph Hay Vint of Cavan, bank manager, and Thomas Vint of Loughview, mercantile clerk, two of the executors. Effects under £2,000.

The Vints were a family of shopkeepers. William began as a baker in Irish Quarter but moved to West Street. They expanded into other goods and traded under the name of William Vint and Sons. Thomas was the first chairman after Carrickfergus became an Urban District in 1899. See Belfast and Ulster Directories; McCrum ed. of McSkimin: *History and Antiquities of Carrickfergus* (1909), pp. 129, 132, 519.]

VINT
[Granite stone against east boundary wall.] In memory of Sara, beloved wife of Thomas Vint, born 21st June 1849, died 25th January 1919. Their infant son who died 14th July 1890 and daughter Lilian Winifred Irene, Baba, born 21st November 1892, died 1st December 1895. Rebecca Margaret BAIN, sister of above Sara Vint and daughter of the late Rev. Jas. Bain of Straid, born 16th January 1844, died 28th August 1918. Also Mary Waring Bain, born 16th November 1847, died 15th December 1922. Also Margaret L. Vint, beloved wife of Robert Vint, died

James Weatherup (b.1812), reproduced by permission of Miss Ann Weatherup

Elizabeth Weatherup nee Donel (b. 1816), reproduced by permission of Miss Ann Weatherup

21st December 1925. Also Thomas Vint J.P., husband of the above Sara Vint, born 11th August 1855, died 1st December 1931. The above Robert Vint, born 28th Sept. 1853, died 20th April 1942.

WALES

[Polished black granite.] To the memory of Anne Wales who died 9th Sept. 1821 aged 52 years. Her husband John Wales who died 5th Jany. 1849 aged 83 years. Their son John who died 1st Feby. 1840 aged 33 years. Their grand-son George H. Wales who died in infancy. And of his wife Grace H. Wales who died 7th Augt. 1870 aged 82 years. Charlotte Greer who died 5th July 1893 aged 92 years. "I am the Resurrection and the life, saith the Lord".

WALES

[Black granite against east boundary wall.] In memory of George Frederick Wales, M.D., F.R.C.S.E., who died 27th June 1905 aged 75 years. Also his wife Charlotte Wales who died 18th January 1914 aged 80 years. And their son William Edward Wales who died 4th September 1938. Also their daughter Elsie Wales who died 5th March 1946. Also their son Alfred Ernest Wales who died 26th August 1949. Also their son Frank Howard Wales, M.A., B.D., who died 28th June 1950. And his wife Jessie Frazer Wales who died 5th October 1850. "O Lord in thee have I trusted". [Mason:-] Jenkins.

WALKER

See LOWE

WALLACE

[White marble with lead lettering.] In loving memory of David Wallace died 5th February 1919. Also his dear daughter Frances LUFF died 3rd March 1969. [Mason:-] Hart, Carnmoney.

WALSH

See POLLIN

WALSHE

[Recorded in McCrum ed. of McSkimin: *History and Antiquities of Carrickfergus* (1909), p. 188. White marble with frame painted black, on east wall of north transept.] Sacred to the memory of Blayney Townley Walshe Esq., late Lieut. Col. Royal Artillery who departed this life Jan. 29th 1839 aged 62. Also of Anna his wife who died in Dublin Jan. 18th 1840 aged 49.

WARREN

See BLACKBURNE

WATSON

Erected by Samuel Watson in memory of his deceased children. Jane Watson who departed this life 11th December 1824 aged 7 years. Also Samuel Watson who departed this life 8th October 1833 aged 11 years. The above Samuel Watson died 26th March 1868 aged 87 years. Also his wife Agnes Watson died 25th November 1872 aged 84 years. Also his son Alexander died 4th June 1873 aged 53 years.

[The will of Alexander Watson, late of Bryantang, Carrickfergus, farmer, who died 3 June 1873 at same place, was proved at Belfast 25 June 1873 by the oaths of Henry McBrin of Carrickfergus and John Graham of Bryantang, both of Carrickfergus, farmers, the executors. Effects under £20.

Samuel Watson, labourer, of the Middle Division, was made a freeman in 1803.]

WATSON

[Set against north transept.] Erected by Sarah Watson in memory of her brother James who died 24th June 1863 aged 40 years. Her brother Samuel who died 13th June 1868 aged 26 years. Her mother Rose who died 14th June 1868 aged 67 years. Her father Alexander who died 28th Sepr. 1869 aged 78 years. The above

Sarah Watson died in Glasgow 13th June 1881 aged 42 years. Her brother Robert who died 8th July 1902 aged 66 years. And her brother William who died 25th Augt. 1903 aged (6)4 years. Also her (sister Kathleen) who died 23rd May (19)11 aged ....

[Alexander Watson was a farmer of the West Division who was made a freeman in 1811.]

WATSON

In loving memory of a dear wife and mother Agnes, died 17th November 1978. At rest. [Mason:-] Wilson 38.9.

WATSON

See FAIR(F)OO(T)

WEATHERUP

[Stylistically this stone belongs to the third quarter of the nineteenth century.] The family burying ground of James Weatherup. 'I love them that love me, and those that seek me early, shall find me.' Prov. VIII.17.

[James Weatherup was born 27th January 1812, the son of John Weatherup of Ballyvanen in the parish of Glenavy and Susan Johnston. His sister married Captain Robert McFerran (q.v.). His third wife Elizabeth (b.1816) was the daughter of John Donel (later changed to Donald) and Jane Downey. James had a tailoring shop in West Street and became superintendent of Sheil's Institute in 1870, a post he resigned two years before his death in 1877. James and Elizabeth had eight children, of whom the second, John (b.1846), was a bookkeeper employed by Taylor's Mills.]

WEATHERUP

In loving memory of my dear husband Samuel Weatherup B.A. died 23rd February 1955. His mother Matilda Weatherup died August 1927. Also Ena Weatherup M.Sc. died 31st December 1974, wife of the above named Samuel.

WEATHERUP

See McFERRAN

WELSH

See GIRVAN/GIRVIN

WHARRY

See GYLE

WHEELER

[Dismantled stone beside north boundary wall.] In memory of Benjamin Wheeler who died 24th Feby. 1810 aged 54 years. Also Catharine his wife who died 17th Decr. 1835 aged 78 years. Also Edmund Wheeler who died 14th December 1865 aged 73 years.

[Benjamin Wheeler, fisherman, of the Town, was made a freeman in 1807 and Edmund Wheeler, also a fisherman, in 1813.]

WHEELER

Beneath are interred the mortal remains of Jane, the beloved wife of Thomas Wheeler, obit. 16th April 1850 aged 62 years. Also the above Thomas Wheeler who died 6th April 1864 aged 81 years.

[The will of Thomas Wheeler, late of Carrickfergus, in the county of the town of Carrickfergus, lately ship owner, who died 6 April 1864 at same place, was proved at Belfast 17 August 1864 by the oaths of Mary Catherine Wheeler, spinster, and John Hamilton, shoemaker, late of Carrickfergus, the executors. Effects under £600.

Thomas Wheeler, mariner, of the Town, was made a freeman in 1811.]

WHITEFORD
A generous bequest by Margaretta Eleanor Whiteford, "Woodlawn", Carrickfergus, who died May 5th 1946, towards the cost of flagging the floor of this church enabled the work to be carried out in 1954.

WILLIAMS
Erected by Eliza Williams in memory of her husband Wm. Williams who died 11th Decr. 1854 aged 47 years. Also their daughter Pamela who died 4th March 1855 aged 7 years. The above-named Eliza Williams died 6th Decr. 1896 aged 85 years. Also their daughter Mary who died 14th March 1905 aged 70 years. Also her daughter Eliza, wife of Charles CAIRN R.N., died 15th Nov. 1917 aged 74 years.

WILLIAMS
Erected by Eliza Williams in memory of her mother Eliza. (M)es(ic..) who departed this life 19th July 1869 aged 82 years. John BRIDGEMAN died 3rd Jany. 1898. Jane Bridgeman died 31st Jany. 1914.

WILLIAMSON
Erected by Rose Anna Williamson in loving memory of her beloved husband Alexander Williamson who died 16th Feb. 1904 aged 72 years. Also his wife Roseann Williamson died 23rd May 1918. And grand niece Rose Anne (Anna) FLECK died 1st March 1971.

WILLIAMSON
See LARMOUR

WILLIS
[South of chancel.] Erected by James Willis in memory of his mother Jan(e Wi)llis who departed this life 26th F...... aged 6(8) years. Also Robert Willis his father who died 23rd March 18(3)0 aged (83) years.

[Robert Willis, chandler, of the Town, was made a freeman in 1787 and Robert Willis, bleacher, of west division was made a freeman in 1807.]

WILLSON
Sacred to the memory of Hill Willson who departed this life on the 27th October 1846 aged 74 years, and of Martha, his wife who departed this life the 23rd December 1834 aged 36 years. Also to the memory of Hill Willson their son, who died on the 4th of June 1833 aged 17 years. Also to the memory of their daughter Mabel F.S. GILLINGTON died 21st June 1861 aged 40 years. And of her husband Revd. George Gillington, for five years curate of this parish and Raloo.

[The Rev. George Gillington was born in Dublin 1823/4, son of George Gillington, entered Trinity College, Dublin, and graduated B.A. in 1850. He was ordained deacon in 1852 and priest in 1853. He was curate of Carrickfergus 1857-62, of Ramoan 1863-79, of Urney (Derry) 1880-3, chaplain of Villierstown (Lismore) 1887-99. He married on 25 January 1860 in St. Mary's, Dublin, Mabel F. Sharman Wilson, 2nd daughter of Hill Wilson of Carrickfergus. He died on 21 December 1899. See Leslie: *Clergy of Connor* (1993); Burtchaell and Sadleir: *Alumni Dublinenses* (1924); Leslie: *Derry Clergy and Parishes* (1937).]

WILSON
[Slate tablet on exterior of baptistry, which was formerly in use as a vault.] In this vault are buried Jane, widow of Davys Wilson, Esquire, and daughter of Samuel CLOSE, Esquire, of Warringstown, Co. Down; Ezekiel Davys Wilson, Esquire, born the 6th day of March 1738, died the 21st day of January 1821. Barbara, eldest daughter of Robert DUNCAN, Esquire, of Lisburn, born the 23rd day of February 1781, died the 27th day of August 1831. The Rev. Robert Duncan Davys Wilson, born the 27th day of October 1795, died the 18th day of January 1835. Catherine, eldest daughter of William D.D. Wilson Esquire, born the 17th day of May, died the 6th day of October 1833. William Duncan Davys Wilson, Esquire, M.D., born

the 2nd day of August 1797, died the 24th day of October 1842.

[Ezekiel Davys Wilson was son of Davys Wilson and Jane Close and inherited the Davys property near the Irish Gate. He was twenty times mayor of Carrickfergus and was M.P. for the borough in 1785, 1790 and 1797. He died unmarried leaving his property to his second cousin.

The Rev. Robert Duncan Davys Wilson was son of Robert Duncan, merchant, entered Trinity College, Dublin, in 1811 and graduated B.A. in 1816 and M.A. in 1821. He assumed the additional surname of Davys Wilson on succeeding to his cousin Ezekiel Davys Wilson's property c.1818. He was ordained in 1821 and was vicar of Island Magee 1821-3. He married, at Carrickfergus Church 2 May 1822, Jane Anne Clements Ellis daughter of Henry Clements Ellis of Prospect, Carrickfergus. William Duncan Davys Wilson was appointed sheriff for 1842. He was a nephew of C.A.W. Stewart and married Jane Dalway who died 1892. His only son Dr William Duncan Wilson became high sheriff in 1867 and died in South Kensington, London on 30th March 1897. See Leslie: *Clergy of Connor* (1993); McCrum ed. of McSkimin: *History and Antiquities of Carrickfergus* (1909); Burtchaell and Sadleir: *Alumni Dublinenses* (1924).]

WILSON

[Grey fossiliferous slab framed in sandstone against south boundary wall.] In memory of Ann HANLY, wife of Saml. Wilson, died 26th Oct. 1839 aged 73 years. William Wilson died Dec. 1830 aged 62 years. Samuel Wilson died 4th Oct. 1849 aged 80 years. James Wilson, son of the last mentioned Samuel Wilson, died 20th Feby. 1869 aged 57 years.

[There were three William Wilsons who were made freemen. One in 1785 was a farmer, one in 1803 was a fisherman and a third in 1811 was a farmer. Samuel Wilson, farmer, of West Division was made a freeman in 1787.]

WILSON

[Slate.] Sacred to the memory of John Wilson who died 10th April 1848 aged 85. Vive memor lethi.

[John Walsh, shoemaker, of the Town/Bank/Joymount was made a Freeman in 1811.]

WILSON

See CARSON, CONNOR and STEWART

WISNOM

Erected by William Wisnom to the memory of his father Alexander Wisnom who died on 14th day of March 1812 aged 68 years. And his mother Elizabeth who died on 29th day of October 1839 aged 76 years. Also her grandchildren William & Sarah Jane who died in infancy. Also his sister Elizabeth who died 26th March 1847 aged 70 years.

WISNOM

Erected to the memory of Alexander Wisnom who departed this life 9th August 1817 aged 48 years. Also Mary his daughter who departed this life 20th September 1827 aged 24 years. Also his grandson John McALLISTER who died in infancy. Also his wife Margaret Wisnom who departed this life 10th February 1854 aged 72 years. Also Ellen McALISTER [sic] who departed this life 12th January 1870 aged 62 yrs. Also Alexr. Wisnom who died 4th March 1907 aged 72 years. Also his wife Agnes who died 27th June 1919 aged 74 years.

[Alexander Wisnom, farmer, of North East Division, was made a freeman in 1787.]

WISNOM

[Slate near Alexander Wisnom d.1812.] In memory of William Wisnom who departed this life on the 11th of April 1848 in the 77th year of his age. Also his wife Jane Wisnom who departed this life on the 7th of April 1852 aged 76 years.

[William Wisnom, farmer, of North-East Division was made a freeman in 1813.]

WOODS
See GORMAN

WOODSIDE
[White marble with surround.] Erected in memory of Charles E. Woodside died 7th October 1924 aged 61. Interred in Ballynure. Also his wife Elizabeth Woodside died 29th April 1959 aged 86. [Mason:-] Hart, Carnmoney.

WORTLEY
[Lead lettering on white marble stone in granite plinth. In a roundel is carved the badge of the Young Citizen Volunteers: on a crowned shamrock, a right hand between the letters Y.C.V.] In proud and loving memory of Segt. T.G. Wortley, 14th R.I.R., eldest son of John and Isabella Wortley, killed in action at Messines 7th June 1917. "His name liveth for ever". Also the above Isabella Wortley fell asleep 30th April 1921. And John their fifth son fell asleep 10th June 1921. "Only Asleep". Also Isabella their daughter fell asleep 10th June 1927. And the above John Wortley fell asleep 18th March 1930. "Re-United."

YOUNG
[Cement tablet inside west door.] William Young, secretary of the select vestry, 1924-1932, and his wife Lily Margaret restored the exterior of this tower in the year of our Lord 1932. J. C. RUTHERFORD, Prebendary of Kilroot, Rector. John BATES, Thomas G. ROBINSON, churchwardens.

YOUNG
See GORDON

....
[Small sandstone beside McSkimins.]
.... Oct. 23 1727 aged 7 ......

....
........................Char(les......................h)e memory (of ....) of July 18(5)6. The stone (is erected) by their mourn(ing) and ....d par(ents) as a token of their ....e loss. "The Lord giveth and the Lord hath taken away, blessed be the name of the Lord." Job 1, 21.

....
[Low sandstone beside that of S.D. Stuart; early part of inscription has been lost.]
.... day af December 1713.

....
[S of chancel amongst woody nightshade. Probably late eighteenth century.]
He............ dy of....... Carrickfergus .... is life the ...... 70th ....

.........IDG(E)
[NE of north transept in front of John Holmes.] Erected ...
Sam(uel.....)idg(e) in m(............ mother An)n (E...........)

....
[Early eighteenth century stone next to wall between campanile and south transept] (Heir) l(ieth ....) M.........

....
Als(o) M(............el)l who de(pa)rte(d .... April 6th 18(.)(2) H(i...............) 2 years.

....
[Small round topped stone incorporated in revetting wall facing path round church.] .... departed this life Dec. 12th 1753 aged 66.

[Stone of about 1850.] (Erected .... who) dep(parted th...............
aged 76 years (T) ....th.......et thy God. Also his nephew Ja(m...............)

[Between Parkhill and Caters.] Erected .... Ja.......... (so) his son John who died 29th Sept. 1834 in the 30th year of his age. Also his grandson Georg(e) who died 31st July 1844 in the 4th year of his age.

J..........
[Small and loose, of red sandstone.] H.M. + J. died the 17 of June 1816.

[Mid-nineteenth century sandstone behind vestry.]

[Loose sandstone set against Craig, Glenfield.] In memory of his w(ife) A(lice) who died Augt. 29th 1825 aged (55) years.

[Used as kerb stone cemented.] ....53................... earl....oss; .....wn family .....mbers:

[Set against the bottom of the church tower. The white marble surface has dissolved badly but the beginning has been protected by the sandstone head.] To the memory of a floweret of the Earth transplanted to the Paradise of God. Here reposeth until the trump of the Archangel ...., ...,

[Sandstone with crossbones at top; east of south transept] (........e)t(h............o(f.....................)fe (t.T.ck V..) a(p who) departed this life the (.) of December Ano (D..) 1689.

M..........
[Stone of about 1700 with cherub carved at top. Behind vestry]
Here lyeth the body of William M.(il.......) who (dep...)ted (thi..... [continues beneath ground level.]

[Deeply eroded sandstone south of chancel.] (Erected)....
James ...... mem... of his d............ (dep)arted ....

CARRICKFERGUS, ST. NICHOLAS' CHURCH OF IRELAND CHURCH, CHICHESTER MEMORIALS

O.S. 52. Grid Ref. J412874

Fine monument to the Chichester family in the north transept

John (1565-1597) and Arthur Chichester (1563-1625) were younger sons of Sir John Chichester of Raleigh, near Barnstaple in Devon. Both men served in Queen Elizabeth's armies in Ireland in the late sixteenth century. John became governor of Carrickfergus and was killed in 1597 at Aldfreck near Ballycarry, county Antrim, in a skirmish with the Macdonnells. Arthur Chichester, who arrived in Ireland two years later, was a veteran of the Armada campaign of 1588, had accompanied Drake in 1596 on his final voyage to the West Indies, volunteered for Essex's expedition to Cadiz in 1597 and had fought with the English forces supporting Henry IV in France the following year when he was knighted by the King after the siege of Amiens. Chichester was one of the most successful (and controversial) of the military adventurers in Ireland in this period. His advancement from the comparatively minor post of governor of Carrickfergus to the office of Lord Deputy of Ireland was accomplished in just six years. In 1612, the year in which he relinquished Lord Deputyship, he was raised to the Irish peerage as Lord Chichester of Belfast and was subsequently appointed Lord Treasurer of Ireland. He became a member of the English Privy Council in 1622.

Chichester acquired an estate of some 30,000 acres, mainly in east and south Antrim, including the site of the growing town of Belfast but he chose to live in Carrickfergus, probably because it was at the time the only defended town in the area. He built a grand house, called Joymount, on the site of the former Franciscan friary at the east end of the town, but it ceased to the family's main residence when they moved to Belfast sometime in the mid seventeenth century. John Wesley, on a visit to the town in 1760 found the house in ruins and observed in his Journal that 'the sheep and horses... make wild work of the parterres and curious trees which the old lord so carefully planted'. Shortly afterwards the family gave the house and ground to the Antrim Grand Jury as the site for a new county Courthouse. This building completed in 1779 is the present Townhall.

John and Arthur Chichester, Arthur's wife Lettice Perrot and their only child, a son who died in infancy, were buried in the family vault in St. Nicholas' Church. Edward, Viscount Chichester of Carrickfergus, brother and heir of Arthur was buried at Eggesford in Devonshire with his first wife Anne Coplestone. His second wife, Mary Denham, was buried at Carrickfergus in 1638 and her coffin may be the one noted by McSkimin, embossed with the initials D and C linked by a heart motif. Edward's son, Arthur, 1st Earl of Donegall (1606-1675) was laid to rest in the Carrickfergus vault (an account of his splendid funeral is given in Shannon Millin's *Additional Sidelights on Belfast History*, (1938)). His first two wives were buried at Eggesford and his widow who remarried was interred in Westminster Abbey in 1691. Arthur, 2nd Earl of Donegall, nephew of the 1st Earl died in Ireland in 1678 and was probably buried at Carrickfergus. His wife, too, remarried and was buried in England.

In 1706 the 3rd Earl was killed at the siege of Monjuich during the War of the Spanish Succession and was buried in Barcelona. Two years later three of his young daughters died in a fire which virtually destroyed the family home in Belfast. The dowager Countess and her son the 4th Earl moved to England where the family lived until the end of the eighteenth century. Throughout this period however, the Donegalls, for political reasons, maintained their links with Carrickfergus and leading members of the family were usually brought back to St. Nicholas's Church for burial.

In the early nineteenth century George Augustus Chichester, 6th Earl and 2nd Marquis, returned to live permanently in Belfast, at Ormeau. He and his brothers were the last members of the Donegall family to be buried at Carrickfergus. Sir Edward and Elizabeth May, father and mother of Anna May, the wife of the 2nd Marquis, were interred with them. See Clarke: *Gravestone Inscriptions, Belfast;* Vol. 3, p.108 for reference to May family as some were buried in Balmoral Cemetery. See *Dictionary of National Biography*, entries for Arthur Chichester, Lord Chichester of Belfast (1563-1625) and Arthur Chichester, first Earl of Donegall (1606-1675); *Complete Peerage*, ed. G.E. C[okayne] Vol. IV; Chichester: *History of the Family of Chichester from A.D. 1086 to 1870* (1871); Maguire: *Living Like a Lord: The second Marquis of Donegall 1769-1844* (1984).

When St. Nicholas' Church was restructured about the year 1614 the north transept was reserved for the Chichester family. Beneath was their place of sepulture, a barrel vault of ashlar sandstone. The insertion of this vault meant raising the floor level of the transept so that the family sat at pulpit level and were separated from the rest of the congregation by carved oak.

The contents of the vault have varied - family members interred elsewhere were sometimes reinterred here, but a century ago there was a major exodus. On 20th December 1869 the Rt Rev. Robert Knox, bishop of Down and Connor and Dromore, consecrated the Chapel of the Resurrection in the grounds of the new Belfast Castle. This chapel was built by the third Marquis of Donegall in memory of his son Frederick Richard, Earl of Belfast, who died in 1853. Beneath, vaults were constructed to replace Carrickfergus as the family burial place. When the Marquis died in 1883 he was laid to rest here and six coffins of his nearest deceased relatives transferred from Carrickfergus to keep him company.

However, when Belfast Castle was presented to the citizens of Belfast by the Earl of Shaftesbury the chapel was transferred to the Church of Ireland, but never became a parish church and falling attendance later brought closure. Vandalism culminated in desecration of the coffins for the sake of their lead. Roselawn crematorium reduced the remains to ashes and seven little caskets were ultimately deposited in the old vault in Carrickfergus. Some of the coffin plates were also returned at this time.

Samuel McSkimin described the contents of St. Nicholas's vault in his history, published 1823 (2nd edition - the 1st edition did not contain these details). F.J. Bigger updated this account and added the contents of the Chapel of the Resurrection (*Memorials of the Dead*, Vol. 1 pp. 113-121). His notes on these are given verbatim below. Any other inscriptions not seen in 1985 are described "now missing".

Today the vault contains seven full size coffins, two small ones clearly intended for infants, the seven caskets, and a damaged cube.

McSkimin, pp. 151-153, quoted in *M.D.* XI, p.117, describes the following as interred in the Chichester vault, though there were no inscriptions even in 1823.

1. Sir John Chichester, beheaded by the MacDONNELLS November 4, 1597; near his coffin, which is broken down, is the blade of a small sword, with some lime.
2. Arthur Chichester, only son of Sir Arthur Chichester first lord baron Belfast, born September 26, 1606, died October 30, same year.
3. Letitia, daughter of Sir John PERROT, and wife of Sir Arthur Chichester, first lord baron Belfast, who died November 27, 1620 - interred January 10, following.
4. Sir Arthur Chichester, first lord baron Belfast, who died in London, February 19, 1624 - interred October 24, 1625.
5. Mary DENHAM, second wife of Sir Edward Chichester, first viscount Carrickfergus, who died at Belfast, February 2, 1637 - interred soon after.
6. Arthur Chichester, first earl of Donegall - died at Belfast, March 16, 1674 - interred May 20th, 1675. He left £50 to the poor of Carrickfergus, and £200 to those of Belfast.
7. Arthur Chichester, second earl of Donegall, died December 13, 1705, aged 72.
8. Arthur Chichester, fourth earl of Donegall, died September 28, 1757, aged 64 years - interred on the 7th of the following October.
9. Hon. Elizabeth Chichester, daughter of John Chichester, died February 12, 1748, interred June 26, the same year.

CHICHESTER

McSkimin, pp.149-151. The version in *M.D.* XI, 3, pp.114, 115 is copied from McSkimin but *M.D.*, III pp.194-197 (1896) agrees closely with our reading. Nearly filling the end wall of the north transept stands the county's finest specimen of Jacobean monumental extravagance sadly subdued by the grime of three centuries. Life size effigies of Arthur Chichester and his wife kneel in prayer facing each other across a fald stool, in front of which lies a baby. Both of the main figures are niched by semi-circular arches the spandrels of which are decorated with fruit and instruments symbolising mortality. This central group is framed on either side by a pair of corinthian columns. On the dados below these are the principal inscriptions. The podium is divided into two panels containing assemblages of militaria characteristic of the eastern and western traditions respectively. On the plinth between the panels kneels another bearded figure, half size, and without hands. Above the entablature rise two more pairs of pillars similar to, but smaller than the first set. Between them is a coat of arms. "W. Cunningham" is inscribed in roman capital letters on the architrave to the right and "(W) Laverty" in italics to the left. At the top of the monument is a roundel bearing a crowned skull and immediately under that appears the legend "en me trivmphantem". Differences of detail exist between the epitaph as it can be read today and as given by McSkimin - possibly the Countess of Shaftesbury contributed to inconsistency in 1895 when she had the original painted lettering replaced by the present engraving (see McCrum footnote, p.182).

Arms at top: a quarterly of fifteen; the first quarter, chequy; second, a bend between six crosses crosslet; third, eight martlets; fourth, three garbs, a chief; fifth, a fess between three roses; sixth, three garbs; seventh, a barry of five, in the chief three roundels; eighth, three lions rampant; ninth, three roses; tenth, a fess between three mullets; eleventh, a bird displayed; twelth, barry, vair and ......; thirteenth, per pale dancettee, a chief; fourteenth, a saltire; fifteenth, two chevrons. Crest: A heron wings expanded holding in the beak a snake. Supporters: Two wolves. Motto: Honor sequitur fvgientem.

[Left hand tablet.] Sacred to God + aeternall memore Sr. Arthvre Chichester Knight, Baron of Belfast, Ld High Threr. of Ireland, Governovr of this towne & of the cvntries adioyning: descended of the avncient & noble howse of the Chichesters in the covnite of Devon, sonne of Sr. Iohn Chichester of Raleiche knight & of his wife Gartrvd COVNTNEY grandchild of Edward Chichester & of his wife Elisabeth, davghter of Iohn BOVRGCHIER Earle of Bathe: After the flight of the Earls of Tiron & Terconnell & other archtraytors their accomplice having svppressed ODOVGHERTIE & other northern rebels, & settled the plantacon of his province, & well & happely governed this kingdom in florishing estate vnder Iames ovr king, the spac of 11 yeres & more whilest hee was Ld. depvtie & governovr generall thereof retyred himself into his private government, & being mindfvll of his mortalitie represented vnto him by the vntimely death of Arthvre his sonne, the only hope of his howse, who lived not fvll 2 months after his birth, as allsoe of his noble & valiant brother Sr. Iohn Chichester knight, late sergeant maior of the armye in this kingdome, & the praecedent govenor of this towne, hath cavsed this chappell to be repaired, & this valt & monvment to be made, & erected as well in remembrance of them whose statves are expressed & theire bodyes interred as allsoe a resting place for the bodye it self, & his most deare & best beloved wife, the noble & vertvovs ladye Lettice, eldest davghter of Sr. Iohn PARROTT knight, sometyme the worthye depvtie of this kingdome: which they hope shall here rest in peace, vntill the second coming of theire crvcifyed redeemer, whome they most constantly beeleeve then to behold with theire bodily eyes to their endles blessednes, & everlastin comfort: Gladivs mevs non salvabit me:

[Right hand tablet.]
Fatvm mortis, a Domino inivnctvm est.
If that desire, or chanche thee hither lead;
Vpon this marble monvment to tread;
Let admiracon, thy best thovghtes still feed;
While weeping thov, this epitagh doest reade:
& let distilling teares, thy commaes be,
As tribvte dve, vnto this elegie
Epitaphe
With in this bedd of death, a viceroy lyes,
Whose fame shall ever live, vertve nere dyes:
Nor he did vertve, & religeon noris he;
& made this land, late rvde, with peace to florish
The wildest rebell he be power did tame
& by trve ivstice gaynd an honord name:
Then now, thovgh hee in heaven with angells be
Let vs on earth, still lovee his memorie.

By him interd his noble ladye is,
Whoe pertake with him, in heavenly blisse
For while the earth vnto them was a seate,
Vnmacht they were, being both good & great.

With them doth rest, theire one & only sonne,
Whose life was short, & soe his glasse soone rvn;
The heavens not earth, was his allotted right,
For which he badd the world soe soone goodnight.

Intombd by them, here allsoe doth remayn,
His worthy brother, by base rebells slayn:
As he in martiall, & brave warrelike feight,
Opposde theire evrie, in his cvntreys right.

& in memorill of theire endles praise,
This monvment is left to after dayes.

CHICHESTER
[Now missing. McSkimin, p.151 - "a small coffin". Not mentioned in *M.D.* (1922) account]. Aetatis 25, obit 8th January 1631.

CHICHESTER
[McSkimin, p.151; *M.D.* XI, 3, p.119, with photograph. A lead coffin 95 cm. long, moulded for head and shoulders and with a handle at each end. The lettering is embossed. A heart symbol separates the initials D and C.] D C QVI OBITT. 8.IAN 1638.

CHICHESTER
[McSkimin, p.151; *M.D.* XI, 3, p.119. Part of a lead coffin 75 cm. long and shaped for head and shoulders. The inscription is embossed.] DEC:3: 1642:E:C:

CHICHESTER
[McSkimin, p.152 - "A small coffin ... much shattered". Now missing, not seen in 1922 (*M.D.* XI, 3).] C.C. March 11th 1701 aetat. 25

CHICHESTER
[McSkimin, pp.147-148; *M.D.* III, p. 194. Formerly above entrance to Chichester transept, now on its east wall, an oval of white marble bordered by a wreath. An earl's coronet surmounts the arms: chequy, or and gules, a chief vair, in the honour point a crescent azure.] Memoriae Perenni Arthuri comitis de Donegall Vicecomitis Chichester de Carickfergus Bars. de Belfast, Comitats. Antrims. Locm. tenentis, Urbis Carickfergus Praefecti, & Serenis Annae Angliae &c Reginae Copiarum in Hispanias missarum Legati; Qui in Barcelona Urbe Hispanica Jacet Sepultus. Ille anno 1704 Calpe quo tempere ab unitis Hispaniarum & Galliae viribus oppugnata in urbem saelicissimum intulit auxilium qua salutem obsessis, obsessoribus ruinan & dedecus comparavit: Anno 1705 in Cataloniam provectus apud obsidionen Barcelonae de re militari insigniter meritus est: Post urbrem captam Girronae & locorum adjacentium Praefectus constitutus summa vigilantia & virtute Bellica res administravit: & cum ex adverso Barcelona a Duce Andegavensi (Rege Catholico Titulari) re-obsessa & a Rege Carolo 3 defensa esset, secum plurimis Cohortibus in Urbem conjecit adeoque Austriacam periclitantem restituit: Ibi propugnaculi Monjuich praefecturum suscipiens tamdiu hostium aggressus sustinuit donec Numero & repetitis conatibus oppressus, animo vel in articulo mortis invictus, florentibus Lauris cumulatus immaturo aevo, et proprio marte non inultus periit Anno 1706, 10mo die Aprilis Aetatis suae 40. Cui iure Matrimoniali et Honoribus Successit Arthurus filius ejus natu Maximus Posuit e sumptibus proprijs Uxor et sumsua fidissima Doma. Catherina e gente Forbesiana, filia unica Arthuri Comitis de Granard, Vicecomitis de Granard & Hamlin, & Baronis de Clanhu.

[Translation: To the undying memory of Arthur, Earl of Donegall, Viscount Chichester of Carickfergus, Baron of Belfast, Lieutenant of County Antrim Governor of Carickfergus, and Lieutenant General of the forces of her most serene Majesty Anne of England etc. in Spain, who lies buried in Barcelona in Spain. In 1704 when Gibraltar was under siege by the united forces of Spain and France he brought most fortunate aid to the place thus saving the besieged and destroying and disgracing the besiegers: in the year 1705 he advanced into Catalonia and gained military fame at the siege of Barcelona: after the capture of the city he was appointed governor of Gironne and the surrounding area which he administered with the greatest vigilance and military vigour: and when Barcelona was again besieged by the Duke of Anjou (the titular Catholic King) and was being defended by King Charles III he attacked with a large force of troops and restored the endangered Austrian cause: he then became governor of the fort of Monjiuch where he sustained so many attacks of the enemy until overwhelmed by their frequent attempts he died aged 40 in the year 1706 on the 10th day of April, still a young man but proven by his military prowess. Even in the moment of death his spirit was unconquered and his many laurels were fresh upon him. His eldest son

Arthur succeeded him by matrimonial right and honours. This monument was erected at her own expense by his most faithful wife Lady Catherine, of the FORBES family, only daughter of Arthur Earl of Granard, Viscount Granard & Hamlin and Baron Clanhu.

Fixed to the wall of the Anderson and McAuley building in Donegall Place, Belfast, is a bronze plaque with the badge of The Royal Sussex Regiment: St George's cross within a garter upon a cut star of eight points all upon an ostrich feather. The legend is as follows:

"This plaque records the fact that on 28th June 1701 Arthur Chichester, 3rd Earl of Donegall by warrant of his late Majesty King William III formed the 35th Regiment of Foot which has since become famous as The Royal Sussex Regiment and that the first recruits were encamped on this site."

This regiment accompanied the earl to Spain. He remained colonel of the 35th Foot until 1706.]

CHICHESTER
[What is now a crushed and broken hollow cube of lead is probably what McSkimin, p. 152 described as "A small coffin ... believed to contain the bones of lady Jane, lady Frances, and lady Henrietta, daughters of Arthur, third earl of Donegall, who were burned in the castle of Belfast by the carelessness of a servant, April 24 same year". *M.D.* XI, p.119 - "Its size is about 15 inches every way."] F.C. 1708

CHICHESTER
[Now missing, not mentioned in *M.D.* (1922). McSkimin, p. 152 -"inscribed on a coffin."] Aetatis suae 50 aged 38 1716.

CHICHESTER
[Now missing. Not mentioned in *M.D.* (1922) account. McSkimin, p.152 - "on a coffin".] I.E.C. Obit Feby. 27th 1719.

CHICHESTER
[Now missing. Not mentioned in *M.D.* (1922). McSkimin, p.152 -"on a coffin".] The son of the Honorable John Chichester Obyt June the 1st 1737.

CHICHESTER
[McSkimin, p.152; *M.D.*, XI, p.118. Coffin plate 42 x 33 cms. of bronze gilt with hatchment: chequy argent and gules a chief vair impaling three bear's heads. Supporters: dexter, a wolf gorged with a ducal coronet a chain attached thereto; sinister, a griffin. Motto: Invitum Sequitur Honos (sic).] The Right Honourable & illustrious Lady Katherine Countess of Donegall, Dowager of the most noble and puissant Arthur Chichester late Earl of Donegall, Viscount Carickfergus, Lord Chichester & Baron of Belfast, died June 15th MXCCXLIII aged 73 years.

CHICHESTER
[Lead plate on lead coffin. The arms on a hatchment are the same on the bronze plate.] The Right Honble. & Ilustrius Lady Katherin Countess of Donegall Dowager of ye Most Noble & Puissant Arthur Chichester Late Earl of Donegall Viscount Carickfergus Lord Chichester & Baron of Bellfast. Died June 15th 1743 aged 73 years.

[McSkimin, p.152 - "Her daughter was also interred in the same vault soon after."]

CHICHESTER
[*M.D.*, XI, 3, p.117. Now missing.] The Honorable John Chichester obitt 22d June 1746 aged 45 years.

[McSkimin gives a different reading:] Hon. John Chichester, son of the third earl of Donegall, died at Bath, June 1, 1746, aged 45, interred October 10th following.

Arms of George Augustus, second Marquis of Donegall, from an unattached brass shield

CHICHESTER

[*M.D.*, XI, p. 120 - then in Belfast. Unattached brass shield, gilt, 45 x 38 x 0.4 cms. The arms are represented on two overlapping oval shields. Dexter shield: quarterly, 1st and 4th chequy a chief vair, 2nd and 3rd fretty. Around the shield is the motto of the Order of St. Patrick - "Quis Separabit MDCCLXXXIII" and outside that is the collar of the order from which hangs the badge, a saltire surmounted by a shamrock. Sinister shield: per fess fretty and chequy impaling a fess between six billets. Crests - dexter: an eagle wings expanded in its dexter talon a flag staff: sinister: a stork wings expanded in its beak an eel. Supporters: two wolves ducally gorged and chained. Motto: Invitum Sequitur Honor.] George Augustus Chichester, Marquis and Earl of Donegall, Earl of Belfast, Viscount Chichester, Baron of Belfast, Baron Fisherwick, Privy Councillor, Lieutenant of the County of Donegal, Knight of St. Patrick, born 13th Aug. 1769, died 5th Oct. 1844.

CHICHESTER

[*M.D.*, XI, p. 118 gives year as 1817. Lead plate in shape of a shield.] Sir Arthur Chichester Bart. aged 80 years 1847.

CHICHESTER

[*M.D.*, XI, p. 120 - coffin plate, then in Belfast. Now missing.] Anna, Marchioness of Donegall, died 6th February 1849 aged 74 years.

CHICHESTER

[*M.D.*, XI, p. 120 - then in Belfast, now missing. F.J. Bigger describes this coffin as "Italian in shape (Lord Belfast died in Naples), made of bronze or copper".] Frederick Richard, Earl of Belfast, was born 25th November 1827 and died 15 February 1853.

CHICHESTER

[*M.D.*, XI, p. 120 - then in Belfast. Trapezoidal brass coffin plate with arms: per pale: 1st quarterly, 1st and 4th chequy a chief vair, 2nd and 3rd fretty; 2nd quarterly, 1st and 4th grand quarters a bordure ermine quarterly, 1st a cross of Calvary, 2nd a chief, 3rd three cups, 4th a saltire, 2nd grand quarter per pale dancettee, 3rd

George Hamilton, third Marquis of Donegall

grand quarter a two-headed eagle displayed between three Maltese crosses. Supporters: two wolves both gorged the dexter ducally. Crest: none, a marquis's coronet.] Harriet Ann BUTLER, Marchioness of Donegall, died in Paris Septr. 14th 1860 aged 61 years.

CHICHESTER
[*M.D.*, XI, p. 120 - then in Belfast. Loose coffin plate, silver plated.] George Hamilton, Marquis of Donegall, K.P., G.C.(H.) born 10th February 1797, died 20th October 1883.

CHICHESTER
[Seven small plain wooden caskets have nameplates as follows:]
Spencer Augustus died 27th May 1825.
George Augustus died 5th October 1844.
Anna died 2nd February 1849.
Frederick Richard died 15th February 1853.
Hamilton Francis died 1st January 1854.
Henrietta Ann died 14th September 1860.
George Hamilton died 20th October 1883.

MAY
[Bronze plate, trapezoidal, 37.5 cm long tapering from 28 to 20 cms wide.] Sir Edward May, bart., died 23d July 1814 in the 63d year of his age.

MAY
[*M.D.*, XI, p. 118. Lead plate.] Sir Edw: May, Bart., died 23d July 1814 in his 63 year.

MAY
[*M.D.*, XI, p. 118. Trapezoidal plate, possibly copper. This wording is exactly duplicated on a lead coffin plate.] Elizabeth, relict of Sir Edward May, Bart., died 26th March 1823 aged 73 years.

CARRICKFERGUS CONGREGATIONAL CHURCH

O.S. 52 Grid Ref. J411875

The modern congregation was formed early in the nineteenth century and worshipped in a chapel beside the Quay from 1821. The present church was built on the Albert Road (1878-1879) in the town and parish of Carrickfergus. It is a romanesque composition of heavy circles and verticals executed in red brick externally, pine and plaster internally.

Baptisms are recorded from 1819 and marriages from 1824. Memorial tablets and windows have been copied. The earliest is dated 1888 (Graham).

BEMBRIDGE
[Window in south wall, based on Holman Hunt's painting "The Light of the World", includes depictions of Ashbourne School, Derby; Northern College, Manchester; and Carrickfergus; and carries the legend "Behold I stand at the door and knock. I am the Light of the world."] In grateful and abiding memory of Rev. George Bembridge B.A., B.D., devoted minister of this church 1936-1979. This memorial is the gift of the members and friends of the church and congregation. He lived and taught the gospel.

CALDER
[Brass plate on lectern to the memory of the son of a former minister.] To the glory of God and in memory of David James Calder, R.A.F., of Carrickfergus and Edinburgh, 22nd June 1923-6th October 1942.

GILLESPIE
[Window in south wall depicting Christ with children, background view of Carrickfergus, and legend "The hope of the world".] To the glory of God in memory of Matthew Gillespie died 9th Sept. 1975 and his wife Jane Eleanor died 14th Jan. 1984, presented by their family 1985.

GRAHAM
[White marble tablet in entrance hall.] Sacred to the memory of the Revd. William Graham, pastor of this church for 22 years, who died on 22nd July 1888 aged 66 years. "He being dead yet speaketh".
[See North Road Cemetery]

HERDMAN
See VINT

HUSTON
[White marble tablet on north wall; inscription flanked by Corinthian pilasters; a shield in the typanum has the year "1919".] Erected by John and Maggie Huston in loving remembrance of their brother and two nephews who lost their lives as the result of a boating accident in Belfast Lough, Friday 29th August 1919. Dr. Thomas Huston of Hunslow, London, aged 48 years, his son James Morrison aged 10 years, Francis Jennings (Frankie) son of Dr. James Huston of Carrickfergus aged 18 years. "Thy will be done." [Memorial by:-] Purdy & Millard.

HUSTON
[White marble tablet.] Erected in grateful memory of John Huston of the Mile Bush, Carrickfergus, born 1863, died 1941. He was a member of the diaconate and served for 36 years as church treasurer. "Well done good and faithful servant." [Memorial by:-] Purdy & Millard.

JACK
See VINT

LYON
[Window in north wall with legend "A sower went forth to sow".] To the glory of God and in loving memory of Reverend James Lyon, pastor of this church from 1888 till 1921- died 12th February 1925. "Now hath he obtained a more excellent minister." [Window by:-] W.F. Clokey, Belfast.

LYON
[Window in north wall depicting Christ with three children and having the legend "Be ye therefore followers of God as dear children. Of such is the kingdom of heaven."] To the glory of God and in loving memory of Adah Gertrude Lyon, widow of the Reverend James Lyon, died 12th December 1952. [Window by:-] Clokey, Belfast.

PATTERSON
[Arms: gules, a castle argent, in the base of barry wavy of six of the second and azure, in the chief two martlets of the second respectant. Crest: a lymphad, on the sail azure a lion rampant or. Supporters: dexter, a gallowglass holding a battle-axe; sinister, a knight in armour holding a lance. Motto: Gloria Prisca Novatur.] This shield is a replica of the official borough shield which hung here during the years 1949-1951 and 1952-1973 when Thomas John Patterson O.B.E., J.P., a deacon of this church from 1932 till 1981, was mayor of the Borough of Carrickfergus.

REID
[Window in north wall depicting woman with three children at mediaeval harbour of Carrickfergus with legend "Charity which is the bond of perfectness. She is like the merchants, ships; she bringeth her food from afar."] This window was erected by Alderman Captain William Reid J.P., of Carrickfergus, in memory of his wife Jane Reid [Window by:-] W. F. Clokey, Belfast.

TODD
See VINT

TURNER
[Window in north wall to the church secretary. "A new commandment I give unto you, That ye love one another."] To the glory of God and in loving memory of William Hanna Turner. This memorial is the gift of his 20th May 1951. [Window by:-] Clokey, Belfast.

VINT
[Brass plate in wooden frame on the rear wall, formerly on the pulpit.] In loving memory of William Vint, John JACK, James HERDMAN, Hugh TODD, for many years associated with this church deacons. Erected by representatives of their families, 20th December 1896.

VINT
[Window in north wall depicting Christ as shepherd, with legend "Yea, though I walk through the valley of the shadow of death, I will fear no evil".] In dear remembrance of Thomas Vint J.P. (1855-1931), a member of this church for 57 years. Wise in counsel and generous beyond all telling. Given by his brother Robert Vint. And when the chief shepherd shall appear ye shall receive a crown of glory that fadeth not away. [Window by:-] Clokey, Belfast.

VINT
[Window in north wall depicting the Good Samaritan. "Go, and do thou likewise."] To the glory of God and in loving memory of Sarah, wife of Thomas Vint, died 25th January 1919 and their child Lilian Winifred Irene (Baba), died 1st November 1895. Also Margaret Livingstone, wife of Robert Vint, died 21st December 1925. "They shall reign for ever and ever." [Window by:-] W. F. Clokey, Belfast.

VINT
[Carved on oak communion table.] Given by this Church in grateful memory of Thomas Vint, J.P. (1855-1931), church secretary for 43 years. "He was a good man and full of the Holy Ghost and of faith."

CARRICKFERGUS FIRST PRESBYTERIAN CHURCH

O.S. 52 Grid Ref. J412875

This stands on the west side of North Street in the town and parish of Carrickfergus. The Presbyterian congregation was founded in the seventeenth century and erected the present church between 1827 and 1829. There is no burial ground although an attempt to acquire land for this purpose was made in 1827. Memorial tablets and windows have been copied. The earliest is 1889 (White).

BARCLAY
[Silver plate attached to oak armchair.] The communion table and chairs have been given in loving memory of Lydia Margaretta Barclay, 1866-1946.

DAVEY
[Brass place on wood mounted on south wall. Regimental badge: St. George and the dragon over the letter V. Motto: Quo fata vocant.] To the glory of God and in memory of William Hamilton Davey O.B.E., M.A., B.L. major the 27th Northumberland Fusiliers (Tyneside Irish). Died from illness contracted on active service 29th August 1920. "Absorpta est mors ad victoriam."

JOHNSTONE
[Two windows flank the puplpit. North window:] To the glory of God and in memory of Robert Johnstone died 5th June 1895 aged 63 years. Presented to the First Presbyterian Church, Carrickfergus, 1897. Behold a sower went forth to sow. [South window:] Presented to the First Presbyterian Church, Carrickfergus, 1897. Cast the net on the right side of the ship and ye shall find.

LEGG
[White marble on grey marble, open book in laurel wreath carved on top.] To the glory of God and in grateful remembrance of Charles McFerran Legg J.P. born 20th November 1858, died 2nd August 1934. This tablet is erected by the members of the congregation who cherish his memory. He was a life-long and loyal worshipper in this church and his interest in every department of Christian work, both at home and abroad, was unique and generous." Thy testimonies have I taken as an heritage for ever for they are the rejoicing of my heart. Ps. CXIX. III. [Memorial by:-] Hastings, Larne.

McGIFFIN
[Window in north wall depicting Samuel and Eli with legend, "It is the Lord: let Him do what seemeth Him good."] To the glory of God and in loving memory of William, Archibald McGiffin - passed away 1918. [Window by:-] W. F. Clokey & Co., Belfast.

McGIFFIN
[Window in north wall depicting presentation of children to Christ with legend, "And He took them in His arms, put His hands upon them and blessed them."] To the glory of God. Erected by James McGiffin in loving memory of William McGiffin, Eliza Jack McGiffin and Martha Lowry McGiffin. [Window by:-] Clokey, Belfast.

PORTER
[Brass plate beneath window in south wall. The window has the legend, "The Prodigal Son - Luke XV, Vrs. 11-32. Him that cometh to me I will in no wise cast out - John VI, Vr.37."] To the glory of God and in memory of William Porter died 9th August 1906 aged 85 years.

PORTER
[Stained glass window with the legend "The Good Samaritan. Luke X, Vrs. 30-37 who went about doing good. Acts X, Vr. 38". The inscription is on a brass plate.]

To the glory of God and in memory of Elizabeth Jane Porter died 22nd October 1906 aged 71 years.

PORTER
[Window in south wall depicting angel pointing upwards with three women. "He is not here but is risen - Luke XXIV,6."] To the glory of God and in memory of Robert Johnstone Porter, born 21st September 1857, died 25th September 1918. [Window by:-] Ward & Partners, Belfast.

PORTER
[Window depicting nativity, on north wall.] In loving memory of Thomas Johnstone Porter, 25th June 1856-2nd August 1919. Also his wife Ellen Hughes Fawcett, 29th January 1863-15th July 1920. They rest in West Laurel Hill, Philadelphia. [Window by:-] Ward and Partners, Belfast.

PORTER
[Window in south wall depicting Christ and kneeling Martha with the legend, "I am the resurrection and the life."] To the glory of God and in memory of Georgina Mary Matilda Porter, born 24th August 1865, died 15th September 1937. [Window by:-] Clokey, Belfast.

WHITE
[Marble tablet on west wall - formerly a part of an imposing monument removed from the entrance hall.] Erected by the congregation of First Carrickfergus in memory of their late pastor the Rev. James White, ordained 31st December 1838, died 11th December 1889. He was their faithful pastor for more than 50 years, an eloquent man mighty in the scriptures, and an able minister of the new testament. "He being dead yet speaketh."

[One of six brothers to enter the Presbyterian ministry, James White, was born 22 May 1816 in the Manse of First Bailieborough, Co. Cavan, where his father Patrick was the minister. He was educated at Edinburgh University. His wife, a daughter of James Blair, Belfast, died 7 October 1888 aged 66. He was buried in the City Cemetery, Belfast. Sons: James and Rev. William Moore White (B.A., 1866; ordained 1869; missionary in Sydney, Australia, 1870-87; LL.D., 1872; M.A., 1873; became a Church of England curate in Devon, 1891). Sons-in-law: Samuel Smyth and L.L. Macassey. See *In Memoriam - Rev. James White* by Rev. W. Moore White, LL.D.]

WILSON
[Window in south wall depicting woman anointing feet of Christ with legend, "She hath done what she could."] In memory of Mary and Isabella Wilson and their nephew James M. Wilson of Kilroot. July 1926. [Window by:-] Ward & Partners, Belfast.

WOODSIDE
[Carved across oak panel.] This organ pulpit and choir seat with adjoining buildings were presented to this church by W. A. Woodside and David Woodside, Castle Rocklands, in memory of their parents James Woodside and Catherine Isabella Woodside, Jan. 1913.

The Rev. James White (1816-1889), Minister of First Carrickfergus Presbyterian Church, from the Memoir by his son

CARRICKFERGUS, NORTH ROAD CEMETERY

O.S. 52. Grid Ref. J414878

Carrickfergus, North Road Cemetery. General view, under snow

This lies in the North East Division of the town, to the east of the North Road, and just beyond the railway track. It was established to augment the old churchyard of St. Nicholas's. A white marble tablet in the east wall of the mortuary chapel explains: "This burial ground was provided for the parish of Carrickfergus in the year 1859 as an additional burial place for persons of all denominations pursuant to a bequest to that effect in the will of Charles Edmonstone Kirk of Thornfield, late captain 1st Royals, agreeably to the terms of said will the moiety of this burial ground lying in the centre and surrounded by the four walks, which run parallel with the boundary walls and are distinct therefrom about 35 feet, has been set apart inalienably as a free burying place for the poor of this parish and for strangers. The residue of the ground namely the plots which lie between the boundary walls and the four walks abovementioned remains under the disposal of the rector of the parish for the time being and the whole is under the control as an ordinary parochial burying ground. A sum of two shillings and sixpence will be payable to the rector for each burial in the last mentioned plots as a burial fee, the same to be applied in keeping the chapel and burial ground in repair and order. This fee will be exclusive of the sexton's charge and will be payable irrespective of the ownership of any particular parcel of ground by any family."

Below this is a smaller square tablet inscribed with a plan of the ground and the accompanying wording, "MAP of the burial ground shewing the position of the drains therein." The drains are marked in red.

Several members of the Kirk family were laid to rest under the chapel. The ground remained in the possession of the Church of Ireland until taken into the care of the Borough Council in 1990.

The earliest date of death recorded in 1853 (Donald). All inscriptions recording deaths before 1901 have been copied.

ALEXANDER
Sacred to the memory of William Alexander who died 24th July 1870 aged 38 years. Also his son William who died 9th Sept. 1869 aged 11 years. Also his son David who was drowned 6th February 1883 aged 23 years. Also his wife Eliza Jane who died 21st July 1906 aged 70 years. Also their last surviving child Mary, widow of James Alex STEELE, died 22nd March 1961 aged 94 years. W. Graham, York St., Belfast. 1 grave to left.

[Letters of administration of the personal estate of William Alexander, late of Carrickfergus, master mariner, who died 24 July 1870 at same place, were granted at Belfast 3 October 1870 to Eliza Jane Alexander of Carrickfergus, the widow of said deceased. Effects under £450.]

ALLISON
See McNEILL

ANDERSON
[Cast iron plaque on railed enclosure.] The burying place of Ed. J. Anderson, Carrickfergus, 1896.

ANDERSON
See PURDY

ADAMSON
See CAMERON

BANKHEAD
See JENNINGS

BARRY
See HERDMAN

BASHFORD
[Lead lettering on white marble in railed enclosure.] In memory of Maggie BOYD, the beloved wife of John Bashford, died 20th August 1886 aged 48 years. Lizzie McMaster, born 10th February 1873, died 14th January 1892. The above-named John Bashford died 17th April 1906 aged 64 years. James Boyd, late town clerk and petty sessions clerk, died 12th Octr. 1915 aged 70 years.

BEATTIE
[Cast iron plaque attached to low railings.] The burying place of Wm. John Beattie, Carrickfergus, 1895.

BECK
(Resting place of John Beck, died 2nd July ...., Crone House.

BEGGS
[Attached to low railings.] The burial ground of W.H. Beggs.
[Cast by:-] James Moore & Sons Ltd., Ironfounders & Engineers, Millfield Foundry, Belfast.

BELL
Erected (by) David Bell in memory of his beloved son William who died 31st March 1873 aged 27 years. Deeply regretted. Also Jane Sands who died in the Lord March 7th 1885 aged 25 years. Also Agnes SANDS her daughter who died March (30th) 1885 aged 1 year. Also Ann Bell his beloved wife who died November 30th 1891 aged 75 years.

[Letters of administration of the personal estate of William Bell, late of Carrickfergus, sailor, a bachelor, who died 22 April 1873 [sic] at same place, were granted at Belfast 4 August 1873 to David Bell of Carrickfergus, labourer, the father of said deceased. Effects under £50.]

BIRNIE
[Six cast-iron plaques attached to railings of enclosure.] Grace Birnie died 25th Jany. 1869 aged 50.

Mary Grace Birnie died 27th Jany. 1870 .... 77 ye... Thos. Mercer Birnie died 14 February 187(3) aged (8)0 years. [Cast by:-] Ulster Foundry. (Millfield) Belfast].

Ellen Birnie died 30th December 1878 aged 83 years. [Cast by:-] Millfield Foundry.

Mary Birnie died 22d. December 1887 aged 57 years. Isabella Birnie died 27th December 1901 aged 85 years.

[Letters of administration of the personal estate of Mary Birnie, late of Carrickfergus, spinster, who died 22 December 1887 at same place, were granted at Belfast 15 November 1889 to Isabella Birnie of Carrickfergus, spinster, the sister. Effects £572 14s. 1d.]

BOYD
[White marble panel framed in sandstone now fallen and broken.] Er(e...) by W.J. Boyd in memory of his beloved wife Lizzie Boyd who fell as[leep] in Jesus 23rd March (188)5 ..ed 27 years. Also his dearly beloved wife Mary Boyd who fell asleep in Jesus 6th January 1894 aged 26 years. Also the said W.J. Boyd died 16th June 1916 aged 57 years. We shall meet to part no never.

BOYD
[Cast iron attached to railed enclosure with Espartero Jones.] The burying ground of William Boyd, Carrickfergus. 1897.

BOYD
[Cast iron plaque attached to low railed enclosure.] The family burying place of David Boyd, Carrickfergus. The Millfield Foundry.

BOYD
[Cast iron plaque attached to low railings.] Burying ground of Andrew Boyd. [Cast by:-] James Moore & Sons Ltd., Ironfounders & Engineers, Millfield Foundry, Belfast.

BOYD
See BASHFORD and GRAHAM

BRENNAN
[Slate.] 1897. Tom Brennan.

BROWN
Burial ground of Edward Brown.

BROWN
See McGILCHRIST and WOODSIDE

BRYANS
[Cast iron plaque attached to low railed enclosure.] The family burying ground of Thomas Bryans Junior. 1896. [Cast by:-] James Moore & Sons Ltd., Ironfounders & Engineers Millfield Foundry, Belfast.

BULL
[Large white marble slab in floor of mortuary chapel.] Mrs Anne Bull, wife of the very Revd. George Bull, Dean of Connor, and second daughter of the late Peter KIRK, Esq., D.L. of Thornfield, Carrickfergus, who departed this life on the 16 November 1881 aged 57 years. Her remains are deposited under this slab.

[Letters of administration of the personal estate of Anne Bull, late of Thornfield, Carrickfergus, who died 12 November 1881 at same place, were granted at Belfast 22 May 1882 to the Very Reverend George Bull of Thornfield, Carrickfergus, D.D., Dean of Connor, the husband. Effects £3,348 6s. 6d.

Letters of administration of the personal estate of Anne Bull, late of Thornfield, Carrickfergus, wife of the Very Reverend George Bull, who died 12 November 1881 at same place, left unadministered by the Very Reverend George Bull, the husband of deceased, were granted at Belfast 5 December 1887 to George Edmonston Kirk of Thornfield, esquire, the acting executor of said Very Reverend George Bull. Former grant 22 May 1882. Effects administered £30 12s. 4d.]

BULL

[Large white marble slab in floor of mortuary chapel.] The Very Revd. George Bull, D.D., Dean of Connor and Incumbent of Carrickfergus, who died at Thornfield on the 24th March 1886 aged 73 years. His remains are deposited underneath this slab.

[The will of the Very Reverend George Bull, late of Thornfield, Carrickfergus, county Antrim, D.D., and Dean of Connor, who died 24 March 1886 at same place, was proved at Belfast 29 October 1886 by George Edmonstone Kirk of Thornfield, Carrickfergus, the sole executor. Effects £2,487 18s. 9s.

Rev. George Bull was born in 1812/3, the son of William Bull, solicitor, and educated at Corpus Christi College, Cambridge, where he graduated B.A. in 1837, M.A. in 1840, D.D. in 1860 ad eundem Oxford in 1860. He was perpetual curate of Dorney, Bucks., in 1846 and exchanged with the Rev. John Chaine in 1855 as Dean of Connor 1855-86 and rector of Carrickfergus. He died on 24 March 1886 at Thornfield, Carrickfergus. He married in Carrickfergus Church on 18 June 1857 Anne Kirk, second daughter of Peter Kirk, J.P., D.L. of Thornfield, county Antrim, M.P. for Carrickfergus, 1835-41, by Ellen Dalway of Bellahill. He had 2 sons:

1. George Edmonstone Bull assumed the name of Kirk in 1858, J.P., D.L. for county Antrim, High Sheriff for county Antrim 1892 and for Carrickfergus 1883, Captain Antrim Artillery Militia, died 23 March 1909. He married (1) 1887 Ethel Margaret Searight who died in 1890; (2) 1893 Agnes Beatrice Armstrong, only daughter of Sir George Carlyon Armstong, Bart. who died in 1935. They had 1 daughter Eileen Beatrice Bull. See Leslie: *Clergy of Connor* (1993).
2. Pardo A. Kirk of St. Catherine's, Carrickfergus and Ballywillwill, county Down, Lieut., Antrim Artillery Militia, High Sheriff for Carrickfergus in 1885. He married on 23 February 1892 in St. Stephen's, Dublin, Ethel Frances, only daughter of T.R. Baillie-Gage of Tirnaskea, Cookstown, and died 7 April 1900 aged 38 years, at his home in Fethard where he had gone to hunt with the Tipperary Hounds. They had 1 son.

CADELL

[Granite within railings.] Erected in memory of Lt. Colonel William Cadell, H.E.I.C.S., eldest son of the late John Cadell, of Tranent, Scotland, born 13th Feb. 1826, died 18th Jan. 1875.

CAMERON

[Over an earlier inscription "Erected by Mary STRAIN 1876" which was concealed with plaster.] Erected by Mary Cameron of Carrickfergus in remembrance of her beloved son Wm. ADAMSON who fell asleep in Jesus the 3rd Septr. 1883 aged 22 years. Ellen GYLS died Novr. 22nd 1902 aged 47 years. Mary Cameron died May 5th 1903 aged 68 years. 2 graves one on each side of the stone

CARSON

[Cast iron.] The family burying ground of James Carson, Carrickfergus, 1896. [Cast by:-] The Millfield Foundry, Belfast.

CLYDE

[Small sandstone.] J. Clyde.

COMBE
[White marble with cast iron enclosure.] In memory of Hannah Combe, wife of John Combe, born at Bradford August 2nd 1832, married at St. Johns Church, Leeds, November 9th 1859, died at Greenisland July 27th 1872. She had a battle to fight, and fought it well, but was not strong enough to conquer.

CONNOR
In loving memory of my dear husband John Connor died 6th Sept. 1950. Also my dear parents William and Annie Guy 1892-1905. Also Elizabeth, beloved wife of the above John Connor, died 25th Sept. 1976. Till he come.

CORKIN
In memory of Ellen Corkin who departed this life 24th August 1892 aged 16 years. Asleep in Jesus. [Cast by:-] James Moore & Sons Ltd., Ironfounders & Engineers, Millfield Foundry, Belfast.

CORKIN
[A small stone beneath foregoing.] In memory of Joseph Corkin died Feby. 28th 1894 aged 13 years.

COURTNEY
[Slate with name painted on.] Courtney.

COWLEY
[Cast iron plaque attached to low railings.] Cowley, 1881.

DAVIDSON
[Granite.] In loving memory of Capt. Andrew Davidson died 21st Oct. 1872. Capt. Samuel Davidson died at sea 11th Feby. 1880. His wife Mary died 12th Feby. 1890. William Davidson, son of the above A. Davidson, died 10th July 1893. Jane, wife of above A. Davidson, died 22nd April 1899. "Deeply regretted". "Jesus wept". St. John XI c., 35 v.

DAVISON
[White marble.] Erected by James Davison in memory of his mother Eliza Davison who died 4th December 1891. Also his father John Davison who died 14th January 1906. The above named James Davison died 1st March 1940. And his wife Sarah Ann who died 19th August 1950. Also his daughter Elizabeth, died 14th April 1990.

DE RYCKERE
See LEATHAM

DOBIE
In memory of David Henderson Dobie, born 10th December 1811 at Dysart, Scotland, died 28th November 1872 at Carrickfergus.

DONALD
In memory of John Donald who died 7th March 1853 aged 69 years. His wife Jane DOWNEY who died 28th February 1866 aged 83 years. Also their children: Thomas Donald who was lost in the S.S. City of Glasgow on his passage from Liverpool to Philadelphia March 1854 aged 40 years and Ann Donald who died 19th Jany. 1883 aged 70 years. J. Irvine.

[The will with one codicil of Jane Donald, late of Carrickfergus, in the county of the town of Carrickfergus, widow, who died 28 February 1867 at same place, was proved at Belfast 15 June 1867 by the oaths of Elizabeth Weatherup, wife of James Weatherup, tailor, and Anne Donald, spinster, both of Carrickfergus, the executrixes. Effects under £200.

Early in the nineteenth century the family were spelling their name DONEL. Thomas dealt in cloth and seems to have been a frequent visitor to New York. His sister married James Weatherup (q.v.). The Downey family were long established in Kilroot. Sources: Donel family Bible; Ann Weatherup, Scotch Quarter.]

DORAN

[The inscription is on white marble tablets on base of rustic cross with entwined vine.] Erected to the memory of John Doran who died 24th May 1866 aged 55 years. Sacred to the memory of a dear and loving mother Annie Jervis Doran died 13th March 1887 aged 82 years. "Her warfare is accomplished". Is. XL, 2. "Her children arise up, and call her blessed". Prov. XXXI, 28. "And God shall wipe away all tears from their eyes, and there shall be no more death, neither sorrow, nor crying". Rev. XXI, 4.

[Letters of administration of the personal estate of John Doran, late of Kilroot, county Antrim, coastguard, who died 23 May 1866 at same place, were granted at Belfast 20 May 1867 to Anne Doran of Fleet Street, Belfast, in said county, the widow of said deceased. Effects under £100.]

DOWNEY

See DONALD

DUGLASS

[Tilting sandstone.] Erected by Mary Ann Duglass in affectionate remembrance of her beloved brother, James Duglass of Woodburn, who died 30th Decr. 1862 aged 34 years.

DUNDERDALE

[Polished granite.] In affectionate remembrance of William Dunderdale who died 20th May 1889 aged 59 years.

[The will of William Dunderdale, late of Albert Road, Carrickfergus, R.I.C. pensioner, who died 20 May 1889 at Larne, county Antrim, was proved at Belfast 17 June 1889 by David Gray of High Street, Carrickfergus, and William Beggs of North Street, Carrickfergus, merchants, the executors. Effects £439 5s. 7d.]

EDMONDS

[Cast iron plaque attached to railed enclosure.] The family burying ground of James Edmonds 1896.

Cast-iron plaque to James Edmonds

ELLIS
[Ledger beside Taylor monument.] This is erected by Mrs. Ellis in remembrance of her late husband Mr Thomas Ellis who departed this life 30th May 1867 at Woodburn, born near Penistone in Yorkshire, England, aged 49 years.

Both day and night I bore great pain
Physicians tried, but all in vain.
But God above he thought it best
To ease my pain and give me rest.

[The will of Thomas Ellis, late of Woodburn, Carrickfergus, in the County of the town of Carrickfergus, contractor, who died 30 March 1867 at same place, was proved at Belfast 11 July 1867 by Samuel Davys Stewart Cunningham of Carrickfergus, merchant, one of the executors. Effects under £800].

ENGLAND
[Sandstone.] In memory of Charlotte E.A. England, infant daughter of Commander England R.N., who died December 3rd 1871 aged 5 months.

ENGLISH
[Lead lettering on white marble. A roundel contains a wheatsheaf and sickle.] Erected by John English in memory of his wife Mary English who departed this life 24th March 1888 aged 41 years. Also his daughter Isabella who departed this life 10th October 1879 aged 15 days. Also his son Thomas who died 18th July 1909 aged 28 years. Also the above named John English who died 18th September 1915 aged 82 years. And their daughter Mary who died 17th November 1961 aged 86 years.

ERSKINE
See JOHNSTONE

EXHAM
See TAYLOR

FALLOON
See MARKHAM

FAUSSET
[White marble set into sandstone.] Sacred to the memory of Revd. Simon James Fausset who died 22nd October 1869 aged 47 years. "With Christ which is far better".

[Letters of administration of the personal estate of the Rev. Simon James Fausset, late of Carrickfergus, clerk, who died 22 October 1869 at same place, were granted at Belfast 21 January 1870 to Anne Jane Fausset of No. 16 Virginia Street, Belfast, the widow of said deceased. Effects under £450.

The Rev. Simon James Fausset was born in 1822/3, the son of Charles Fausset of county Fermanagh, entered Trinity College, Dublin in 1839 and graduated B.A. in 1844. He was curate of Belfast 1858-9, perpetual curate of St. Mark's, Ballysillan (Connor) 1859-65, curate of Moira 1865-69 and vicar of Kilmood 1869 but died of apoplexy at Carrickfergus before taking up the appointment. He married Anne Jane ---- and had at least 3 daughters:

1. Margaret Mathewson Fausset died on 25 May 1879 at 79 Stamford Terrace, Donegall Pass, Belfast.
2. Mary Fausset died at Sidley, British Columbia, on 25 April 1921.
3. Henrietta Wray died 1 March 1879 at Leeson Park, Dublin.

See Burtchaell and Sadleir: *Alumni Dublinenses* (1924); Leslie and Swanzy: *Biographical Succession Lists of the Clergy of Diocese of Down* (1936).]

FLEMING
[White marble shaped as scroll with lead lettering, in a railed enclosure.] Erected by Margaret L. Fleming in memory of her husband William Fleming, late brigade

sergeant-major, R.A., who died 5th Sept. 1906 aged 69 years. Also their children: Margaret who died in infancy, Archibald Crozier who died 26th Jany. 1880 aged 8 years. Alfred Ernest who died 24th March 1892 aged 22 years. Maud Mary who died 22nd Decr. 1892 aged 10½ years. Edith Annie who died 3rd April 1895 aged 20 years. Frederick A. Fleming who died 9th April 1917 aged 36 years. Clara E. Fleming who died 9th November 1921 aged 43 years. The above named Margaret L. Fleming died 24th October 1936 aged 97 years.

FRENCH
[Gothic lettering on sandstone within low railing.] In memory of Harriet French, daughter of Wm. French and Margaret French, of Dublin who died at Carrickfergus 9th September 1865 in the 82nd year of her age. Maria Noy JOHNS, daughter of Alexander and Emma Johns, born 3rd March 1828, died 7th September 1916. "The path of the just is as the dawning light that shineth more and more into the perfect day".

GARDNER
[White marble with lead lettering, now fallen on its face.] Erected by James Gardner in memory of his father James Johnston Gardner, died 2nd Jan. 1861 aged 71 years. Also his mother Jane died 15th April 1879 aged 75 years. Also his sister Margaret died 16th Oct. 1862 aged 23 years. Also his brother Thomas, lost at sea 23rd April 1875 aged 48 years. Also the above named James Gardner died 20th Jan. 1890 aged 56 years.

[The will of James Gardner, late of Eden, Carrickfergus, labourer, who died 20 January 1890 at Belfast, was proved at Belfast 13 June 1890 by James Watt, wife of Edward Watt, of 116 York Street, Belfast, the sole executrix. Effects £105 18s. 3d.]

GARDNER
[West edge of grave yard, decoration includes anchor and crown.] Sacred to the memory of Clarence C. Gardner, sub-lieutenant H.M.S. "Edgar" who was killed by accident on the railway between Belfast and Carrickfergus on the 11th of September 1863 in the 20th year of his age. This tablet was erected by his messmates as a slight token of their esteem and regard. "In the midst of life we are in death". [Mason:-] Jn. Robinson, York St., Belfast.

GARDNER
[Slate.] Erected by John Gardner in memory of his wife Esther Gardner who died 28th Octr. 1880. Also his son Samuel who died 24th May 1879. Also his son James who died 8th March 1884. The above John Gardner died 22nd June 1901. His son William Gardner died 28th May 1947.

GASTON
[Sandstone with fresh coat of white paint in a high railed enclosure.] Erected by James Gaston, Carrickfergus, in memory of his son Alexander who fell asleep in Jesus 22nd Feby. 1884 aged 17 years. The above James Gaston who died 13th July 1899 aged 60 years. Also his daughters Annie Eliza who died 24th July 1904 and Maria who died 7th March 1913. Also his son-in-law James LOGAN who died 20th April 1920. Also his wife Mary Gaston who died 7th January 1928. And his daughter Rosetta who died 16th December 1945. Also his daughter Letitia Jane, wife of the above named James Logan, who died 3rd December 1966.

[Maria, third daughter of James Gaston married on 1 January 1892, Samuel Stewart. They were married by the Rev. James Lyon, Congregational minister.]

GILLESPIE
[Headstone and surround of granite.] In memory of Robert Gillespie died 20th October 1893 58 years. Also his wife Catherine Gillespie died 21st December 1922 aged 84 years. Also their son James died 1st April 1875 aged 6 years. Robert Gillespie, eldest son of the above, died 28th December 1951 aged 82 years. Peace perfect peace.

GRAHAM

[Tall white marble stone with lead lettering and low surround.] Erected by the Revd. William Graham in memory of his beloved children:- Susan Mary died December 31st 1875 aged 18 years, Janetta Wilhelmina died February 26th 1876 aged 12 years, Joseph James died February 24th 1878 aged 10 years, William Robert died May 18th 1882 aged 20 years. The above Revd. Wm. Graham, for 22 years pastor of the Independent Church, died July 22nd 1888 aged 66 years. Also his wife Sarah Graham who died 31st March 1892 aged 62 years. And his son-in-law Revd. R.H. BOYD B.A., for 22 years minister of Ballyjamesduff Presbyterian Church, died Decr. 7th 1904 aged 46 years. Also his grandson Lieut. Wm. Graham Boyd, 9th Royal Irish Fusiliers, killed in action at Ypres 16th August 1917 aged 21 years. Also his grandson Dr. Thomas W. Boyd died 20th Decr. 1928 aged 31 years. Sarah Louise, wife of the above Revd. R.H. Boyd, died 25th September 1951 aged 85 years. Also his grandson Joseph Douglas Boyd died 14th Nov. 1960. [Mason:-] Rankin.

[The Rev. William Graham was born in 1822 in county Tyrone and grew up among the Primitive Methodists. In 1844 he was ordained to their ministry and when he came to Carrickfergus he was made pastor of the independent meeting house at the Quay Gate in 1865. A new church was opened on Albert Road in 1879. He resigned in 1887.

The Rev. Robert Henry Boyd was born at Dunover, near Ballywalter, county Down in 1857. He was educated at Queen's College and Assembly's College, Belfast and graduated B.A. of the Royal University of Ireland in 1883. He was licenced by the Ards Presbytery in 1884 and ordained minister of Ballyjamesduff, county Cavan in the same year. He married in 1895 Sarah Louise Graham, daughter of the Rev. William Graham.

See McCrum ed. of McSkimin: *History and Antiquities of Carrickfergus* (1909); Barkley; *Fasti of the Presbyterian Church 1871-1890.* (1987).]

GRAHAM

[Square and compasses in a roundel.] In affectionate remembrance of my beloved husband David Norman Graham, sergeant, Antrim Artillery Militia (late R.A.) who died at Carrickfergus 14th January 1881 aged 45 years. "Not dead but sleepeth". Also Benjamin Mills TAGGART, grandson of the above, who died 30th May 1905 aged 5 years. Safe in the arms of Jesus.

GRAHAM

In memory of Maggie McALPIN, the beloved wife of James Graham, who died 2nd June 1883 aged 33 years. Also his son Willie died 12th August 1887 aged 9 years. Also his daughter Nellie died 4th Sept. 1899 aged 23 years. Also the above named James Graham who died 4th December 1926 aged 84 years. [Mason:-] Jenkins, Larne.

GREEN

See JOHNSTON

GREER

[Cast iron plaque attached to low railed enclosure.] The family burying ground of Mrs. Jane Greer, 1875.

GREER

See PURDY

GYLS

See CAMERON

HAMILTON

[Lead lettering on white marble.] In loving memory of Mary Hamilton who died 31st July 1895 aged 66 years. And of her father Rev. William Hamilton, Baptist minister who died 15th July 1888 aged 80 years. [Mason:-] Holden.

[The will of Mary Hamilton, late of Carrickfergus, county Antrim, spinster, who died 31 July 1895 at Cavan, was proved at Belfast 4 October 1895 by Eliza K. Close, wife of the Reverend W. Close of Carrickfergus, the sole executrix. Effects £117.10s.

The Rev. William Hamilton was the first pastor of the Baptist Congregation formed in 1863. He began preaching at the age of 16 as a Wesleyan in the Athlone Circuit, but changed his views and was baptised by Dr Carson of Tobermore. From 1837 to 1846 he was Baptist missionary in Athlone and Moate, then moved to Ballina and finally to Carrickfergus. See McCrum ed. of McSkimin *History and Antiquities of Carrickfergus* (1909); *Carrickfergus Advertiser*, 26 October 1888.]

HANNAN
[White marble with lead lettering.] In memory of William Hannan and Margaret his wife. Also their children Thomas & Ellen. [Mason:-] A. McBain.

HART
[Polished granite in railed enclosure.] Erected by Martha Hart in memory of her husband James Poag Hart who died 1895 aged 52 years. Also their daughter Maggie who died 1877 aged 5 months. Their daughter Agnes who died 1887 aged 15 years. Their son Thomas who died 1891 aged 22 years. Their daughter Jannie who died 1895 aged 25 years. Our dear mother Martha Howard McKee Hart, born October 2nd 1846, died January 18th 1924.

HART
[Cast iron plaque on railed enclosure.] The burying place of Alexr. Hart. 1891

HERDMAN
[Polished black granite enclosed by low railings.] To the memory of Agnes BARRY, beloved wife of William P. Herdman, died 25th June 1873 aged 22 years. Also William P. Herdman died 31st January 1916 aged 80 years. Also William (Quartus) eldest son of the late William PORTER of Hawthorn, died 26th March 1933 aged 49 years. Also his brother Christian Anderson died 17th December 1935. [Mason:-] Purdy & Millard, Belfast.

HERDMAN
[Lead lettering on white marble within low railings.] In affectionate remembrance of Eliza, the beloved wife of James Herdman, died 10th December 1884 aged 48 years. Also the above James Herdman died 25th December 1889 aged 60 years. Also his sister Ann Jane Herdman died 31st December 1906 aged 82 years. "Blessed are the dead which die in the Lord". Rev. XIV c., 13v.

[Letters of administration of the personal estate of James Herdman, late of Carrickfergus, draper, who died 25 December 1889 at same place, were granted at Belfast 5 February 1890 to Ann Jane Herdman of Market Place, Carrickfergus, spinster, the sister. Effects £253 10s. 5d.]

HERRON
[Cast iron plaque attached to railings.] The burying ground of William Herron. [Cast by:-] Victor C. Taylor, Atlas Foundry, Townsend St., Belfast.

HERRON
[Sandstone, propped on its side.] Sacred to the memory of Francis Herron who died 19th January 1884 aged 18 years. Also his father John Herr(on) who died 12th June 1895 aged (6)0 (years).

HILL
[Cast iron.] Margaret J. Hill died May 1891.

HODKINSON
(Sacred to) ... (memory of) John Hodkinson who was accidentally killed by an explosion of dynamite on the 2nd January 1885 whilst superintending the erection of the new (harbour) works, Carrickfergus, aged 24 years. Lived a Christian and

died in Lord. Also in memory of Amy, daughter of James Hodkinson, who departed this life (7th) February 188(1) aged (5) years.

[The harbour improvements of the 1880s were contracted to T.D. Lewis who employed John Hodkinson as clerk of works from mid 1884. He was secretary of Carrickfergus Amateur Rowing Club. His father James Hodkinson came to Carrickfergus as manager of the Salt Works owned by M.R. Dalway. He took over the Eden Salt Mines in March 1903, but died a few months later. His sons continued the management. See *Carrickfergus Advertiser*, 9 January 1885; McCrum ed. of McSkimin: *History and Antiquities of Carrickfergus* (1909) pp. 515-516.]

HOGG
[White marble on granite plinth.] In loving memory of Geo. Wm. Hogg, son of G. & E. Hogg, who died 19th Jan. 1892 aged 14 months. "He sleeps in Jesus". [Mason:-] G. McCann, Belfast.

HOLMES
[Cast iron plaque on low railings.] The burying ground of John Holmes 1892. [Cast by:-] James Moore, Millfield Foundry, Belfast.

HOLMES
[Cast iron plaque on railed enclosure.] The burying ground of James B. Holmes.

JENNINGS
[White marble.] In beloved memory of Eliza, widow of the Rev. John Jennings, Warrenpoint, and daughter of the late Rev. John BANKHEAD, Ballycarry, who departed this life at Carrickfergus June 29th 1873. [Mason:-] Purdy & Millard, Belfast.

[Behind.] The family burying ground of Joseph Young.

[Letters of administration, with the will and one codicil annexed, of the personal estate of Eliza Jennings, late of Carrickfergus, widow, who died 29 June 1873 at same place, were granted at Belfast 10 April 1874 to William Porter Jennings of Lombard Street, Belfast, county Antrim, hardware merchant, paternal uncle and curator of Evangeline Jennings and Henry John Arthur Jennings, the children of said deceased (limited). Effects under £100.

She was one of twenty two children fathered by Rev. John Bankhead (1737-1833), who was Presbyterian minister of Ballycarry from 1763 and married, in 1858, Rev. John Jennings (1832-1870), who ministered to several Unitarian congregations in southern England and Remonstrant congregations in east Ulster, dying at Warrenpoint on 14 May 1870.]

JOHNS
[Imposing stone within railed enclosure of corresponding dimensions.] Here lies the body of Mary Catherine, the gentle and loving wife of Wm. Johns Esq. of Carrickfergus, who died the 5th of Jany. 1863 aged 27. "The sun shall no more be thy light by day, neither for brightness shall the moon give light unto thee, but the Lord shall be unto thee an everlasting light and thy God thy glory". Also of the above William Johns of Mountjoy Court, Carrickfergus, who departed this life on 26th March 1898 aged 80 years. "Peace perfect peace". In loving memory Tyndall Stuart Johns, born 13th March 1868, died 7th February 1947. Also Lieut. Cor. Arthur Henry Tyndall Johns, youngest son of the above, killed in action at sea 31st December 1942.

JOHNS
[A collection of four crosses in a large railed enclosure.] I.H.S. To the dear memory of Alexander Johns of Sunnylands who died 14th December 1889 aged 67. And of his infant daughter Harriet Annie Frances who died 29th April 1871 aged 6 months. "Till He Come".

In loving memory of Harriett F. Johns who died 30th Novr. 1888 aged 63, and of her sister Marianne S. Johns who died 24th Feby. 1894 aged 64. "He giveth His beloved sleep". [Mason:-] Robinson.

In memory of Digby Johns who died 17th Novr. 1893 aged 55 years. And of his son Alexr. Digby who died at Ceres, South Africa 11th March 1894 aged 28 years. "There the wicked cease from troubling, and there the weary be at rest." Also his daughter Bessie F. Johns who died 17th July 1895 aged 26 years.

Sir William Arthur Johns, K.C.S.I. son of Alexander and Anne Johns, born 6th December 1858, died 2nd June 1918. "A man greatly beloved" who "after he had served his own generation by the will of God fell on sleep".

[The will of Alexander Johns, late of Sunnylands, Carrickfergus, bank director, who died 14 December 1889 at same place, was proved at Belfast 5 August 1890 by Anne Johns, of Carrickfergus, widow, and Edward Bates of Royal Avenue, Belfast, solicitor, the executors. Effects £13,120 5s. 6d.

The will of Harriet French Johns, late of Carrickfergus, spinster, who died 30 November 1888 at same place, was proved at Belfast 22 August 1890, by Maria Noy Johns and Marianne S Johns, both of Carrickfergus, spinsters, the executrixes. Effects £1,226 12s. 3d.

The will, with one codicil, of Marianne Johns otherwise Stuart Johns, formerly of St Bride's and late of Alton, both Carrickfergus, spinster, who died 24 February 1894 at latter place, was proved at Belfast 4 October 1895 by Maria Noy Johns of Alton, Carrickfergus, spinster, the surviving executor. Effects £1,503 4s. 8d.

Letters of administration of the personal estate of Bessie French Johns, late of 9 Palmerston Park, Dublin, spinster, who died 17 July 1895 at Belmont, county Antrim, were granted at the Principal Registry 6 September 1895 to Edward H. Johns of Palmerston Park, B.L., the brother. Effects £543 10s.]

JOHNS
See FRENCH

JOHNSTON
[A marble full rigged ship is set into the sandstone] 1874. Sacred to the memory of William John Anderson Johnston only and beloved son of Wm. and Jane Johnston, in childhood of Carrickfergus, late of Manchester, who died of yellow fever at Rio de Janeiro on the 30th January 1873 aged 18 years. Deeply regretted by all who knew him.

    Oh, sad was his fate,
    He, the youthful and brave,
    Had crossed the wild billows,
    And found but a grave;
    Yes, with strangers a grave
    On a far foreign shore,
    And the land of his heart's hope
    He never saw more.

Blessed are the pure in heart for they shall see God. Lines by his mother. Erected by Mrs. GREEN in memory of her beloved son.

JOHNSTON
[Sandstone with inset of white marble.] Erected by Hannah Johnston in memory of her beloved husband Thomas Johnston of Mile Bush who died 16th Jany. 1876 aged 6(5) years. Their son Andrew, born 19th Jany. 1841, killed in railway accident at Heule, Belgium, 9th March 1901. Also of his wife Elizabeth, born 10th July 1837, died 16th Augt. 190(0). Their son James who died 1(5)th Feby. 19(4)4 aged 69 years.

[The will of Thomas Johnston, late of the Mile Bush, North Road, Carrickfergus, grocer, who died 16 January 1876 at same place, was proved at Belfast 5 June 1878 by the oath of Hannah Johnston of the Mile Bush, North Road, Carrickfergus, same county, widow, the sole executrix. Effects under £300.

Hannah, widow of Thomas Johnston, died at the residence of her son-in-law George Blackwood, 16 Tilly Street, Belfast, on 21 December 1885.]

JOHNSTON
[Sandstone enclosed within low railings.] Erected by Isabella Johnston in memory of her beloved husband David Johnston died 17th July 1885 aged 52 years. Also the above Isabella Johnston died 10th Nov. 1920 aged 89 years. And their daughter Margaret Kilpatrick LARKIN died 26th Aug. 1962 aged 88 years.

JOHNSTON
[Cast iron plaque attached to railed enclosure.] The family burying ground of Joseph Johnston. 1888.

JOHNSTON
[Cast iron plaque.] The burying ground of Thomas Johnston.

JOHNSTON
[Broken white limestone.] In loving memory of our dear mother and father, Margaret and Jared Johnston. [Stone broken through last names, no other information.]

JOHNSTONE
[Polished granite.] In memory of Francis Johnstone died 18th January 1901 aged 63 years. Also his sons:- Francis Edward died 14th September 1868, James Alexander died 15th December 1872, infant son died 14th August 1882. Also his wife Elizabeth ERSKINE died 3rd April 1906 aged 64 years. And his son William Francis died 31st October 1932 aged 56 years. And his daughter Margaret F. Johnstone died 17th June 1941 aged 70 years. And his daughters, Rina died 15th December 1942, Anna J. died 3rd February 1943. Jane Alexander Johnstone died 29th Dec. 1958 in her 94th year.

JOHNSTONE
In loving memory of Thomas Johnstone died 26th January 1929.
William Johnstone died 12th August 1908 aged 86 years. Hannah his wife died 1871. Also Louisa, wife of the above named Thomas Johnstone, died 20th February 1950.

JOHNSTONE
[Granite stone and surround.] In loving memory of John Johnstone died 21st February 1891 aged 72 years. Also his wife Eleanor died 10th July 1928 aged 88 years. Also their daughters Magaret died 21st July 1881 aged 15 years. Jane Eleanor, wife of James Johnstone, died 11th March 1916 aged 48 years. Also James Johnstone died 3rd December 1936 aged 75 years. Till He Come. Thomas Frederick Johnstone died 28th February 1983 aged 74.
[Letters of administration of the personal estate of John Johnstone, late of Longfield, Greenisland, Carrickfergus, farmer, who died 21 February 1891 at same place, were granted at Belfast 10 April 1891 to Eleanor Johnstone of Longfield, Greenisland, the widow. Effects £40.]

JONES
[Cast iron plaque - same enclosure as Wm. Boyd.] The burying ground of Espartero Jones, Carrickfergus. 1897

KAIN
[Cast iron plaque mounted on railed enclosure.] John Kain.

KENNEDY
[Cast iron plaque on railed enclosure.] The family burying ground of John Kennedy. 1872.

KIRK
[Recumbent slab within railings beneath tablet on NE wall of mortuary chapel. Ringed by a laurel wreath in high relief are arms:- Indented, a sword and crozier in saltire, in a chief a Scottish thistle. Crest:- Sword and crozier in saltire. Motto:-

Optimum quod primum.] Sacred to the memory of Charles Edmonstone Kirk, son of the late Sir William Kirk of Thornfield, Carrickfergus. He died at Thornfield February 11th 1864 aged 65 years. "But as for me I will behold thy presence in righteousness and when I awake up after thy likeness I shall be satisfied with it". Lth Psalm, 16th. V. "Beloved now are we the sons of God and it doth not yet appear what we shall be: but we know that when He shall appear, we shall be like Him, for we shall see Him as He is." 1st John 3rd c., 2nd V.

[The will of Charles Edmondstone Kirk, late of Thornfield in the county of the town of Carrickfergus, esquire, who died 11 February 1864 at same place, was proved at Belfast 14 April 1864 by the oath of Ellen Kirk and Maria Kirk, both of Thornfield, Carrickfergus, spinsters, Alexander Johns of Sunnylands, Carrickfergus, a director of the Belfast Bank, all in the county of the town of Carrickfergus, and James Torrens of Edenmore, Whiteabbey, in the county of Antrim, solicitor, the executors. Effects under £30,000.

See under St. Nicholas's Graveyard.

KIRK

Sacred to the memory of Ellen Kirk, who died at Thornfield 16th August 1875 aged 53 years, eldest daughter of the late Peter Kirk, Esq, D.L. "Unto them that look for him shall he appear the second time without sin unto salvation." Heb. IX, 28. [Mason:-] J. Robinson & Son, Belfast.

[The will, with one codicil of Ellen Kirk, late of Thornfield, Carrickfergus, spinster, who died 16 August 1875 at same place, was proved at the Principal Registry 12 October 1875 by the oaths of Maria Kirk of Thornfield, spinster, and William Nevin Wallace of Downpatrick, county Down, esquire, the executors. Effects under £50,000.]

KIRK

[Large marble slab in floor of mortuary chapel.] The remains of Miss Ellen Kirk, eldest daughter of Peter Kirk Esq. D.L. of Thornfield, Carrickfergus, who departed this life on the 16 August 1875, are deposited under this slab.

KIRK

[Mural tablet in mortuary chapel.] Sacred to the memory of Maria Kirk who died at Thornfield 1st April 1881 aged 55 years, youngest daughter of the late Peter Kirk, Esq., D.L. "Fear not for I have redeemed thee I have called thee by thy name thou art mine", Isaiah, XLIII, I.

[The will of Maria Kirk, late of Thornfield, Carrickfergus, spinster, who died 1 April 1881 at same place, was proved at Belfast 17 May 1881 by William Nevin Wallace of Downpatrick, county Down, solicitor, one of the executors. Effects under £90,000.]

KIRK

[Large slab in floor of mortuary chapel.] The remains of Miss Maria Kirk, youngest daughter of Peter Kirk Esq, D.L., of Thornfield, Carrickfergus, who departed this life on the 1st of April 1881, are deposited under this slab.

KIRK

See BULL

KIRKBY

[Low sandstone with surround.] In loving memory of James Alexander Kirkby died 6th May 1900 aged 79 years. His wife Ellen died 19th April 1887 aged 52 years. And their children Fred, Edwin, George, Jim.
Father in thy gracious keeping
Edwyn Kirkby died 11th March 1963 aged 86 years.

LAPPIN

[Sandstone, beginning to flake.] Erected by James Lappin in memory of his three children Margt., born 24th April 1870, died 16th Septr. 1875. Quinn, born 21st

Headstone to the children of James Lappin, now flaking

Feby. 1873, died 4th Octr. 1875. Mary E., born 20th Octr. 1871, died 6th Octr. 1875.

LARKIN
See JOHNSTON

LARMOUR
[Fallen on its face, white marble.] In loving memory of Catherine, wife of William Larmour, died 23rd June 1918 aged 68 years. Also William Larmour, founder of Whitehead, died 4th Nov. 1918 aged 76 years. Also their children who died in infancy. "Until the daybreak".

LEATHAM
[White marble with lead lettering.] Edith Violet Leatham aged 3 years July 11 1888. "Let not your heart be troubled". Hilda Balfour Leatham, Xmas 1908. "Rejoice evermore". And their sister Mary Kathleen, beloved wife of Joseph Albert DE RYCKERE, March 13 1932. Also their father Charles Western Leatham, commissioner R.I.C., born 1846, died 1933. "God is Love". And Charlotte Grace Leatham, at rest January 10th 1948.

LOWRY
[Slate.] In memory of Lizzie Lowry who departed this life 20th August 1875 aged 18 years.

LYLE
[Sandstone.] Erected by Letitia Lyle in memory of her beloved husband Samuel Lyle who departed this life 9th Sept. 1883 aged 76 years. Also the above-named Letitia Lyle who departed this life 11th July 1888 aged 73 years. Also their grandchildren: Ellen Lyle who departed this life 7th May 1897; John Lyle who departed this life 7th April 1900. Also Ellen Lyle, the beloved wife of Samuel Lyle, who departed this life 5th Nov. 1910. And the above-named Samuel Lyle who departed this life 7th May 1925.

LYNAS
[Sandstone with badly dissolving white marble inset.] (Erected by Robert) Lynas (in memory of his beloved wife) Jenny (........ April 1877 aged 26). Also his three children, Mary .....7(th) February ...., Jenny (died 22nd July 1877, William ...... October 1877).

LYONS
[White marble with lead lettering.] In affectionate remembrance of Thomas Lyons who died 17th July 1892 aged 73 years. Also his wife Ann Jane Lyons who died 23rd December 1904 aged 79 years. Also Martha Hill, beloved wife of John W. Lyons, who died 1st November 1914. The above named John W. Lyons died 27th February 1937.

McALISTER
[Sandstone, first date is on round inset of white marble.] Erected 1879 by Henry McAlister in memory of his beloved wife Elizabeth who died 10th July 1866 aged 50 years. Also his daughter Ellen Jane who died 18th February 1877 aged 40 years. Also the above Henry McAlister who died 17th Dec. 1890 aged 80 years. Also his daughter Martha who died 11th August 1900 aged 50 years. Also his daughter Mary who died 8th April 1917 aged 85 years. Mary McAlister, nee WALLACE, who died 17th September 1937 aged 64 years. Henry, husband of the above Mary McAlister, died 21st Aug. 1943 aged 83 years. Not dead but sleepeth.

McALISTER
[Lead lettering on white marble inset on concrete.] Erected by Felix & Mary McAlister in loving memory of their son Arthur McAlister, born 17th Jany. 1897, died 21st Jany. 1897. Also the above Felix McAlister, born 31st Oct. 1872, died 24th April 1930.

McALISTER
[Cast iron plaque with the legend partly obscured by a wooden surround.] The burying ground of James McAlister, (Carrick)fergus. (189)5.

McALLISTER
[Cast iron plaque.] The burying ground of William McAllister. Makers: Musgrave & Co. Ltd., Belfast.

McALLISTER
[Cast iron marker.] The burying ground of Alexander McAllister. [Cast by:-] Musgrave & Co. Ld., Belfast: Makers.

McALLISTER
[Cast iron plaque.] The burying ground of Andrew McAllister.

McALPIN
The burying place of Samuel McAlpin Carrickfergus 1895. [Cast by:-] Houston & Hamilton Foundry, Belfast.

McALPIN
See GRAHAM

McARA
[Sandstone within railing.] Erected by Thomas McAra in memory of his beloved wife Susan who died 5th May 1867 aged 40 years. Also the above Thomas McAra who departed this life 7th July 1888.
[Letters of administration of the personal estate of Thomas McAra, late of Carrickfergus, county Antrim, publican, who died 7 July 1888 at same place, were granted at the Principal Registry 27 March 1889 to Sarah McAra of same place, the widow. Effects £506 18s. 7d.]

MCBRINN
[Small slate.] Anthony McBrinn, Ballyhackamore.

McCALMONT
[Lead lettering on white marble within low railings.] In loving memory of Edith McCalmont who died Nov. 1881. Charlie who was lost at sea May 1883. Maggie who died July 1897. [Mason:-] Purdy & Millard, Belfast.

McCARTNEY
[Polished granite.] Erected in memory of John McCartney who died 10th Oct. 1894 aged 60 years. Also his beloved daughter Margaret who died 6th April 1885 aged 15 years. Also his dearly beloved wife Margaret Esler McCartney who died 12th Sept. 1931 aged 87 years. Also their dear son James McCartney who died 24th Sept. 1946 aged 72 years.

McCLURE
[Low enclosure with white marble tablet bearing lead lettering.] The burying ground of Robert McClure.

McCULLOUGH
[White marble tablet on low railings.] The family burying ground of Robert McCullough, Belfast.

McDERMOTT
[Cast-iron plaque.] The family burying place of Head Constable James McDermott, Carrickfergus, 1885. [Cast by:-] James Moore, Millfield Foundry, Belfast.

McDOWELL
[Low sandstone.] In memory of James McDowell who died 17th October 1875 aged 80 years.
[The will of James McDowell, late of Slievetrue, county of the town of Car-

rickfergus, farmer, who died 16 October 1875 at same place, was proved at Belfast 19 November 1875 by the oath of David Weatherup of Slievetrue, Woodburn, Carrickfergus, farmer, one of the executors. Effects under £200.]

McDOWELL

The family burying ground of John McDowell, Carrickfergus, 1890. [Cast by:-] Victor C. Taylor, Atlas Foundry, Townsend St., Belfast.

McGILCHRIST

[White marble with lead lettering, fallen and lying on its face. Convolvulus is carved on a panel near the top.] In loving memory of our mother Christina McGilchrist, died 19th March 1876 aged 73. Also our dear son George G. BROWN died November 1889 aged 4½. Also our dear son William H. Brown died in Switzerland November 1909 aged 31. Also infants. Janet, beloved wife of James H. Brown, died 21st April 1931. James H. Brown died 23rd October 1937. Forever with the Lord.

McILWAINE

[Sandstone.] Erected by Mary McIlwaine in loving memory of her husband William McIlwaine who died 21st February 1885 aged 65 years. Also their son William who died 26th September 1866 aged 4 years. Also their daughter Ann Jane who died 14th October 1866 aged 2 years. Also their son Crawford, Chief Officer of British India Co's. Steamer "Lindula", who died on the voyage from Bombay to Calcutta 28th May 1892 aged 35 years. Also their son Thomas, apprentice on board ship "Lord Dufferin" of Belfast, who met his death by accident at sea 5th June 1893 aged 19 years.

Although they there at anchor lie,
With many of their fleet,
They will one day again set sail,
Their pilot Christ to meet.

Also their daughter Maggie Jane, wife of J.R. McQUITTY, who died July 1902. And the above Mary McIlwaine who died December 1904. And their little grand-son Alex McQuitty who was accidentally killed 11th September 1913 aged 14½ years.

[The will of William McIlwaine, late of Castle Street, Carrickfergus, victualler, who died 21 February 1885 at same place, was proved at Belfast 17 April 1885 by William Hogsett of Kilroot, county Antrim, farmer, and Mary McIlwain of Carrickfergus, widow, the executors. Effects £298 6s.

Letters of administration of the personal estate of Crawford McIlwaine, late of Carrickfergus, mariner, who died 28 May 1892 at sea, were granted at Belfast 23 September 1892 to Margaret Jane McQuitty of Carrickfergus, married woman and half sister. Effects £5.]

MACKEY

[Cast iron plaque on railed enclosure.] The burying ground of John Mackey. [Memorial by:] Purdy & Millard, Belfast.

McMEEKIN

[Polished granite.] Erected by William & Mary McMeekin in memory of their son James who died 19th Octr. 1878 aged 10 years. Their daughter Elizabeth Ann who died 31st March 1883 aged 6 years. Their daughter Catherine who died in infancy. Their son William who died 2nd Feby. 1900 aged 29 years. The above-named Mary McMeekin died 15th Feby. 1900 aged 58 years. The above-named William McMeekin died 19th Decr. 1902 aged 65 years.

McMILLAN

Erected by James McMillan in memory of his mother Agnes McMillan who departed this life 7th June 1869 aged 63 years.

McNEILL
[Celtic cross in granite.] In loving memory of Captain R.H. McNeill, born August 14 1861, died April 6 1916. And his wife Mary who died 10th Sept. 1952 aged 86 years. Also Basilan Sydney Norman, youngest son, born May 29 1896, died April 17 1900.

McNEILL
[Polished granite enclosed with foregoing.] Erected by James McNeill 1891 in loving memory of his son James who died 4th May 1891 aged 27 years. And of the above named James McNeill who died 4th Novr. 1898 aged 74 years. His wife Elizabeth ALLISON (family of Allison of Brae Face, Parkgate 1798), born 4th May 1827, died Easter Monday (1st April) 1907. Also Daniel McNeill, eldest son of above, died 8th Feb. 1934. And Nellie, wife of above Daniel McNeill, died on Christmas day 1947. Ion Alexander Carlisle McNeill, younger son of the late Daniel and Nellie McNeill, born 20th Sept. 1906, died 23rd Jan. 1971. Donald Robert McNeill, elder son of the late Daniel and Nellie McNeill, born 30th Jan. 1902, died 6th Sept. 1978. And his wife Rhoda Margaret McNeill, 1913-1992. Eileen Sara McNeill, daughter of Daniel & Nellie McNeill, died 20th May 1980 aged 80 years.

[Letters of administration of the personal estate of James McNeill, formerly of Magherafelt, county Londonderry, and late of Meadowbank, Carrickfergus, bank official, who died 4 May 1891 at latter place, were granted at Belfast 3 June 1891 to James McNeill of Meadowbank, county surveyor's assistant, the father. Effects £163 14s. 8d.]

McPHERSON
[Sandstone beginning to flake.] Erected (to) t(he) memory of Eliza McPherson who departed this life March 22nd 1867 aged 46 years.

[Letters of administration of the estate of Eliza McPherson, late of Carrickfergus, spinster, who died 22 March 1867 at same place, was granted at Belfast 26 April 1867 to Joseph McPherson of North Street, Carrickfergus, grocer, the brother and one of next of kin. Effects under £100.

McQUITTY
See McILWAINE

MANN
[Lead lettering in white marble. Roundel contains dove with sprig.] Erected by Thomas Mann in memory of his beloved wife Mary Mann who died 4th January 1894 aged 49 years. And their three children who died in infancy. And their beloved son Thomas Horan Mann who died 17th October 1897 aged 14 years. The above-named Thomas Mann died 11th August 1904 aged 61 years. [Mason:-] A. McBain, Belfast.

MARKHAM
[Lead lettering on white marble. Large wheeled cross at top.] Sacred. Erected by their eldest son to the dear memory of Alexander Markham Esq., for 42 years an officer of the militia of this county and 30 years a coroner thereof. Died at Greenisland 15th July 1876 in his 80th year. Also Sophia Hulbert, his wife, only daughter of the late Marcus FALLOON, clk, rector of Layde, died at Greenisland 26th May 1878 in her 67th year.

"If we be dead with him, we shall also live with him." II. Tim. II, 11.

[The will of Alexander Markham, late of Roseville, Greenisland, Carrickfergus, coroner of the county of Antrim and quartermaster of the Royal Antrim Artillery, who died 15 July 1876 at same place, was proved at Belfast 28 August 1876 by the oath of Sophia Hulbert Markham of Roseville, Greenisland, widow, the sole executrix. Effects under £200.]

MATHIAS
[White marble cross, now off its plinth, within railings.] In memory of Edgar Richard Mathias, commander R.N., who died 28th February 1888 aged 44 years.

"O death, where is thy sting? O grave, where is thy victory". "Our help standeth in the name of the Lord, who hath made heaven and earth".

[E.R. Mathias was the son of Capt. Mathias R.N. of Norfolk. He passed from Royal Naval College in 1857; was appointed midshipman in 1859; sub-lieutenant, 1863; lieutenant, 1865; commander, 1879. He succeeded Commander Meyer R.N. in the Carrickfergus Coastguard District in 1883. He was given a military funeral: the procession from his residence, The Deanery, Scotch Quarter, included the band of the 2nd Brigade N. Irish Division Royal Artillery, a firing party from 1st. Batt. West Surrey Regiment, stationed in the Castle, and many coastguards. See *Carrickfergus Advertiser* 9 March 1888.]

MATTHEWS
See MULREYNE

MILLAR
The family burying ground of Samuel Millar.

MILLAR
[Lead lettering on white marble.] Erected by John Millar in loving memory of his wife Margaret Jane who died 28th Oct. 1862 aged 41 years. Also his son Robert Henry died 9th Aug. 1873 aged 4 years. Also the above-named John Millar who died 21st February 1898 aged 56 years. [Mason:-] A. McBain.

MILLAR
See THOMPSON

MINNIS
[Cast iron plaque within railed enclosure.] The family burying ground of William Minnis. [Cast by:-] The Millfield Foundry.

MONTGOMERY
The family burying ground of William Montgomery. In loving memory of his mother Elizabeth who died 15th January 1893 aged 60 years. Also his daughter Lizzie who died 18th August 1903 aged 6 years and his sister Mary Jane who died 19th April 1909 aged 54 years.

MOORE
[Sandstone, fan & quartrefoils at top.] Erected by Anne Moore in memory of her beloved husband Samuel Moore who departed this life December 30th 1870 aged 32 years.

MULREYNE
[Laid flat in front of modern Matthews stone.] Erected by Eliza Mulreyne in memory of her beloved son Mitchell Mulreyne who died 18th June 1874 aged 4 years. He shall gather the lambs with his arms and carry them in his bosom. Isa. XL.11. The above Eliza Mulreyne died 23 July 1908. And (her s)on-in-law Jos(ep)h MATTHEWS died 9th April 1935. Also his son Charles who was lost with submarine L24 10th January 1924. And Jane, wife of the above Joseph Matthews, died 16th September 1940. Their daughter Elizabeth died 8th September 1943.

MUNRO
[Sandstone and white marble, now fallen from its plinth.] Sacred to the memory of Ann, wife of Captain Munro, Adjutant Antrim Artillery Militia, who died at Carrickfergus 10th April 1875 aged 59 years.

OGLE
See TAYLOR

O'NEILL
[Fossiliferous limestone.] The burial place of Robert McNeill. Sacred to the memory of Sarah RAUBB, the beloved wife of Robert O'Neill, who died at Car-

rickfergus 8th Dec. 1880. Also Annie O'Neill, daughter of the above named, died 8th Dec. 1880. Also Charlie O'Neill, son, who died at Carrickfergus March 1885. Also Rose O'Neill, daughter, who died at Belfast Dec. 1915. "His compassions fail not. They are new every morning". Sam. [sic] 3;22, 23. [Mason:-] Walsh, Ballymena.

PALMER
[Low slate.] Eliza Palmer.

PATTERSON
[White marble with lead lettering. Roundel contains dove in flight with twig.] Erected by John Patterson to the memory of his loving wife Ellen Patterson who died 20th March 1890 aged 38 years. Also the above named John Patterson who died 31st July 1926 aged 76 years. Also Ellen, beloved wife of the above named John Patterson, who died 2nd February 1929 aged 71 years. [Mason:-] A. McBain.

PEARCE
[Sandstone.] Erected to the memo(ry of) W.H. Pearce Esq. R.N., late commander of her Majestys cutter Rac(er) who was accidentally drowned in Belfast Lough in the performance .. his duty on the 2nd of March 18(6.) aged 38 years. This tablet is erected to his memory by his sorrowing shipmates who regret his loss. Requiescat in pace.

PORTER
[White marble.] Sacred to the memory of William Porter who departed this life 10th April 1878 aged 71 years. Also his wife Jane who departed this life 29th March 1877 aged 63 years. This stone is erected by their only surviving son William as a token of love and respect. [Mason:-] J. Robinson, Belfast.

PURDY
Erected by (Jane) GREER in memory of her dear sister and niece. In loving memory Sarah ANDERSON widow of Hugh Purdy who died April (9)th 18(8)9 aged 49 years. Also her beloved daughter Sarah Agnes aged 20. "Whom the m(ou..)ed ..... death." "And God shall wipe away all tears from their eyes."

RAUBB
See O'NEILL

REID
[Polished granite tall and round.] Erected by William Reid in loving memory his father William Reid, born 17th March 1830, died 30th April 1894. His mother Maria Reid, born 16th June 1827, died 16th April 1911. His brother Captain John Reid, born 23rd July 1851, died 18th May 1906, interred in the Moravian Cemetery, Staten Island, New York. And George who died in infancy. Also his beloved wife Jane Reid, born 3rd October 1854, died 28th June 1927. The above William Reid J.P., born 24th Oct. 1855, died 24th Feb. 1936. And his sister Mary Reid died 6th March 1958. [Mason:-] Gemmell.

REID
See TAYLOR

RITCHIE
[Sandstone.] Erected by John Ritchie of Portadown in memory of his beloved daughter Carline who departed this life 22nd July (1863) aged 14 years. [The remainder is merely painted on the stone and is now faded, especially close to ground level.] Also his daughter Elizabeth, dearly beloved wife of George ......

ROBB
[White marble with lead lettering.] In memoriam Isabella Robb who died 11th May 1888 aged 83 years. Also her son David Robb late Harbour-Master and Rate-Collector who died 2nd September 1908 aged 71 years. "In my father's house are many mansions".

RODGERS

[Polished granite.] In loving memory of Mary Rodgers died 31st July 1899 aged 57 years; wife of Alexander Rodgers died 21st Jany. 1904 aged 67 years. Also their sons: Alexander died 13th Jany. 1904 aged 35 years; John died 17th Nov. 1907 aged 32 years. Also 4 children died in infancy.

ROTHWELL

[Heavy granite stone with lead lettering on inset of white marble, now fallen face downward.] In affectionate memory of Margaret "Maggie" the beloved wife of William Rothwell and eldest daughter of Charles & Mary STEWART, who entered into her rest the 17th day of April 1879 in her 28th year.

RYND

See TAYLOR

SANDS

See BELL

SMYTH

[Cast iron plaque on low railed enclosure.] The family burying ground of Robert Smyth.

SMYTH

[Draped urn at top. Main inscription is on SE face.] In loving memory of Nellie Owens WATERSON, died 24th March 1913 aged 19 years. Also James Waterson, died 17th April 1926 aged 72 years. His wife Mary Waterson died 1st August 1927 aged 72 years.

[On SW face.] Mary Jane Smyth died 27th October 1898 aged 66 years. [Mason:-] Purdy & Millard, Belfast.

[Adminstration, with the will, of the personal estate of Mary Jane Smyth, late of 28 Canning Street, Belfast, widow, who died 27 October 1898, granted at Belfast 22nd December 1898 to Mary Waterson of 28 Canning Street, Belfast, married woman, the universal legatee in trust. Effects £126 14s. 7d]

STAFFORD

[White marble.] Erected by William WOODS in loving memory of Patrick Stafford who died 15th Augt. 1891 aged 71 years. Also Ellen Stafford who died 27th July 1897 aged 80 years. "Blessed are the dead who die in the Lord."

STEELE

See ALEXANDER

STEVENSON

[Sandstone within low railings.] Erected by Capt. David Stevenson in memory of his brother James who died at Rio-de-Janeiro 27th March 1859 aged 17 years. Also his sister Charlotte who died 4th October 1872 aged 17 years. Wm. YOUNG S.M.R.N. died 31 Dec. 1884 aged 42 years. His mother Charlotte died 29th April 1888 aged 77 years. The above David Stevenson died at Algiers 6th January 1893. Annie Stevenson, wife of Wm. Young, died 13th June 1895. Robert Stevenson died 22nd October 1897 aged 86 years. Margaret Stevenson died 15th September 1900. James S. Young died 15 Dct. [sic] 1912. Catherine Stevenson died 16 Dec. 1912. Also Elizabeth Stevenson died 22nd June 1939. [Mason:-] R. Love, Belfast. [Probate of the will of Robert Stevenson, late of Minniebrook, North-West Ballycarry, county Antrim, farmer, who died 22 October 1897, granted at Belfast 20 January 1898 to John Stevenson, mercantile clerk, and Edward Hamilton Sturdy, farmer, both of Ballycarry. Effects £141 10s.]

STEVENSON

[Small sandstone cross.] "Jesus loves me". In loving memory of Birdie, daughter of the late Capt. D. Stevenson, born Oct. 13 1890, died Oct. 17 1896.

STEVENSON
[Cast iron plaque on railed enclosure.] The burying place of J. McN. Stevenson. [Cast by:-] James Moore, Millfield Foundry, Belfast.

John McNeill Stevenson (b.1824) came from Kilraughts to be master of Trooperslane School. He transferred to Lancasterian Street School in 1849 and to the Model School in 1861. For many years he served as clerk of session in North Street Presbyterian Church and died 24 July 1910 leaving a son and six daughters. See McCartney: *Nor Principalities Nor Powers*, pp. 228-229, 274.]

STEWART
[White marble stone with lead lettering, within same railed enclosure as ROTHWELL.] Erected by Charles and Mary Stewart in memory of their beloved children:- Robert Alexander Jenkins, born 12th September 1860, died 27th May 1862. Charles Edward, born 23rd December 1862, died 23rd May 1867. Ellen, wife of Joseph WILCOX C.E., born 1st May 1853, died 1st April 1884. John, lost at sea 29th December 1899 aged 41. The above Charles Stewart died 26th February 1900 aged 76. Jane Stewart died 7th June 1909 aged 53 years. Also the above Mary Stewart who died 4th June 1916 aged 88 years.

STEWART
[White marble tablet attached to iron railings.] In affectionate remembrance of our beloved mother Sarah Stewart who died August 1879 aged 47 years. Also Minnie our dear sister who died April 1881 aged 17 years. And our beloved father Samuel Stewart who died 23rd February 1909 aged 78 years.

    Here would we end our quest:
    Alone are found in Thee
    The life of perfect love - the rest
    Of immortality.

STEWART
See ROTHWELL

STRAIN
See CAMERON

STRANGE
[Lead lettering on white marble.] Erected by Hugh Strange in memory of his daughter Anne who died 3rd March 1865 aged 1 year and 9 months. Also his daughter Jane who died 12th March 1865 aged 3 years and 5 months. Also his son George who died 7th October 1887 aged 19 years. Also the above Hugh Strange who died 14th May 1907 aged 81 years. Also his son William Robert who died 20th February 1918 aged 57 years. Also Margaret, beloved wife of above Hugh Strange, who died 1st June 1928 aged 91 years.

SUTHERLAND
[Peeling grey paint, tall, within low railings.] Erected by Hugh Sutherland to the memory of his beloved wife, Margaret Sutherland, who departed this life 5th January 1860 aged 55 years. Also Georgiana his daughter who died 22nd June 1861 aged 26 years. The above named Hugh Sutherland died 2nd January 1865.

SUTHERLAND
[Granite headstone and surround.] In memoriam Alexander Sutherland, born 15th March 1838, died 31st December 1891. Also his son George Hay Sutherland, Lieut. 9th Royal Inniskilling Fusiliers died 2nd November 1918 of wounds received in action, buried in Boulogne. And his wife Mary Sutherland died 24th June 1933. [Mason:-] Jenkins.

[Letters of administration of the personal estate of Alexander Sutherland, late of Ballyrobert, county Antrim, mining engineer, who died 21 December 1891 at same place, were granted at Belfast 14 Mary 1892 to Mary Sutherland of Ballyrobert, the widow. Effects £276 18s.]

TAGGART
[Tall white marble with lead lettering.] In loving memory of David Redmond Taggart M.D., Carrickfergus, late coroner for County Antrim and County of the Town of Carrickfergus, Surgeon Major Royal Antrim Artillery, Surgeon Shiels Institute, died 10th April 1886 aged 47 years. "With Christ which is far better." [Mason:-] Robinson, Belfast.
[There is a memorial tablet to him in St. Nicholas Parish Church, q.v.]

TAGGART
See GRAHAM

TAYLOR
[Slate.] In memory of Ellen Taylor, the beloved daughter of the Revd. J. Taylor, who died April 16th 1863 aged 22 years.

TAYLOR
[Suite of three Celtic crosses. The central one is tall, the others are within gable-shaped headstones.] In loving memory of Alexander Taylor of The Barn, Carrickfergus, born 28th September 1838, died 27th June 1878.
In loving memory of Mary REID, The Barn, Carrickfergus, born July 17th 1828, died August 14th 1885. Erected by her daughters Ellen Shaw RYND, Agnes Richmond OGLE, Elizabeth Grant EXHAM.
In loving memory of James Taylor Reid J.P., The Barn, Carrickfergus, born July 28th 1851, died September 21st 1883. [Mason:-] Robinson, Belfast.
[The will (with one codicil) of Alexander Taylor of Carrickfergus, Co Antrim, flax spinner, who died 27 June 1878 at London was proved at Belfast 16 August 1878 by Thomas Digby Johns of Carrickfergus, solicitor and James Barbour of Ardville, near Holywood, Co Down, engineer, the executors. Effects £60,000.
The will of James Taylor Reid late of Carrickfergus, flax spinner, who died 21 September 1883 at Harrowgate in England was proved at Belfast 19 November 1883 by Thomas Digby Johns and James Barbour, both of Belfast esquires, the executors. Effects £68,820.10.10.
James Taylor established a large flax spinning mill at Barn on the outskirts of Carrickfergus town in the year 1852. In 1853, three years before his retirement, it became James Taylor and Sons Limited. His sons, James Junr. and Alexander did not enjoy longevity (d.1871 and 1878). Alexander was travelling to the continent for reasons of health when he died in London. The body was shipped home and the funeral took place on 2nd July 1878. He was a Justice of the Peace, municipal commissioner, and Poor Law guardian. Control of the mill passed to his nephew James Taylor Reid, son of John Reid, a Glasgow merchant. From 1883 the managing director was John McFerran (d.1904), the husband of Ellen Love, a niece of the Taylor brothers. Mary Reid married in 1884 William Wolfe Rynd, captain in the 7th Foot, son of Christopher Rynd of Mount Armstrong, county Kildare. He died at Donadea Castle, county Kildare on 18 May 1886 aged 42 years. (See also under Ogle, St. Nicholas's Graveyard; *Belfast Newsletter*, 29 June and 3 July 1878; Bassett: *The Book of Antrim (1888)*: McCrum ed. of McSkimin: *History and Antiquities of Carrickfergus* (1909): pp. 501, 505-6, 517 and 519. *Burke's Landed Gentry of Ireland*, 1912 ed.]

TAYLOR
[Large granite monument in railed enclosure.] In memory of James Taylor, Junr. died 27 September 1871 aged 34 years. In memory of James Taylor, born at Carrickfergus 16th June 1869, died at Glasgow 30th January 1895. In memory of Alexander Taylor, Captain, Royal Scots Highlanders, born at Carrickfergus 25th March 1872, killed in action in France 21st April 1917.
[James Taylor, late of 13 Granby Terrace, Hillhead, Glasgow, died 30 January 1895. Administration was granted at Glasgow the 13 June 1895. Resealed at Dublin. Effects £2,843 19s. 8d]

THOM
[Sandstone with white marble inset.] In memory of John Thom died 5th August 1(8)6(8) aged 41 years.

[Letters of administration of the personal estate of John Thom, late of Carrickfergus, pawnbroker, who died 5 August 1868 at same place, were granted at Belfast 28 May 1869 to Alice Thom of Carrickfergus, the widow of said deceased. Effects under £200]

THOMPSON
[White marble.] Erected by Samuel Thompson in memory of his mother Margaret Thompson who died January 1873 aged 45 years. Also his sister Mary Eliza who died 29th March 1890 aged 27 years.

THOMPSON
Erected by Whiteside Thompson in memory of his father John Thompson who died 27 March 1877 aged 59 years. Also his mother Sarah Thompson who died 24th Feby. 1891 aged 70 years. Also his brother-in-law Robert MILLAR who died 4th November 1908. And the above named Whiteside Thompson who died 11th March 1925. Also his sister Annie Millar who died 9th May 1930.

THOMPSON
[Sandstone. Roundel at top contains dove in flight with olive branch.] The family burying ground of Robert H. Thompson. Erected in memory of his daughter Eleanor who died 14th Jan. 1890 aged 24 years. Also the above named Robert H. Thompson who died 8th Jany. 1896 aged 55 years.

TODD
[Cast iron plaque attached to railed enclosure.] In memory of my beloved husband James Logan Todd died May 19 1876 aged 39.

[The will of James Logan Todd, late of Greenisland, Carrickfergus, engineer, who died 19 May 1876 at same place, was proved at Belfast 14 June 1876 by the oath of Thomas Todd of Priory Park, Holywood, county Down, commercial traveller, the executor. Effects under £20.]

TODD
[Cast iron plaque attached to railing beside foregoing.] Sacred to the memory of William Todd, his children and grandchildren of Carrickfergus, 1887. [Cast by:-] A. Hoy, Belfast.

TODD
[Cast iron plaque attached to low railings.] The burying ground of W. J. Todd.

[Similar plaque on same railing:-] In loving memory of my daughter Mary, born 18th Novr. 1887, died 18th Novr. 1897. At Rest. [Cast by:-] James Moore & Sons Ltd., Ironfounders & Engineers, Millfield Foundry, Belfast.

TUKE
[Low cross of white marble within railings.] Beatrice J. Tuke, 23rd Dec. 1888 aged 9 months. Walter Fergus G. Tuke, 17th Nov. 1893 aged 1 year 8 months.

TURNER
The family burying ground of William Turner, Carrickfergus. 1893. [Cast by:-] Millfield Foundry, Belfast. 1907.

WALLACE
[Polished granite.] Erected by Agnes Wallace, Belfast, in loving memory of her husband James Wallace, master mariner, born Nov. 22 1832, lost at sea Dec. 8 1886. Also their children: Mary Ann born Feb. 27 1859, died July 14 1863; William born July 11 1857, died June 23 1887; James born Mar. 12 1863, died April 12 1895; Isabella born Feb. 12 1861, died Aug. 19 1897. The above named Agnes Wallace died 21st March 1913 aged 82 years. [Mason:-] Robinson, Belfast.

WALLACE
[Cast iron plaque on low railed enclosure.] The burying ground of Jenny Wallace, Carrickfergus. 1896.

[Polished granite headstone in same enclosure.] Erected by Jenny Wallace in memory of her dear husband William WORKMAN who died 18th July 1877 aged 30 years. His remains are interred in Raloo. Also her dear husband Samuel Wallace who died 9th July 1895 aged 76 years. And her beloved daughter Agnes Knox Workman who fell asleep in Jesus 1st July 1902 aged 29 years. Also her beloved son Henry Workman who died 28th April 1908 aged 33 years. Also her beloved son Samuel Workman who died 11th June 1911 aged 37 years. Elizabeth, dear wife of Samuel Workman, died 24th March 1915 aged 41 years. And their dear son William died 2nd April 1928 aged 28 years. Their dear son Herbert died 16th March 1935 aged 32 years. "Them also which sleep in Jesus will God bring with him." The above named Jenny Wallace died 2nd Nov. 1939 aged 89. [Cast by:-] McNally & Pirie, York St.

WALLACE
See MCALISTER

WATERSON
See SMYTH

WEST
[White marble.] Sacred to the memory of S.M.B.E. West died 16th April 1884.

WHAN
[Cast iron marker.] The family burying ground of David Whan, Carrickfergus. 1894. [Cast by:-] The Millfield Foundry, Belfast.

WHITE
[White marble within low railings.] In memory of John White who died 19th July 1895 aged 70 years. Also his wife Elizabeth who died 26th July 1905 aged 80 years. And their son Charles who died 27th October 1901 aged 39 years.

WILCOX
See STEWART

WOODS
See STAFFORD

WOODSIDE
[Heavy monument surmounted by draped urn.] In memory of James Woodside died 18th May 1866 aged 80 years. And his wife Catherine Isabella BROWN died 12th May 1876 aged 80 years. Also their son Wm. Allan Woodside J.P. of Castle Rocklands, born 11th January 1832, died 29th June 1914. Also their son David Woodside of Castle Rocklands, born 10th June 1834, died 7th October 1916.

[Letters of administration, with the will annexed, of the personal estate of James Woodside, late of Carrickfergus, in the county of the town of Carrickfergus, gentleman, who died 18 May 1866 at same place, were granted at Belfast 27 May 1867 to Catherine Isabella Woodside of Carrickfergus aforesaid, widow of deceased and the residuary legatee. Effects under £800.

W.A. Woodside was High Sheriff in 1880 and David Woodside in 1895.]

WORKMAN
See WALLACE

YOUNG
See STEVENSON

CARRICKFERGUS, ST. NICHOLAS' ROMAN CATHOLIC GRAVEYARD (MINORCA)

O.S. 52. Grid Ref. J407873

In 1826 Father Arthur O'Neill obtained a lease of Barley Hill, and upon it was erected a church which bears two masonry shields with the legends:- "1826, W. Crolly, Bp., A. O'Neill, P.P." and "Rebuilt 1926, J. MacRory, D.D.; G. MacKay, P.P." The cement-rendered rectangular building has now been superceded by Liam McCormick's curving structure of brown brick on the other side of the parochial house. On the higher ground behind them all is the little burial ground bordered on the west by the steep cutting of the Carrickfergus Harbour Tramway.

Of the stone-cutter who was responsible for Fr. O'Neill's headstone, O'Laverty says "he has made it a monument, that only testifies to his own ignorance of the Latin tongue". The earliest death mentioned is 1834 (Lynch). All stones with dates of death before 1900 have been copied.

BALF
I.H.S. Erected to the memory of Mary Balf who departed this life 10th Jany. 1865 aged 71 years. Requiescant in pace.

BROWN
I.H.S. Ann Brown departed this life the 16th of February 1844.

BURNHAM
I.H.S. Sacred to the memory of Elisha Burnham who departed this life 2nd Feb. 1837 aged 64 years. Also his wife Ellen Burnham who departed this life 14th Oct. 1841 aged 63 years. Requiescant in pace. Amen.

CASSIDAY
[Sandstone.] I.H.S. Erected by his pare(nts) in memory of Francis Cassiday, who departed this life 13th April 1869 aged 14 years. R.I.P.

CAVANAGH
[Slate with latin cross and shamrock incised.] I.H.S. The family burying place of James Cavanagh.

DOWLING
See McINTOSH

GIRVIN
See McINTOSH

KINNEY
See NOLAN

LYNCH
(Er)ected by Wi(lli)am Lynch to the memory of his son Jo(hn w)ho departed this life 1(1)th Sept. 1851 aged 5½ years. Also his father John Lynch who departed this life 7th April 18(3)4 aged 49 years. Also his sister Ann who departed this life 7th Octr. 1834 aged 21 years. (Al)so his brother Thomas who departed this life 12th Octr. 1836 aged 4 years. Also his sister Sarah who departed this life 10th Feby. 1838 aged 18 years.

McCLEMENT
[White marble and sandstone with dove in roundel and surmounted by wheeled cross.] Of your charity pray for the soul of Patrick McClement who died 16th May 1887 aged 89. His wife Catherine, who died 10th Feb. 1885 aged 77. Their children:- Maria, who died 12th Aug. 1851 aged 11. Ellen, who died 21st Oct. 1860 aged 25. Richard, surgeon R.N., who died in Japan 17th Aug. 1871 aged 35. Also

F. McClement M.D., R.N., H.M.S. Clyde, who died 30th October 1894 aged 49 years. Rev. W.J. McClement, Rector, Penarth, Wales, died 5th Feb. 1901 aged 58. Also Elizabeth A. McClement, late of Dundrum, who died 14th Nov. 1921. Requiescant in pace.

[The will of Patrick McClement, late of Dundrum, county Down, gentleman, who died 16 May 1887 at same place, was proved at Belfast 5 October 1887 by the Reverend William Joseph McClement of Penarth, county Glamorgan in England, R.C.C., and Elizabeth McClement of Dundrum, spinster, two of the exectors. Effects £1,778 1s. 9d.

Father William McClement was born in Carrickfergus in 1842 and ordained on 11th June 1867. After fifteen years as parish priest at Aberavon with Neath, came his appointment as P.P. of St. Joseph's (R.C.), Penarth, in November 1885. He became a well-respected and familiar sight around the town as he visited parishioners with his black and white terrier Barney by his side. He died from heart failure. See David Fanning: *St Joseph's Penarth* (1990).]

McILROY

Sacred to the memory of Neil McIlroy who departed this life 16th April 1863 aged 41 years. Erected by his beloved wife Mary McIlroy of Carrickfergus. Also the above Mary McIlroy who departed this life 5 May 1884 aged 61 years. Requiescant in pace.

[Letters of administration of the personal estate of Mary McIlroy, late of 10 North Street, Carrickfergus, widow, who died 5 May 1884 at same place, were granted at Belfast 19 September 1887 to Mary Eliza Doherty of 18 Bismarck Street, Ormeau Road, Belfast, wife of Edward Doherty, a child. Effects £1,116 14s.]

McILROY

[White marble close to foregoing. A roundel contains a cross of calvary surrounded by shamrocks.] Erected by Mary McIlroy in memory of her beloved husband John McIlroy who died 26th June 1885 aged 35 years. Also in memory of his grandmother Mary McIlroy. R.I.P.

[Letters of administration of the personal estate of John McIlroy, late of Market Place, Carrickfergus, painter, who died 26 June 1885 at same place, were granted at Belfast 10 August 1885 to Mary McIlroy of Carrickfergus, the widow. Effects £277 12s. 11d.]

McINTOSH

[Lead lettering on white marble.] I.H.S. The family burial ground of Archibald McIntosh, born 7th August 1782. And his wife Cathrine, born 25th November 1791. Also in memory of the DOWLINGS, GIRVINS, & MAGILLS. Erected by Janet TORBET who died on 14th March 1960. R.I.P.

McINTOSH

[White marble with lead lettering. Latin cross near the top.] Erected by John McIntosh in memory of his beloved wife, Mary McIntosh who departed this life 24th Jany. 1889 aged 65 years. R.I.P.

McQUAD

I.H.S. Erected by Charles McQuad in memory of his sister Mary Ann McQuad who departed this life 11th April 1842 aged 29 years.

MADDEN

[Granite Celtic cross with inscriptions on three sides of the base. Front face:-] I.H.S. In memoriam William Madden, Linen Hall Hotel, Belfast, died 15th June 1876 aged 55 years. Erected by a number of his friends in testimony of qualities which distinguished him as a Catholic, a citizen and a friend, and won for him their enduring respect and esteem. Requiescat in pace.

[South face:-] His daughter Margaret Madden who died 23rd March 1857 aged 8 years and 9 months.

[North face:-] His son William Madden who died 9th June 1849 aged 4 years.

[Letters of administration of the personal estate of William Madden, late of Donegall Square, Belfast, hotel keeper, who died 15 June 1876 at same place, were granted at Belfast 11 August 1876 to Margaret Madden of Donegall Square East, the widow of said deceased. Effects under £ 1,500.]

MAGILL
See McINTOSH

MARSHALL
See NOLAN

MULHOLLAND
[Next to Patrick Mulholland.] Erected in memory of Charles Mulholland who died 11th Octr. 1858 aged 20 years. Also Hugh Mulholland who died 14th June 1868 aged 20 years. Edward Mulholland who died 7th J(une 192)3 aged 70 years.

MULHOLLAND
[Sandstone against west wall beside foregoing.] Erected (in) memory (of) Patrick Mulholland who died 3rd November 1870 aged 22 years.

MULHOLLAND
[Next to Charles Mulholland d.1858.] Erected by Edward Mulholland in memory of his father Patrick Mulholland, who died 11th February 1901 aged 83 years. Also his mother Agnes Mulholland who died 13th February 1898 aged 85 years. Also Elizabeth Mulholland who died 13th November 1931. Also Margaret Mulholland who died 23rd March 1932. "Thy will be done". R.I.P.

(MU)RPHY
(Sac)red (to the memory) of (Ne)il(l) (Mu)rphy who departed this life (Nov)ember 5th 1835 aged (45) years. This stone was erected by his widow as a tribute to his beloved memory. Reader if integrity of purpose, dis(interes)ted friendship, kindess of heart (claim th)y regard, revere th(ese.....) Also his brother Ch(arles who) departed this life Augt. 2nd 18(7. aged.)0 years.

NOLAN
[A monument in sandstone and white marble representing a broken fluted column. The inscriptions are on the dado and it is enclosed by iron railings. Front face:-] I.H.S. Erected by Michael Nolan with an affectionate regard to the memory of his beloved mother Mary Nolan who departed this life 27th April 1858 aged 60 years. Her life was the path to heaven. Also his father Valentine Nolan who was drowned off Carrickfergus 12th July 1839 aged 30 years.

"Reader boast not to day
Nor say to morrow's thine
Thou may'st be called away
By sudden death like mine"

And his sister Mary who died infancy.

[South face:-] Peter KINNEY died 19th Jan. 1841 aged 29 years. John Nolan died 15th Sept. 1847 aged 33 years. William MARSHALL died 10th Jan. 1853 aged 29 years.

[North face:-] I.H.S. Michael Nolan died at Hoylake, England, 24th June 1874 aged 51 years. Also his beloved sisters Bridget Marshall who died August 1876 aged 46 years. And Catherine Nolan who died 14th Nov. 1887 aged 47 years.

[The will of Catherine Nolan, late of Belfast, spinster, who died 14 November 1887 at same place, was proved at Belfast 14 December 1887 by John J. Young of Belfast, commission agent, one of the executors. Effects £2,242 1s. 7d.

O'NEILL
Arthurus O'Neill Parochus depositus est hic in pace Decima nona aet ris MDCCCXXXXXII. Sexage simo octavo aetatis anno.

[The Rev. Arthur O'Neill was born on 14 May 1783 at Killymurris, in the parish of Finvoy, county Antrim. He was ordained on 29 August 1808 and officiated in Rasharkin and later Derriaghy. He was appointed parish priest at Ballymoney and Bushmills in June 1815 and in March 1817 to Carrickfergus on 28 October 1851 where he died. See O'Laverty: *An Historical Account of the Diocese of Down and Connor, Vol. III, 115-116.]*

TORBET
See McINTOSH

CARRICKFERGUS, PROSPECT ROMAN CATHOLIC CEMETERY

O.S. 52 Grid Ref. J396887

This cemetery lies in Middle Division on the west side of Prospect Road. In 1874 the Roman Catholic Church purchased a plot for use as a burial ground. It is now the principal place of interment for Catholics in the parish.

The earliest death recorded here is 1871 (HAYS). All inscriptions recording deaths before 1901 have been copied.

BOYCE
I.H.S. Erected by James & Annie Boyce in memory of their dearly beloved son Jas. Joseph who died 10 Apl. 1882 aged 1 year & 7 months. Also there [sic] infant children Jas. Joseph and Michael.

DAWDS
See McGARRY

DEANE
[Lead lettering on white marble surrounded by stucco decorated with sacred heart, etc.] In loving memory of Joseph Joy Deane died 7th Novr. 1892. Also his wife Ellenora V. Deane nee REDMOND died 17th Feby. 1898. Their grandson Joseph Hugh McGREEVY died 12th June 1913. Their son Joseph James Deane died 28th June 1919. Their daughter Teresa McGreevy died 3rd Octr. 1920. Also their daughter Henrietta C.L. HOUSTON died 19th April 1944. Also her daughter-in-law Mary Jane Deave nee McNERN died 1st Octr. 1946. R.I.P. Ellen Deane died 16th Jan. 1954. Philip E. Deane died 22nd Octr. 1958.

ESLER
[Wheeled cross.] I.H.S. In loving memory of James Esler who died 30th Nov. 1908 aged 75 years. Also his beloved wife Mary Esler who died 25th Aug. 1898 aged 65 years. R.I.P.

HAYS
Erected by Samuel & Wm. Hays in memory of their mother Elizabeth Hays who died 14th July 1874 aged 59 years. Also Eliza Jane, daughter of the above William Hays, who died 15th January 1871 aged 3 years. Also her sister Mary Ann who died 26th October 1875 aged 6 months.

[Samuel and William were fleshers. Samuel died at home in West Street on 9 July 1886 aged 44.]

HAYES
[White marble mounted in decorated sandstone; an inset panel carried a recumbent lamb; above is a wheeled cross.] Erected by John Hayes to the memory of his beloved daughter Mary Ann, who departed this life 30th June 1880 aged 12 years and 9 months. Also his daughter Maggie who departed this life 14th July 1885 aged 14 years. Also his daughter Matilda who departed this life 12th July 1888 aged 15 years. Also his daughter Isabella who departed this life 18th June 1890 aged 13 years. Also his son Thomas Joseph who departed this life 16th May 1897 aged 17 years. Also his son-in-law Thomas McCORRY who departed this life 25th March 1903 aged 40 years. Also his beloved wife Mary Ann Hayes who departed this life 3rd June 1912 aged 72 years. Also the above John Hayes who departed this life 30th August 1916 aged 76 years. Also his daughter-in-law Margaret who departed this life 20th June 1932. R.I.P. [An added panel:-] Also his son George who departed this life 15th July 1934. Also his daughter Elizabeth McCorry who departed this life 16th Novr. 1937. [Mason:-] George Rankin, 108 York St., Belfast.

[Lizzie, second daughter of John Hayes of North Street, married on 3 January 1888 in St. Nicholas's Roman Catholic Church, Thomas McCorry of Jordanstown.]

HOUSTON
See DEANE

KEEGAN
[Celtic cross adorned with the sacred heart and passion flowers. Inscription on base.] In loving memory of Frances Elizabeth Mary, daughter of Edward W. Keegan, who died at Scoutbush on 25th May 1891 aged 4 years & 6 months. R.I.P.

LENNON
[Red sandstone.] Erected by John LEWIS in memory of Daniel Lennon who died 17th Novr. 1884 aged 66 years. His daughter Gennetta Lennon died 27th April 1888 aged 41 years. Also Agnes Lewis, beloved wife of John Lewis, who died 30th January 1890 aged 43 years. [Mason:-] Gemmell, Belfast.

[Administration, with the will, of the unadministered estate of Agnes Lewis, late of Carrickfergus, wife of J. Lewis, who died 30 January 1890, granted at Belfast 14 July 1897 to Mary Lennon of Carvoy, county Monaghan, widow, the curatrix of the residuary legatees in remainder. Former grant 25 June 1890. Effects £100.]

LEWIS
See LENNON

McCORRY
See HAYES

McGARRY
[Red sandstone.] Erected in memory of Catherine McGarry who died 6th of April 1877 aged 23 years. Also of Anne Jane DAWDS who died 18th of March 1878 aged 33 years. Requiescant in pace.

McGREEVY
See DEANE

McLAUGHLIN
[White marble within low railings.] In loving memory of our dear father Cornelius McLaughlin died 23rd April 1898. Also our dear mother Mary McLaughlin died 15th January 1955. Their dear son Cornelius died 26th April 1965. R.I.P.

McNERN
See DEANE

McSPARREN
[Base of broken cross.] In loving memory of Mary Jane, only daughter of the late James McSparren, died 8th Novr. 1884 aged 13 years. R.I.P. Erected by her mother Mary McSparren.

MADDEN
[Granite wheeled cross.] I.H.S. Pray for Catherine Madden who died 5 Nov. 1895 aged 70 years. R.I.P.

REDMOND
See DEANE

SPENCE
[Celtic cross decorated with sacred heart and panels of interlace.] In loving memory of our beloved father George Spence who died 12th Nov. 1883. Also our beloved mother Elizabeth Spence who died 9th Nov. 1917. Also Teresa, dearly beloved wife of Joseph Spence, who died 8th Jan. 1927. And their daughter Lily who died in infancy. Also our beloved brother Hercules who died 14th April 1930. On whose souls sweet Jesus have mercy.

[The will of George Spence, late of Belfast, brick manufacturer who died 12

November 1883 at same place was proved at Belfast 20 June 1884 by Elizabeth Spence at Belfast, widow, one of the executors. Effects £1,104 16s. 11d.]

TANNY

To Elizabeth Tanny who for many years was the faithful and trusted nurse to those who knew her worth and cherish her memory and who in affectionate remembrance erect this monument. Died at Sea Park, Carrickfergus, 3rd January 1875. "When Christ shall appear who is your life, then you also shall appear with him in glory." Col. III. 4. [Mason:-] Geo. Rankin, 108 York St., Belfast.

[The will of Elizabeth Tanney, late of Seapark, Carrickfergus, widow, who died 3 January 1875 at same place, was proved at Belfast 22 January 1875 by the oath of Alexander Tanney of Armagh, county Armagh, cabinet maker, the sole executor. Effects under £300.]

WHITE

[White marble with vine motif.] Erected by John and James White in memory of their beloved mother Mary White died 14th May 1874 aged 67 years. Also her grandson David White died Jan. 7th 1881 aged 10 years. Also her son John White who died Decr. 1st 1887 aged 62 yrs. [Mason:-] Purdy & Millard, Belfast.

CARRICKFERGUS, VICTORIA CEMETERY

O.S. 52. Grid Ref. J420887

This lies in the North-East Division and on the west side of Victoria Road. Before 1978 a wrought iron archway over the entrance gate held a cast iron plaque giving the information, "Opened 10th Decr. 1904. Presented to Carrickfergus by Hugh G. Legg Esq., Cape Town, in memory of his father and mother, residents of this town." McCrum (p.135) tells us the Urban District Council of Carrickfergus, acting as a burial board, provided the cemetery at a cost of £2,500. On 19th July 1904 the U.D.C. presented Mr and Mrs H.G. Legg with an illuminated address recognising their gift of £1,000 towards the new cemetery.

There is only one stone with a date of death before 1900. It is attached to the east perimeter wall and is of sandstone carved in a style typical of the early nineteenth century, so may have been moved from another site.

PORTER
   Erected by John and William Porter's in memory of their father John Porter who died 4th of June 1800 aged 67 years. Also their brother and sister who died in infancy. Resting at Ballynure.

   [Modern stone below:] In affectionate memory of Martha Lizzie Porter died 30th March 1934 aged 72 years. Also her husband John Porter died 30th September 1934 aged 74 years.

LOUGHMORNE PRESBYTERIAN GRAVEYARD

O.S. 46. Grid Ref. J404942

Loughmourne Presbyterian Graveyard. General view, under snow

This is 4 miles north of Carrickfergus and on the east side of Carneal Road. A covenanting meeting house was established here in 1804 but the church is now associated with the General Assembly of the Presbyterian Church. It is a long low building at the foot of a slope, which is used as the burial ground. The earliest date of death is 1808 (Stewart). All those inscriptions which record deaths before 1901 have been copied.

AITCHESON
See IRWIN

BARRON
Erected to the memory of John Barron of Lochmorne who died 27th May 1836 aged 70 years. Also his wife Margaret GRAHAME, who departed this life, 10th September 1843 aged 76 years. Also his son, David Graham Barron who died 21st April 1870 aged 70 years. Also his son James Barron, who departed this life on the 12th January 1879 aged 83 years. Also his wife Eliza Barron, who departed this life 31st March 1916, aged 83 years. Their daughter Deborah died 22nd March 1934. Also their son David Graham died 5th July 1937.

[The will of James Barron, late of Loughmourne, county of the town of Carrickfergus, farmer, who died 12 January 1879 at same place, was proved at Belfast 5 March 1879 by the oaths of James Owens of Loughmourne and William Boal of Marshalstown, Carrickfergus, county Antrim, farmers, the executors. Effects under £3,000.]

BARRON
Erected by John Barron to the memory of William Barron of Pullendoes who departed this life 19th May 1840 aged 72 years. Isabella, wife of the above-named John Barron, died 21st December 1889 aged 72 years. The above John Barron died 1st Feby. 1899 aged 90 years. Also William Barron, son of the abovenamed John

Barron who died 22nd January 1914 aged 67 years. Also Alexander Barron, son of the above John Barron, who died 11th June 1919 aged 65 years.

BARRON
[On same stone as SCULLY, within railed enclosure.] The family burying place of Robert Barron, Loughmorne. His son Robert, departed this life on the 17th August 1843 aged 20 years. And the above named Robert Barron who died 15th December 1852 aged 78 years. Also his wife Agnes who died 5th September 1863 aged 82 years. Also their daughter Agnes who died 5th Septem. 1882 aged 63 years. Also their son John who died 20th May 1900 aged 79 years.

[Letters of administration of the personal estate of Agnes Barron, late of Loughmourne in the county of the town of Carrickfergus, widow, who died 5 September 1863 at same place, were granted at Belfast 19 September 1864 to John Barron of Loughmourne, Carrickfergus, farmer, the son, one of the next of kin of said deceased. Effects under £20.]

BARRON
[Lead lettering on marble enclosed with SCULLY.] The family burying place of Daniel Barron of Loughmourne. In memory of his two sons William Hugh and Daniel who died in infancy. Also his daughter Agnes BLAIR who departed this life 13th December 1881 aged 19 years. The above-named Daniel Barron departed this life 18th February 1907 aged 91 years. Also his beloved wife Helena Barron who departed this life 25th February 1908 aged 91 years.

Also their son Robert Barron who departed this life 21st October 1915 aged 66 years. Also their son William Hugh Barron who departed this life 14th January 1922 aged 65 years.

BARRON
Erected by Joseph HILL to the memory of Elizabeth the beloved wife of Samuel Barron. She died 19th Sept. 1883 aged 78 years. Also the above-named Samuel Barron who died 2nd Feby. 1902 aged 88 years.

BEGGS
[Modern stone of polished granite.] In loving memory of James Beggs, died 15th August 1891. His wife Ellen died 4th April 1912. Their daughter Jane died 21st January 1897. James A. Beggs died 12th April 1958. His wife Agnes died 4th March 1953. Their son Thomas died 25th December 1986.

BLAIR
See BARRON and STUART

BOYD
Erected by Alexander Boyd of Trench Park in memory of his father William Boyd who died 26th March 1893 aged 85 years. Also his mother Mary who died 23 September 1894 aged 76 years.

[The will of William Boyd, late of Middle Division, county of the town of Carrickfergus, farmer, who died 27 March 1893 at same place, was proved at Belfast 11 August 1893 by James Boyd, and Alexander Boyd, farmers, and Henry Smyth, factory clerk, all of Carrickfergus, the executors. Effects £1,107 15s. 7d.]

CATHCART
[White marble.] Erected to the memory of Joseph Cathcart who died 27th Oct. 1910. Also his father Samuel Cathcart who died May 1850. Also his mother Sarah Cathcart who died Oct. 1859. Also his brother Edward Cathcart who died 28th Feb. 1915.

CLOSE
[Large granite stone.] In memory of the Rev. William Close, born 17th January 1822, ordained minister of Loughmorne Congregation 7th November 1848, died 12th May 1899. Also his wife Eliza Kinnear Close, born 27th April 1829, died 26th May 1906. And of their son Robert Close, born 9th October 1866, died 5th

December 1905. And of their daughter Mary Close, born 25th July 1858, died 23rd May 1928.

[Probate of the will of the Reverend William Close, formerly of Loughmorne, Carrickfergus, and late of Clinen, The Knock, county Down, Presbyterian minister, who died 12 May 1899, granted at Belfast 16 June 1899 to Robert Close of Clinen, Knock, bank official. Effects £2,460 5s. 6d.]

CLOSE
[White marble tablet in entrance hall of church.] Erected by the congregation of Loughmourne in loving memory of Rev. Wm. Close, ordained 7th Nov. 1848, died 12th May 1899. He was their faithful and esteemed pastor for almost 50 years, an able expounder of scripture, an earnest preacher and a diligent worker for the spiritual and temporal welfare of his people. He being dead yet speaketh.

DUNN
Erected by George Dunn of Lyndon's Park, in memory of his son William Dunn who departed this life 19th January 1853 aged 17 years. Also his daughter Ellen Dunn who departed this life the 31st Oct. 1860 aged 22 years.

DUNN
Erected in memory of Robert Dunn, Ardboly, who departed this life 20th January 1845 aged 33 years. Also his brother William who departed this life May the 7th 1814 aged 13 years.

GALT
[Rough slate with shallow scratched inscription and deeply marked with an 'X']........ Jane Galt ...(823) 56.

GARDNER
In memory of William Gardner who died 29th Jany. 1897 aged 75 years. Also his wife Eliza Gardner who died 9th Decr. 1899 aged 84 years. Also their daughter Mary Stuart Gardener [sic] who died 22d. July 1878 aged 19 years. Also their son William John Gardner who died 9th May 1922 aged 69 years. Also his wife Mary Gardner who died 21st July 1926 aged 72 years. 1 grave north.

[Probate of the will of William Gardiner, late of Carrickfergus, county Antrim, farmer, who died 29 January 1897, granted at Belfast 24 March 1897 to William Gardiner of Carrickfergus, farmer. Effects £160.]

GIRVIN
Erected by James Girvin in memory of his mother Margaret Girvin who died 24th March 1813 aged 40 years. Also his father Robert Girvin who died 14th April 1813 aged 44 years.

GRAHAME
See BARRON

HAMILTON
[Polished granite, fallen.] The burying ground of John Hamilton, Woodburn, his wife and family.

HART
See SEAGRAVE

HILL
See BARRON

HOOD
Erected in 1871 by John Hood in memory of his infant son who died Decer. 1866 aged 4 days. Also his daughter Jane who did 26th February 1870 aged 2 years. The above-named John Hood died 22nd Nov. 1902 aged 78 years.

Headstone to Robert Irwin, who died in 1877, and his family

HUNTER
Erected by William Hunter, Ballyvallough, in memory of his daughter Martha Maria who departed this life 30th April 1881 aged 14 years. Maggie Jane Hunter died 25th April 1886 aged 21 years. Lizzie Hunter died 22nd March 1890 aged 14 years. Mary Smyth Hunter died 25th May 1891 aged 19 years. James Hunter died 12th June 1892 aged 29 years. William Hunter died 18th January 1896 aged 26 years. John Hunter died 16th February 1897 aged 28 years.

IRWIN
Sacred to the memory of Martha Irwin who departed this life, the 11th April 1837 aged 51 years. Also her son Robert Irwin who departed this life 9th Janry. 1877 aged 73 years. Also Annie Irwin who died 5th Jany. 1883 aged 23 years. Also Mary AITCHESON, who died 4th May 1886 aged 37 years. Also Agnes Irwin who died at Glasgow 19th January 1922 aged 78 years. Sadly missed. One grave north.

IRWIN
[Marble and sandstone.] 1887. In loving memory of Robert Irwin who died 9th January 1877 aged 73 years. Also his wife Margaret who died 5th July 1882 aged 63 years. Their son Robert who died 23rd March 1887 aged 33 years. Their daughter Agnes Irwin who died at Glasgow 19th Jany. 1922 aged 78 years. Their daughter Elizabeth McDOWELL who died at Glasgow 30th Jany. 1922 aged 74 years. Their daughter Margaret McLEAN who died at Glasgow 26th April 1922 aged 72 years.

JUNKIN
Erected by William Junkin of Raloo in memory of his father David Junkin who died 15th April 1845 aged 60 years. 1 grave south & 1 north.

KILLEN
Erected by Nathan Killen, Drumcrow, in memory of his beloved father James Killen who departed this life 1st Feby. 1886 aged 69 years.
[The will of James Killen, late of Drumcrow, county Antrim, farmer, who died 1 February 1886 at same place, was proved at Belfast 10 December 1886 by John McCarrol and James Morrow, both of Drumcrow, and Hugh Groddy of Ballyrickard, all in said county, farmer, the executors. Effects £271 10s.]

LONG
In memory of Jane Long who died 15th July 1891 aged 68 years. Also her daughter Mary, who died 17th July 1861 aged 8 years. Also her son James Alfred, who died 17th June 1885 aged 23 years. Hugh died 22nd Feb. 1924. Annie died 9th March 1931. Joseph H. died 21st March 1956.

LONG
[Polished granite.] Erected in memory of John Long, Ballylig, who died 10th April 1933 aged 78 years. Also his wife Hannah Long who died 15th February 1890 aged 34 years. And their daughter Ellen Jane who died 24th February 1928 aged 47 years. Their grand-daughter Nellie Long died 8th April 1941 aged 30 years. And their daughters Minnie Long died 10th April 1950 aged 64 years, Annie Long died 13th Oct. 1951 aged 69 years. James Alfred Long died 10th Nov. 1962 aged 74 years. J. McKay, B'mena.

McALISTER
[Stone has flaked.] Erected by Arthur McAlister in memory of his wife Mary TEMPELTON who died 9th Jan. 1841 aged 69 years. Also the above Arthur McAlister .... 1846.

McALISTER
[Laid flat in modern surround.] Erected by Samuel McAlister, Isle of Glass, in memory of his beloved wife Jane who died 25th October 1870 aged 69 years. Also their daughter Mary, who died 8th August 1852 aged 19 years. Also their grand-

daughter Ellen J. McAlister who died 8th Sept. 1869 aged 2 years & 4 months.

McALLISTER
Erected by John (S) McAllister in memory of his beloved nephew Robert McAllister who departed this life 22nd March 1880 aged 5 years.

McAULEY
See MURPHY

McBRIDE
Erected by John McBride of Bank Hall in memory of his mother, Anne McBride, who departed this life 22nd Jany. 1848 aged 66 years. And of his father Alexander McBride, who departed this life 24th August 1855 aged 77 years. Also his wife Jenny McBride who departed this life 2nd Decr. 1857 aged 48 years. And his son who died in infancy.

McBRIDE
In loving memory of our dear father Alexander McBride died 16th October 1900. Also our dear mother Esther McBride died 13th February 1945 interred in Knockbreda Cemetery. And their beloved son Alexander W., Captain, R.I.R., died 3rd January 1964.
 [Administration of the estate of Alexander McBride, late of Pullindross, Carrickfergus, county Antrim, farmer, who died 25 October 1900 granted at Belfast 24 December 1900 to Esther McBride, widow. Effects £127.]

McDOUGALL
Erected by Jane McDougall in memory of her beloved husband Samuel McDougall who departed this life 7th Jan. 1861 aged 66 years. Here likewise now rest the remains of Jane McDougall who died on the 17th day of December 1885 aged 76 years.
 [The will, with two of codicils of Jane McDougal, late of Woodlands, Carrickfergus, widow, who died 17 December 1885 at same place, was proved at Belfast 25 January 1886 by the Reverend William Close of Carrickfergus, Reformed Presbyterian minister, and Samuel Hamilton of Duncrew, county Antrim, farmer, the executors. Effects £1,334 10s. 4d.]

McDOWELL
[Sandstone tilting steeply forward next to Mattie Stewart d.1900] Erected by James McDowell to the memory of his wife Margaret K. McDowell who died 29th July 1867 aged 24 years. Also their nephew James Stuart McDowell who died 30th July 1867 aged 9 years.

McDOWELL
In memory of Sarah McDowell who died 30th Augt. 1887 aged 69 years. Also her husband John McDowell who died 20th Dec. 1891 aged 79 years. Also their son John McDowell who died 27th March 1893 aged 34 years.
 [Letters of administration of the personal estate of John McDowell, late of Duff's Hill, Carrickfergus, farmer, who died 27 March 1893 at same place, were granted at Belfast 19 May 1893 to Hugh McDowell of Loughmourne, Mile Bush, Carrickfergus, farmer, a brother. Effects £52 10s.]

McDOWELL
The burying ground of William McDowell, Woodburn, his wife and family.

McDOWELL
See IRWIN

McLEAN
See IRWIN

McMAW
[White marble with lead lettering.] Erected by Robert McMaw in loving memory of his mother Elizabeth McMaw who died 29th May 1874 aged 57 years. Also his father William McMaw who died 18th Nov. 1883 aged 88 years. Jane McMaw died 24th May 1939. John, husband of above Jane McMaw, died 15th December 1928. Also Elizabeth McMaw, daughter of above John, died 7th July 1977 in her 96th yr.

MILLIKEN
See STEWART

MOORE
[Granite.] Erected by his sons in memory of Thomas Moore of Ballynerry who died 6th May 1894 aged 63 years. And of his wife Sarah Moore who died 14th April 1901 aged 73 years. Till he come. Also their brother Adam Moore who died 22nd July 1902 aged 43 years.

MURPHY
Erected by John Murphy, Killyglen, to the memory of Christian McAULEY his wife who died 18th Sept. 1834 aged 72 years. Also the above John Murphy who departed this life 28th Feb. 1837 aged 77 years. 2 graves north.

NEILSON
[Stone slanted forward.] Erected to the memory of Mary Neilson who departed this life 6th Decr. 1826 aged 28 years. Also her mother Mary Neilson died 1st Feb. 1837 in the 71st year of her age.

PAUL
[Large headstone surrounded by high railings. The lettering was clumsily restored in 1970.] To the memory of the Rev. John Paul, D.D. of the Eastern Reformed Presbyterian Synod and minister of Loughmourne congregation, who fell asleep in Jesus on the 16th day of March 1848 in the 71st year of his age and 44th of his ministry. He was an earnest pastor and able divine, a christian patriot and philanthropist, equally distinguished for a powerful intellect and a generous and loving heart. His valuable writings testify how zealously his great talents and learning were employed in the defence of sound doctrine and of civil and religious freedom. It accords with a desire once expressed by himself to say, "here lies a man who loved truth, hated error, detested tyranny and abhorred persecution". "He rests from his labours and his works follow him". Psalm XXXVII, 37; Prov. XXIII, 23; Daniel VII, 3; Jude 3rd verse; Revelations XIV, 13. Also to the memory of Rachel, his wife, who died October 6th 1861 aged 83. Also his daughter, Ellen, who died Feby. 3rd. 1891 aged 81 years. Also of his daughter Mary Anne, who died Dec. 12th 1891 aged 77 years.

[The Rev. John Paul was born at Tobernaveen, county Antrim in 1777, son of John Paul, farmer, and was educated at Glasgow University, R.P. Divinity Hall. He was licenced at Garvagh in 1803 and was minister of Loughmorne 1805-1848. He obtained the D.D. of Union College, U.S.A. in 1836. He resigned from the R.P. Synod of Ireland in 1840 and joined the Eastern Reformed Synod at its formation in 1842. He married in 1807 Rachel Smith of Ballyearl, Carnmoney and had 2 daughters, one of whom married the Rev. D. Stewart Bates of Glasgow. See Loughridge: *Fasti of the Reformed Presbyterian Church* (1970).

The will of Rachael Paul, formerly of Carrickfergus in Ireland, late of Glasgow, widow, who died 6 October 1861. Confirmation granted herein by the Commissariat of Lanarkshire 12 June 1862. Resealed at the Principal Registry, Dublin 7 August 1862. Effects in Ireland under £100.]

PORTER
[Fallen stone, next to William Stuart d.1864.] Erected by James STUART to the memory of his uncle Wm. Porter, who died in 1823 aged 56 & his daughter, Ellen Stuart, who died in 1826 aged 14 weeks & his wife, Elizabeth Stuart, who died

Nov. 15th 1832 aged 30 years. Also his daughter, Mary Stuart, who died 15th March 1839 aged 15 days. And his son, James Stuart, who died 25th July 1849 aged 2 years. The above named James Stuart senr. departed this life 29th August 1870 aged 74 years. Also his wife, Jane Stuart, who departed this life 17th Decr. 1885 aged 80 years.

ROSS
Erected by William Ross in memory of his mother Martha A. Ross who departed this life 3rd October 1895 aged 69 years.

[The will, with two codicils, of Martha Ann Ross, late of Carneal, Raloo, county Antrim, who died 3 October 1895 at same place, was proved at Belfast 18 November 1895 by Charles Knox of Ballyvallough, Raloo, Larne, and James McKee of Blackhill, Ballycarry, in said county, farmers, the executors. Effects £101 7s.]

SCULLY
[On the same stone as Robert Barron inside enclosure.] Robert Scully, the infant son of Andrew Scully, Antrim, departed this life 14th of June 1845 aged 11 months. Also his son Andrew who died 15th of July 1845 aged 6 years. Also his (wife Elizabe)th Scully, who died 3(0) ....(4) years.

SEAGRAVE
The burial-place of John Seagrave, M.D. The property of Wm. HART.

SLOAN
Erected by William Sloan of Lindins Park to the memory of his son William Henry, who died 25th Jany. 1852 aged 20 years. Also his son James, died in infancy. For as in Adam all die even so in Christ shall all be made alive. Cor. XV. 22. 1 grave north.

SNODDY
Erected by William Snoddy in memory of his beloved daughter Mary Locke Snoddy who departed this life (on) the 7th March 1868 aged 1(7) years. The above-named William Snoddy died 5th April 1881 aged 80 years. Also his wife Agnes Snoddy who died 15 Augt. 1885 aged 73 years.

[The will of William Snoddy, late of Ballyrickard, county Antrim, farmer, who died 5 April 1881 at same place, was proved at Belfast 24 August 1881 by James Killen of Drumcrow, national school teacher, and Robert Snoddy of Ballyrickard, farmer, late in said county, and Samuel Snoddy of Mountpottinger, county Down, town missionary, the executors. Effects £363 3s. 0d.]

SNODDY
[An open book at the top of the stone is inscribed "Holy Bible 1 Cor. XV, 43." Erected by Samuel Snoddy, Mountpottinger, Belfast, in memory of his beloved son John A. Snoddy, died 27th May 1882 aged 2 years. The above-named Samuel Snoddy died 21st December 1899 aged 64 years. And of his son Samuel who died 20th April 1901 aged 17 years.]

[Administration of the estate of Samuel Snoddy, late of 162 My Lady's Road, Belfast, missionary, who died 21 December 1899, granted at Belfast 22 January 1900 to Mary Snoddy, the widow. Effects £540 6s. 5d.]

SNODDY
[Next to foregoing.] Erected by Hugh Snoddy in memory of his brother Robert J. Snoddy who died 22nd May 1892 aged 62 years. Also his beloved wife Mary Jane Snoddy who died 5th June 1894 aged 39 years. Also his wife Anne Jane Snoddy who died 11th February 1897 aged 42 years. Also the above named Hugh Snoddy who died 7th April 1927 aged 80 years. And his daughter Mary Jane Snoddy who died 22nd July 1940 aged 51 years. Also his son Robert John who died 10th June 1948 aged 63 years.

[Letters of administration of the personal estate of Robert John Snoddy, late of Ballyrickard More, county Antrim, farmer, who died 27 May 1892 at same place, were granted at Belfast 25 November 1892 to Eliza Snoddy of Curran, Larne, said county, executor, a sister. Effects £234 9s. 6d.

SNODDY
    See STUART

STEWART
[Heavily lichened stone. Arms:- A fess chequy between three lions rampant. Crest:- A viscount's coronet, an arm holding a heart. Motto:- Nil (es)t (d)es(p)e(r)andum. Supporters:- A seventeenth century soldier and a robed figure.] (Here) lieth the body of James Stewa(rt) who departed this life the .. of January 1808 aged (3)1 years.

STEWART
Erected by Mary Stewart in memory of her husband William McAuley Stewart who died 20th Feby. 1885 aged 78 years. Also their daughter Mary who died in infancy. Also their son William who died 14th July 1879 aged 32 years. The above-named Mary Stewart who died 17th Dec. 1898.
    [The will of William McAuley Stewart, late of Loughmourne, Carrickfergus, farmer, who died 20 February 1885 at Capertongate, Loughmourne, was proved at Belfast 6 July 1885 by William Pennell of Ballyrickard, farmer, and William May of Larne, Clerk of Union, both in said county Antrim, the executors. Effects £172 6s.]

STEWART
[Cast iron plaque mounted on low iron railings.] The family burying place of William Stewart, 1887.

STEWART
[Within low railings.] In loving memory of Isabella MILLIKEN, beloved wife of Alexander Stewart, who died at Grangemouth, Scotland, 11th March 1895 aged 49 years. Also three infant children. Also the above named Alexander Stewart who died 1st September 1928. And his widow Jane Stewart who died 16th April 1949. Asleep in Jesus.

STEWART
[In same large enclosure as foregoing.] Erected by Charles Stewart in memory of his beloved wife Elizabeth who departed this life 7th February 1899 aged 28 years. Also his infant daughter Mattie died 14th October 1896 aged 1 year & 10 months. The above mentioned Charles Stewart died 28th April 1937 aged 74 years.

STEWART
[White marble with head lettering.] Erected by Charles Stewart, Sen., in memory of his beloved wife Mattie born 1817, died 1900. Also their five infant children. The above mentioned Charles Stewart died 28th August 1916 in his 99th year. Also in memory of his daughter Martha Jane who died 27th March 1937 aged 84 years.

STEWART
    See WHITE

STUART
[Sandstone lying flat in front of Charles Stuart who died in 1870, formerly mounted on the wall.] (In) memory of Charles Stuart of ...(n)eel who departed this life 23rd Augt. 1823 aged 10 years. (Al)so his mother Jane BLAIR, 11th Decr. 1826 aged 47 years.
    ....end when dead is but removed from sight
    .... in the lustre of eternal light:
    ....en the parting storms of life are o'er;

May (yet) rejoin us on som(e) happier shore.
Also S(amue)l Stuart his father who died 4th M(arch) 1844 aged 70 years.

STUART
[Steeply tilting stone.] Erected by James Stuart to the memory of his son William Stuart, who died 24th April 1864 aged 37 years. Mary Jane Stuart, daughter of William Stuart who died 18th April 1865 aged 7 years. Also James son of above William Stuart, who died at Spokane, U.S.A., 2nd April 1897 aged 38 years. Elizabeth, wife of the above-named William Stuart, she died 27th Dec. 1907 aged 72 years. Also John, son of above William Stuart, who died 17th June 1921 aged 60 years.

STUART
[Granite tablet mounted on wall.] In memoriam Charles Stuart who died 1st Jany. 1870 aged 29 years. Also his father Samuel Blair Stuart who died 30th April 1884 aged 74 years. His mother Eliza Stuart died 17th Feby. 1893 aged 77 years. His wife Isabella Stuart died 8th Nov. 1910 aged 77 years. Also his son Samuel Blair Stuart who died 29th Feby. 1936 aged 67 years. And Mary Ellen, wife of the above Samuel Blair Stuart, died 14th October 1943 aged 67 years. Parents of Isabella SNODDY and Helen Mary.

[The will of Samuel Blair Stuart, late of Carneal, Raloo, county Antrim, farmer, who died 30 April 1884 at same place, was proved at Belfast 1 April 1887 by David Gray of Carneal, Thomas McWilliam of Ballyrickard More in said county, and John Snoddy of Browndod in said county, farmers, the executors. Effects £321 13s. 4d.]

STUART
[Granite.] Erected by Robert Stuart, Bella Hill in memory of his wife Ellen Stuart who died 2nd Nov. 1894 aged 59 years. The above-named Robert Stuart died 21st Oct. 1904 aged 76 years.

STUART
See PORTER

TEMPELTON
See McALISTER

WHITE
Erected by Margaret STEWART in memory of her father Thomas White who died Novr. 1900. Also her mother Eliza White who died Novr. 1910. Also her 3 children who died in infancy. Above named Margaret Stewart died 18th October 1926.

W.
[Scratched on a rough slate] M.W.

STRAID CONGREGATIONAL GRAVEYARD

O.S. 46. Grid Ref. J336918

This is the only church building in the village of Straid, (townland of Straid and parish of Ballynure). The church has a T-plan with galleries, and, with the church hall, forms one building unit. It is pebble-dashed with good quoins and presents an attractive massing of barge boards and pointed arches. A tablet facing the main street bears the inscription, "Ebenezer, erected 1816, rebuilt and enlarged 1837."

BAIN

Sacred to the memory of Rev. James Bain, minister of this church for 43 years, died 17th July 1881. "He being dead yet speaketh" Heb. XI,14.

[His daughter Sara married Thomas Vint of Carrickfergus becoming a loyal member of the Independent congregation in that town. Several members of the family are buried in St. Nicholas's old graveyard. See McCrum ed. of McSkimin: *History and Antiquities of Carrickfergus* (1909), p.213.]

Appendix 1
Some Carrickfergus Deaths, 1853-1872

The following list of names is written on the fly leaf of a bible which was presented to Widow Robinson (great-grandmother of Mrs. Duncan) who now has it, by the Carrickfergus Bible Society on 6th October 1838. The list was evidently built up over time. As the page filled the size of writing diminished and any free corner was employed. As presented here the chronology of the entries has been restored and date forms have been standardised, but Mrs. Robinson's spelling of personal names has not been altered. Uncertainty in reading the handwriting is indicated by brackets or dots. Many of the names are also on gravestones but often with a small difference in date.

1853	Sept. 12	Johanah Thompson died
1854	Feb. 28	Sam Anderson died
	March 8	(Jiney) Ingram died
	March 20	David Legg died
	March 28	Marget Davey died and husband also
	March 29	James (Slown)
	April 2	Miss (Slown) and her brither also.
1856	Nov. 12	Peater Kirk buried
	Dec. 5	Wm. Alexander died
	Dec. 17	Jane Daff died
	Dec. 27	Dr. Fursyth died
	Oct. 3	Mrs Burleigh died
1857	May 6	William Hamilton died
	May 29	Mrs. Samuel Stuart died
	Oct. 17	Dr. McGowan died
185(8)	May 18	Mr. ..... died
1858	June 3	M(a)r(th..) Ingram died
	June 9	Mrs. Jafery died
	Oct. 21	Hughy Smyth died
	Nov. 18	Mr. Creage shought himself
	Dec. 2	Mrs. Robinson died aged 99 years
	Dec. (3)	Mrs. Gray died
1859	Jan. 26	Miss B(imey) died
	Feb. 20	Mrs. Parker died
1860	Jan. 22	Jane Shaw died
	March 13	Wm. Parker died
1863	April 18	Mrs. Cupels died
1864	Feb. 12	Mrs. Patrick died
	Feb. 12	Charles Kirk died
	April 4	Capt. Wheeler died aged 80
	August	The Distubens in Belfast
	August 13	Mrs. H(olb) died
	August 15	John McMaster killed in Philadelphia
	Sept. 2	M(ichey) Andrews died
	Sept. 17	James Cunningham died
1865	Feb. 28	Mrs. McQuitty died
1866	May 13	Mr. Johns died 8(1) yers
	June 2	Doctor Patrick died
1867	April 25	James Alexander died
	May 17	Wm. McQuitty died
	June 7	Gerg McGee died
	June 28	Mrs. Hamilton died
	Sept. 26	Samuel McThosh died
	Oct. 17	Thom McColley lost
1869	Feb. 20	James Wilson died
	July 28	James Ingram died
	Oct. 28	Capt. Long & wife lost
	Dec. 11	Mr. Dalway died
1870	August 13	Mrs. McCapen died
1872	July 7	Mrs. Gourley died

**Summary Guide to
Documentary Sources for the
Family and Local Historian**

Parish of Carrickfergus

Registers of births, deaths and marriages

In Ireland civil registration of births, deaths and marriages was not obligatory for the whole community until 1864, although marriages of Protestants and Jews had to be registered from 1845. The official set of copies of all these registers for the whole of Ireland, for the period 1864-1922, is held in the Registrar General's Office, Lombard Street East, Dublin. Copies of the printed indexes of birth registers for all Ireland, 1864-1922, are available in PRONI (MIC 165). The Mormon Family History Centre, Holywood Road, Belfast holds copies of indexes and registers of civil records as follows:

Indexes:
Births 1864-1958
Protestant marriages 1845-1958
Catholic marriages 1864-1958
Deaths 1864-1959

Registers:
Births 1864-1880
Marriages 1845-1870
Deaths 1864-1870

The original registers of births and deaths from 1864 kept by the local District Registrars in Northern Ireland have been centralized in the General Register Office, Oxford House, Chichester Street, Belfast. Each register is indexed but at present there are no adequate general indexes before 1922. Marriage registers from 1845 are held by District Registrars in local District Council Offices but again no adequate general indexes are available.

The agencies involved in the Irish Genealogical Project in Northern Ireland will be indexing the registers of births, deaths and marriages, from 1864, for Northern Ireland. The Ulster Historical Foundation is responsible for indexing these registers and pre-1900 church registers for the city of Belfast and all of Cos Antrim and Down.

Under the Registration Acts, 1845-1976, the Registrar General issues certificates of births, deaths and marriages from information extracted from the registers in his custody. A summary of the information available on each certificate is noted below.

Birth certificate: date and place of birth, name of infant, sex, first name(s) and surname of father, residence of father, first name, surname and maiden name of mother, rank, profession or occupation of father, signature, qualification and residence of informant, when registered, signature of registrar, baptismal name if added after the registration of the birth.

Death certificate: date and place of death, first name(s) and surname of deceased; sex, condition (whether married, bachelor, spinster, widow, etc), age, rank, profession or occupation, cause of death, signature, qualification and residence of informant; when registered.

Marriage certificate: when married; first name(s) and surnames of the groom and bride, ages, condition (widow, widower, bachelor, spinster, etc) rank, profession or occupation for both, residences for both at the time of the marriage, names of both fathers, rank, occupation; the church where married, the names of two witnesses and the minister performing the ceremony. The age given may be 'full' (over twenty-one) or minor (with father's consent). Very often the witnesses were family members or relatives of the bride and groom.

Census Returns

An official census for all Ireland was conducted every ten years from 1821-1911. The returns for the years 1821-1851 were destroyed in PROI, Dublin in 1922. The returns for 1861 and 1871 had been previously pulped in spite of the pleas of the archivists in the Public Record Office of Ireland. The returns for 1881 and 1891 were used for waste paper in World War I. Thus the only full census records surviving for Co. Antrim are for 1901 and 1911 and these are available for inspection in the National Archives, Dublin. The 1901 census is available on microfilm in PRONI (MIC 354/1/126 for Carrickfergus). The 1926 census for Northern Ireland was used for waste paper in World War II. The first census for Northern Ireland that has survived is for 1937 and this should be available for inspection in the year 2038.

After the introduction of old age pensions in 1909 claimants had to provide proof of age and this resulted in applications being made to the Public Record Office of Ireland to search the 1841 and 1851 census records in their custody in order to provide proof of the age of individuals. Some 40,000 of these search forms recording details (if any) found about individuals were completed c.1910-1922. The largest holding of search forms is for Co. Antrim with 4282; 2187 of these are held in the National Archives, Bishop Street, Dublin (reference Cens 1/1-2187) and the remainder in PRONI (T550)

A detailed list of the surnames for which there are extracts from 1841 and 1851 census for the parishes of Carrickfergus and Ballynure is given below. Quite often the return is negative but where an individual is identified details of his parents, their date of marriage and the names of all their children are given.

Detailed list of the surnames for which there are extracts from the 1841 and 1851 census for the parish of Carrickfergus in the National Archives, Dublin. Ref: CENS-1-

Number	Location	Surnames	Census Year
879	Davy St.	Dowling	1851
880	,,	Loughans (Bailey)	,,
881	,,	Marsh	,,
882	Eden Village	Brown (Hasson)	,,
883	Eden	Bankhead (Bennet)	,,
884	Elles(?) St.	McClure	,,
885	Front 1/4 St.	Cameron	,,
886	,,	Simms (Robertson)	,,
887	Middle Div.	Black (McAuley)	,,
888	,,	Irwin (Dunn)	,,
889	,,	,,	,,
890	,,	Lockhart	,,
891	,,	McAllister (Weatherup)	,,
892	,,	McClean	,,
893	,,	Mulholland (Wilson)	,,
894	,,	Rice	,,
895	,,	Rice	,,
896	,,	Patterson (Robinson)	,,
897	,,	Whiteford (Reilly)	,,
898	North St.	McIlroy	,,
899	N.E. Div.	Cameron	,,

900	"	Graham (Berry)	"
901	"	Hopkins	"
902	"	Kirk (Cannon)	"
903	"	Mearns (Stewart)	"
904	"	Millar (Proctor)	"
905	"	Risk	"
906	Scotch 1/4	Andrews (Thompson)	"
907	"	Cameron (Wilson)	"
908	"	Close	"
909	"	Cunningham	"
910	"	Dean (Saunderson)	"
911	"	Donald (Evans)	"
912	"	Dowling (McIntosh)	"
913	West Div.	Adams	"
914	"	Boyd "	
915	"	Catherwood	"
916	"	Girvin (McIntosh)	1841
917	"	Lochans (Wilson)	1851
918	"	Loughran "	"
919	"	McAuley (Adams)	"
920	"	McMullan	"
921	"	Milliken (Holmes)	"
922	"	Simpson	"
923	"	Wallace	"
924	West St.	McCalmont	"
925	"	Sweeney	"

Detailed list of the surnames for which there are extracts from the 1841 and 1851 census for the parish of Ballynure in the National Archives, Dublin. Ref: CENS-1-

Number	Location	Surnames	Census Year
278	Ballybracken	Dougall (Mayne)	?
279	Ballyclare	Millar (Ingran)	1851
280	"	Forsyth (Ryan)	"
281	"	Gordon (Stewart)	"
282	Ballygowan	Baxter (Greenlees)	"
283	"	Knox	"
284	"	McCallion	"
285	"	McConkey (Johnston)	"
286	"	McConkey	"
287	Ballylagan	Bell (McClure)	"
288	"	Lennon	"
289	"	"	"
290	"	McAllister	"
291	"	McClean	"
292	Ballynarry	Agnew (Whiteford)	"
293	"	Curran (McAllister)	"
294	Ballynure	Park (Bonnar)	"
295	Bryantang	Watson	"
296	Castletown	Kennedy	"
297	"	Scott (Bradley)	"
298	Straidland	Kirk	"

Wills and testamentary records, c.1536-

From the Reformation the proving of wills and the granting of administrations in Ireland became the exclusive concern of the established Church of Ireland. Wills were probated in local diocesan courts except where goods or land worth more than £5 were held in more than one diocese; such wills were probated in the Prerogative Courts of the Archbishop of Armagh.

In 1858 testamentary jurisdiction was transferred from the ecclesiastical to secular courts. A Court of Probate was established with a Principal Registry in Dublin and eleven district registries, including three for the province of Ulster, in Armagh, Belfast and Londonderry.

Original wills probated by the ecclesiastical courts for the whole of Ireland up to 1858 and the original wills probated in the Principal and District Probate Registries, 1858-1900, were deposited in the Public Record Office, Dublin and destroyed there in 1922. Transcripts of probated wills were kept in will books in district probate registries from 1858 and these are now deposited in the National Archives, Dublin and in the Public Record Office of Northern Ireland.

PRONI holds the records of the registries of Armagh, Belfast and Londonderry. The jurisdiction of the Armagh District Registry covered Cos Armagh, Lough, Monaghan and Tyrone, except the baronies of Strabane and Omagh; the Belfast registry covered Antrim and Down and the Londonderry registry was responsible for Cos Donegal and Londonderry and the baronies of Strabane and Omagh.

The records from these registries for the period 1858 to September 1921 are now deposited in PRONI, except original wills and some grant books for Cos Louth and Monaghan, 1901-21, which were transferred to the Public Record Office of Ireland.

Many of the Irish wills destroyed in 1922 survive in some form somewhere. The main collection of copies and abstracts of wills is in the National Archives, Dublin. The major collection there are the genealogical abstracts of some 37,000 Prerogative Court wills for the period 1536-1800, and some 5,000 administrations in cases of intestacy, 1595-1802, compiled by Sir William Betham. These Betham will abstracts relate to people of considerable wealth and status (Betham also compiled thirty-two volumes of will pedigrees based on this material and these are now held in the Genealogical Office, Kildare Street, Dublin).

There are also thousands of copies and abstracts of wills in the collections of the working papers of record searchers like Miss Gertrude Thrift and Tenison Groves in the National Archives, Dublin and PRONI with card indexes to facilitate access.

List of wills for Carrickfergus and Ballynure, Co. Antrim, saved from destruction in the National Archives, Dublin

Name and Address	Nature of record	Year	Court of registry	Ref No National Archives
Alexander, Jane, Ballyclare, Ballynure	Admon. Dbn.	1857	Connor	B 8937
Baxter, Johanna (Mrs) C'fergus	Will & Grant	1855	Connor	B 8492
Bell, James, Dunturkey, Ballynure	Will & Grant	1853	Connor	B 8223
Bowman, James C'fergus, N E Division	Will & Grant	1857	Connor	B 9001
Campple?, Robert Ardboley, C'fergus, farmer	Will & Grant	1855	Connor	B 8548
Carnaghan, John, C'fergus	Admon.	1819	Connor	B 1830
Cook [Cooke], William Ballygavan [Ballygowan], Ballynure	Will	1819	Connor	B 1887
Cunningham, William, C'fergus	Admon.	[1819?]	Connor	B 1907
Davey, Samuel, Leefield, N E Division, C'fergus, farmer	Will & Grant	1856	Connor	B 8702
Davys, Henry, C'fergus	Will & Grant	1708	Prerog.	B
Duncan, Charlotte, C'fergus	Will & Grant	1856	Connor	B 8819
Eccleston, John M, C'fergus	Will & Grant	1854	Connor	B 8242
Finlay, William, C'fergus	Will	1818	Connor	B 1728
Finlay, William C'fergus	Admon.	[1819]	Connor	B 1836
Forsyth, George, MD C'fergus	Will & Grant	1857	Connor	B 9002
Gowan, John, Sullatobber, C'fergus	Will & Grant	1856	Connor	B 8794
Gowan, John, physician C'fergus	Admon.	1857	Connor	B 9080
Girven, John, Minorca, C'fergus	Will & Grant	1855	Connor	B 8647
Gordon, Alexander, Woodburn, C'fergus, blacksmith	Admon.	1854	Connor	B 8405
Henderson, John, Calhame, Ballynure, farmer	Will & Grant	1854	Connor	B 830
Herdman, John,	Will & Grant	1856	Connor	B 8838

C'fergus, WD, farmer				
Herdman, Mary Ann, Longpark, C'fergus, spinster	Will & Grant	1856	Connor	B 8839
Hamilton, William, C'fergus, blacksmith	Admon.	1857	Connor	B 8985
Kirk, Charles Edmonston, Thornfield, C'fergus	Will & Grant	1857	Connor	B 9093
Kirk, Eleanor, C'fergus, Middle Division	Will & Grant	1857	Connor	B 8935
McAuley, Henry, Thompson's Point, C'fergus, farmer	Will & Grant	1855	Connor	B 8547
McBride, Robert, C'fergus	Admon.	1855	Connor	B 8535
McDowell, Andrew, Straidnahanna, C'fergus	Will	1819	Connor	B 1832
McKinney, George, N E Division, C'fergus	Will & Grant	1854	Connor	B 8338
McKnight, William, C'fergus, W.D., publican	Admon.	1854	Connor	B 8346
McQueston, Andrew, Toberdowny, Ballynure	Will	1819	Connor	B 1905
Mairs, Thomas, Greenisland, C'fergus, printer	Will & Grant	1855	Connor	B 8601
Martin, Elizabeth, Dunkisky, Ballynure	Admon.	1818	Connor	B 1685
Martin, William Kirk, C'fergus	Will & Grant	1856	Connor	B 8546
Millar, John, Calhame, Ballynure, farmer	Will & Grant	1855	Connor	B 8451
Montgomery, Elizabeth Ree Hill, Straidnahanna, C'fergus, widow	Admon.	1855	Connor	B 8683
Mulholland, Hugh, C'fergus	Will & Grant	1856	Connor	B 8760
Mulholland (Mulhallon), John, Ninescore Acres, C'fergus	Will	1818	Connor	B 1675
Nelson, Samuel, C'fergus	Will & Grant	1856	Connor	B 8739
O'Brien, Margaret, widow, C'fergus	Will & Grant	1729	Prerog.	B
Orpin, Thomas, glazier, C'fergus	Will & Grant	1727	Prerog.	B
Park, Alexander, Ballynure, farmer	Will & Grant	1854	Connor	B 8292
Park, William Forsythe, Ballynure, miller	Will & Grant	1857	Connor	B 8950

Picken, James, C'fergus	Will	1818	Connor	B 1651
Sloan, James, dealer, C'fergus	Admon.	1854	Connor	B 8371
Stewart (alias Kimmon), Mary, Eden, widow	Will & Grant	1857	Connor	B 9042
Stewart, Robert, Reehill, Straidnahanna, C'fergus	Admon.	1855	Connor	B 8681
Thompson, Mary, C'fergus, spinster	Will & Grant	1855	Connor	B 8602
Thompson, Robert E Division, C'fergus, farmer	Will & Grant	1855	Connor	B 8490
Wisnom?, Alexander, Duffs Hill, C'fergus	Will & Grant	1856	Connor	B 8775

	PRONI Ref. no
Wills & grants of probate of Adair & Ellis families including Ann Moore 1703, Henry Ellis 1720, Henry Gill 1761, Hercules Ellis 1782, John Moore 1792-, Ezekeil Davys Wilson 1819-, Henry Ellis 1825 & James Cowan 1851	D3860
Will of James Dobbin, student at Trinity College, Dublin, bequeathing property at Carrickfergus, 1768	D2548
Wills and testamentary papers of Boyd, Dobbs, Ferguson and Shaw families of Carrickfergus and district, 1791-1886	D1296
Testamentary papers of Greer family of Seapark, D2339 1854-87	D2509
Wills of Kirk family including Sir William Kirk 1819, Charles Kirk 1864 & Maria Kirk 1879	D1255/5/2

Extracts from Connor Will and Grant book 1818-20 in National Archives, Dublin

These copies of Wills and Administrations Nos 1611-1967 were prepared by the Deputy Keeper of PROI, Miss Margaret Griffith, in 1966. She notes that the original Will and Grant Book was 'severely damaged' in the fire at PROI in June 1922. Where possible details have been added from the Connor Diocesan Register of Wills and Administrations in PROI.

p 296 No. 1830
John Carnaghan late of Carrickfergus who died intestate: administration granted to his eldest son Samuel Kernaghan 27 April 1819.

pp 296-7 No. 1832
Will of Andrew McDowell late of Straidnahannagh, Carrickfergus, farmer included bequests to: son-in-law Samuel Kennedy and his present wife Jane Carmedy, son-in-law Charles (Adamson) and his wife Elizabeth Adamson; Widow Stewart 5 and the house which I now occupy; Son James McDowal, all properties, bonds, bills, accounts, etc.

PS To Elizabeth Stewart 15 in addition to the above sum.
Executors James McDowal, Samuel Russell, John Blair all of Straidnahannagh
Probate granted to son James 29 April 1819. Effects 94 3s 9d

pp303
Administration [May] 1819. William Finlay late of Carrickfergus who died intestate; chattels to his widow Jane.

pp303-4 No 1838
Will of William Brannon of Boydtown in the west division of the town and county of Carrickfergus farmer; bequests: eldest brother John Brannon's daughter; daughter Jane otherwise Simpson, farm in Boydtown for her to dwell to brother's son John Brannon
Testator made his mark.
Executor James Grant, Witnesses Hugh Larmour, David McDowell, Robert Mearns
Probate granted 4 June 1819. Effects 15 3s

Will pp 357-7 No 1882
Phillip Bell late of Ballyclare and formerly of Ballynarry in the parish of Ballynure, yeoman; bequests:
brother John Bell half a crown sterling
sister Eleanor otherwise Lyle wife of James Lyle half a crown sterling
sister Sarah otherwise Blakely wife of Samuel Blakely half a crown sterling
brother Charles Bell Dr of Medicine half a crown sterling
sister Agnes Bell otherwise Mill half a crown sterling
brother Bell
Executors brother David Bell, brother John Bell and Samuel Hunter of Ballyclare
Probate 2 September 1819. Effects 100

pp 365-6
William Cooke of Ballygowan, Ballynure, farmer died 1818. Probate 16 September 1819

No 1896 Will of Isaac McNeice late of Crew, Glenavy, dated 26 August 1814, probated 8 November 1819. Effects 849.15.8.

No 1905 Andrew McQueston, Toberdowey, Ballynure, Co Antrim. Will dated 22 May 1817, probated 6 November 1819. Bequest to daughter Martha 20 sterling. Son Robert assets 175.8. Executors Thomas Dollar, David Forsythe and R. McQueston

No 1908
Mr Edward Craig of Carrickfergus died intestate Administration to Mrs Mary Craig widow, 11 November 1819. Effects 699 8s

pp 434 No 1944
Will of Andrew Crooks late of Carrickfergus [half page blank]; probate granted 12 January 1820

Selected collections of wills and testamentary papers in PRONI

Wills, leases, title deeds, etc., of the related families of Davys, Bowman, Kerr and Malcolm, all of Carrickfergus, 1768-1856, incl. the will of Davys Bowman, 1850; copy will and probate of Sarah Bowman, 1850, also letters and papers of Malcolm Bowman, locomotive superintendent of the Belfast and Northern Counties Railway, 1886-1930	D3603
Will of James Dobbin, student at Trinity College, Dublin, bequeathing property at Carrickfergus, 1768	D2548
Testamentary papers of the Park family, 1782-1912, including copy wills of Alexander Park, 1782, Andrew Park, 1795, and John Park, 1823, all of Ballynure	
Wills and testamentary papers of Boyd, Dobbs, Ferguson and Shaw families of Carrickfergus and district, 1791-1886	D1296
Testamentary papers of the Fulton family of Jordanstown and their property at Carrickfergus, 1802-39, including will of John Fulton, 1802	D3140
Title deeds, wills and leases, re: property of Adair family, 1606-1928	D3860
Title deeds, testamentary and legal papers, re: James and William Cowan and John Thompson Cowan, 1792-1910	D3855
Probate, Henry Ellis, 1720, and wills of Alderman Henry Gill, 1761, Hercules Ellis, 1782, Ezekiel Davys Wilson, 1819, Henry Clements Ellis, 1825	D3860
Will of John Moore, 1792, and James Cowan, 1851	D3855

Copy Muster Rolls, 1630-1631

Following the completion of the English conquest of Ireland in 1603, the lands of six of the nine counties of the province of Ulster (Antrim, Down and Monaghan were excluded) were granted to undertakers who were bound to 'plant' their estates with British tenants, military men serving in Ireland (called servitors) and occasionally the Irish. These undertakers held their lands directly from the Crown, and since they were settled in a barely conquered country, arrangements had to be made for self-defence.

Undertakers, that is the large landlords, were required to muster all the able-bodied Protestant males on their estates between the ages of sixteen and sixty. The men were paraded before a government official, a muster master, who recorded their names and arms. The original muster rolls were destroyed in PROI, Dublin in 1922, but copies survive for eight of the nine counties of Ulster (all save Monaghan) in the British Library (Add. MSS 4770) and these are available in PRONI in copy and transcript form (ref. D1759). In general the material is arranged by barony without sub-division by parish, so it is impossible to identify the exact location of individuals. The reference for Carrickfergus is D1759/3C/3.

Books of Survey and Distribution, 1641-1703

The books of survey and distribution show the changes in land ownership during and after the Cromwellian period when large areas of land were taken from Roman Catholics and granted to Protestants. The names recorded in the books, whether of the dispossessed or the new owners, are inevitably only the wealthy few. The reference for the Co Antrim volume in PRONI is D1854/1/

Subsidy Roll, 1663

These rolls provide only the names of the nobility, clergy and laity, that is the major property owners who were liable to pay direct tax to the crown. Transcripts of subsidy rolls for Cos Antrim, Down and Tyrone and the town of Enniskillen, 1662-69, are available in PRONI with indexes. (PRONI reference to the copy of the 1663 subsidy roll for Co. Antrim is T307.)

Hearth Money Rolls, 1663-1669

Copies of these records, arranged by barony, parish and townland, are available in full or in part for eight of the nine counties of Ulster (all except Co. Down). These are lists of the names of householders compiled by local Justices of the Peace in preparation for the levying of a tax of two shillings per hearth or fireplace, paid half yearly. The roll for Co. Antrim edited by Trevor Carleton was published by PRONI in 1991 *Heads and Hearths*.

Memorials in the Registry of Deeds

This registry was established in 1708 under the Registration of Deeds Act (Ireland), 1707. The main object was to determine priorities between documents relating to the same piece of land in order to secure purchasers and to prevent fraudulent conveyances of land. The Act was largely designed to prevent the laws which prohibited the sale and transfer of lands to Roman Catholics being bypassed by secret deeds. Registrations in the Registry provided a safe record of a deed and, although registration was not compulsory, the fact that the Act provided for unregistered deeds being regarded as fraudulent against registered deeds meant that registration became general in most areas.

The Registry was established as part of the Penal Code against Roman Catholics and the statute specifically stated its purpose was 'preventing forgeries...frequently practised in this kingdom, especially by Papists to the great prejudice of the Protestant interests thereof'. Leases of less than twenty-one years were not accepted for registration and this in effect prevented the use of the registry by Roman Catholics who could not hold leases for twenty-one years or more until the relaxation of the Penal Laws in 1778. Registration was not carried out on a wide spread scale until about 1745. From that point onwards until c.1830 the memorials can be a unique source of information. The original memorials in the Registry of Deeds are held in the basement of the office at Henrietta Street, Dublin, but transcripts are available on vellum sheets bound in large volumes in a public search room at the top of the building. Up to c.1832 there are an estimated one million pages of documentation.

In addition to the absence of deeds concerning Catholics before 1778, certain small religious groups such as the Society of Friends and the Palatine German settlers did not make use of this facility, nor did most of the Presbyterian farmers in Ulster.

There are two indexes to the memorials in the Registry of Deeds. The first of these is an index of grantors, that is the first parties to the deeds. This is arranged alphabetically by surname and, although it gives the surname of the grantee, this name is not indexed. The name of the relevant townland is not specified until 1828. Thus, if a surname is a common one it makes use of the index extremely difficult.

The lands index is arranged alphabetically by townland, within each county, and the towns are listed separately at the end. This is not a strict alphabetical index. The townlands are just gathered according to their initial letter. If the townland has the prefix 'Bally', much searching is involved.

PRONI holds microfilm copies of the volumes of transcripts of memorials (MIC 311) and also of the lands and grantors index (MIC 7).

The Registry of Deeds is the one archive in Ireland which is superior to equivalent registries in the rest of the British Isles. There was such uncertainty about title to land in Ireland that registration was carried out on a much wider scale here than elsewhere in the United Kingdom and from the outset detailed indexes were maintained. Even in Scotland it is only now that detailed indexing of registered memorials is taking place.

Religious census returns, 1740, 1766 & 1775

In 1740 the Irish House of Commons required the compilation of returns of Protestant householders in the north of Ireland. The work seems to have been undertaken by the Hearth Money collectors in their various 'walks'. The original records of this survey were destroyed in PROI, Dublin, in 1922. Copies survive for many parishes, particularly in Co. Londonderry, giving a total of over 14,000 names of Protestants. These are in the Tenison Groves collection in PRONI (T808). Only statistics are provided in many cases.

In 1766 the Irish House of Lords ordered the clergy in each Church of Ireland parish to prepare a return of the number of Protestant and Roman Catholic families in their parishes. Many of these were only numerical returns, but some give the names of the heads of the families.

Also available in PRONI are copies of transcripts of the names of Protestant dissenters listed in petitions submitted to Government, October-November 1775.

Statistics for Carrickfergus and Ballynure are available in PRONI:

1766 T808/15264 p 103

1775 T808/15207 p 20 & p 13

Registers of voters

Registers of freeholders and voters list the names and addresses of individuals entitled to vote at parliamentary elections, and poll books (often in printed form before the introduction of the Ballot Act of 1872) list the names of voters and the candidates they voted for. Occasionally registers include observations such as 'gone to America' or 'married a papist'. Arrangement of these registers is, as usual, by county, barony and parish.

It is important to appreciate some of the limitations of this source. Until the introduction of reforming legislation in 1832, 1867 and 1884, the franchise at parliamentary elections was restricted and, particularly in Ireland, Catholics were excluded altogether until 1793. Until then Protestants with freeholds worth forty shillings or more a year were entitled to vote and, from 1793 to 1829, Roman Catholic freeholders enjoyed the same privilege. After the Catholic tenant farmers in Co. Clare had defied their landlords and elected Daniel O'Connell at a by-election, the government was forced to introduce an act for Catholic Emancipation, but they accompanied this with a punitive measure raising the franchise qualifications for everyone from forty shillings to ten pounds. At a stroke, the electorate was reduced from around 100,000 to about 16,000.

Unfortunately very few early registers of voters survive for Co. Antrim. There is one Freeholders Register for Co. Antrim 1776 but this includes only half the electorate and only two entries for Carrickfergus and Ballynure are recorded (D1364/L/1 in PRONI).

No 18 James Craig of Ballyhackett; freehold at Carrickfergus, Monday 17 June 1776.

No 42 John Forsythe of Bryantang: freehold at Ballynure, Friday 14 June 1776.

Tithe Applotment Book

Farmers of most agricultural land in Ireland were liable to pay to the rector of the established Church of Ireland a tax of a tenth of the yearly produce of the land and stocks. This tax was especially unpopular with Presbyterians and Roman Catholics, so much so that in parts of the country such as Co. Tipperary it became impossible to collect. Agitation against the tax forced the government to change the law and make the tithe charge a financial one (instead of crops etc) levied on the landlord rather than on the tenant. In order to determine the amount of money to be charged in lieu of tithe all agricultural land liable to tithe had to be surveyed and valued. This work was done by local surveyors and the detail given is variable and unfortunately there are no maps accompanying the survey showing the locations of farms.

In general the surveys provide the names of lease-holding tenants in each townland of the parish. The tithe surveys for parishes in Northern Ireland for the years 1823-38 are deposited in the Public Record Office of Northern Ireland. In order to conserve the original documents only microfilm copies of these surveys are produced to the public.

The survey for the parish of Carrickfergus was done in 1827 and the PRONI reference is FIN5A/70.

Valuation Records

The earliest comprehensive valuation of property in Ireland was carried out in the 1830s. This valuation was carried out in each townland and parish of the country and the surveyor's manuscript field books of this 'townland valuation' for parishes in Northern Ireland are deposited in the Public Record Office of Northern Ireland (ref. VAL 1B). No detail is given of the buildings unless these are valued at £3.00 or more and this lower limit was raised to £5.00 in 1838 thus excluding most rural houses. Fortunately, most of Ulster was valued before the threshold was raised to £5.00, with the result that many buildings here around £2.00 valuation are included. In towns and cities many houses were substantial enough to reach the valuation of £3.00 or £5.00 and in these cases detailed measurements of rooms and outbuildings are sometimes given as well as named of occupiers.

For Carrickfergus the names of some occupiers are given in the field books of the townland valuation for the parish of Down c.1838 (VAL 1B/187).

The National Archives Dublin has another set of these field books of the 1830s for Carrickfergus (ref. OL 4.0459).

The first detailed valuation of all properties in Ireland (popularly known as Griffith's tenement valuation) was started in the province of Leinster during the Great Famine in 1848, and the valuation was completed in Northern Ireland 1858-64. The manuscript field books of this valuation for Northern Ireland are held in PRONI (ref. VAL 2B) and also the annual revisions recording changes in occupancy, consolidation of farms and the upheavals resulting from the Land Acts from the 1880s up to c.1930 (ref VAL 12B). The references for the parish of Carrickfergus are:

VAL 2B/1/22A-22E c.1860
VAL 12B/7/5A-5F 1865-1894
VAL 12B/7/6A-6D 1894-1929 Rural
VAL 12B/7/7A-7C 1894-1929 Urban
VAL 12B/7/8A-8B 1908-1929 Eden village

School Records in the Public Record Office of Northern Ireland

The national system of elementary education was established in Ireland in 1831, nearly 40 years before there was a similar system in England. Prior to its introduction, there were numerous schools throughout Ireland, though many were in poor condition and badly conducted. The province of Ulster, for example, had 3449 schools in 1821, of which over 1000 were to be found in Cos Antrim and Down. No county, in fact, had a better ratio of schools to population than Down. Among these pre-1831 schools were those managed by the Kildare Place Society, schools sponsored by the London Hibernian Society and hedge or 'pay' schools which generally served the Catholic community. The schools sponsored by the London Hibernian Society were avoided by Roman Catholics because of their proselytising character.

The aim of the new national system was to provide schools that would serve the whole community rather than particular religious groups. Secular instruction was to be given on week days and on Saturdays clergy of the main denominations provided religious instruction for their children. Over 2,500 national schools were established in Ulster in the period 1831-1870. The records that are available for these schools provide illuminating detail for the local and family historian as well as for the historian of education. They fall into four main categories. .

(1) Grant Aid Applications 1832-89 (ED1)

Each school applied to the Board of Commissioners of Education for a grant in aid of its running costs. The printed forms that they completed have been preserved in the Public Record Office of Northern Ireland, in the ED 1 series which contains over 4500 grant aid applications. The principal details recorded in this source include the date of establishment if it had been in operation before applying to become a national school, name of teacher, size and condition of building, number of enrolled pupils and average number in attendance. The great majority of teachers appointed were male but, as the schools attracted more pupils, more female assistants were appointed to teach needlework, sewing and cutting out. The Grant Aid applications are, therefore, a useful source for an investigation of 'women at work' in the 19th century. The files for Carrickfergus schools are [old reference]:

i	Aldoo (Carrickfergus) 1838-1841	[ED/1/1/p 111]
ii	Carrickfergus 1838-1841	[ED1/1/p 83]
iii	Carrickfergus 1838-1841	[ED1/1/p 95]
iv	Duncrew (Carrickfergus) 1838-1841	[ED1/1/p 96]
v	Carrickfergus - evening 1845-1853	[ED 1/3/p 39]
vi	Trooper Lane 1845-1853	[ED 1/3/p 59]
vii	Joymount, 1853-1860	[ED 1/4/p 81]
viii	Minorca Place, 1853-1860	[ED 1/4/p 2]
ix	Joymount, 1858-1863	[ED 1/5/p 125]
x	Mount Pleasant, 1858-1863	[ED 1/5/p 46]
		[ED 1/5/p 130]
xi	Troopers Lane, 1858-1863	[ED 1/5/p 49]
xii	Woodburn, 1858-1863	[ED 1/5/p 16]
xiii	Front Quarter, 1861-1868	[ED 1/6/p 90A]
xiv	Sullatober, 1861-1868	[ED 1/6/p 4]
xv	Minorca Place, 1868-1873	[ED 1/7/p 138]
		[ED 1/7/p 159]
xvi	Albert Road, 1886-1888	[ED 1/9/p 7]
xvii	Carrickfergus, West St 1886-1888	[ED 1/9/p 71]
xviii	Carrickfergus 1886-1888	[ED 1/9/71]
xix	The Commmons, 1886-1888	[ED 1/9/87]
xx	Woodburn, 1876-1889	[ED 1/10/187]

(2) Registers of correspondence with national schools from 1835 (ED6)

Registers giving abstracts of correspondence between schools and the Commissioners of National Education exist in an almost complete series from 1835 to the early 1850s (ED6/1). In addition to much of the information to be found in the grant aid applications, these registers list all previous teachers as well as those currently in post. They also record entries for the appointments of new patrons, and the amount of money received by each school every year from pupils (not recorded elsewhere) is noted. The information about the schools in these registers of correspondence is very detailed specifying townland and parish of location, date of establishment, date when the school was taken under the Board of Education, the names of clerical applicants (Church of Ireland, Presbyterian, Roman Catholic etc.), names of lay applicants stating their religion. For the period 1835-55 these registers are arranged by county. Each National School has a Roll Number.

National School Correspondence Registers, County Books, 1835-1855 [EDG/1/1/1/]

Folio No	Date	School	Roll No
72	1835-1843	Carrickfergus (male)	31 [EDG 1/1/1]
73	"	Carrickfergus (female)	32
83	1835-1839	Carrickfergus No 2	35
98	1836-1842	Carrickfergus or Aldoo	1225
79	1835-1840	Woodburn	34
84	1835-1843	Duncrew	36
103	1841-1847	Carrickfergus	31 [EDG1/1/2]
184	1843-1852	Carrickfergus or Aldoo	1225
211	1844-1851	Carrickfergus (female)	32 [EDG/1/1/2]
216	1844-1851	Duncrew	36
f90	1848-1851	Carrickfergus (male)	31 [EDG/1/1/3]
f124	1848-1851	Trooper Lane	5542
f22	1852-1854	Carrickfergus (male)	31 [EDG/1/1/5]
f23	1852-1854	Carrickfergus (female)	32
f24	1852-1854	Duncrew	36
f95	1852-1854	Trooper Lane	5542 [ED1/1/6]
f151	1852-1853	Woodburn	6634
f180	1854-1855	Minorca Place	7020

(3) School Registers (SCH)

Registers of pupils who enrolled in some 1450 national schools in Ulster are held in PRONI, and for over 1000 schools these registers date from before 1900. They thus can serve as a substitute for non-existent census records prior to 1901. They record the age (indeed, often the date of birth) of the pupil on entry, occupation of the pupil's father or guardian, and often the address of the last school attended. This last piece of information provides a unique record of the migration from country to town that was a feature of late- 19th century Ireland. It is a particularly useful means for tracing individuals in a rapidly growing city like Belfast which was, in the last quarter of the century, the fastest growing city in the United Kingdom. The references for pupils' registers for schools in Carrickfergus:

		Earliest date of registers	Reference SCH
i	Albert Road	1874	1042
ii	Barn Mills	1864	129
iii	St Nicholas	1884	128
iv	Carrickfergus (Model)	1861	130
	Minorca Place		
v	St Nicholas' Boys (formerly Minorca Place)		1245
vi	St Nicholas' Girls (formerly Minorca Place)		1246
vii	Woodburn No 1 & No 2	1864	68
vii	Sullatober		1014
ix	Commons		547

Salary Books, National and Public Elementary Schools (ED7)

c.250 vols. recording salary payments to teachers in National and later Public Elementary Schools. The volumes consist of specially printed folios and though the layout of the folios was altered on a number of occasions the information provided remained essentially the same throughout.

In the volumes entries are arranged by numerical order of rolls. Underneath the roll number the name and address of the school, the Circuit or District in which it lies, its connection with the Board of Education (vested or non-vested and its status as a free or excess fee paying school are recorded; also voted is the name, address and religious denomination of the Manager. This is followed by a series of columns dealing with the teachers, monitors etc. Besides names of individuals the entries record their official position and academic qualifications, the date of appointment or resignation.(when either event occurs in a time span of the volume) and various particulars of salary and other payments made. Salaries could be effected by a variety of factors so much incidental information is recorded e.g. the annual capitation grant and average attendance figures; relevant Board Orders are noted and reference is made to any absence of the teacher and any temporary closing of the school.

The volumes in the Public Record Office of Northern Ireland begin in 1899 but not until 1905 are all the volumes relating to Northern Ireland available here. The pre-1899 and the missing 1899-1904 volumes will be found in the National Archives, Bishop Street, Dublin (ED4).

Up to 1844 a single series of volumes was used to cover the whole country; from 1844 to 1855 provincial volumes, and from 1856 to 1870 County volumes were in use. These volumes will be found in National Archives, Dublin.

From 1870 to 1902 salaries paid were recorded in District Volumes, a District consisting of a portion of a county or portions of several adjoining counties. Only the volumes for 1899 to 1902 and for Districts 3, 4, 7, 8, 8A, 9, 9a, 10 and 11 are in the P.R.O.N.I. (see ED7/1). For 2 years, 1903 and 1904, Circuit Volumes were used; only those relating to the Ballymena and Belfast Circuits are in P.R.O.N.I. (see ED7/2).

In 1905 the National Board reverted to the County Volume arrangement and from this point onwards P.R.O.N.I. has all the material relating to what is now Northern Ireland.

When the N.I. Ministry of Education took over responsibilities from the National Board of Education they inherited the records now deposited here and continue to use Salary Books until 1948 when the Books were superseded by 'Teachers Cards'.

Sub-Classes
ED7/1 District Volumes 1899-1902
ED7/2 Circuit Volumes 1903-1904
ED7/3 Co Antrim Volumes 1905-1926

School Records in the National Archives, Dublin

It is important to realize that not all correspondence, salary books and files for national schools in Northern Ireland were transferred North in the early 1920s. It is worth checking on the holdings of the National Archives, Dublin for Northern Ireland schools. The registers and files are held in the headquarters of the National Archives at Bishop Street and can be produced on request, but the salary books are in 'off-site' storage and must be ordered at least a day in advance.

Salary Books in National Archives, Dublin (ED4)

Up to 1844 there are volumes covering the whole of Ireland. For the period 1844-55 material is arranged by province and within the province in groups of counties. Material is arranged by county for the period 1856-70 and by district from c.1890 (61 districts for the whole country). There are no volumes for the period 1.10.1840-30.9.1843. Arrangements within the volumes is by numerical order of the roll number of the school. The volumes are not indexed. There are over seventeen hundred volumes for the period 1834-1918. Details provided include earnings of teachers, status, names of schools where individuals taught previously or are going to. All the names of teachers in the school are given.

Date	Area	Reference
1834-44	All Ireland	ED 4/1-6
1844-5	Ulster	ED 4/7
1846-7	Cos Antrim & Down	4/11
1847-8	Cos Antrim & Down	4/13
1848-50	Antrim, Armagh & Cavan	4/15
1848-51	,, ,, ,,	4/18
1851-2	,, ,, ,,	4/21
1852	,, ,, ,,	4/24
1853	,, ,, ,,	4/27
1854	,, ,, ,,	4/30
1855	For Co. Antrim etc	

From 1855, Ireland was divided into sixty-one Education Districts and the old school correspondence registers were re-organised into 'district books'. A number of these have been deposited in PRONI (ED6). Information on the standard of instruction in the schools and the state of repair of school buildings.

Files (ED 9), 1877-1924

These are case files concerning individual schools. They cover a wide variety of subjects ranging from routine appointments to investigation into allegations of misconduct against teachers.

Local Authority Records

Letters patent granting corporate status to Carrickfergus, 1602, and defining the boundaries of the Corporation, 1610.	T1150
Chronological schedule of certificates of election for chief magistrates, etc. for various boroughs including Carrickfergus, 1711-1816.	T3416
Carrickfergus Grand Jury presentment book, 1766-1817, including treasurer's accounts, 1780-1817.	ANT4
Deed appointing James Erskine, Carrickfergus, as gaoler of Carrickfergus, 1827, and later as Governor of the gaol, 1837 and 1848; correspondence and accounts for the upkeep of Carrickfergus gaol, 1835-7.	T2532
Petty sessions order books, 1862-1946.	HA1
Papers of Miss M.V. McCaughen, school teacher, Carrickfergus, who became the first female member of Carrickfergus Borough Council, including volume of newspaper cuttings relating partly to Council membership.	D2912

Carrickfergus Church Records

	PRONI Ref.
Church of Ireland (St Nicholas') baptisms 1740-99 and 1825-75; marriages 1740-1845, burials 1740-1800 and 1825-70; confirmation lists, 1828-54	T679/323-4, 339-343
Plans of the church, 1931; Accounts of building church spire	CR1/25
Roman Catholic; Carrickfergus and Larne baptisms 1852-72; marriages, 1852-72; indexes to baptisms and marriages, 1828-1852	MIC1D/90
Extracts from a printed booklet entitled	T3148

The Sure Way to Heaven
by Rev. James Mathew MacCary, R.C. Rector of Carrickfergus and Larne, 1797, with list of names of subscribers.

Presbyterian, 1st Carrickfergus: baptisms 1823-1901 marriages 1825-1845 committee minutes, 1824-1946; session minutes, 1860-1935; building committee minutes, 1826-9 and 1879-81, account books, 1815-89; pew book, 1914-34; Sustentation Fund minutes, 1876-88	MIC1P/157

Stipend book 1829-48 held by Presbyterian Historical Society

Presbyterian, Woodburn: MIC1P/160
baptisms 1863/5-1952,
marriages 1866-1932

Presbyterian, Loughmorne: MIC1P/161; CR3/43
baptisms 1848-53 and 1892-1952
marriages 1863-1930

Methodist:
baptisms 1815-58   MIC.429/1/352
baptisms 1826-43 In local custody
marriages 1864-

Baptist: CR7/8
baptisms, marriages and minutes 1864-

Congregational: CR7/8
baptisms 1819-1969 [not to be consulted
marriages 1824-43 without permission] list of members, 1824, 1847 and 1862;
minutes 1823-36 and 1862-3; collections for the poor, 1860

Ballynure Church Records

Church of Ireland
baptisms 1812-72
marriages 1803-45
burials 1840 and 1852-80   T.679.209-213
vestry minutes 1818-;   held locally

Straid Congregational
Baptisms 1837-1915
marriages 1839-65
deaths 1839
list of members with details of emigration, 1837-50   CR 7/9

Ballynure Methodist
Baptisms 1843-, marriages 1864-76   held locally

Presbyterian
Baptisms 1819-1918, marriages 1819-99   MIC 1P/103

Carrickfergus: Maps, Surveys; Postcards & Photographs

Date	Description	Reference Number
c.1570	Map of Carrickfergus showing the castle with armory, a church, houses in elevation and beehive-shaped Irish houses. Original in Public Record Office, London.	T1493/46
c.1570	Map of Carrickfergus with elevations and names of occupiers of buildings including a church, 'a freers house'. Annotated by Sir William Cecil. Original in Trinity College, Dublin.	T1668/29
c.1570	Map of Carrickfergus showing shipping, 'the freres' etc.	T2528/2
1587	Pictorial plan of Carrickfergus	T1273/1
c.1600	Map of Carrickfergus. Original in Trinity College, Dublin.	T1668/30
1612	Map of Carrickfergus showing fortifications with schemes for improvements by John Dunstall.	T2528/10
c.1680	'An exact survey of the island of Maghe, the river of Belfast, Carrickfergus, and the coast as far as the Capelan islands.'	T2528/15A
c.1680	Two plans of Carrickfergus with inset view of the town and castle.	T2528/16A,17
1685/6	Thomas Phillips' survey of the fortifications of towns and harbours in Ireland, including Belfast and Carrickfergus	T1720/1/1-36
c.1696	Copy of general plan of Carrickfergus Bay and road, with surroundings.	T2528/28
18th century	Plan of the principal towns, forts and harbours in Ireland, including Carrickfergus.	D2278/8
1722	Maps of Ballyclare and Carrickfergus, the property of Agmondisham Vesey, surveyed by John Maclanachan.	
c.1750-c.1800	Volume of maps of Loughguile estate of Sir George Macartney including Lissanoure and Dervock; also includes properties in the town of Carrickfergus	D1062/2/4
1751	Map of estate of Francis Clements by Wm Hoy	D3860
1763-1821	Maps of Downshire estate at Carrickfergus, Straid etc.	D671/M3/1-21
1767-70	Volume of maps of estates of the Marquess of Donegall in Carrickfergus, Ballyclare and Antrim areas, Islandmagee and the northern outskirts of Belfast, by James Crow.	D835/3/1

1780	Maps of 'Lands in the Liberties of Carrickfergus ... belonging to William Byrth Esquire' surveyed by John Barker.	D2121/5/3
1786;c.1805; 1810;1819	Maps of Carrickfergus estate of William Kirk including Aldoo and Thornfield demesne and seat surveyed by James Williamson, James, John and Thomas Frain, John Wavening and J O'Kane.	D2121/5/4-7,9-11
1795	Engraved view and description of Carrickfergus Castle by I Nixon.	D1105/9
c.1800	Map of Straid district, Carrickfergus.	T1965/359
1802	Map of Carrickfergus estate of Macartney family	T1064/7p.23
1802	Map and survey of parts of the Carrickfergus estate of the Marquess of Downshire surveyed by John Bell and others.	D671/M3/7-8
1803	Map and survey of Castlereagh and Carrickfergus estates of the Marquess of Downshire by Brownrigg, Murray and Longfield	D671/M4/31
1803;1808	Working maps and survey of the Carrickfergus estate of the Marquess of Downshire including Straid area.	D671/M3/9,11-15
1805	Four maps of Ballylagan on Carrickfergus estate of the Marquess of Downshire, by James Williamson.	D671/M3/10
1811	Map of 'A plan of the Castle and Outworks of Carrickfergus ... to accompany the Inspectional Returns for March 1811'.	T1922/7
1815	Maps of Kirk estate from c.1815.	D2121
c.1812	Map of coastline showing Carrickfergus Bay, Carrickfergus, with roads to Ballynure and Islandmagee.	D2121/5/8
c.1817	Map of Carrickfergus showing the castle, quay, Irish and Scotch quarters and roads to Larne, Belfast, Islandmagee and Straid.	D2121/5/9
c.1820	Map of Bolyhouse, Boydstown, Carrickfergus, Downshire estate.	D671/M3/20-214
1821	'A map of the County of the town of Carrickfergus from actual survey by James O'Kane 1821' with plan of town of Carrickfergus, front elevations of county gaol and courthouse and sketch of Carrickfergus Castle inset.	D1954/6/13
1825	Map of farm in the middle division of Carrickfergus held under Peter Kirk by Thomas Lattimer, surveyed by William Curran.	D2121/5/12

c.1835	Map of Carrickfergus from the Ordnance Survey showing parliamentary and other boundaries by Thomas Larcom.	D3447/
1828-1966	Manuscript and published town plans from as small as 12 inches to 1 mile to as large as 1:500, including Ballynure 1902 and Carrickfergus 1884 and 1901.	OS8 OS9

Ordnance Survey maps on scale of 6 inches to one mile:

1. Surveyed 1832	OS/6/1/52/1
2. Revised 1857	2
3. Revised 1901	3
4. Revised 1901	4
5. Revised 19016	5
6. Revised 1920	6
7. Revised 1945 & 51 7 8. Revised 1945 & 51	8

	Prints of Carrickfergus Castle mid 19th century.	D3764/
	Glassplate slides of Carrickfergus Castle.	D3031
c.1900	Photographic prints from Lawrence collection of glassplate negatives in the National Library of Ireland, including views of Carrickfergus. T2418	
c.1885- c.1930	Photographs of the old harbour, Carrickfergus, c.1885, Carrickfergus lifeboat, c.1890 and aerial photograph of Carrickfergus.	D2652
c.1897-1900	Photographs of Carrickfergus by R.J. Welch.	T2377/
c.1900-1909	Postcard view.	T1942 T3009
c.1900	Postcard views Red Hall, Ballycarry and Altfreckan Glen, Ballycarry.	T3546
1900	Postcard views of Carrickfergus.	T3009

Family Papers

Papers of Dobbs family of Castle Dobbs   D162
The Dobbs family are the principal landlords in the Carrickfergus area.
They include the papers of Arthur Dobbs (1689-1765) who was, from
1754-1765, Governor of North Carolina. The papers in the archive outline
his concern for the effective settlement of the state by peoples of European
stock, including tenants from his Co. Antrim and Co. Wicklow estates. Arthur
Dobbs' career is well documented in *Curious in Everything: The Career of
Arthur Dobbs of Carrickfergus, 1689-1765*, published by the Carrickfergus
& District Historical Society (1990).

Collection of letters of Judge Michael Ward (c.1680-1758) including more than a dozen letters from Arthur Dobbs, 1734-48, referring mainly to his attempts to find a north-west passage around North America; also includes reference to the defenceless state of Carrickfergus when seized by the French in 1760.	D2219
Papers of the Greer family of Seapark, near Carrickfergus, Co. Antrim, and Tullylagan, Co. Tyrone, 1732-1926, including plans and elevations by Thomas Jackson, relating to Seapark House and the proposed erection of Turkish baths, a conservatory, stable, yard, etc., 1851; personal accounts, receipts, etc. of the Greer family, Tullylagan and the Owden family, Seapark, 1853-c.1947.	D2339 D2509
Photographs of Greer family of Tullylagan and Seapark, Carrickfergus, c.1860-1925.	D2547
Manuscript notes on the formation of the Volunteers in Co. Antrim, 1778-90, by Samuel McSkimin, historian of Carrickfergus with his recollections of political and military events in Co. Antrim, 1795-98.	T2822
Eleven letters from Dr. J.W. Bowman in Edinburgh, London and the West Indies, etc., to his family in Carrickfergus, 1792-9; emigrant letter from E.D. Moore in New York to his mother in Carrickfergus, 1815, describing the voyage out and his immediate impressions of New York; a Carrickfergus election broadsheet, 1831; title deeds and testamentary papers, etc., relating to the Moore and Bowman families of Carrickfergus, 1734-1904.	D2107
Correspondence, legal papers and domestic accounts of Verner family in Heidelberg, New South Wales, Australia, Carrickfergus and Belfast, 1839-60.	D975
Papers of the related families of Chisholm and Smith, Whiteabbey and Carrickfergus, Co. Antrim, 1842-67, including a farm rent and general account book, probably relating to the Chisholm property at Carntall, 1842-54; a map of the property of George Smith in the West Division of Carrickfergus, 1867.	D2979
Papers of the Sproull family, Carrickfergus including a family photograph album, c.1870-c.1900; a volume of newspaper cuttings including details of local elections, social and church affairs, 1865-75 (pasted into an election check book for Carrickfergus, 1860s).	D3009
Papers of Miss M V McCaughen, school teacher, Carrickfergus, including correspondence of the Gwynn family, Antrim, 1846-1917 (Miss McCaughen's father's family); letters from Steven Gwynn describing life in the trenches, 1918; correspondence of Miss McCaughen, 1905-66, including letters from Profs. D.L. Savory and F.T. Lloyd-Dodd.	D2912
Malcolm Papers, c.1750-1919. c.100 Documents of the Malcolm family, Whitehead, Co. Antrim, including the journal of John Moore, Carrickfergus, 1760-70, in which he records his experience in colonial America and his return as an empire loyalist.	D3165

Diary of James Boyd of Carrickfergus, 1910-24, describing his service in   MIC126
the Ulster Volunteer Force.

Genealogical notes and pedigrees

Notes on genealogy of Brown family, Carrickfergus, c.1800-c.1900.	D1040
File of genealogical notes and pedigrees of the Carlin family of Carrickfergus, Ballynahinch, Co. Down, and USA, c.1720-	D3000/102
Pedigree notes on the Coates family, c.1800-c.1870.	T3008
Pedigrees compiled by G.S. Young of Culdaff, Co. Donegal, including the Dobbs family, Carrickfergus, c.1550-.	T2366
Pedigree of Douglas family, Ballynure, 1826-92	T3146
Notes and pedigrees of McCance family of Dunmurry, Co Antrim, and the related family of Finlay of Carrickfergus, c.1680-1984	T3266(add)
Notes on genealogy of Gardner and Catherwood families of Carrickfergus.	MIC104
Genealogical notes relating to the Greer family and related families of Bell, Carroll, Pierson, Atkins and Jackson, c.1600-1900	D2339 D2509
Pedigree of the Johnstone family, including details of the Cary, Chaplin, Gunning, Hutton, Maxwell, Pogue, Stannus, Thompson and Wilson families of Carrickfergus, 1804-1910.	T1195
Pedigree of the Newton family, Carrickfergus and Galgorm, Co. Antrim and and Coagh, Co. Tyrone, c.1600-1966.	D3010
Pedigree and notes of Roberts family of Lurgan, Co. Armagh, and Brishane, Australia, with detail of the related family of Smyth, Carrickfergus and Lurgan, 1830-1980.	D300/60
Pedigree of the Sproull family, Dungannon, Co. Tyrone, Lisburn and Carrickfergus, Co. Antrim and Belfast, 1747-1858; with notes taken from a Sproull family bible, 1755-1954, and a pedigree of the related family of Laurie, Scotland, 1674-1960.	T2578
Genealogical notes relating to the Tenison family, Carrickfergus, Thomastown and Dillonstown, Co. Louth; and about related families of Cole of Enniskillen, Co. Fermanagh, Moss of Cork and Moore of Co. Monaghan, c.1630-c.1890.	T2934
Pedigrees of Tisdall family of Carrickfergus, Cos Louth and Meath, c.1620-	D3000.120
Notes on genealogy of Thompson and Carey families of Carrickfergus, c.1720-1952.	T2152
c.40 vols. of genealogical note books and papers of Robin Hall, c.1960, concerning families in Cos. Antrim and Down with copy wills from c.1750-.	D2764

Estate Papers

Carrickfergus Municipal Commissioners, 2136 acres, 715 valuation

1596-c.1830	Leases, fee farm grants, conveyance, legal papers.	T686/1-20

Dalway Estate, Ballyhill, Carrickfergus 800 acres 883 valuation

	Title deeds and legal papers, Dalway family, Red Hall estate, including copy grant to John Dalway, 1609.	D1905/
1811-57	Family papers.	T1701
1849	Leases Carrickfergus, properties.	D639/33,130
1869-71	Bundle of copy deeds relating to Kilwaughter.	D1905/2/5
1883	Land Judges' rental, maps and sale particulars relating to Marriott Dalway's property, Carrickfergus and Ballyhill.	T3546/4/1
	Another copy.	LR1/832/7/A-C

Land Registry Archive

Date	Name	Box No.	Record No.
1907-1909	Dalway, Marriott R	0974 LR1/974/2/A-C	LJ 00746

Dobbs Estate, 5061 acres, 5065 Valuation

Land Registry Archive

Date	Name	Box No.	Record No.
1904-1935	Dobbs, Major Arthur Frederick	1828	NI 01025 LR1/1828/1/A-C
1874-1936	Dobbs, Sarah	2306	NI 01676 LR1/2306/11/A-C

Marqess of Donegall's Estate, Belfast, Antrim etc., including Carrickfergus, 9789 acres, 14,012 valuation (See also maps and surveys section)

The very extensive estates of the Marquis of Donegall included lands in the Carrickfergus area as well as Belfast, Antrim and Inishowen, Co. Donegal. The main collection of leases for the estates were deposited in PRONI, c.1952.	D509
Title deeds for the various estates were deposited c.1956	D811
Rentals and ledgers for all the estates, 1775-1933, are available and these include detailed maps of the Co. Antrim and Inishowen estates by James Crow, 1767-1770.	D835

1617-c.1890	Donegall estate papers.	T712/1-32
1603-c.1917	Donegall estate papers.	T956/1-179
1603-c.1870	Leases and other estate papers.	D509/1-3117

1617-1932	c.1800 leases and papers re the estates of the Donegall family in Donegal, Antrim and Down.	D652/1-1746
c.1668-1930	Estate papers including legal deeds, conveyances, wills, fee farm grants and Irish Land Commission papers.	D791/5
1706-23	Volume of typed copies Chancery Master's exhibits, including rentals, accounts etc.	T455/1-2
1719	Rental for Belfast, Moylinny, Ballylinny, Island Magee and Carrickfergus.	D2249/61
1775-82; 1864	Rentals.	D835/3/1 D835/3/4
1767-70	Maps by James Crow.	D835/3/1
1782-1822	Volume of searches, Donegall estate	D835/5/1
1783-1925	Rent ledgers.	D835/2/1-23
1796-1800	Cash rent book, Antrim estate.	D835/4/1
1833; 1895-1929	Tithe rentals.	D835/8/1 D835/8/2-16
1830-45	Copy deeds and mortgages.	D1255/7
c.1845-c.1860	Donegall-Verner correspondence	D1798/3-14
1852	Encumbered Estates' Court rental.	D835/6/1
1882	Schedule of determinable leases, Donegall estate.	
1886-1930	Copy out-letter books.	D1080/1

Land Registry Archive

Date	Name	Box No.	Record No.
1832-	Marquess of Donegall	1470	NI01809
1937		2363	LR1/2363-4/1/A-C

Marquess of Downshire's Estate, Carrickfergus etc. 2071 acres 1424 valuation

16th-20th century	Title Deeds. The Carrickfergus estate includes the following properties: Carrickfergus, 1601-1874; manor of Glynn etc., 1637-82; Bryantang, 1743-1887; Gideon's Land, 1804-31; Slievetrue 1723-1873; Straid, 1709-1893.	D671/D3/1-11
	c.5000 leases, early 18th century-early 20th century. These exist for all the estates, although the bulk are post-1750, and there are only c.700, for the early 18th century. Lease books begin in 1794 but record the state of leases from c.1700.	D671/LE/1-14 D671/L3/1-14
1834-1919	103 rentals for Carrickfergus	D671/R3/1-103
	c.700 maps, early 18th century-early 20th century. The collection of maps is dominated by two surveys of the estates, both providing detailed townland maps,	

by Brownrigg & Co., in 1803 and by Robert Manning in 1856-7.

There is relatively little material for the two smaller estates, Carrickfergus and Newry, but worthy of note are a group of maps of the Straid area near Carrickfergus.

c.1000 volumes of accounts etc., 18th century-20th century. These begin with the usual series of ledgers, specie books and cash books for the Carrickfergus estate in 1742. The lease books begin in 1794 but record the state of leases from c.1700, and there is a complete series of rentals for all the estates from c.1800. In 1813 the 3rd Marquess of Downshire emerged from his minority, interested himself in the management of his estates, and created a new set of account books. His book-keeping reforms are explained in the first volume of each class of account; for example, minute books are introduced for each estate which summarise estate management topics and against these summaries the Marquess himself lays down a course of action for his agents. His reforming zeal seems to diminish in the 1820s, but for a period the minute books are an excellent statement of estate management policy. The remaining accounts cover the demesne and household at Hillsborough, Co. Antrim, from the late 18th century, and cover agents, solicitors, tithes, rent charges, judicial rents etc., in the 19th century.

c.30,000 letters, c.1800-c.1900. These consist in the main of estate management correspondence passing between the Marquess and his chief agent in Hillsborough, and between the chief agent and the agents of the individual estates. The correspondence is particularly detailed for the period 1813-45, during the majority of the 3rd Marquess. Apart from the basic estate management topics, it reflects the interest and patronage of the Downshire family relative to road, canal and railway developments, to the building of schools, churches and markets, and to the involvement of the 3rd Marquess in agricultural improvements, the linen trade and local politics.

Land Registry Archive

Date	Name	Box No.	Record No.
1670-1929	Downshire, Marquess of (Carrickfergus estate)	0061	EC.03958 LR1/61L/4/A-C

Downshire estate records for Carrickfergus estate:

Deeds	D671/D3/1-11
Leases pre 1750	D671/LE3/1-14
Post 1750	D671/L3/1-14
Rentals	D671/R3/1-103

Edmonstone Estate, Red Hall, Carrickfergus

1821	Agreement	T561/2
c.1769	Letter relating to position of A Edmunstone on his estate at Red Hall.	
1777	Rent roll for the half year.	
1779	Letter enclosing deeds.	

1779	Articles of agreement for sale of land and property. Barony of Broad Isle.	
1780	Draft releases.	D233/1-14
1823	Legacy agreement.	D794/4

Kirk Estate, Carrickfergus

Title deeds, legal papers, etc. relating to Kirk estate,
Carrickfergus, including group of early 17th century title deeds. D1255/5/1-6

c.500 documents and volumes including rentals and ledgers from 1875. D2121

c.300 title deeds and leases from c.1780, maps of the Carrickfergus estate from c.1810.

1629-c.1950	c.400 leases.	D1255
c.1718-1735	Estate correspondence	T2524/1-25
1827-8	Rental account.	
1842-54	Rent roll for the Carrickfergus estate.	
1855-1934	Rental and cash accounts.	
1875-99; c.1931; c.1906-1925	Three ledgers.	
1884-1933	Two rent cash books.	
1884	Rentals.	
c.1875-1900	Five boxes of Irish Land Commission sale papers.	
1898-9	Notes relating to leases and rent.	
1925-7	Bundle of correspondence and Land Law papers relating to the estate.	D2121/1-8
1909	Valuation.	D1255/5/1-6
1786	Map by James Williamson. Scale 20 perches to 1 inch.	
1810	Map of Atlas by James and John Frain. Scale 20 perches to 1 inch.	
1819	Map of Aldoo. Scale 200 perches to 1 inch.	
1839	Map of a farm in the middle division held under Peter Kirk, by William Curran. Scale 10 perches to 1 inch.	
c.1839	Plan of part of Thornfield, Scale 2 statute chains to 1 inch.	
c.1839	Map of North Lodge by William Larmour. Scale 4 statute perches to 1 inch.	
c.1851	Map of Fairy Mount and Bridewell. Scale 2 statute chains to 1 inch.	

Macartney Estate, Lissanoure 12,532 acres £6355 valuation

1607;1663 1670; 1654; 1683	Abstract from leases of lands near Carrickfergus	
1664-c.1850	Miscellaneous estate papers.	D2225/ 7/1/1-96
1593-c.1940	Box of miscellaneous patents and correspondence etc.	
1679-1872	87 title deeds.	
c.1750-c.1800	Volume of maps of Loughguile estate, including properties in Carrickfergus.	D1062/2/4
1757	Copy will and probate for lands and premises in Cos. Down, Antrim and Carrickfergus.	
1771	Papers relating to Carrickfergus estate.	
c.1770-1810	Agents' correspondence.	D.572
1767	Survey and valuation of Antrim estates.	
1801;1816; 1828	Rent rolls and returns.	D572/21
1880-1925	Box of rentals and cash accounts.	
1884	Six maps of Antrim estates of George Macartney. [See Calendar for townlands]	T1064/1.2,6-7
c.1903-1945	Miscellaneous estate papers including testamentary and Irish Land Commission papers.	D1062/2
c.1885	Legal papers	D1905

Porter Estate, Red Hall, Carrickfergus

1780	Memorial of bargain and sale of Broad Island	
1792	Memorial lease for same.	D1747/1/11

Saunders' Estate, Belfast and Carrickfergus

1771-8	Rent roll for Newtownards, Comber, Belfast and Carrickfergus.	D1759/3B/7

Titles Deeds for properties in Carrickfergus

Conveyances, 1654 and 1685.	D1905/
Deeds, 1655, 1719 and 1754	D1421
Lease of property from Carrickfergus Corporation to Sir Robert Colvill, Galgorm, 1685.	T2014
Deeds, 1686-1887.	D1820/
Deeds, leases, etc., relating to property in Carrickfergus, mainly Hare, Poaghe/Pogue/Poague/Poag, Barry and Carry/Carrey families, 1699-1908.	D2999
Deeds and testamentary papers relating to the Moore and Bowman families of Carrickfergus, 1734-1904.	D2107/
Deeds relating to property in Carrickfergus and Portadown, Burleigh family, 1757-1861, together with copy wills of Thomas Burleigh, Edenderry, Co. Armagh, 1760; commissions of the peace for Carrickfergus to William Burleigh and James Wills, 1830; leases of property in the Ballynure area, Co. Antrim, Dobbs family, 1775-1833.	D2489/
Deeds and legal papers, 1796-1934.	D1800
Deeds and legal papers, Miller estate, Carrickfergus, c.1800-.	D971
Deeds to various properties in Belfast and Carrickfergus, Mairs family, 1813-87.	D2336
Deeds and legal papers, McFerran family, Carrickfergus and Belfast, 1824-1912.	D1905
Papers concerning Robert Getty's purchase of Red Hall, estate of Dalway family, 1836-7.	D1905
Deeds, wills, etc., Davys and Bowman families, Carrickfergus.	D2603
Deeds, leases and testamentary papers, Fulton family of Jordanstown and their property at Carrickfergus, 1802-39, including will of John Fulton, Jordanstown, 1802.	D3140
Carrickfergus properties, 1863-1902.	T1780
Deeds and leases, Atkinson property, Carrickfergus, Belfast, etc., 1864-1924.	D1253
Deeds to quarries in Belfast and Carrickfergus, Co. Antrim and to the land and stock of the Belfast and Cavehill Railway, 1877, Torrens and Hughes families.	D2269
Copy deeds relating to property at the Great Commons, Carrickfergus, Simms, Hamilton, Hilditch family, c.1874-1938.	D2233/

History and Archaeology of Carrickfergus

Letters of Captain Piers and Malby at Carrickfergus, c.1565-77 to Sir William Fitzwilliam, Treasurer at War and Lord Justice of Ireland.	MIC47
Extracts from the Plantation Commissioner's Report, 1611, describing building work at Carrickfergus, Belfast, etc.	T2182
Muster of Scottish Army at Carrickfergus, c.1642	MIC521
Correspondence concerning the landing of the French under Thurot at Carrickfergus, 1760.	T1180
Letter by Edward Willes, Chief Baron of the Exchequer on circuit in Ireland, c.1759, registering dismay at ruinous state of Joymount House; He visits the Chichester monument in St Nicholas' Church and remarks 'better care is taken for their corpses when dead than for their habitation when alive'. He describes the extraordinary behaviour of a local Carrickfergus 'character' called Moll Willis: whilst he was 'walking in state to Court' ''she took me round the neck and kissed me (as is her usual custom) til I put something into her hand, the trumpets playing God Save Great George, etc., all the while'.	MIC 148
Manuscript notes on the formation of the volunteers in Co. Antrim, 1778-90, by Samuel McSkimin (1775-1843), historian of Carrickfergus, together with his recollections of the political and military events in the county, 1795-98 and the position of Roman Catholics. He writes, 13 May 1784, 'it is here proper to observe that still all that was thought on at this time respecting Roman Catholics voting for Members of Parliament was that he [sic] should have a vote when possessed of 50 per annum in fee and even this was rather generally disapproved of...'	T2822
Ordnance Survey Memoir for Carrickfergus, c.1835, including substantial extracts from McSkimin's history.	MIC6
Extracts from a printed booklet entitled *The Sure Way to Heaven* by Rev. James Mathew MacCary, Roman Catholic Rector of Carrickfergus and Larne, 1797: including a list of subscribers' names	T3148
Notes and sketches of an archaeological survey at Carrickfergus, 1889.	T2682
Antiquarian notes on Carrickfergus and Ballycarry, c.1896-1930.	D1611
Newspaper article, c.1873, relating to William Dobbs, Carrickfergus, and to his sea fight with Admiral Paul Jones, 1778.	D2453

Newspaper articles by Rev. Cannn J C Rutherford on the history of Carrickfergus, 1960.	T2535
Newspaper articles on the history of Carrickfergus.	T2191
226 issues of the *Carrickfergus Advertiser* and *East Antrim Gazette* between 1906 and 1913.	N22
2 vols of *Carrickfergus Advertiser*, 1892-1905.	D1565
Carrickfergus Advertiser 20 June 1968 with an article on the Result, one of the last ships built at Carrickfergus shipyard.	D1389
Correspondence and photographs gathered by the architect John Seeds during his research into Georgian houses, etc., in Northern Ireland, 1933-57; buildings include Thornfield House, Castle Dobbs, Carrickfergus and Red Hall, Ballycarry.	D2134

Business and Port Records

Legal papers and maps concerning Carrickfergus Salt Works, c.1868-86.	D980
Correspondence concerning lease of salt works, c.1880.	D1769/
Prospectus of Carrickfergus Salt Works Company, 1897.	D2610
Newspaper reports on salt mine, October 1927.	D1636
Plan & elevation of Woodburn works, property of James Gamble, cotton spinner, 1856.	D2339
Report by James Campbell relating to James Taylor's flax spinning mill, Carrickfergus, 1855.	D2168
Bankruptcy papers Woodburn Weaving Company, Carrickfergus, 1892.	D1769/
Papers in dispute concerning bleach works at Ballyclare and Ballynure, c.1865.	D1905/
Legal papers in dispute on pollution of Woodburn river by linen mill, c.1866.	D1905
Plan of Barn flax spinning mill, Carrickfergus, 1870.	D1273
Plans of works, water supplied, machinery, etc. for Sullatober Bleaching and Print Works Company, Carrickfergus, 1899-1923.	D2329
Correspondence files concerning liquidation of Joymount Dye Works, Carrickfergus, linen bleachers, c.1932-65.	D2717

Correspondence and deeds, re-sale of John Reid's flour mill, Carrickfergus, c.1858.	D1905/
Minutes, accounts and correspondence of Carrickfergus Gas Company, 1854-1950.	D1733
Title deeds to quarries in Belfast and Carrickfergus.	D2269/
Photograph of employees at Paul Rodgers' shipyard, Carrickfergus, c.1888.	T2600
Reports on shipyard, 1885.	D1389
Port books for Carrickfergus, 1612-15, (Temple Newsam Collection, Leeds Public Library).	MIC199
Bill of lading for his Majesty's frigate *Monk* bound for Carrickfergus, under Sir Clowdesley Shovell, 1690.	D2645
Correspondence and agreements relating to building work at Carrickfergus harbour, 1868-97.	D2652
Photographs of the old harbour, Carrickfergus, Co. Antrim c.1885, and the Carrickfergus life boat, c.1890.	D2652

Political Papers

Carrickfergus election broadsheet, 1831.	D2107
Letter from John Rowan, Carrickfergus, to Andrew Mayne, Liverpool, describing in detail the election contest for Carrickfergus borough between Sir Arthur Chichester and Conway Dobbs, 1832.	D2381 T2575 D1905/
Election papers Carrickfergus Borough, 1879.	D1905/

List of Subscribers to this Volume

William A Allen
16 Rosepark Central
Dundonald
Belfast

Mr W Beattie
55 Long Lane
Littlemore
Oxford
OX4 3TN
England

R J G Cameron
33 Upper Road
Greenisland
Co. Antrim

Ian Forsythe
Carrickfergus
Co. Antrim

David Hart
31 Downshire Road
Carrickfergus
Co. Antrim

Robert Howieson
21 Doagh Road
Ballyclare
Co. Antrim

James B Holmes
4 Findlers Place
N Richmond
NSW
Australia

Dr J S Logan
27 Maryfield Park
Belfast

Arthur McAlister
26 Whinfield Lane
Greenisland
Carrickfergus
Co. Antrim

Mervyn McDowell
26 Whinfield Lane
Greenisland
Carrickfergus
Co. Antrim

T H McGowan
35 Port Road
Cloughtin
Islandmagee
Co. Antrim

Mrs Caroline Nicholson
Duncrue Cottage
57 Liberty Road
Carrickfergus
Co. Antrim

D Helen Rankin
Carrickfergus
Co. Antrim

Albert Rutherford
26 Dermott Avenue
Comber
Co. Down

Ernest McA Scott
2 Cunningham Place
Ballyclare
Co. Antrim

Dee Stevenson
846 Diamond Drive
Gaithersburg
MD 20878
USA